ECONOMICS OF ARECANUT CULTIVATION IN KARNATAKA

ECONOMICS OF ARECANUT CULTIVATION IN KARNATAKA

S.V. Padmini
Guest Lecturer
PG. Department of Studies in Economics & Research
School of Business & Economics
Kuvempu University, Shankaraghatta
Shivamogga District, Karnataka

SERIALS PUBLICATIONS
NEW DELHI

First Published - 2008

ISBN: 978-81-8387-209-6

Published by

SERIALS PUBLICATIONS
4830/24, Prahlad Street, Ansari Road
Darya Ganj, New Delhi-110002 (India)
Phone : 23245225 Fax : 91-11-23272135
E-mail: serials@satyam.net.in

Dedicated to my

Beloved Father

Dr. S. Uasantha Kumar

Retd. Senior Medical Officer, Sorab, Shimoga

Beloved Mother

Dr. Seetha U. Kumar

Retd. Taluk Health Officer, Sagar, Shimoga

Beloved Brother

Dr. S.U. Deepak

Dental Surgeon, Shimoga

CONTENTS

PREFACE

Arecanut palm (Areca Catechu Linn) is cultivated primarily for its kernel obtained from its fruit which is chewed in its tender, ripe or processed form. Arecanut belongs to the family palmae. It is native of Malayan Archipelago, Philippines and other East Indian Islands. Commercial cultivation is confined only in India, Bangladesh and Sri Lanka. The book is based on the research carried out by the author on Economics of Arecanut Cultivation in Shimoga District–A Case Study.

India is the largest producer of Arecanut in the world. India stands first both in area (57%) and production (53%) of Arecanut in the world.

In India, Karnataka State stands first both in the area and production of Arecanut when compared to other states.

In Karnataka among the 27 districts, Shimoga District stands first in area under areca cultivation more than 20,000 hectares in 2002. In addition to this, Shimoga district recorded the highest increase in area under Arecanut cultivation in the last decade (1990-91 to 2000-01) as compared to other districts.

Apart from this Shimoga district comprises both traditional and non-traditional areas of Arecanut cultivation as compared to other districts. Further Shimoga district very well represents all the stages of areca gardens (first, second and third stages) as compared to other districts.

The above reasons made me to select Shimoga district for the case study.

It has been brought out that Arecanut is highly remunerative crop in the entire study area and in both the taluks and this was the reason behind rapid area expansion of areca cultivation of both taluks. Namely Sagar and Shimoga despite the high establishment cost in the first stage of the Arecanut garden.

The results of the study indicates that the investment on Arecanut cultivation is economically feasible and financially sound irrespective of category of farmers in the study area.

The size of land holding is a vital element in determining the management capacity of the farmers.

Author recommended to grow intercrop (banana) and mixed crops (pepper, cocoa) in areca gardens to get some economic relief to the farmers which also provides employment generation for the rural folk.

The inputs like human labour, farm yard manure, green leaves, chemical fertilizers, plant protection chemicals are used efficiently by large farmers category in the study area and they are, getting, good returns and they are economically benefited.

All large farmers adopted systematic, scientific cultivation practices. Hence large farmers are in better position in getting yield and returns and it should not be confined to large farmers category only. At the same time the small and medium category of farmers can reap the substantial benefit by implementing the cultivation practices intensively and meticulously.

Attention should be given to the production of by-products,and value-added products such as tobacco less gutkha, scented supari, pan parag, which may boost the farmers economy and it will open up a new way in marketing and makes the areca cultivation sustainable.

Analysis made with the help of correlation, linear, multiple regression, and evaluation of investment made. Tabular analysis made, percentage variation, averages, percentages used Bar, Pie, Area diagrams employed. Further constructive suggestions are welcome from the readers for the improvement of the book.

ACKNOWLEDGEMENT

I place on record my foremost intellectual and personal gratitude to Dr. N.G. Chachadi M.A., Ph.D., Principal, Karnataka Arts College, Dharwad, Karnataka.

He has been very kind, patient and supporting to me in my research work. His encouragement with smiling profile has inspired me and his incessant striving for truth enlightened me to assimilate enormous data. His untiring supervision and guidance led me to complete my research work successfully.

I ever remain grateful to you Sir.

Author is highly grateful to External Referees Dr. Koteshwara Rao, Professor of Economics, Nagarjun University, Hyderabad and Dr. V.B. Jugale, Professor of Economics, Dean for Social Science, Shivaji University, Kollapur.

Sri S. Bangarappa Ex-chief minister, inspite of being a reknowned politician has been associated with our family since a long time and along with his wife Smt. Shakunthalamma Bangarappa, he has been very kind, encouraging and supporting us. His love and affection, blessings and good wishes has resulted in the completion of my research work. I extend my sincere gratitudeness to both Sri. S. Bangarappa and his wife Smt. Shakunthalamma Bangarappa.

I extend my sincere gratitudeness to Prof. K. Chidananda Gowda, Retired Vice-Chancellor, Kuvempu University, Shankaraghatta for his continuous encouragement and support. I remain grately indebted to you Sir.

I am highly grateful to Hon'ble Vice Chancellor Professor S. K. Saidapur and Registrar Sri Vinay Luthra IAS, Karnatak University Dharwad for giving me opportunity to publish my Ph.D. Thesis.

I am highly grateful to Hon'ble Vice Chancellor Professor B.S. Sherigar and Registrars of Kuvempu University.

I am highly grateful to Hon'ble Director and Member of the Economic Advisory Committee of the Prime Minister of India, M. Govinda Rao and Staff of National Institute of Public Finance and Policy, New Delhi.

Dr. P.S. Mundinamani, Professor and Chairman, Dr. G.R. Patil, Professor and Chairman, Dr. R.V. Dadibavi, Professor and Chairman, Dr. S.R. Narappanavar, Professor and Chairman, Dr. Mukta Adi, Professor and Chairman, Dr. Ulevappa, Professor and Chairman, PG Department of studies in Economics and Research, Karnatak University, Dharwad, Dr. L.D. Vaikunte, Reader, Dr. Pushpa M. Savadatti, Reader, PG Department of studies in Economics and Research, Karnatak University, Dharwad have been radiant support to me not only in my research work but also in my seminar pertaining to my Ph.D. work. I remain grateful to you all.

I extend my deep and heartfelt gratitudeness to all my elder teachers who have been resourceful and creative guides to me in my research work. I ever remain grateful to you Sirs.

I am highly grateful to Hon'ble Vice Chancellor, Hampi University, Professor Dr. A. Murigeppa, Prof. B.M. Kumarswamy, Retired Principal, D.V.S. College, Shimoga, Dr. Mahabaleshwara Hegde, Head Department of Horticulture, College of Agricultural Science and Regional Research Station, Navile, Shimoga, Dr. Vignesh. M.S., Head, Department of Sociology, College of Agricultural Science and Regional Researh Station, Navile, Shimoga, Dr. Chandrakantha, Head, Department of Agricultural Economics, GKVK, UAS, Bangalore, Prof. Ananth, Department of Agricultural Economics, GKVK, UAS, Bangalore, Dr. Prakash Kammaradi, GKVK, Bangalore, Dr. G.K. Hiremath, Head, Department of Agricultural Economics, UAS, Dharwad, Dr. K.C. Gummagolmath, Department of Agricultural Economic, UAS, Dharwad, Dr. R. S. Deshpande, Head, ADRT unit, Institute of Social and Economics Change, Bangalore, Dr. Anitha H.S. Department of Commerce, Kuvempu University, Davanagere, Dr. P.M. Honakeri, Professor, P.G. Department of Economics and Research, Karnaak University, Dharwad,

I am highly thankful to Dr. T.R. Manjunath, Professor and Chairman, P.G. Department of Economics and Research, Kuvempu

University, Shankaraghatta Dr. B. Jayarama Bhat, Professor of Economics Sri. S. Shankar and Dr. S.N. Yogish, P.G. Department of Economics and Research, Kuvempu University, Shakaraghatta.

I am indebted to my 'ALMA MATTER' Lal Bahadur Arts, Science and S.B.S. Commerce College, Sagar and Dr. T.S. Raghavendra, Prof. Puttaswamy and Prof Shivakumar H.M. Department of Economics L.B. College, Sagar.

Author is gratitude towards Professor Romesh Bhandari, Director, Sri. Saurabh Thakur, Sri Sunil Bhat, Indicus Analytics Pvt. Ltd., Nehru House, New Delhi.

My special thanks and indebtedness to Dr. M.N. Mageri who has been kind enough in statistical analysis of my research work.

My sincere thanks to Prof. R.N. Kadam, Department of Economics, Prof. L.R. Pawar, Department of English, JSS College, Dharwad, and Prof. V.K. Kumbi Department of Mathematics, Karnataka College, Dharwad for their encouragement and timely help.

Author is highly thankful to Sahyadri Arts & Commerce College, Shimoga.

I may fail in my duty if do not thank my librarians of various universities and colleges. I remain grateful to you for helping me in referring to various books and research works of your libraries and bureaus. I sincerely thank Karnatak University, Dharwad, UAS Dharwad, CMDR Dharwad, Karnatak College Dharwad, GKVK, UAS, Bangalore, College of Agriculture and Regional Research Station, Navile, Shimoga, Bureau of Economics and statistics, Bangalore.

I thank all the government officials who have been kind enough to provide me necessary information.

District statistical office, Shimoga, Office of the Assistant Director of Agriculture, Shimoga and Sagar, Director of Horticulture, Shimoga, office of the Assistant Director of Land Records. Shimoga and Sagar, Agricultural Produce Marketing Committee, Shimoga and Sagar, Co-operative Marketing Societies : CAMPCO, MAMCOS Shimoga and Sagar, APSCOS, Sagar, office of the Tahashildar Shimoga and Sagar, Adike Belegarara Sangha, Sagar, P.G. Department of studies in Economics and Research, Ph.D. Academic section, Karnatak University, Dharwad. Department of Economics and Business Management, Office of the Principal, Karnataka Arts College, Dharwad.

I am grately thankful to all the farmers of the study area of Shimoga and Sagar for providing me the necessary information and data required for my research work.

I sincerely thank all the progressive farmers of the study area, Dr. Devangi R. Prafulla Chandra, Lakshmipura, Smt. Vasanthalakshmi Govindagowa, Hosudi, Sri A.S. Vishwanath, Harakere, Shimoga, Sri K.G. Vasudeva Rao, Hosudi, Sri. M.S. Nelakantappa, Hosudi, Sri L.T. Thimmappa Hedge and his son, Sagar, Sri Thimappa Hedge, Kandika, Sri Thimmappa, Ex-President, Gram Panchayath, Hosahalli and farmers of Hosudi, Lakshmipura and Sogane in the study area of Shimoga taluk and farmers of Hosahalli, Sasaravalli, Kandika and Kerekoppa in Sagar taluk.

I would not have done my research had not my beloved parents begotten, educated and encouraged me to do the research. I extend my gratitudeness to my father Dr. Vasantha Kumar S. Retired Senior Medical Officer, Sorab and my mother DR. Seetha V. Kumar, Retired Taluk Health Officer, Sagar.

I also extend my gratitudeness to my beloved brother Dr. Deepak S.V., Lecturer, Sharavathi Dental College, Shimoga, my beloved sister-in-law Dr. (Smt.) Bhagyalakshmi Deepak, Ophthalmic Surgeon, Shimoga, Sri Karthikeya Deepak, My beloved maternal uncle Late Sri. K.H. Ganapathi Rao, Retired Asst. Director of Agriculture, Shivamogga Sri. K.H. Maruthi Rao, Retired Joint Director of Agriculture, Shimoga, Aunty Late. Smt. Akku Bai, Aunty Smt. Kamala Bai, my beloved uncle Sri. Shivaswamy S. Regional labour Commissioner, Central, Bangalore, my beloved sisters Smt. Saraswathi H. AGM, DCC Bank, Shimoga Smt. Leelavathi H. Senior Auditor, Shimoga, Smt. Indumathi Nagaraj, Principal, Shimoga, Smt. Sujatha Devarao, Davanagere, My brothers Smt. and Sri. G.S Jayaprakash, Senior Manager, Andhra Bank, Kuppam, AP, Dr. G.S. Ramachandra, Divisional Surgeon, Railway Hospital, Mysore, Dr. (Smt.) Savita Ramachandra, Ophthalmic Surgeon, Railway Hospital, Mysore, Smt. and Sri Manoj Kumar, G.S. System Engineer, Bangalore, Sri Sampatkumar K.M. Indian Bank, Shivamogga.

I am grately thankful to Dr. J. Narendra, Cardiologist Dr. Devendrappa H.R. Consulting Physician, Nanjappa Hospital, Shivamogga.

My special thanks go to Sri R.K. Hegde and Smt. Asha R. Hegde of Krupa Computers Srinagar and their associates Dharwad.

Author is highly thankfull to Image Cyber Café, Sri Vishnu Bhakt and Sri Ramprasad Shivamogga.

Author is highly thankful to Jupiter Computers, Shivamogga. For cover page designing of the book.

Author is highly grateful to Sri Vijay Kumar, Serials Publication Ltd. New Delhi. For under taking publication of my research work.

I remain grateful to all the elders and learned scholars who have helped me directly or indirectly and whose names have not been included in my acknowledgement.

"Arise, Awake, Stop not until the goal in reached" –Swami Vivekananda.

Is the guiding force prompted me to complete this precious work.

Dharwad
February 2008

Padmini S.V.

1 ARECANUT IN THE INDIAN ECONOMY AND TRADE

INTRODUCTION

Arecanut palm (Areca Catechu Linn) is cultivated primarily for its Kernel obtained from the fruit which is chewed in its tender, ripe or processed form. Arecanut belongs to the family palmae. It is native of Malayan Archipelago, Philippines and other East Indian Islands. Commercial cultivation is confined only in India, Bangladesh and Sri Lanka.

Arecanut or Betelnut described as Tamboola in Vedic literature has several medicinal properties. It has the quality of supplying stimulation to nervous system and increasing secretion of saliva in the mouth. It aids to the digestive system and removes bad odour from the mouth. Our Ancient Ayurvedists used Arecanut for some of its medicinal qualities for manufacturing aphrodisiac medicines for skin diseases, diabetes, blood pressure, leprosy, fever, leucoria, urinary stones, rheumatism, intestinal worms, seminal weakness, jaundice, gastritis, hyper acidity etc, by blending with other herbs. Arecanut is welknown as an appetiser which is also digestive and carminative.

Arecanut may be a habit forming nut, but it is not a drug. This does not cause any addiction if it is used alone. The danger lies in by blending it with tobacco, charas, ganga, lime.

Since more than 2500 years ago, pan chewing with supari which originated in South India, as a habit spread to North India and then to Far East and South East Asian countries gradually. Arecanut can also be used in manufacturing soap, chewing gums, dyes, chocolates, toothpaste, cosmetics, after shave lotion, ulcer cleaning tincture.

Arecanut is both used in Ayurvedic as well as in Folk medicines. In native medicines various parts of Areca palm bark, roots, leaf sheath, juice of ripe arecanut, tender, raw and dried nuts flowers etc are used for different purposes.[1]

As the consumption of panbeedas, pan masala, scented supari etc, has been increasing in recent years, arecanut is gaining potentiality of capturing the world market. Recent years have witnessed an increase in the consumption of such value added products such as pan beedas, pan masala and scented supari in foreign countries. This is a good indication for the export sector of Indian arecanut. But despite this fact growers are taking no interest in the cultivation of arecanut. Some of the major reasons are fluctuations in the price of arecanut and liberalized imports.

Arecanut production in India has now almost reached a level of self-sufficiency. Uses of Arecanut other than chewing are negligible. Its export prospects are also very much limited. Therefore the present policy is not to expand the area under arecanut, but to adopt intensive cultivation and take up replanting of the aged and unproductive gardens. Inter-cropping in arecanut gardens is advocated to augment the income from the existing arecanut gardens.

Area and Production of Arecanut

Arecanut is cultivated on a large scale in India. The other producers include China, Indonesia, Bangladesh, Myanmar, Thailand, Malaysia and Sri Lanka.

According to FAO estimation, the total area under this crop in the world is 4,68,316 hectares and the production is 5,93,275 tonnes. Of this India's contribution in terms of area and production is 57 per cent and 53 per cent respectively.

In terms of area and production the share of Indonesia is 16 per cent and 5 per cent, China 16 per cent and 29 per cent, Bangladesh 8 per cent and 5 per cent, Myanmar 6 per cent and 5 per cent, Thailand, 2 per cent each and Malaysia 1 per cent each. Productivity is the maximum at 3752 kg/ha in China and the lowest at 433 kg/ha in Indonesia[2].

In India the cultivation of arecanut is mostly confined to Karnataka, Kerala and Assam. It is also cultivated to a small extent in Tamil Nadu, West Bengal, Maharashtra, Andhra Pradesh, Meghalaya, Goa, Tripura, Pondichery, Mizoram, Andaman and Nicobar Islands. The share of Karnataka, Kerala and Assam in terms of total area under cultivation and production is around 83 per cent.

However since 1990-91, the share of these three states both in terms of area and production has been declining and that of the others is increasing mainly because of the attractive price and unremunerative price for food crops.

The total area under arecanut crop at present during 1998-99 is about 3,72,000 hectares and the production is about 4,15,000 metric tonnes. Karnataka stands first both in terms of area and production followed by Kerala and Assam[3].

In Karnataka, Arecanut is cultivated as a garden crop whereas in Kerala, except in Kasaragode and Cannanore Districts it is grown in almost all the tracts of land near to the paddy fields and near to the coconut gardens. But recently due to dependable price of Arecanut, scientific farming is done in Kerala, Karnataka and Assam states. Further large scale expansion of Arecanut farming is also taking place in non-traditional areas. Adequate and regular supply of plant nutrients are essential for proper growth and yield of Arecanut.

Trends in Area and Production of Arecanut

The area under arecanut was 1,05,000 hectares in 1950-51 which increased to 3,72,000 hectares in 1998-99 indicating a growth of 254.29 per cent. The production during the same period has increased from 73,000 tones to 4,15,000 tones, accounting for a growth of 468.49 per cent. The yield per hectare has increased from 695 kg in 1980-81 to 1116 kg in 1998-99 accounting for a growth of 60.58 per cent.

In recent years the production of arecanut in some regions is severely affected by pests and diseases and also due to lack of adequate rains. The average annual loss was estimated to be around Rs.300 crores.

Area and Production of Arecanut in Karnataka

In Karnataka, arecanut being cultivated on 98047 hectares of land Dakshina Kannada accounts for 22.13 per cent, Shimoga 19-54 per cent, Chikmagalur 12.87 per cent, Uttar Kannada 9.92 per cent of the total area of arecanut cultivation in Karnataka in 1998-99.

In Karnataka the cultivation of arecanut has spread from the traditional Dakshina Kannada, Shimoga, Chikmagalur, Uttara Kannada to Mysore, Kolar, Tumkur and Dharwad.

The area under arecanut cultivation in Karnataka has increased substantially from 65,100 hectares in 1990-91 to 98047 hectares in 1998-99, indicating a growth of 50.66 per cent, whereas the yield per hectare has fallen from 7034 kg per hectare to 6680 kg per hectare during the same year indicating a decline of 5.03 per cent. The total production has risen from 4,57,922 tonnes to 6,48,365 tonnes between 1990-91 and 1998-99 indicating a growth of 41.58 per cent. This increase in production is due to increase in area under cultivation.

The area under arecanut cultivation has increased more rapidly in Shimoga district as compared to Dakshina Kannada and Uttara Kannada districts during the period under study. The percentage of area under acecanut cultivation has increased by 0.796 in Dakshina Kannada, 16.00 in Uttara Kannada and 49.26 in Shimoga between 1990-91 and 1998-99.

Varieties of Arecanut

There are mainly two varieties of Arecanut namely; White Supari and Red Supari. White variety supari is prepared by harvesting fully ripe Arecanut and by sundrying for 40 to 50 days. After drying the nut, the shell of nut has to be removed by hand or machine. The nut derived from this dried fruit is called Arecanut/Supari/ Betelnut.

Red variety supari is prepared by peeling the tendernut and are processed as per the variety required. (i.e. wholenut, two pieces, eight pieces etc) boiled in water and then sundried.

The white variety i.e., chali variety of Areca is mainly grown in South Kanara, North Kanara of Karnataka State and Northen parts of Kerala.

The Red variety Arecanut is mainly produced in Shimoga, Chikmagalur, North Kanara, Chithradurga, Tumkur, districts of Karnataka, Trivandrum, Quilon, Allepy Kottayam, Ernakulam, Trichur, Waynad district of Kerala.

There are mainly two varieties in Red Supari, Red supari prepared in North Kanara, parts of Shimoga, Chithradurga, Tumkur districts are called Rashi, Edi, Api, Bette variety. This variety is prepared by dehusking tendernuts, boiling, colouring and drying.

After drying primary garbling is done by land picking by the farmer and mainly four varieties are made. They are mainly Api, Rashi, Edi, Bette and Kempu gotu or Gorabalu. The secondary garbling is done by hand picking/sizeing.

Shimoga variety, red supari is prepared by dehusking tendernuts making them into two pieces, boiling, colouring and drying. Farmer does the primary garbling and varieties are called as Saraku, Bette, Gorabalu. The main varieties after garbling at the traders level are called Small Alu, Big Alu, Rajalu, Phector, Saraku, Nuli, Vanthi Dala, Vanthi Bette, Benmuri, Kempu Bette, Nice Bette etc.

The white supari is used mainly in the panbeedas and the Red variety is used both in the preparation of panbeedas and value added products like panmasala ghutkha etc.

Price Behaviour of Arecanut

The above table reveals that the production of arecanut increased steadily from 1,60,000 metric tonnes to 4,15,000 metric tonnes during the period 1975-76 to 1998-99 and at the same time the average wholesale price of arecanut has also increased steadily from Rs. 7.10 to 98.40 per kg. It clearly indicates that the increase in price resulted in increase in production of arecanut over a period of time.

Table 1
Production and Average Wholesale Price of Arecanut in India

Year (01)	*Production (Metric Tonnes)* (02)	*Average whole Sale Price (Rs.per kg)* (03)
1975-76	1,60,000	7.10
1980-81	1,91,000	15.80
1985-86	2,16,000	22.70
1990-91	2,39,000	39.60
1991-92	2,51,000	61.90
1992-93	2,48,000	58.80
1993-94	2,75,000	52.70
1994-95	2,89,000	65.50
1995-96	2,95,000	71.80
1996-97	3,07,700	82.30
1997-98	3,33,900	81.40
1998-99	4,15,000	98.40

Source: Dr. Vigneshwara Vermudy, Adike Marukattee Andhu, Indhu, Mundhu 2001.[4]

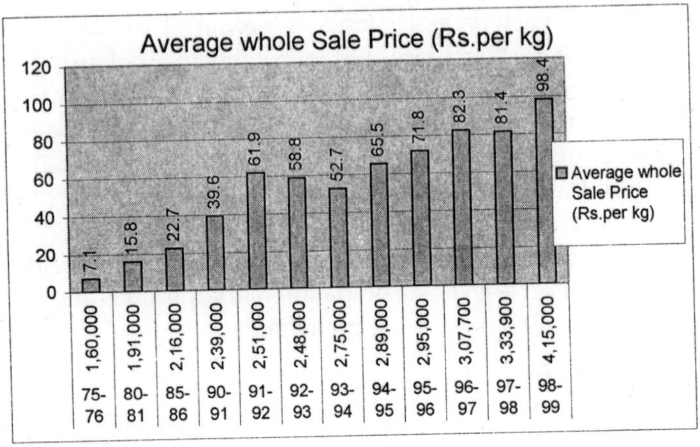

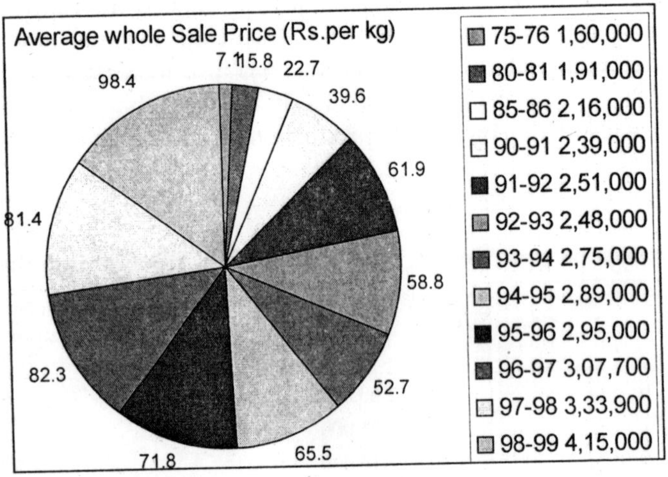

Shimoga Market

The price of arecanut varies from market to market, according to the variety offered for sale. According to the Annual Report, APMC, Shimoga, in Shimoga market arrivals of arecanut during 1980-81 was 1,09,650 quintals which went up to 2,32,170 quintals in 1999-2000. The sales of arecanut during the same period went up from 1,04,689 quintals to 2,20,610 quintals. The price per quintal of arecanut during 1980-81 was Rs. 1580 which went upto Rs. 13,600 in 1999-2000.[5]

In Shimoga market from 1980-81 onwards arrivals, sales and value of arecanut is raising steadily.

Central Arecanut and Cocoa Marketing and Processing Co-operative Society Ltd. (CAMPCO)

The Central Arecanut and Cocoa Marketing and Processing Co-operative Society (CAMPCO) has set up Arecanut Research and Development Foundation in Mangalore to find alternative uses of arecanut. CAMPCO, was basically setup by the State government to stabilize the price and prevent the exploitation of arecanut farmers by traders. After the establishment of CAMPCO, the price of arecanut started picking up and reached the peak level of Rs. 1,16,000 per tonne by 1999-2000.

CAMPCO used to purchase or sell up to about 10 per cent of the crop and could control the price. However, after the growth of gutkha industry the demand and production of arecanut has gone up to such an extent, that now price stabilisation by CAMPCO is beyond its resource.

In 1995-96, CAMPCO purchased 2,52,155 quintals of arecanut valued at Rs. 180.95 crores. A ban on gutkha industry can severely affect the lives of lakhs of farmers in India who find this crop quite lucrative.[6]

As a whole the price of Chali arecanut has been unstable over the years, that is why the interest of the growers in its cultivation is minimised. Several reasons were pointed out by the traders as well as co-operatives for the steep fall in the price of arecanut, such as excess production, declining pattern of consumption and the impact of liberalised policy etc.

However as per the market survey conducted by the All India Areca Growers Association in January 2001, the price fluctuation is mainly because of trade manipulation. The price of arecanut which has been showing a fluctuating trend witnessed substantial increase during the last decade. The price of 'choor' in Trichur market in Kerala has increased from Rs. 4938 per qtl to Rs. 12,826 per qtl during the last two year period ending 1997-98. In Mangalore market the price of supari also showed an increase of 237 per cent during the same period. In Bombay and Delhi markets the increase in price is 276 per cent and 116 per cent respectively during the last decade.

The price behaviour of arecanut has created favourable impact on area expansion, growth in productivity and production of arecanut.

Role of Arecanut in Indian Economy

Contribution of Arecanut to Indian Economy is Enormous.

According to the statistics made available by the Ministry of Agriculture, Govt. of India, India is one of the largest producers of arecanut in the whole world and Karnataka is the major arecanut producing state in the country. This can be seen from the Table 2.

Table 2

Area and Production of Arecanut in India (1998-99)

State	*Area (Ha)*	*Production (Tonnes)*
Karnataka	1,09,000	1,60,000
Kerala	94,000	1,00,000
Assam	1,06,000	85,000
Others	63,000	70,000
Total	3,72,000	4,15,000

Source: Ministry of Agriculture, Govt. of India, 1998-99.

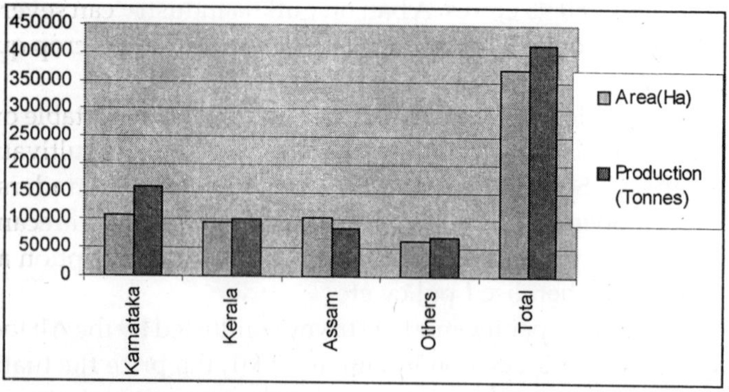

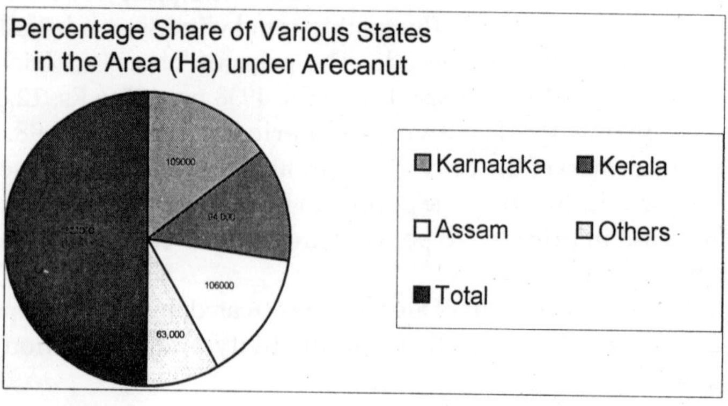

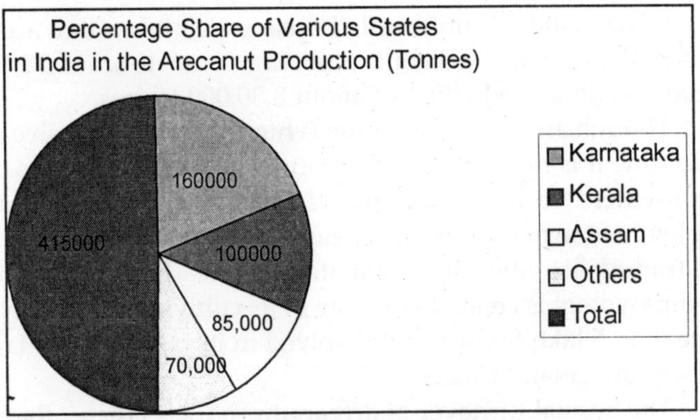

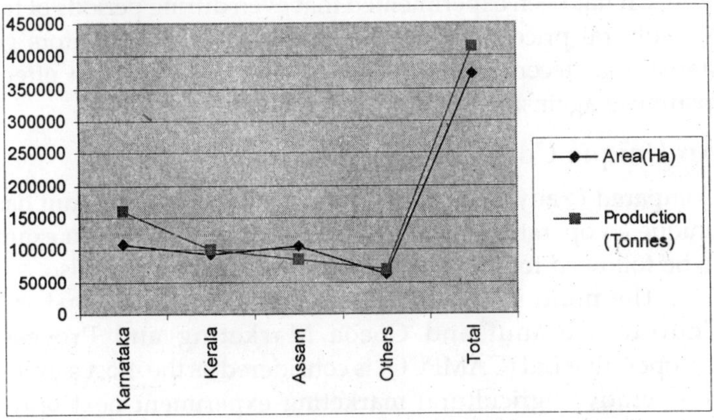

Area and Production of Arecanut in India (1998-99)

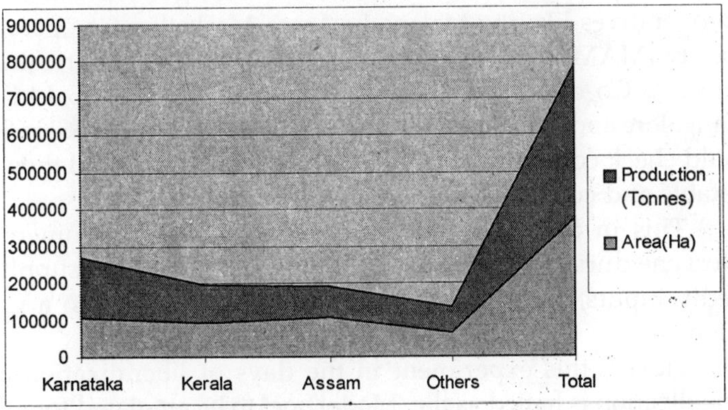

Area and Production of Arecanut in India (1998-99)

In Karnataka if unrecorded area is also taken into account, the actual area under arecanut cultivation comes to around 2,42,915 hectares with a production of about 8,30,000 tonnes.

Though arecanut cultivation is highly capital intensive at the same time it is high employment oriented also. It provides direct employment to large number of farmers as well as indirect employment to many who are engaged in its processing, marketing and trading activities. It is estimated that nearly 5 crore mandays of employment is created annually in its cultivation. In Karnataka more than 5 lakh families are involved in its cultivation. Majority of them are small farmers.

The annual turnover of arecanut products crosses Rs.10,000 crores. It has been experimented that even during periods of fall in agricultural prices in South India the arecanut cultivators got a stable and decent income. Hence, it proved to be an effective insurance against agricultural price fluctuations.

An Unique Co-operative Experiment

Compared to any other agricultural commodities arecanut has an unique co-operative marketing mechanism, which is an example to be followed for all other agricultural commodities also.

The multi state arecanut co-operative sector, that is, the Central Arecanut and Cocoa Marketing and Processing Co-operative Ltd (CAMPCO) is considered as the most significant co-operative agricultural marketing experiment next only the Gujarat's 'AMUL' in India.

The performance of CAMPCO along with the other Co-operatives like the Malanadu Areca Marketing Co-operative Society (MAMCOS) Ltd. in Shimoga, South Kanara Agricultural Produce Co-operative Marketing Society (SKACMS Ltd) in Mangalore and Totagar's Co-operative Sales Society (TCSS) in Sirsi could check concentration, enhance the competition and thus get a stable and competitive prices to the farmers.

This in fact, reduced the burden on the government to intervene during the periods of distress and also in the supply of credit, inputs, storage and other marketing facilities to a great extent.

Hence, this experiment in the days of liberalization and globalization is hailed as the 'Model one' to be emulated for other crops also.

Govt.'s MSP Scheme

The Government of Karnataka in the recent budget announced a Market Intervention Scheme (MIS) to protect the interest of arecanut farmers in the State. By responding positively to this initiative the Central Government announced a Minimum Support Price (MSP) of Rs. 60/- Kg 'Chali' variety (white supari) recently.

The state government and the CAMPCO are working out the modalities of procuring nearly 10,000 tones of arecanut in the state. The responsibility of procurement at the stipulated Minimum Support Price is assigned to the CAMPCO Hence the burden to the government in this respect is very much minimal.

The MIS is hailed as the model one to be extended to other crops also as the scheme is aimed not only to protect the farmers but also strengthen the co-operative experiment in agriculture. (Cost of cultivation of arecanut Report 2002).

Imports of Arecanut

So as to meet the domestic requirements, the country imported arecanut in large volume up to 1956-57. From then onwards because there was an increase in the domestic production it has declined steadily. But in recent years, because of the liberalized policy of the government the import of arecanut has been increasing slowly and steadily.

India imports arecanut from, Bangladesh, Hongkong, Indonesia, Malaysia , Myanmar etc. The quantum of import varied from 545 tonnes to 10,823 tonnes during the years 1994-95 to 1999-2000.

The imported arecanut is much cheaper and is 55.76 per cent less than the domestic price. However its quality is much inferior than that of domestic arecanut and hence it is mainly used in the preparation of value-added products. [7]

Exports of Arecanut

During 1936 to 1940 India exported arecanut to the tune of 6344 tonnes, in 1946-47 it was 675 tonnes. From then onwards the export of arecanut has declined to 125 tonnes, but in 1983-84, it has increased to 783 tonnes which during 1994-95 has further increased to 823 tonnes. From then onwards it has shown a declining trend and during 1999-2000. it was 350 tonnes.

India exports arecanut to different countries like England, Nepal, Saudi Arabia, Singapur, Maldives, South Africa, Russia, Australia, Tanzania, Philippines, United Arab Emirates, America, Mali, Canada, Bangla Desh etc.

Exported arecanut from India includes wholenuts, splitted nuts, value added products i.e. Panmasala, Gutkha, Scented Supari etc. Therefore, all out efforts should be made to boost the export of arecanut so as to protect the interests of arecanut growers.

The limited use of chewing only is the main hurdle to the future of the commodity. Now the time has come to explore the new market for this. We have to undertake extensive market research in the foreign countries to study the chewing, consuming mode, habits etc.

Since Arecanut is having stimulative character and also contains tannins, this may be used in the preparation of chewing gums. These chewing gums may be exported to USA, Canada etc where the habits of chewing prevails.[8]

Opportunity to Export

The Demand for value added arecanut products is fast growing globally also. For instance our neighboring countries like Pakistan, Middle East and other Muslim countries have became an assured destination for value added arecanut products. As a result of which the export of value added products from India has almost doubled in a span of just five years. Interestingly, the demand is increasing gradually in the developed world including US, UK, Canada and France and that too for the products such as Gutkha and Pan masala. Given its capacity to generate income, employment and the previous foreign exchange arecanut is seen having all the potential to emerge as an Ideal Swadeshi traditional industry.9

Demand for Arecanut

The consumption base of arecanut has expanded over the years, It is because of increasing income over years, increase in population and because of urbanization.

Arecanut is consumed by the people in different forms viz., tender, ripe or processed in pan-beedas along with tobacco without betel leaves. In the preparation of these varieties of pan-beedas or other arecanut based products, the pan-beeda, shop –keepers use dried, fried, wet, powdered, semi-powdered, scented etc. arecanut according to the tastes and preferences of the buyers or consumers, and again on the basis of availability of these with the shop-keepers.

As a whole the investigation with regard to 'Marketing of Arecanut' the need for a consumer based approach' is pointed out that as far as consumers tastes and preferences were concerned, in the existing marketing conditions majority of them consumed Katcha followed by Pacca variety. The non-availability of information or different varieties is a constraint in the marketing of this product of this area and hence it calls for an immediate study from the authorized agencies to make propaganda and publicity in this regard.

The demand for arecanut shows a fluctuating trend during the period between 1980-81 and 1999-2000.

The demand for arecanut during 1980-81 was 1,04,689 quintals by 1999-2000 went up to 2,20,610 quintals (increased by 110.73%). The increasing trend continued from 1980-81 to 1986-87. In 1987-88 it has declined to 93,822 quintals. From 1988 onwards it has shown increasing trend upto 1989-90 During 1990-91 it has declined. From 1991 onwards up to 1996 it has shown increasing trend. But once again in 1996-97 it has declined, and later in 1999-2000 the demand has increased to 2,80,610 quintals.

The supply of arecanut during 1980-81 was 1,09,650 quintals. whereas the demand for arecanut during the same year was 1,04,689 quintals. Up to 1983 the supply of arecanut exceeded the demand. But during 1988-89 and 1989-90 demand exceeded the supply. Again during 1999-2000, the supply has shown increasing trend than demand i.e., the supply was 2,32,170 quintals and demand was 2,20,610 quintals.[10]

Over a period of time, both demand and supply of arecanut has been fluctuating steadily and it is too difficult to show a combat between supply and demand of arecanut in Shimoga market.

Supply Response of Arecanut

Farmers in the recent years have taken up growing perennial crops like arecanut on large scale because of the alarming price for the product and also high income from the less area.

The area under arecanut and the production have been increasing over the years and especially true after the CAMPCO came into existence. Studies on supply response of arecanut have shown that the price has played a crucial role in increasing the supply of output of arecanut.

Unlike annual crops, perennial crops are characterized by long gestation period between initial input and first output.

Gradual deterioration of productive capacity of plants. The area and production of arecanut is increasing alarmingly because of the price and non-price factors.

Irrespective of diseases and proposed move to ban gutkha by many State governments the farming community in coastal and malnad area have been switching over to arecanut cultivation from traditional paddy farming. Arecanut production in Karnataka has increased due to expansion in the area under arecanut cultivation.

Constraints for Arecanut Cultivation

The Arecanut growers in recent years are facing so many problems. The productivity of arecanut is declining due to prevalence of pests and diseases in Malnad region and immature nut dropping in maidan areas.

The souring of prices these years have been saved the growers from the seriousness of the infection which might become critical in future.[11]

Post Harvest Problems

1. Non availability of adequate organised local markets, which makes the way for the entry of intermediaries.
2. Non-availability of market intelligence to the growers one of the main reason for the periodic fluctuations in the price of arecanut.
3. Transportation problem.
4. Lack of proper training to the farmers on aspects like grading, storage etc.
5. Higher level of sales tax, multiple tax etc.
6. Lack of proper arrangements to undertake direct sales to the consuming centres.[12]

Economics of Intercrop Cultivation in Areca-Gardens

Multiple cropping, relay overlap cropping. Inter cropping and mixed cropping are some of the terms that are being more widely used by the agricultural scientists in recent years, All these in reality mean an intensive land use to take two, three or even more crops either simultaneously or successively each year. These systems not only increase the productivity per unit area and per unit time but also provide additional work to the agricultural labour. They have been advocated mostly for cereals, pulses and such other annuals.

The practice of inter cropping or mixed cropping in arecanut gardens has been in vogue even in early times. But the objective in those days was not intensive cropping. The long pre-bearing age of 5 to 8 years. The low income in the early years of bearing, the fluctuation in the yield of the crop due to pests and diseases (which had no proper control measures in early years) and seasonal conditions forced the planter to take up the inter cropping. They had no markets near about or they were sometimes cut off from the marketing centres due to lack of communication or transport (as in interior or 'Malnad' of Karnataka State). The farmers were therefore compelled to grow their day to day requirements of vegetables and fruits in the areca gardens. Further the income from the arecanut gardens is restricted to a few months in a year. The inter crops when raised can provide additional income during the off-seasons.

The crops chosen as inter crop or mixed crop also vary from tract to tract though the crop like banana may be more universally grown. If growers at Sirsi prefer cardamom and pepper as inter crops, the planters at South Kanara select pepper and yam as best suited to that locality.

The basic concept of farming is now changing from subsistence farming to business farming based on sound principles of economics and technology. The grower is not raising crops to meet the demands of his family alone. Every items of input like land, water, fertilizer, labour capital etc has to be considered in terms of the additional gain that can be achieved from the crop raised. The crop or crops of inter cropping are to be chosen more carefully especially when one of the partners is a perennial crop like arecanut. The inter crops chosen should create only minimum problems of soil exhaustion and pest build up while ensuring at the same time maximum production or maximum returns per unit input to the farmer.

The kind of inter crop chosen will vary depending upon several factors like the agro-climatic condition of the area, the demand and performance of the local market and the personal likings and needs of the farmer. In inter crops there are two categories.

1. The first coming under the group of money or cash crops like pepper, cardamom and ginger having an export potential and,

2. The second falling under the category of food crops like banana, elephant-foot-yam and pineapple. It is the farmer to choose the variety or crops found best from the 'cafeteria' of alternative crops. Yet under the present scarcity condition for food prevailing in the country it is considered a bounden duty and responsibility of the grower to raise food crops of high caloric value.

Alternatively if the intention of the areca grower is to get additional income in view of the recent fall in the price of arecanut, he may choose a mixed crop like pepper or cardamom depending upon the agro-climatic region in which the garden is located.

However, it has to be understood that inter or mixed cropping with a perennial crop like arecanut is to be considered primarily as a safeguard against the uncertainties of returns from the produce of pure or mono culture gardens due to reasons beyond the control of the planters, Raising two or three crops in the same will help to stabilize the income of the small holders like that of areca cultivators. The farmer should choose only such crops that are not only non-detrimental to the main crop i.e., arecanut, but can also co-exist to the benefit of both of them.[13.]

Inter Crops in Arecanut Gardens: Malnad Region

In the Malnad region of Karnataka State, inter crops, like banana, cocoa, cardamom, pepper, betelvine and pineapple are commonly grown. The yield obtained from these crops are not given manurial and cultural operations. As a result the inter crops are to depend on the manure and water given to the main crop of arecanut. The position can be improved by giving them the same treatment as is given if they are pure crops. Based on the general performance of the inter crops betelvine and pepper are found to be the most suitable for the Malnad area.[14]

Inter Crops in Arecanut Gardens: Maidan Area

In the maidan region of Karnataka State mixed crops like mango, jack, coconut, banana and other crops are commonly grown. The cultivation practices in maidan area are markedly different from the method adopted in Malnad tracts. [15]

Value Added Products of Arecanut

The emergence of value added arecanut products such as Gutkha has given a real boost to the arecanut economy in India.

There are two main types of arecanut called boiled red type (red supari) and white chali type (white supari) prepared by the farmers in Karnataka.

During the 80's as the arecanut was consumed mostly in the raw forms to prepare either traditional tambulam or the beeda, the price realized by the farmers was not that much remunerative.

When the era of 'value addition' through the large scale industrial processing of arecanut began, the diversified products in attractive packets and labels such as the scented supari, panmasala, herbal supari, khaju supari and Gutkha, started flooding the Indian retail market.

This enhanced the choice and convenience for the consumers as a result of which the consumption of arecanut, especially in Northern States such as Uttar Pradesh, Gujarat, Delhi and Maharashtra increased by many folds.

As the value addition is the stated objective under our agricultural development policy, this in the case of arecanut is viewed as a step in the right direction. This infact enhanced greatly the earning capacity of arecanut farmers in India.

At present, out of the total production of arecanut in India, 50 per cent goes towards the preparation of gutkha and scented supari, 47 per cent for beeda and pan making and remaining 3 per cent for home consumption.

At the retail levels gutkhas are sold at an average of Rs.800 per Kg whereas the price of panmasala and scented supari is around Rs. 400 per kg.

One estimate says that around 2 crore people are consuming these products in India.

Value Addition Helped Farmers to get Good Price

For instance in a span of just 15 years from 1985 to 2000 area under arecanut in Karnataka has almost doubled and the increase in the price for raw nuts has increased by more than 500 per cent.

It enabled the small farmers with below one hectare under arecanut to earn an assured income sufficient enough to lead a decent standard of living.

For example, average price of white chali variety reached as high as Rs.13,000 per quintal in the year 2000 an average yield of around 10 quintals the farmers in the coastal district could easily realise a net income of around Rs.50,000 to Rs.70,000.

As a result, the consumer durable such as two wheelers, TV refrigerators and cars which are otherwise confined only to the urban upper middle-class became common household items in the regions growing arecanut.[16]

NOTES AND REFERENCES

1. Shankar Bhat P. 'Medicinal Values and Prospects of Arecanut', Rajatha Singara, 1998, CAMPCO, Mangalore.
2. Dr. Vigneshwara Varmudy, 'A Crisis in the Arecanut Sector', Facts for you, *Economic and Political, Weekly*, April, 2001, P. 23-25.
3. Dr. Vigneshwara Varmudy 'A Crisis in the Arecanut Sector', Facts for you, *Economic and Political Wekly*, April 2001, P. 23-25.
4. Dr. Vigneshwara Varmudy, 'Production and Average Wholesale Price of Arecanut in India' Adike Marukatte, Andhu, Indhu and Mundhu-2001, Published by Varmudy Prakashana, Adyanadya, South Canara District.
5. Annual Report APMC, Shimoga Market 2001.
6. 'CAMPCO', Rajatha Singara, CAMPCO 1998, Mangalore.
7. Dr. Vigneshwara Varmudy, 'A Crisis in the Arecanut Sector', Facts for you, April 2001, P. 23-25.
8. Bhat, A.S. "Export Potentialities of Arecanut" Rajatha Singara, CAMPCO, 1998, Mangalore.
9. Dr. Vignesh M.S. Dr. Mahabaleshwar Hegde, Dr. T. K. Prabakara Shetty and Dr. Prakash Kammaradi, 'Contribution of Arecanut to Indian Economy is Enormous', The Arecanut Heritage of India, 2002, Pub. by Arecanut Research Centre, UAS, Navile Campus, Shimoga, Karnataka.
10. Dr. Vigneshwara Vermudy, Demand for Arecanut, Adike Marukatte Andhu, Indhu, Mundhu 2001, Published by Varmudy Prakashana, Adyanadya, South Canara District.
11. Rajashekarappa M.T. 'Constraints for Areca Cultivation, Supply Response and Emerging Constraints for Arecanut Cultivation in Karnataka'. Seminar Report (Unpublished).
12. Rajashekarappa M.T. 'Problems of the Arecanut Sector', Supply Response and Emerging Constraints for Arecanut Cultivation in Karnataka, Seminar Report (Unpublished).
13. Sham Bhat K. 'Intensified Inter Cropping or Mixed Cropping in Areca Garden the Need of the Day', P. 67-69, Arecanut and Spices Bulletin, 1974.

14. Devdas K Bhandary, 'Study of Inter and Associated Crops in Areca Gardens of Malnad Tract of Karnataka', P. 76-77. Arecanut and Spices Bulletin, 1974.

15. Nagaraj. B. 'Inter Cropping in Arecanut Gardens of Maidan Areas of Karnataka', P. 78-79, Arecanut and Spices Bulletin, 1974.

16. Dr. Vignesh M.S. Dr. Mahabaleshwar Hegde, Dr. Prabakarashetty T.K. Dr. Prakash Kammaradi, 'Value Added Products of Arecanut' P-15-16, The Arecanut Heritage of India 2002, Pub. By Arecanut Research Centre, UAS, Navile Campus Shimoga, Karnataka.

2 REVIEW OF LITERATURE

There has been a plethora of studies made by many expert committees and individual scholars on several aspects of arecanut.

Some of these studies have been reviewed here to have an idea about their main areas of study.

- D.A. Hegde (1987) has studied the 'Impact of price behaviors on Arecanut Plantations and Growth in Karnataka. A case study of North Kanara District with the following objectives.

    1. To analyse the extent to which the price behaviors between 1957-58 have made their impact on the economic conditions of the plantation owners.
    2. To study the extent of area shift if any, which have taken place in the rice growing area to derive the opportunity cost-benefit from price improvements of arecanut of their implications.
    3. To analyse the role of marketing agencies in bringing better price advantage to arecanut plantation owners.
    4. To re-emphasize the need for giving greater attention to the commercial crop in Karnataka.
    5. To assess the future role of arecanut cultivation in improving the economic status of plantation owners and the contribution it can make to the economy of the state as a whole and,
    6. To make suitable policy recommendations in the light of the analysis so as to influence the public policy.

    The analysis has shown that the fluctuations and uncertainties created by the price movements has been a serious constraint on the income generation to small and marginal farmers. They are the first victims of any violent fluctuations in prices. Moreover the depression in the arecanut prices result in mounting overdue with the co-operative banks and other financing agencies. This leads to the demand for government intervention to provide relief by sanctioning additional installments for repayment, exemption from penal interest, writing off the debt etc.

The study reveals that the main cause for fluctuation in prices during pre-independence era was the import of cheap varieties of Arecanut from Singapore, Cylon, Malaysia and such other neighbouring countries. But this situation has changed due to positive attitude shown by the Central Government by severely restricting imports through certain tariffs impositions in the post-independence era.

It is pointed out in the analysis that CAMPCO which is the central marketing agency for South India is not able to compete effectively with the private traders in Central Indian and North Indian markets due to higher sales tax or commercial tax rates in some of these states. This is clear indication of lack of proper marketing for arecanut. So the study adds further justification for creation of a central organisation like 'Arecanut Board' to tackle such issue.

The study suggested that it is essential to enforce grading and standardisation of certain varieties so that the market can be widened and stabilised. The farmers should be encouraged to produce those varieties only. Mechanical devices for processing and grading should be introduced by undertaking technological innovations.

The study has emphasised price factor and marketing system of arecanut and how they have affected the incomes of arecanut growers. In fact apart from price factor there are various non-price factors which will also influence the cultivation and income levels of arecanut cultivators.

- N.S. Vishwanath (1992), has studied Arecanut Marketing in Karnataka with the following objectives.
    1. To study the phace and pattern of supply of and demand for arecanut.
    2. To analyse the marketing behaviour of producers.
    3. To assess the structural change in marketing.
    4. To elucidate the market conduct of functionaries and,
    5. To evaluate the performance of the Arecanut Marketing System (AMS).

The Hypothesis Framed for the Study are as Follows

1. Structural changes have taken place in the Arecanut Marketing System (AMS).
2. Market conduct has changed in the Arecanut Marketing System (AMS).
3. Consequent to changes in the market structure and conduct performance of the Arecanut Marketing System (AMS) has changed in favour of producers.

The study has selected Karnataka State which is predominant in production and has institutions dealing in marketing and has infrastructural facilities.

The markets, Mangalore, Shimoga and Sirsi have been selected for the study, because these markets handle about 73 per cent of the total market arrivals of arecanut in the state. Moreover, they cover Districts of Dakshina Kannada, Shimoga, Chickmangalore and Uttar Kannada respectively.

The study has selected Bombay and Bangalore terminal markets in view of major varietal trade transactions of arecanut concerning the three subsystems Mangalore, Sirsi and Shimoga respectively.

In order to study the varieties of Arecanut, the monthly data on unboiled and boiled nuts collected from The Directorate of Economics and Statistics from 1972 to 1989 is used.

In each of the selected markets, selling Co-operatives (SCs) Co-exist along with other Commission Agents (CAs), and are engaged in establishing backward and forward linkages. Since these Co-operatives are performing marketing functions it was thought that these Scs need be studied for the impact created on the market functionaries and other elements. The South Kanara Agricultural Co-operative Marketing Society Limited (SKACMS) at Shimoga and the Totegars Co-operative Sale Society Ltd. (TSS) at Sirsi have been selected for detailed study. In addition to his, the existence of Taluk Agricultural Produce Co-operative Societies (TAPCMS) wherever they coexist with these Scs were studied for analysis of their role in the marketing process.

Three Primary Agricultural Credit Societies (PACS) one in each of the three subsystems were selected for the study at random depending upon the business link of the PACS with higher level selling Co-operatives.

In order to select the produces latest data on size distribution of land holdings were obtained for each selected District where the market is located. The total number of one hundred and fifty were interviewed.

The study has revealed that the irregular variations in arrivals and sales are marked by volatility in the three markets (i.e. Mangalore, Shimoga and Sirsi). In respect of price, it is found that the magnitude of irregular various has increased after 1971.

The study has failed to make suitable recommendations so as to solve the problems in Arecanut Marketing System (AMS) in Karnataka.

Anitha H.S. (1997) has also worked on Arecanut Marketing (A case study of Shimoga Dist.) with the following objectives.

1. To study the production and processing pattern of arecanut in Shimoga Dist.
2. To analyse the problems of arecanut growers.
3. To analyse the existing marketing pattern of arecanut.
4. To study the contributory factors for price fluctuations and,
5. To suggest suitable remedial measures to overcome the deficiencies in arecanut marketing.

The Main Hypotheses of the Study are

1. Most of the growers of arecanut particularly small and medium sell their produce when prices are unremunerative.
2. Intermediaries enjoy a higher share in the customer rupee than producers.
3. Absence of uniform tax policy for all the arecanut producing states has contributed to the wide fluctuation in prices.
4. Malpracties in regulated markets have affected the economic position of growers.
5. Absence of proper marketing mechanism has forced the growers to sell their produce in the village itself.
6. It is profitable to sell the produce to private merchants rather than in regulated markets.

The study has analysed the marketing structure patterns problems of arecanut marketing, contributory factors for price fluctuation of arecanut in the sample district and suggested suitable remedies to overcome the deficiencies in arecanut marketing.

The study has made certain suggestions to make arecanut marketing system more effective. According to the study an effective functioning of any system, the human values are important, Unfortunately in recent years these values are eroded at all levels. In the interest of our farmers and our country the values are to be restored. Everybody in the system should not be just guided by economic desires but these desires should have a moral fabric. To improve the arecanut marketing system, the Government Regulated Markets, Market intermediaries have a collective role to play. Their responsibility is co-equal.

The study has stressed on ethical aspects in the system so as to bring better returns to the farmers. Such things seem to be far from reality.

Ramachandra. V. Bhat (1977) has studied the Arecanut crop in India with special reference to Karnataka and Kerala.

The study reveals that the production of arecanut in the country has increased at a rate of 4.58 per cent per annum, over the period between 1959-60 to 1974-75, this increase was due to the expansion in area which has increased at the rate of 4.06 per cent per annum. In contrast the productivity per hectare increased only by 0.58 per cent per annum.

According to the study, during 1972-73 there was an unprecidental slump in arecanut prices both in Karnataka and Kerala. This was probably because of the high rate of inflation specially in food grains, cutting the purchasing power of people. Hence the demand for arecanut might have gone down. This situation was accentuated by a sudden increase in supply of about 16,000 tonnes in 1973-74.

The imports of arecanut by our country which accounted to more than 30 per cent of total supply during 50's have been practically slipped since 1968-69.

The study reveals that now at this junction when our country is not only self sufficient in arecanut requirements but it has surpluses because of considerably high rate of increase in production, there is an urgent need to enhance its exports.

The study has failed to suggest suitable measures to stabilise arecanut prices. It has also failed to analyse scientifically, how market arrivals and sales effect prices.

- K. Purandara Rao (1974) has studied an Analysis of Marketing Problems of Arecanut in Karnataka State with following objectives.
  1. To analyse the behaviour of arrivals and price of arecanut in the selected assembling centers of Karnataka.
  2. To study the existing marketing channels and margins retained by different agencies.
  3. To compare the cost of harvesting, curing and processing, grading, transportation and storage in selected districts of Karnataka.
  4. To suggest measures to improve the existing marketing system.

The study was restricted to the three important arecanut growing districts viz. South Kanara, Shimoga and North Kanara, three of the important markets viz. Mangalore in South Kanara, Shimoga in Shimoga and Sirsi in North Kanara were selected for the study. Each selected market is characteristically different from the other in respect of the trade of arecanut marketed.

The study has tried to examine some important aspects of arecanut processing and methods of processing, processing costs, profitability of different methods of processing, seasonal price fluctuations, seasonal arrivals and costs and contribution of various market intermediaries in regulated markets at Mangalore, Shimoga and Sirsi.

According to the study an analysis of the realtionship between prices and arrivals in the three markets though prices generally ruled high during the lean period when arrivals were low. No definite pattern of relationship could be established between the market arrivals and prices.

The study further reveals that the seasonal variations in arrivals of arecanut showed that the arrivals were distributed according to the season of harvesting. Peak arrivals were between January to April in Mangalore, December to March in Shimoga and December to May in Sirsi.

The market information system in the three important markets for arecanut should be integrated to improve the price making mechanism.

The study has effectively analysed the marketing problems of Arecanut in Karnataka. But the study has not given much attention to what measures should be taken to establish definite patterns of relationship between the market arrivals and price.

- Ashok Kumar (1989) studied the price and arrivals of Arecanut in selected major markets of Karnataka with following objectives.
  1. To study long term fluctuation in the price and arrivals of arecanut.
  2. To identify the short term movements in the price and arrivals of arecanut.
  3. To assess the extent of market integration.

The data used for the study are the price, arrivals of arecanut over the years taken from the records of APMC Mangalore, Shimoga and Sirsi. In the market of Mangalore and Sirsi the type of arecanut is chali so the price and arrival data in these two markets are for the chali type and in Shimoga market the data pertains to Saraku type.

The study has analysed the long-term behaviour, the short-term behaviour (seasonality) of arecanut in Karnataka state, Three major arecanut markets in Karnataka namely, Mangalore, Shimoga and Sirsi have been included to provide the price arrival data required for the study.

In all the three markets the arrival was more or less constant. The trend was neither increasing or decreasing one. Arrivals were maximum during January to May in Mangalore and Sirsi. In Shimoga also the maximum arrivals period was of five months but advanced by a month. This is because of type of arecanut (Saraku–Saraku type is a resultant of tender boiled dried arecanut) market in Shimoga need early harvest of nuts, whereas the type made in Mangalore and Sirsi (Chali type Chali type is a resultant of ripened sundried nuts) require late harvesting. High rise in arrivals immediately following the harvest indicate that the farmers sell the bulk of their produce just after harvest. The pattern of arrivals is same over the years. In Mangalore and Sirsi there are two peaks in arrivals. The first one may be associated with the farmers need for cash to meet their immediate needs. The other may be associated with the sale of arecanut to repay the crop loan. There was no cycle in the arrivals. Though seasonal patterns in price was non-significant in Mangalore and Sirsi markets bloom in prices was present during stump in arrivals.

- Krishnamurthi (1991) has studied the marketing of Arecanut in Shimoga District. A study of Sagar Market. The study has following objectives.
    1. To analyse the existing marketing system of Arecanut in Shimoga district in general and Sagar market in particular.
    2. To identify the marketing problems faced by the Arecanut growers.
    3. To identify the marketing problems of commission agents, wholesalers and retailers.
    4. To study the role of Arecanut Co-operative marketing societies and Regulated market.
    5. To study the buying and consumption pattern of Arecanut consumers and their behaviour towards Arecanut.
    6. To offer suggestions for improving the marketing of Arecanut.

It is an empirical study of analytical nature involving rigid field survey. The data are collected from the samples selected and by administering the interview schedules personally at the places of respondents.

Sagara taluk in Shimoga district of Karnataka State is purposively, selected for the study. The study covers a sample of 100 growers, throughout the taluk, 35 retailers and 3 co-operative marketing societies functioning in the limits of regulated markets.

Further 70 consumers are also interviewed of which 40 consumers are grower consumers and the remaining 30 consumers are non-grower consumers.

The study has revealed that the problems faced by the growers are low yield rate, lack of skilled workers for plucking of arecanut, lack of knowledge about scientific grading, substantial loss of produce every year due to diseases, pests and monkeys, pigs etc inadequate irrigation and transport facilities and above all uncertainty in prices.

According to the study, the overall marketing system for arecanut is well organised and the market functionaries are operating quite satisfactorily.

- Jagadesh Alse (1998) studied the Management Appraisal of Agri business Unit. A case study of the Campco Ltd. Mangalore.

The Main Objectives of the Study are

1. To study the procedure-followed, pattern and costs involved in purchase of arecanut.
2. To study the existing marketing channels and costs involved in marketing of arecanut.
3. To study the grade standards followed in marketing of arecanut both at domestic and export markets.
4. To study the business performance of CAMPCO.
5. To identify the problems faced by CAMPCO in performing its functions and to suggest improvements.

To elicit the information regarding the procurement, processing, grading, sales etc the personal observations were followed. To identify the problems faced by the co-operatives in procurement and sale of arecanut discussion were held with the officials of the co-operatives.

The secondary data, relating to physical performance indicators, The annual report of the co-operative were used and the data were collected for the period from 1986-87 to 1996-97.

The data relating to the financial aspects of the co-operative such as balance sheet, profit and loss account and trading accounts were abstracted from annual reports for the same period. The indicators are employed in the ratio analysis to evaluate the performance of the co-operatives.

The data regarding procurement, sale of arecanut both in terms of quality and value, prices of arecanut, cost incurred for procurement and sale and other required data were also collected from the records of the co-operative.

The study reveals that in India Arecanut is grown in a area of about 2.16 lakh hectares with annual production of 2.48 lakh metric tonnes (1993-94). Karnataka stands first both in area and production of arecanut followed by Kerala, Assam, Meghalaya, West Bengal and Tamil Nadu.

India exports about 6190 qtls. of arecanut and 5029 qtls of arecanut products valued at about Rs. 320 lakhs and Rs.317 lakhs respectively.

According to the study though the production of agricultural commodities in country has significantly increased, the benefits have not fully reached to the farmers. Most of the ills in the economy could be attributed to the absence of an orderly–

marketing management for agricultural produces, seasonality, biological nature, time lag involved in production process, bulkiness and perishability of agricultural commodities.

The study has effectively highlighted the drawbacks of marketing system and absence of an orderly marketing management not only for arecanut but also for other agricultural produce.

- Krishnaraja E. (1981) has studied 'An Evaluation of investment in Arecanut Gardens in Dakshina Kannada District, Karnataka with following objectives.
  1. To estimate the recurring and non-recurring investments in different size groups of areca gardens.
  2. To asses the economic feasibility of investment in arecanut gardens.
  3. To evaluate the benefits of 'purfo' irrigation system against the conventional method of 'surface' irrigation in areca gardens.

Out of the 8 taluks in South Canara district, Puttur taluk which occupies the first position with respect of total area under arecanut (3428 ha) and accounting for 26.60 per cent of the total area in the district was selected for the study, on the basis of magnitude of the area under different category were prepared. The farmers were classified as small, medium and large farmers depending upon their total land holding. The farmers having an area upto one-hectare, 1 to 2 hectares and above 2 hectares of irrigated land were classified as small, medium and large farmers respectively.

The study reveals that the Dakshina Kannada district occupied first place with an area of 12,923 hectares, thus claiming about 26 per cent of the total area under arecanut in Karnataka (49,971 hectares).

The results of the study indicated that the investment in arecanut enterprise is economically feasible irrespective of the size group. However the results of discounted cash flow measures revealed that priority should be given to the large areca gardens followed by medium and small gardens.

Arecanut enterprise provides employment for both skilled and unskilled labourers. The large gardens provided the highest mandays of employment followed by medium and small gardens.

The enterprise provides employment throughout the year and employment could be increased further by adopting intercropping in the garden with intercrops such as pepper, banana, cocoa etc.

With regards to the irrigation systems in areca gardens the purfo-irrigation system was found superior over the conventional surface irrigation system in terms of less cost of irrigation and more net returns. Further purfo irrigation method is labour saving technique and hence could be adopted when labour is scarce.

However the purfo irrigation system required huge investment and it was observed that only big farmers (who have more capital base) adopted the system of irrigation. Hence efforts should be made to provide adequate financial facilities for the needy farmers who wish to adopt purfo irrigation method.

The study on the whole indicated the remunerativeness of the arecanut enterprise in the Dakshina Kannada district of Karnataka and hence there is a scope for extending financial facilities, through institutional agencies to encourage arecanut production.

- Gajanana T.M. (1985) studied An Analysis of Supply Response of Arecanut in Karnataka.

  The study was undertaken with the overall objective of assessing the behaviour of arecanut farmers in response to changes in price and non-price factors. The other objectives of the study were as follows:

  1. To analyse the growth rate of arecanut in terms of area, production, productivity and price before and after the establishment of central arecanut and cocoa marketing and processing co-operative Ltd. Mangalore (Campco).
  2. To estimate the degree of supply response to price and non-price factors.
  3. To calculate the co-efficients of rigidity to know the number of years required for adjustment of area, yield and output.
  4. To suggest appropriate policy measures with respect to area, production and price.

The three districts Viz. Dakshina Kannada, Shimoga and Uttara Kannada were selected for the study mainly on the basis of their contribution to the total area and production of arecanut in Karnataka State.

The study revealed that in India arecanut is being cultivated in the states of Kerala, Karanataka and Assam. These three states together account for 90 per cent of the total area and 95 per cent of the total production of arecanut. In Karnataka, arecanut cultivation is mainly concentrated in the Malnad and coastal regions.

Dakshina Kannada, Uttar Kannada and Shimoga are the important arecanut growing districts of Karnataka. These three districts together constitute 62 per cent of total area and 70 per cent of total production of arecanut in the state.

According to the study the growth rate of output of arecanut was found to be the result of growth rate of area but not because of the growth rate in yield. Farmers brought marginal and submarginal lands under arecanut cultivation without taking much care to increase the yield. In these areas farmers should not be encouraged to expand the area under arecanut.

The study reveals that farmers were found to respond to prices in terms of area but not in terms of yield. Concerted measures may be taken up to equip the farmers with yield increasing input like seedlings, fertilizers, plant protection chemicals, provision for adequate and timely credit supported by technical knowledge.

The study highlighted only supply aspect in determining arecanut price. The study did not give much attention to demand aspect of arecanut. This is the limitation of the study.

- N.K. Hegde (1998) has studied, 'Crop Diversification Studies in Arecanut (Areca Catechu L.) Plantation with the following objectives.
    1. To compare monoculture of Arecanut over crop diversification.
    2. To study the performance of tuber crops as intercrops in comparison with their sole crops and to screen it for growing as sole crop and as intercrop.
    3. To characterize the microclimate of plantations is respect of air temperature relative humidity and interception of Photosynthetically Active Radiation (PAR) by component crops under different Arecanut based cropping systems.
    4. To study the root distribution/rooting pattern of Arecanut.
    5. Assess the performance of black pepper, banana, cardamom and cocoa under mixed cropping systems and

to evaluate the extent of crop intensification per unit land area under different Arecanut based mixed cropping systems.

6. To assess the availability of PAR for interception by underplanted Arecanut seedlings under different mixed cropping systems and to assess the availability of PAR for interception by component crops.
7. To find out the vaiability in the population of Arecanut (CV Sirsi Local) and to find out divergence in the population by Principal Component Analysis (PCA).
8. To find out the correlation of different growth and yield parameters on Arecanut yield.
9. To study the yielding behaviour and bearing tendency of Arecanut population.

The result of the above study revealed that both inter and mixed cropping in Arecanut plantation is a viable practice if properly adopted by the farmers of up ghat.

The above, study mentioned 'Future Line of Work' also,

1. Long term studies on intercropping in Arecanut plantation are needed in view of its perennial nature.
2. Various combinations of plant geometry have to be studied depending on the layout of the land for long term productivity.
3. Ideal varieties of components crops for Arecanut based cropping systems need to be identified along with their nutritional and other cultural requirements as a associated mixed/inter crop.
4. Studies are required on the effect of plantation eco climate on disease and pest incidence and spread.
5. Studies on performance of under planted Arecanut seedlings in a mixed cropping system consisting of cocoa as a component crop may be taken up as there is very less (less than 0.02 ly/min i.e. 1.7% of total) PAR available for interception by Arecanut seedlings.
6. progeny test of very high yielding palms of Arecanut with lesser coefficient of variation may be carried out to assess the heritability.

7. Bearing tendency differed among different yielding groups. There is a need for further investigation to know the causes in low yielding and very low yielding groups to deviated from normal tendency of biennial bearing.

The above study's investigations were carried out during 1993-94 to 1996-97 at ARS (Pepper), Sirsi, Uttara Kannada. Three different components viz. intercropping in Arecanut plantations, mixed cropping in Arecanut plantations and variability and correlation studies in Arecanut (CV. Sirsi Local) were included under the study. Field trial on intercropping including seven seasonal tuber crops (cultivated as rainfed sole crop and rainfed intercrop) and studies on variability and correlation in Arecanut CV Sirsi Local were carried out.

Established plantations were availed for studies on Arecanut based mixed cropping in system.

- Balachandra K. Naik (1998) has studied 'Farming System in Uttara Kannada District – An Econometric Analysis' with the following objectives.
    1. To delineate study areas based on agro-climatic parameters.
    2. To analyse the farming systems in the delineated areas.
    3. To estimate optimum system under.
        (a) Existing farming practices under present resource levels.
        (b) Recommended farming systems under present resources levels.
        (c) Possible farming system with enhanced resources levels.
    4. To develop alternative strategies to operationlise the improved farming systems.

The above study examined the possibilities of augmenting income and employment potential under different technological and capital environments.

The study focused on various issues. Such as, average farm situation of small and large farmers under both irrigated and rainfed conditions in three regions of the district. The relevant average statistics per farm were determined separately for both small and large farmers under both rainfed and irrigated conditions.

Linear programming technique was used to develop thirty six optimal plans for the three delineated clusters of Uttara Kannada district of Karnataka.

In addition the study focused net farm returns under different optimal plans, capital and credit requirement under different optimal plans, labour use under different plans, shadow prices of resources in each optimal solution of various models and problems and constraints in different farming systems.

- Ganapathi K.N. (1993) studied on 'Economics of Farming System in Malnad Region–A Case Study in Sagar Taluk' with the following objectives.
    1. To identify and analyse the farming systems in the taluk.
    2. To workout the economics of different farming systems.
    3. To analyse the cropping pattern income, savings and investment and structure under different farming systems.
    4. To examine the problems associated with different farming systems.

In the present study based on the implications of the findings the followings made.

1. It was found that most of the farmers were practicing only crop production with animal husbandry.

   To stabilize the income and to absorb the manpower during the lean season, dairy, sericulture can be under taken wherever it is possible.
2. Arecanut farmers can increase their net returns by growing intercrops like pepper, cardamom, cocoa, clove, nutmeg which do not need much extra effort for cultivation. However, some of the disease and pests are destroying the crop. So the farmers need to be educated to prevent and need to be educated to prevent and control these diseases.
3. Investment on irrigation structure like wells and pump sets was very low in the taluk. So, if rice farmers go in for irrigation they can grow pulses and vegetables in summer.

4. Investment is needed to establish the crops like rubber, coconut and cashew in the barren lands available. These crops help the farmers to increase their incomes in future in both the farming systems.
5. It was also observed that the area under pulses and oilseeds was negligible and paddy was the mono crop accounting for more than 90% of the gross cropped area in rice farming system. These crops can be grown if protective irrigation is provided.

   Farmers can also increase the area under sugarcane for jag gery purpose and ginger which are more profitable than paddy. Vegetable production is also negligible in the taluk and it depends on other parts of the state for its requirement. So, vegetables production also need to be undertaken.
6. Most of the farmers in the area complained about silting of tanks. So, water is not available in the later period of the Kharif Season. Government should take measure to desilting the tanks which will help farmers to greater extent.

- Smt. Prajna R. Mattihalli (2002) studied 'Marketing of Arecanut through Co-operative Societies in Karnataka state: A Diagnostic study.

The specific objectives of the study are:

1. To analyse growth pattern of Arecanut co-operative societies.
2. To analyse the relationship between production and Marketing System.
3. To analyse benefits accruing to the growers by selling through the society.
4. To throw the light over the problems encountered by Arecanut co-operatives in Marketing Process.
5. To understand Marketing behaviour of producers.
6. To analyse operating and financial efficiency of Arecanut Marketing societies.

In the above mentioned study the following suggestions highlighted in the present study.

1. There has been a constant expansion of the Arecanut cultivation in the last decade especially because of the economic viability of this crop.

2. World is now in the liberalized economic policy and trade in the globalization situation. Hence there is bound to be complex competition in the market. The co-operative sector in the twenty first century has to consolidate itself against various odds to carve a niche for itself in the socio-economic fabric of the countries.

The above mentioned study concluded that professional touch to the marketing operations of the Arecanut marketing co-operatives by a dedicated band of marketing professionals, with a focus on formulating market-driven marketing strategies in view of ever changing marketing scenario would go a long way in making, the sample marketing societies, more environment sensitive and operationally efficient in the country.

The above mentioned studies conducted by individual scholars and research agencies have mainly focussed their attention on aspects such as marketing, price behaviour, investment in arecanut cultivation etc. But none of the studies has focussed in detail on cost and returns from arecanut cultivation among different categories of farmers into different stages of arecanut gardens and also the benefits of inter-crops along with marketing of arecanut etc. Such an attempt is made in the present study. Apart from that the present study has also tried to examine the employment and income generation from arecanut cultivation. Therefore, the present study has tried to take up the analysis of those vital aspects which were hitherto not been examined.

3 THE RESEARCH METHODOLOGY AND GENERAL PROFILE OF KARNATAKA STATE AND SAMPLE DISTRICT

NEED FOR THE STUDY

India is the largest producer of Arecanut in the world. India stands first both in area (57%) and production (53%) of Arecanut in the world. In India, Karnataka state stands first both in the area and production of Arecanut when compared to other states. In Karnataka, among the 27 districts Shimoga district stands first in area under areca cultivation more than twenty thousand hectares in 2002.

In addition to this Shimoga district recorded the highest increase in area under Arecanut cultivation in the last decade (1990-91 to 1998-99) as compared to other districts. Apart from this, Shimoga district comprises both traditional and non-tradition areas of Arecanut cultivation as compared to other districts.

Further, Shimoga district very well represents all the stages of areca gardens (first, second, third stages) as compared to other districts. These reasons made me to select Shimoga district for the case study.

Nature and Source of Data

The present study is mainly based on primary data but secondary data is also used. The secondary data is collected from Bureau of Economics and Statistics, Bangalore, District Statistical Office, Shimoga, Office of the Joint Director of Agriculture, Shimoga, Office of the Assistant Director of Agriculture, Shimoga and Sagar, Office of the Horticulture, Shimoga and Sagar, Arecanut Research Station, Shimoga and Sagar, Office of the Tahashildar, Shimoga and Sagar, Agricultural Produce Marketing Committee (APMC) Shimoga and Sagar, Malnad Areca Marketing Co-operative Society Limited (MAMCOS) Shimoga and Sagar, Central Areca and Cocoa Marketing and Processing Co-operative Society Limited

(CAMPCO) of Shimoga and Sagar, Arecanut Processing and Sales Co-operative Society Limited (APSCOS), Sagar.

For evaluating the objectives of the study necessary primary data were obtained from the selected sample farmers through personal interview method during the months of April, May, June, 2002, with the help of pre-tested schedule. The data so collected refer to the agricultural year 2002.

The data collected from the sample farmers are related to the expenditure made in the first, second and third stages i.e. establishment and maintenance costs.

Selection of the Study Area

India is the largest producer of arecanut in the world. India stands first both in area (57%) and production (53%) of arecanut in the world.

In India, Karnataka State stands first both in the area and production of arecanut when compared to other states.

In Karnataka, among the 27 districts, Shimoga district stands first in area under areca cultivation more than 20,000 hectares in 2002. In addition to this, Shimoga district recorded the highest increase in area under arecanut cultivation in the last decade (1990-91 to 2000-01) as compared to other districts.

Apart from this Shimoga district comprises both traditional and non-traditional areas of arecanut cultivation as compared to other districts. Further, Shimoga district very well represents all the stages of areca gardens (first, second and third stages) as compared to other districts. The above reasons made us to select Shimoga district for the case study.

Selection of the Taluks

The Shimoga district for administrative purpose is divided into 7 taluks and two sub-divisions.

(i) Sagar sub-division

(ii) Shimoga sub-division.

Sagar and Shimoga taluks were selected for the study as the traditional and non-traditional areca gardens respectively.

In order to represent the traditional areca gardens Sagar taluk is selected for the following reasons.

1. There is co-existence of hilly and maidan areas. It is the peculiar nature of Sagar taluk as compared to other traditional taluks viz, Thirthahalli, Sorab, Hosanagara.

2. Traditionally Sagar taluk is a stable areca growing area, as compared to other traditional taluks and it is because of this reason Arecanut Research Station has been established in Sagar in the year 2002.
3. All the stages of arecanut gardens are existing in Sagar taluk as compared to other traditional taluks.
4. The economy of Sagar taluk is standing on the cultivation and production of arecanut.
5. Existence of Agro-based industries is also one of the important reasons to select this taluk as compared to other traditional taluks.
6. Sagar taluk's 'Agricultural Produce Marketing Committee' (APMC) is considered as one of the reputed markets. Malnad Arecanut Marketing Co-operative Society Limited (MAMCOS), Central Arecanut and Cocoa Marketing and Processing Co-operative Soceity Limited (CAMPCO), Arecanut Processing and Sales Co-operative Society Limited (APSCOS) are operating in APMC yard of Sagar.
7. Last but not the least, Sagar taluk is more advanced (in infrastructure) as compared to other traditional areca growing taluks.

In order to represent the non-traditional areca gardens, Shimoga taluk has been selected for the following reasons.

1. Shimoga taluk is canal-irrigated area. It receives canal irrigation from both Thunga and Badhra reservoirs.
2. Shimoga taluk represents, all the stages of Areca gardens (first, second, third stages) when compared to other non-traditional areca growing taluks.
3. Existence of Agro-based industries in Shimoga taluk is one of the important reasons to select Shimoga taluk, as compared to other non-traditional taluks.
4. Inspite of price fluctuations of the arecanut, areca cultivation in Shimoga taluk is considered as stable when compared to other non-traditional taluks of Shimoga district.
5. Arecanut Research Station has been established in the year 2002 in Shimoga and it is functioning.
6. Agricultural Produce Marketing Committee (APMC) of Shimoga is considered as one of the reputed market in India

and Malnad Arecanut Marketing Co-operative Society Limited (MAMCOS), Central Arecanut and Cocoa Marketing and Processing Co-operative Limited (CAMPCO) are operating in the APMC yard of Shimoga market.

Selection of the Sample Villages

As per 1991 census there are 233 and 198 villages in Sagar and Shimoga taluks respectively.

From each sample taluk (Sagar and Shimoga taluk) four villages are selected on the basis of information gathered from the village accountants and information obtained from respective taluka offices of Sagar and Shimoga. The major arecanut growing villages, having all the stages (first, second and third) and all the category of farmers (small, medium and large) were selected for the study. From each village 25 sample farmers were selected randomly.

VILLAGES SELECTED

In Sagar Taluk

1. Hosahalli
2. Sasaravalli
3. Khandika
4. Kerekoppa

In Shimoga Taluk

1. Hosudi
2. Hosahalli
3. Lakshmipura
4. Sogane

The above sample villages are having the basic infrastructural facilities such as veterinary facility, primary health centre, agro-service centre, storage facility, primary co-operative credit society, regional rural bank, approach road, main road, market, school, post and telegraph office, agricultural co-operatives etc, all these facilities are available in these villages within a range of 0-4 km distance.

Selection of Sample Farmers

The total sample size is 200 farmers, 100 from each taluka. Within the taluk out of four villages selected for the purpose 25 farmers were selected randomly from each village equally from different farm categories and also from different stages of areca garden. This can be seen from the following Table 1.

Accordingly, in the small farmers' category, 06 respondents in first stage, 04 in second stage and 02 in third stage in each village (total 12) have been selected. In the medium farmers' category, 04 respondents in first stage, 04 in second stage and 01 in third stage have been selected in each village (total 09). In the large farmers' category, 02 in first stage, 01 in second stage and 01 in third stage have been selected in each village (total 04).

Selection of Sample Areca Gardens

The areca gardens of the villages were divided into three stages based on the age of the respective areca gardens.
Assuming the life span (economic bearing) of the areca palm as 50 years the present study has divided this period into three stages.

1. First Stage (1 to 7 yrs.)
2. Second Stage (8 to 40 yrs.)
3. Third Stage (40 to 50 yrs.)

The areca garden in the gestation period (i.e.,1 to 7 yrs) is considered as First Stage. During this stage the areca palm will be in an infant stage and it starts bearing the yield from 6th year.
The areca garden between 8 to 40 yrs is considered as Second stage. In this stage the areca palms start yielding and the yield of areca palm will go on increasing year after year upto 40 years.
The areca garden above 40 years is considered as Third stage. This may be considered as period of declining stage upto 50 years. After that the plant need to be replaced.

In all 48 first stage gardens, 36 second stage gardens and 16 third stage gardens were selected from each taluk.

Categorisation of Sample Farmers

The farmers of the sample villages were divided into three categories as small, medium and large based on the size of their land holdings.

1. Small (upto 1 hectare of irrigated land).
2. Medium (1.01 to 2.00 hectares of irrigated land).
3. Large (Above 2.00 hectares of irrigated land).

Table 1
Selection of Sample Farmers

	First Stage			Second Stage			Third Stage			
I *Sagar Taluk*	*Small*	*Medium*	*Large*	*Small*	*Medium*	*Large*	*Small*	*Medium*	*Large*	*Total*
1. Hosahalli	06	04	02	04	04	01	02	01	01	25
2. Sasaravalli	06	04	02	04	04	01	02	01	01	25
3. Kandika	06	04	02	04	04	01	02	01	01	25
4. Kerekoppa	06	04	02	04	04	01	02	01	01	25
Total	24	16	08	16	16	04	08	04	04	100
II Shimoga Taluk										
1. Hosudi	06	04	02	04	04	01	02	01	01	25
2. Hosahalli	06	04	02	04	04	01	02	01	01	25
3. Lakshmipura	06	04	02	04	04	01	02	01	01	25
4. Sogane	06	04	02	04	04	01	02	01	01	25
Total	24	16	08	16	16	04	08	04	04	100
Total Sample Size	48	32	16	32	32	08	16	08	08	200

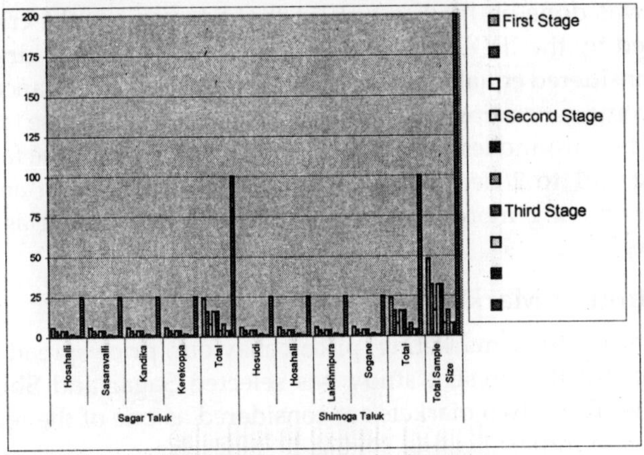

Selection of Sample farmers

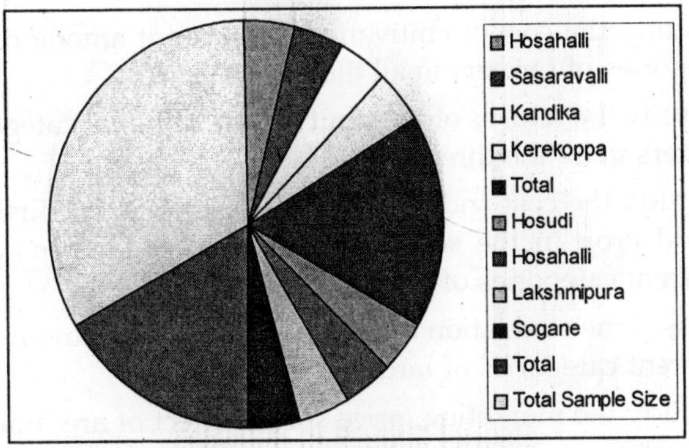

Selection of Sample farmers

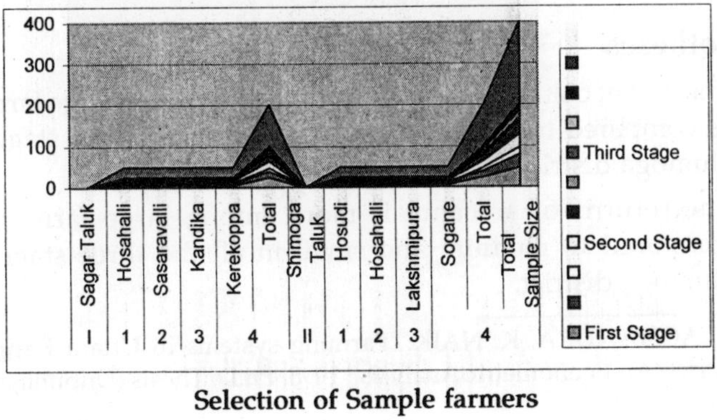

Selection of Sample farmers

The categorisation of the sample farmers into small, medium and large was done on the basis of landholdings as per the criterion adopted by the IRDP. In this classification 2 hectares of dry land was considered equal to one hectare of wetland in accordance with the income generating capacity of dry and wetlands. Those farmers with 1 hectare and less were considered as small, while the farmers having 1.01 to 2 hectares were considered as medium and the farmers having more than two hectares were grouped as large farmers.*

Selection of Markets

In order to study marketing, price behaviour, price spread effect of arecanut the present study has selected Sagar and Shimoga markets. These two markets are considered as one of the reputed markets in India.

Objectives of the Study

1. To study the cost of cultivation of arecanut among different categories of farmers in all the three stages.
2. To study the returns of arecanut among different categories of farmers in all the three stages.
3. To study the cost and returns of inter crop in the first stage, mixed crop in the second stage in areca-gardens among different categories of farmers.
4. To asses the evaluation of investment in areca garden among different categories of farmers.
5. To study the marketing, price spread effect of arecanut.
6. To make suitable policy recommendations in the light of the analysis to influence the public policy.

Hypotheses

1. The cost of cultivation of arecanut is more among large farmers as compared to medium and small in all the three stages in Shimoga district.
2. The returns of arecanut is more among large farmers as compared to medium and small in all the three stages in Shimoga district.

---

* BALACHANDRA. K. NAIK: 'Farming systems in Uttara Kannada District- An Econometric Analysis' 1998. Ph.D. Thesis (Unpublished).

3. The large areca farmers are benefited more by cultivating inter crop/mixed crop as compared to medium and small in Shimoga district.
4. Arecanut plantation is economically viable among all the categories of farmers in Shimoga district.

COMPUTATION OF COSTS AND RETURNS

Costs

The costs of arecanut garden are worked out on the basis of the establishment and the maintenance of arecanut gardens.

The establishment of an arecanut garden requires huge amount of investment as it is a perennial crop. Areca palm takes seven years to establish and start bearing economic yield.

In Sagar and Shimoga taluks banana is grown during the gestation period (first stage) mainly to provide shade to the young areca palm and to get some early returns. The banana suckers will be removed once the areca palms obtain four years of age.

In the second stage of areca garden (8 to 40 years) sample farmers of Sagar and Shimoga taluk have planted pepper and cocoa as mixed crop respectively to get an additional income.

In the third stage, sample farmers in both the taluks maintain the existing areca garden. Mono-cropping is observed in this stage.

The costs involved in establishing and maintenance of the areca garden are mainly classified into

(A) Establishment Cost
(B) Maintenance Cost

Establishment Cost

Establishment cost includes costs incurred on land levelling, fencing, open well and pump sets, sprinkler, conveyor pipes, pump house, processing yard, seedlings, red earth, interest on fixed capital, land revenue etc. It also includes interest on fixed capital and land revenue paid to the government.

Maintenance Cost

Maintenance cost includes, costs incurred on labour and materials.

Labour Cost

The expenditure incurred on human labour bullock power and hired machine constitutes labour costs.

The hired labour was charged at the prevailing wage rates paid per day, in the study area. For family labour the wages were imputed at the same rate as those paid to hired labour.
Bullock power and Hired machine were calculated separately by taking into account the number of days hired and the hiring charges.

In the gestation period the expenditure on labour in the first year included activities like land levelling, digging pits, planting the seedlings, irrigating the garden application of manure and chemical fertilizers, plant protection chemicals etc.

In the subsequent years main operations carried out were irrigating the garden, weeding, mulching, maintenance of trenches, harvesting and processing etc.

Material Cost

It includes the expenditure incurred on the purchase of materials such chemical fertilizers and manures, plant protection chemicals, farm yard manure, electricity or fuel charges and interest paid on short term loan etc.

Total Cost (A+B)

Total cost comprises of total establishment cost and total maintenance cost.

Returns

Returns from processed arecanut were recorded in physical quantities and the monetary value of produce is calculated considering the prices received by the cultivators.
The returns are calculated by multiplying the quantity with respective price.

Total Returns

The total quantity received from the areca garden per hectare in quintals with respective price.

Net Returns

The returns received by the farmers after deducting the total cost from the total returns.

Returns Over TMC

The returns received by the farmers after deducting the total maintenance cost from the total returns.

Cost of Cultivation of Intercrop and Mixed Crop

The Cost of cultivation of Intercrop and Mixed crop includes the expenditure on planting material (i.e. banana suckers, cocoa seedlings/sapling, pepper vines), material cost (i.e. Chemical Fertilizer Plant Protection Chemicals. Farm Yard Manure, Green Leaves, Red Earth) and labour cost (application of all these inputs) irrigation cost, harvesting and processing.

Returns of Inter Crop and Mixed Crop

The yields and prices received for intercrop (banana) and mixed crop (pepper and cocoa) was calculated accordingly.

Methods of Analysis

For assessing quantitatively the objectives and hypotheses outlined for the purpose of the present study simple tabular analysis was used with the aid of averages, percentages, percentage variation for obtaining meaningful results for comparison, between various stages and farmer's category in two taluks of the study area.

In addition to this the other statistical devices such as Correlation Analysis and Multiple Regression Analysis and Linear Regression Analysis, t-test with respect to Multiple Regression and Linear Regression were used.

Apart from this, in order to assess economic feasibility of investment among various category of sample farmers *Net Present Value, Internal Rate of Return, Benefit-Cost Ratio, Pay Back Period* were employed.

Evaluation of Investments

Investment evaluation in arecanut gardens was felt necessary since the life span of the orchard extends over a long period. Gittinger (1974), has illustrated the usefulness of discounted cash flow techniques in evaluating the long term projects in agriculture. Hence for evaluating the investment and to find out the feasibility and economic viability of the investment in arecanut gardens, a few measures of project evaluation using the discounted cash flow technique were used. These techniques are advocated as an aid to evaluate and find out the worthiness of the investment, especially those of long term projects. This technique has an advantage in that the future variable cash flows are reduced to a single sum at a specific point of time, thereby facilitating comparison between investment alternatives.

The discounted cash flow measures used in the analysis are Net Present Value (NPV), Internal Rate of Return (IRR), Benefit Cost Ratio (B:C ratio).

Net Present Value

The net present value is simply the present worth of net benefit of a project discounted at the opportunity cost of capital. This criterion ranks the investments for selecting the best alternatives. Generally, higher the net present worth, better would be the preference. In calculating the net present value, the difference between the present value of the cost stream and present value of benefit stream were considered at a discount rate of 12.50 per cent. This is the rate that is being charged by the financial institutions on loans advanced for investment on areca garden.

The general verbal and mathematical form of net present worth criterion is presented below:

NPV = [Present worth of benefits] – [Present worth of costs]

$$NPV =_{-} \sum_{t=1}^{n} \frac{B_n - C_n}{(1+d)^n}$$

Where,

B_n = Benefits in nth year (from areca and intercrop/mixed crop)

C_n = Costs in nth year (of areca and intercrop/mixed crop)

n = Number of years.

d = Discount rate.

OR

$$NPV = \left[\sum_{=1}^{n} Y_{n(1+r)^{-n}} - I_0 \right]$$

Where,

Y_n = Net Cash inflows in the nth year.

r = Discount rate (12.50%)

I_o = Initial Investment

i = Number of years.

In order to select worthiness of the project, the net present value should be positive.

Internal Rate of Return

The internal rate of return is the rate of return, which equates the present worth of benefits to present worth of costs, which means the net present worth is zero. This represents the average earning capacity of an investment from the projects.

The mathematical form of IRR is:

$$\text{IRR} = \sum_{t=1}^{n} \frac{B_n - C_n}{(1+d)} = 0$$

where,

B_n = Benefits in n^{th} year (from areca and intercrop/mixed crop)
C_n = Number of years.
d= Discount rate.

The internal rate of return is arrived at by interpolation technique by using different discount rates so as to see that the net present worth is equated to zero. The interpolation formula employed in this study is as follows.

$$IRR = \left(\frac{\text{Present worth of the cash flow at lower discount rate}}{\text{Lower discount rate + Difference between higher x and lower discount rate}} \right) \text{x} \begin{array}{c}\text{Absolute difference between} \\ \text{the present worth of cash} \\ \text{flow at two discount rates}\end{array}$$

Benefit-Cost Ratio

It is the ratio of discounted cash inflows and outflows which must be unity or more for an enterprise to be considered worthwhile. The minimum ratio required is 1:1. This 1:1 indicates the coverage of costs without any surplus benefits. But usually, the ratio should be more than unity in order to provide some additional returns over the costs for clear decision. The benefit-cost ratio can be stated both verbally and mathematically as:

$$\text{B} : \text{C} = \frac{\text{Present worth of benefits}}{\text{Present worth of costs}}$$

$$\text{B} : \text{C} = \sum_{=1}^{n} \frac{B_n / (1+d)^n}{C_n / (1+d)^n}$$

Where,

B_n = Benefits in each year (from areca and intercrop/mixed crop)
C_n = Costs in each year (of areca and intercrop/mixed crop)
n = Number of years.
d = Discount rate.

Payback Period

Payback period represents the length of time required for the stream of each proceeds produced by the time required for the project to pay for itself. In the present study, the pay back period is calculated by successively deducting the initial investment from the net returns until the initial investment is fully recovered.

CHAPTER SCHEME

Chapter I : Arecanut in the Indian Economy and Trade.

This chapter presents the profile of arecanut in the Indian Economy and Trade, area and production of Arecanut in Karnataka, trends in area and production of Arecanut, varieties of arecanut, price behaviour of arecanut, role of arecanut in Indian Economy, imports of arecanut, exports of arecanut, demand for arecanut, supply response of arecanut, constraints for arecanut cultivation, economics of intercrop cultivation in areca garden, value added products of arecanut.

Chapter II : Review of Literature.

This chapter presents a brief review of the studies conducted by the individual scholars, which mainly focused on aspects on marketing, price behaviour and investment in arecanut cultivation.

Chapter III : The Research Methodology and General Profile of Karnataka State and Sample District.

This chapter presents, nature and source of data, selection of the Study area, selection of taluks, selection of sample villages, selection of sample farmers, selection of sample areca gardens, categorisation of sample farmers, objectives of the study, hypotheses, computation of costs and returns, methods of analysis, Scheme of presentation, concepts used in the study, limitation of the study, profile of the Karnataka state, general profile of the sample District.

Chapter IV : Socio-Economic conditions and cultivation practices of the sample farmers.

This chapter presents size of land holdings, housing conditions, family size, educational status, consumption expenditure, consumer durables and agricultural equipments of sample farmers, accessibility to mass-media of sample farmers in the study area, institutional participation of sample farmers in the study area, sources of borrowing of sample farmers, cultivation practices of sample farmers.

Chapter V : Cost of Cultivation of Arecanut: An Analysis.

This chapter deals with the cost of cultivation of arecanut in the first stage, second stage, third stage, cost of cultivation of intercrop and mixed crop and the primary data has been examined under the framework of correlation analysis and multiple regression analysis i.e., correlation co-efficient of maintenance cost among various farmers category in Sagar taluk, Shimoga taluk and Shimoga District and multiple regression of maintenance cost among various farmers category in Sagar taluk, Shimoga taluk and Shimoga District.

Chapter VI : Returns of Arecanut : An Analysis.

This chapter deals with the returns of arecanut in the first stage, second stage, third stage, average annual total returns, net returns, returns over total maintenance cost, returns per Re unit cost in the study area over a period of 50 years, returns of intercrop in the first stage, returns of mixed crop in the second stage, evaluation of investment in areca gardens, employment generation in areca gardens. The primary data has been examined under the framework of correlation, multiple regression and linear regression analysis i.e., correlation co-efficient of dependent variables returns of areca, intercrop/ mixed crop, EC, MC, CCIC/CCMC of various farmers category in Sagar taluk, Shimoga taluk and Shimoga District. Multiple Regression of returns of arecanut of various farmers category in Sagar taluk, Shimoga taluk and Shimoga District. Linear regression of returns of intercrop/mixed crop of various farmers category in Sagar taluk, Shimoga taluk and Shimoga District.

Chapter VII : Marketing of Arecanut.

This chapter deals with the price movement and growth in plantation, a brief note on marketing societies, CAMPCO, MAMCOS, APSCOS, marketing of white variety, marketing of red variety, procedure of sales and its proceedings in APMC yard, major Secondary markets of arecanut in Karnataka, Agricultural Produce Marketing Committee (APMC), Price behaviour of arecanut, Price spread effect of growers, intermediaries and consumers of the study area, Farmers opinion on the marketing system in the study area, export of arecanut, imports of arecanut, conclusions and suggestions.

Chapter VIII : Summary, Conclusions and Recommendations.

It is the final chapter of the study presenting summary, conclusion with suggestions and recommendations.

Concepts Used in the Study

The study makes frequent reference to certain concepts, the definitions which are given below.

Small Farmer

A farmer having upto 1 hectare of irrigated land holding is considered as small farmer.

Medium Farmer

A farmer having 1.01 to 2 hectares of irrigated land is considered as medium farmer.

Large Farmer

A farmer having more than 2 hectares of irrigated land is considered as large farmer.

First Stage

The arecanut gardens which are in the gestation period (i.e. 1 to 7 years) come under this group.

Second Stage

The arecanut gardens between 8 to 40 years come under this group.

Third Stage

The arecanut gardens above 40 years come under this group.

Traditional Area

The area in which the arecanut is grown as their main crop since long time without considering the price boom.

Non-Traditional Area

The area in which the arecanut is being grown recently because of price boom.

Inter cropping

Growing annuals or biennials in the interspace of the plantation crop (Arecanut)

Mixed Cropping

Growing of perennials in the interspace of plantation crops.

Limitation of the Study

The present study is beset with certain obvious limitations. They are enumerated here:

Only two taluks were selected for the study. Hence results are largely applicable to those areas where similar conditions prevail.

PROFILE OF KARNATAKA STATE

Description of Karnataka State

- Land Resources
- Climate
- Soils
- Forest
- Cropping Pattern
- Water Source
- Minerals

Karnataka State was constituted as per the recommendations of the States Re-organisation Committee on November 1, 1956. The State, then named, as Mysore State, was formed by consolidating the Kannada speaking areas of former States, of Bombay, Hyderabad, Madras and Coorg which was a centrally administered territory and the erstwhile native State of Mysore. It was renamed as Karnataka on November 1, 1973.

Karnataka, is a maritime State, situated in the western part of Deccan peninsula of the Indian Union, lying between 11.5 and 19' IV latitudes and 74^0 and 78^0 'E' longitudes. It is bounded by Goa and Maharastra States in the North, by Arabian sea in the west. The southern and eastern boundaries are defined by Kerala, Tamil Nadu and Andra Pradesh. The State, occupying a geographical area of 191791 thousand hectares. The total population of the State is 5.27 crores. The density of population in the State is 275 persons per sq. km.

Resource Base

Human and material resources together, form the resource base of an economy and its economic prosperity depends on the extent and intensity with which, the resource base is exploited. Karnataka is rich in resources like forests, minerals, water resources, live stock and fisheries. It is no wonder that, the State is described as "priceless gift of nature".

Land Resources

Physiographically, Karnataka is a State in contrasts and may be divided into 4 regions as (a) The Coastal Belt, (b) The Malnad, (c) The Northern plateau and (d) The Southern plateau.

Each of these regions, has its distinct demographic and physical characteristics. The map indicates the geographic region of the State.

The Coastal Region

It is lying between the edge of western Ghats and the Arabian sea and is about 320 kms long and 13 to 32 kms wide in the north and 50 to 60 kms wide in the South. It is varied and picturesque region of great beauty. This low land region of the west coast is further beautified by several ridges and spurs of the western Ghats. It is a different terrain full of rivers, creeks, isolated peaks and detached ranges of hills. Along the coastal area of Karnataka, there are seen an endless palm grooves and snow white beaches, inter spaced with lagoons and back waters, against a back drop of majestic mountains with ever green forest. The soils are lateretic except in isolated stretches near the sea side. The dominant crop is paddy, sugarcane, followed by coconut and arecanut gardens. In recent years, groundnut, vegetable and onions are grown as summer crops in this region. Fishing and boat building, supports, sizable section of the population.

The Malnad

The Malnad region, stretches for about 650 km long and 50 to 60 km wide to the eastern side of the western ghats edge with thick forest. Its situation is 152 mtrs, above the sea level in the west and gradually, rises towards the east, thus culminating in a series of ranges of hills, with an average height of about 900 mtrs. It is separated from the coastal plains, by the steep wall of the ghats. The Malnad, has an average rainfall of 2500 to 1000 millimetres from west to east. The climate is generally hot and wet. Soils of Malnad are lateretic. They are of average fertility. The major crop of this region is paddy sugarcane. There are plantations of coffee, arecanut and coconut. There are rich forests of excellent wood consisting of sandalwood, teak, nandi and varieties of forest trees, which have provided inputs to building activity, as well as, to artistic woodcraft in malnad region at Sagar, Sorab. The malnad region is described as, an area consisting of hills and dales of forests and perennial rivers, majestic mountains and significant water falls.

The Northern Maidan

The Northern Maidan, lies to the east of the semi-malnad and stretches to the northeastern boundary of the State to the north of Bellary district. In the northern parts, the region is an extensive plateaus, with an elevation of 365 to 610 metres above the sea level. It slopes towards the east and consists of several isolated ridges. There are three important rivers, viz the Krishna, the Bhima and the Tungabhadra, which drain the area and at the same time, they have become massive irrigation projects during the five year plan periods. This region has rich black cotton soil and has open treeless fields. The soils have capacity to retain moisture, for longer period. Average rainfall ranges from 350 to 900 millimetres. Prior to coming of large scale irrigation projects, these lands were irrigated by tanks, wells and canals. The major crops that are grown are jowar, wheat and cotton.

The Southern Maidan

The Southern Maidan, represents the core of old Mysore State. The western part of southern maidan, stretches up to the eastern edge of the malnad and is about 915 to 975 metres in right. The plateau rises to a height of nearly 915 metres in the eastern part. The river system consists of the Tungabhadra, Cauvery, Pennar and the Palar rivers. It is divided into numerous valleys, differing widely in size and shape. The soil is predominantly red and is generally less fertile. The rainfall decreases and variations are greater, from west to east. The total annual rainfall, varies from 500 to 750 millimetres. The major crops grown are rice and ragi.

CLIMATE

The climate of the State as a whole may be described as, essentially tropical monsoon type. It gets rain from both south–west and north–west monsoons over the greater part of the State. Summers are very warm and winters are very cold. In the coastal region, humidity makes summers enervating. In the northern region, winters are delightfully cool. But, summers are uncomfortably hot. The following four seasons recognised by the climatologits are also applicable to Karnataka.

1. Cold weather period–January to February.
2. Hot weather period–March to May.
3. South–west monsoon–June to September period.
4. North–east monsoon period–October to December.

The State receives rains from both the monsoons, but it receives the major portion of its rainfall from the south-west monsoon. The annual average rainfall in Karnataka is about 1,200 millimetres. But, there are regional variations in the distribution of annual rainfall; the annual rainfall varies from 7620 mm on the western ghats to about 380 mm in the eastern and north–eastern part of the state.

Soils

The soils of Karnataka State exhibit a marked diversity in different parts of the State. It depends upon the nature of the present soil and the climatic conditions prevailing in that area. The variations in soil and climatic conditions are such that, no other state in the country can compare with it, in the variety and crops prevailed. The soils of the state can be classified into four main groups as follows.

Laterite

These soils are found in the hilly and heavy rainfall regions of the Eastern Ghats and in Chikmagalur, Shimoga, South Kanara, North Kanara, Coorg, Belgaum and Dharwad districts. They are acidic in nature and are different in lime and other nutrients. These soils are best suited for paddy crop and also for plantation crops like coffee, tea, coconut and arecanut.

Red Loams and Red Sandy Loams

They occur in long strip in the southern districts of the State viz. Tumkur, Bangalore, Kolar, Mandya, Mysore, Hassan and some parts of Chikmagalur, Dharwad and Bellary districts. The red sandy loams occurs in the central and south eastern portion of the State. The water holding capacity of the soil is poor. Paddy, ragi, pulses, millets and oil seeds are some of the important crops grown in this soil.

Black Soils

Most areas of northern part of Karnataka State, covering Dharwad, Bellary, Belgaum, Bijapur, Raichur, Gulbarga and Chitradurga, are covered by these soils. The blocks are fertile and can grow good crops of cotton, jowar etc.

Alluvial Soils:

These are mostly found in river valleys and in some plains in the West Coast region. These soils are mostly transported. They contain alternative layers of sand and solt. The alluvial soils on the west coast are poorer in basins than, those in the eastern part. They are sandy loam in texture and rich inorganic matter. They are found to yield good crops of paddy, sugarcane, plantains and arecanut.

Out of the four varieties of soil conditions in the State, three are favourable to growth of arecanut plantations. It is only in red sandy and black soils that, the arecanut can not be grown. But these soils are restricted to fewer districts and smaller areas of the State. In other words, major parts of the State, has favourable climatic and soil conditions for growth of arecanut plantations.

Forest

Karnataka State, has relatively smaller area under forests, compared to the national average. The area under forests in the country, as a whole constitutes 22 per cent of the total geographical area; whereas, the corresponding proportion in the State is only 18 per cent. But the said area is well endowed with better quality of forest wealth which is enormously rich in teak and agony, black–wood, nandi, halasu and variety of forest trees.

Climate, altitude and also, the type of soil, which exists in particular area, govern the geographical distribution of the forest. With a rainfall, varying from the 250 mm to 7620 mm and with attitudes varying from the sea level to 915 metres, there are wide differences between the forests of different places. In the State, the most of the forest area is confined to the malnad area in the west. The proportion of forests in malnad region is 43 per cent of the total concentration of forests and is to be found mostly in North Kanara, South Kanara, Coorg, Shimoga, Chickmagalur and Mysore districts. The arecanut plantations are mostly situated in malnad districts under the cover of the thick forest.

Cropping Pattern

It is one of the factors determining the value of farm output. The bulk of the cultivated area in the State is devoted to the production of food crops but the lands under non food crops are also sizable.

Water Sources

The main water resources in Karnataka State are rainfall, rivers and underground water.

Rainfall

The climate of the state may be described as essentially tropical monsoon type. On an average, Karnataka receives 1040 mm of rainfall, mainly from the South-West monsoon.

Rivers: State is bestowed with major rivers and small rivers.

Underground Water Resources: Underground water resources of the state are limited to the low percentage i.e., 10 per cent of annual rainfall.

Minerals

Karnataka is one of the mineral rich States in India, possessing extensive and valuable mineral deposits of Gold, Iron ore Manganese, ore Chromite, Bauxite, Limestone, Copper etc. The State ranks fifth in regard to mineral production in the country.

GENERAL PROFILE OF THE SAMPLE DISTRICT

Introduction

Shimoga is one of the twenty seven districts of the Karnataka State. It is situated roughly in the mid-south western part of the state, with an eventful history and rich cultural tradition. The district is bestowed with abundant natural resources. The western part consists of a mountainous terrains and on eastern side it is densely forested hilly region with heavy rainfall is called Malnad. An area having natural characteristics to some extent of both Malnad and Maidan called 'Semi-Malnad' and open region, (a level land) called 'Maidan'. The western part is replete with fascinating natural beauty, being clothed with dense tropical forests stimulated by heavy rainfall. The eastern part also consists of an open area with attractive lakes and hills.

Location

The district is situated between $13^{0}27'$ and $140^{0}39'$ as North Latitude and between $74^{0}38'$ and $76^{0}4'$ East Longitude in the mid-south western part of the state.

Boundary

The length from east to west is 152.9 kilometers and from north to south 128.8 kilometers. The Shimoga district is bound on the east by the Davanagere district, on the west by North Canara and Udupi districts, on the north by Haveri district and on the South by Chikkmagalur district.

Area, Population

Shimoga district covers an area of 8,465 sq. kms i.e., 3.21 per cent of the state's total area. According to the 2001 census, the population of the district is 16,40,000 it accounts for 3.11 per cent of the state's population. The density of population is 193 per sq. km. Out of the total population male population accounts for 50.61 per cent and female population about 49.39 per cent.

There are 07 taluks, 40 hoblis, 1440 villages, 260 village panchayaths, 09 town/urban communities, 09 corporations. All the seven taluks are grouped into two revenue subdivisions, for administrative purposes i.e. Shimoga and Sagar.

The district administration centre is at Shimoga City and it is 275 kms away from the capital city of Bangalore. Of the total area of the district, Sagar taluk covers 1940 sq.kms which is 22.92 per cent of the total area and it is the largest taluk in the district, and Shimoga taluk covers 1108 sq. kms which is 13.09 per cent of the total area of the district.

According to 2001 census, literacy rate of the sample district is 74.86 per cent. Literacy rate of male and female population is 82.32 per cent and 67.24 per cent respectively.

Agriculture and Agricultural Development

According to the village records the total geographical area of Shimoga district is 84,65,000 hectares. Out of this the forests cover an area of 2,77,000 hectares, the net sown area is 2,17,000 hectares and net irrigated area is 1,32,000 hectares.

The distribution of land-holdings clearly shows that small and marginal farmers having land-holding less than 2 hectares constitute 78 per cent of the total number of holdings in the district. Thus it can be said that large size holdings are very less in the district. This can be seen from the Table 2.

Table 2

Distribution Of Land –Holding In Shimoga District During 2001-02

Sl. No.	*Taluk*	*Less than 1 hectare (No of Land Holding)*	*Between 1 & 2 hectares (No of Land Holding)*	*Between 2 & 4 hectares (No of Land Holding)*	*Between 4 & 10 hectares (No of Land Holding)*	*Above 10 hectares (No of Land Holding)*	*Total (No of Land Holding)*
01	Shimoga	10829	7449	4195	1739	211	24423
		(44.34)	(30.50)	(17.18)	(7.12)	(0.86)	
02	Bhadhrawathi	18588	6338	2985	937	43	28891
		(64.34)	(21.94)	(10.33)	(3.24)	(0.15)	
03	Thirthahalli	9985	5190	2614	966	138	18893
		(52.85)	(27.47)	(13.83)	(5.12)	(0.73)	
	Division Total	39402	18977	9794	3642	392	72207
		(54.57)	(26.28)	(13.56)	(5.05)	(0.54)	
04	Sagar	11005	5727	2832	1264	177	21005
		(52.39)	(27.26)	(13.48)	(6.03)	(0.84)	
05	Hosanagara	5061	3780	2133	805	108	11887
		(42.57)	(31.80)	(17.94)	(6.77)	(0.92)	
06	Shikaripura	12802	9737	4670	1779	183	29171
		(43.89)	(33.38)	(16.01)	(6.10)	(0.63)	
07	Sorab	11031	7596	4664	2306	546	26143
		(42.20)	(29.06)	(17.84)	(8.82)	(2.08)	
	Division Total	39899	26840	14299	6154	1014	88206
		(45.23)	(30.43)	(16.21)	(6.98)	(1.15)	
	District Total	79301	45817	24093	9796	1406	160413
		(49.44)	(28.56)	(15.02)	(6.11)	(0.87)	(100.00)

Source: Agricultural Progress Report 2001-02. Office of Asst. Director of Agriculture, Shimoga, Page 3.

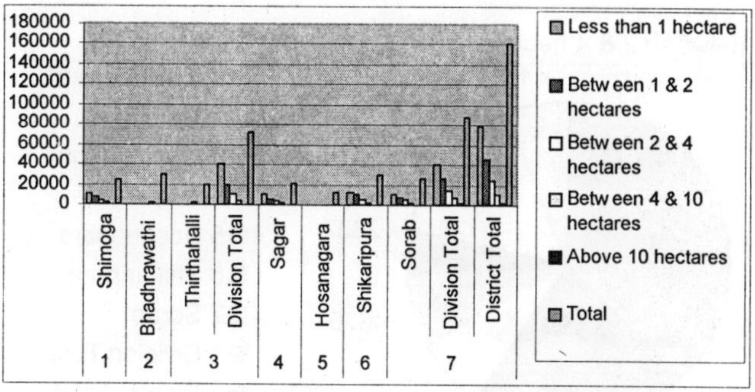

Distribution of Land–Holding in Shimoga District During 2001-02

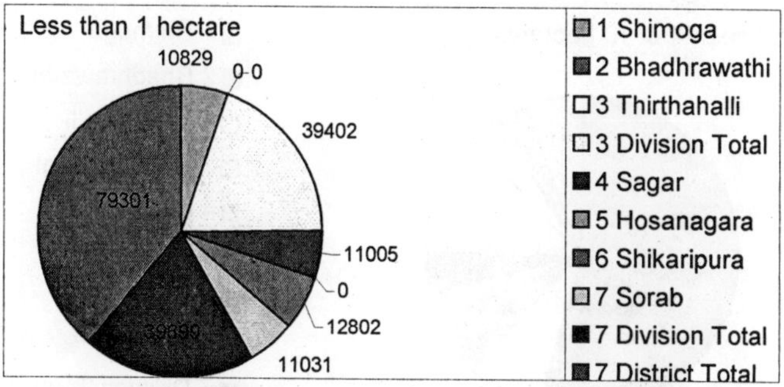

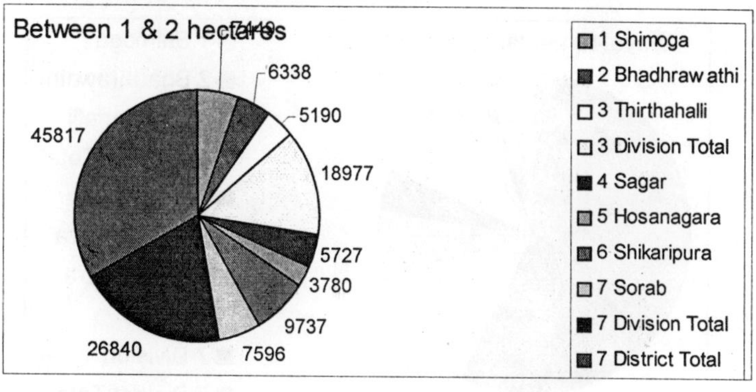

Cropping Pattern

The cropping pattern in the district reveals that food crops dominate as compared to non food crops. The percentage of area under non food crops is more in Shimoga and Sagar taluks as compared to other taluks. This can be seen from the Table 3.

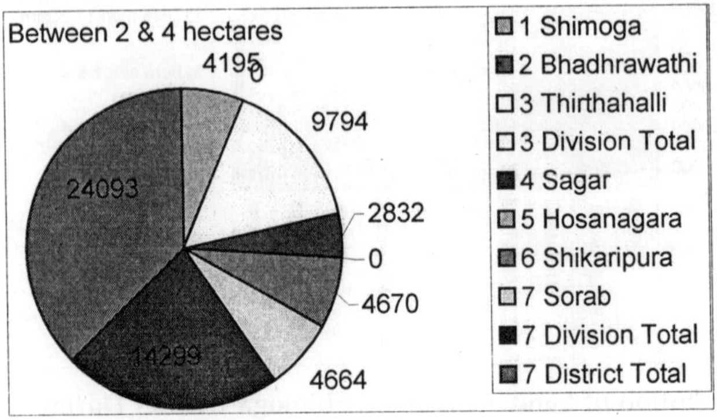

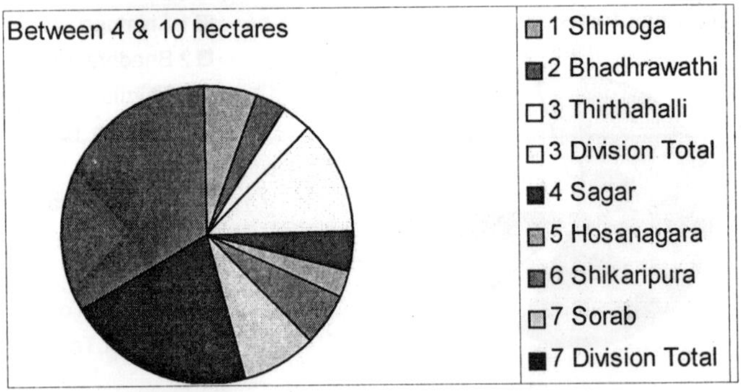

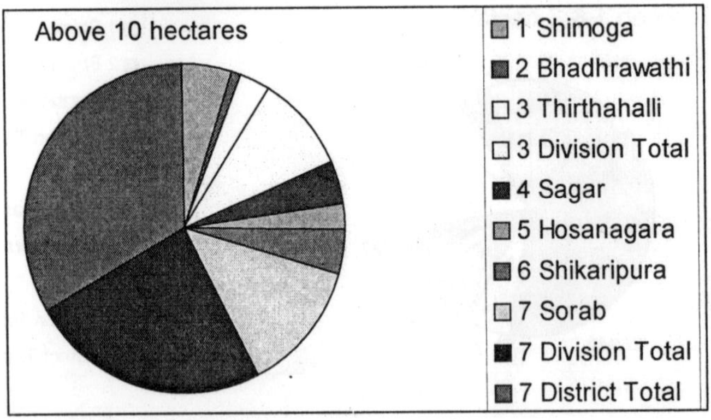

Horticulture

Horticulture, though a part of agriculture in general began to receive separate and special attention in the sixties. The growing of fruits and vegetables was encouraged and efforts were made to

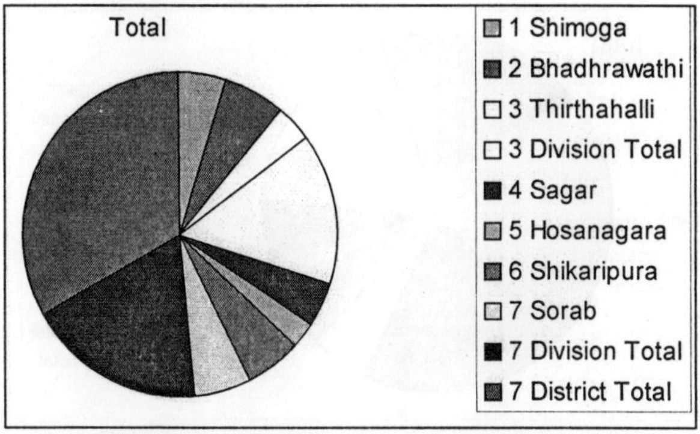
Total
1 Shimoga
2 Bhadhrawathi
3 Thirthahalli
3 Division Total
4 Sagar
5 Hosanagara
6 Shikaripura
7 Sorab
7 Division Total
7 District Total

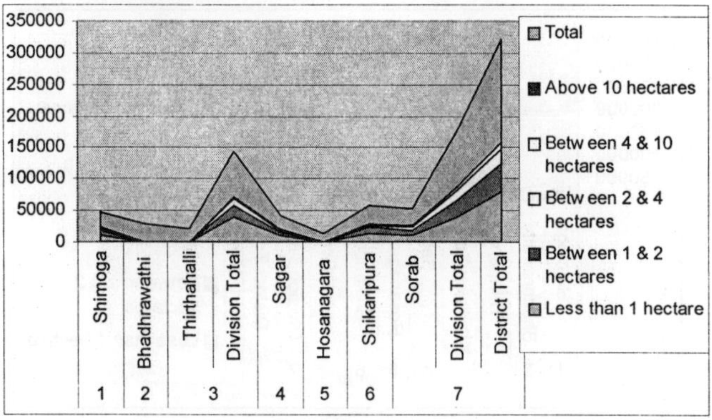
350000
300000
250000
200000
150000
100000
50000
0
Shimoga
Bhadhrawathi
Thirthahalli
Division Total
Sagar
Hosanagara
Shikaripura
Sorab
Division Total
District Total
1 2 3 4 5 6 7
Total
Above 10 hectares
Betw een 4 & 10 hectares
Betw een 2 & 4 hectares
Betw een 1 & 2 hectares
Less than 1 hectare

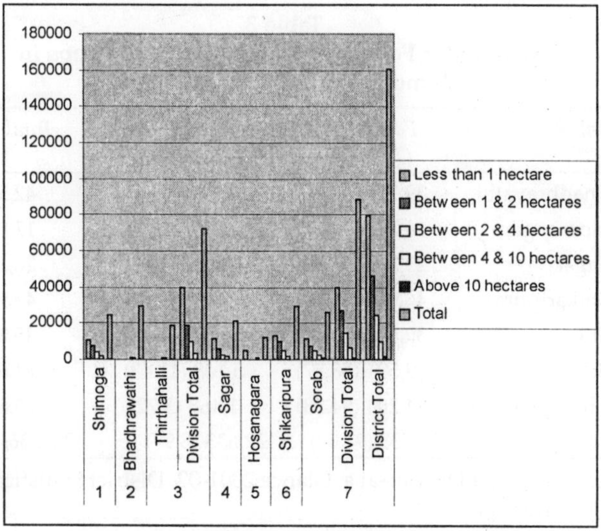
180000
160000
140000
120000
100000
80000
60000
40000
20000
0
Shimoga
Bhadhrawathi
Thirthahalli
Division Total
Sagar
Hosanagara
Shikaripura
Sorab
Division Total
District Total
1 2 3 4 5 6 7
Less than 1 hectare
Betw een 1 & 2 hectares
Betw een 2 & 4 hectares
Betw een 4 & 10 hectares
Above 10 hectares
Total

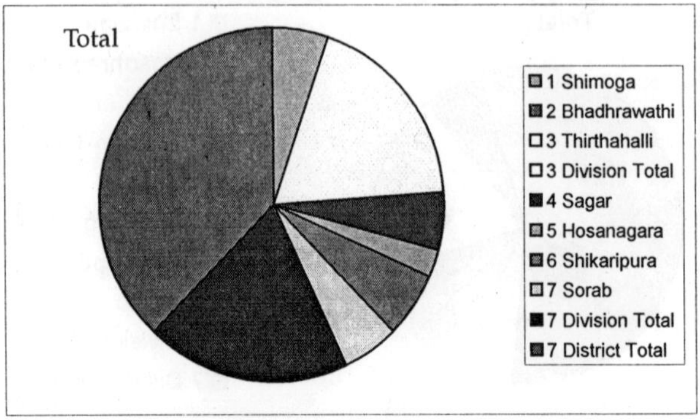

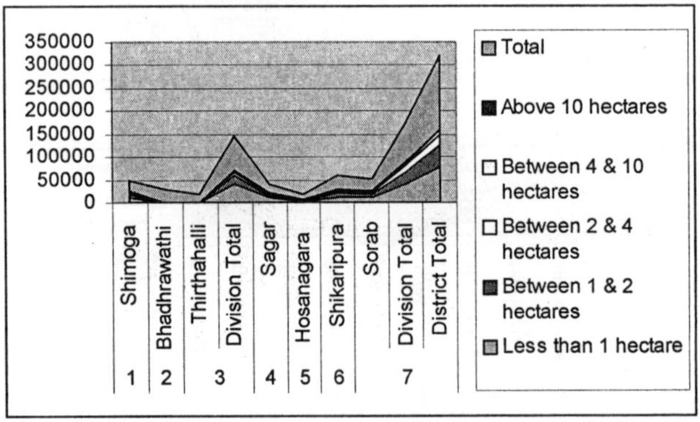

Table 3
Area under Food Crops and Non-Food Crops in Shimoga district During 2001-02

Sl. No.	*Taluk*	*Food Crops (Total) Ha.*	*Non-Food Crops (Total) Ha*	*Total (Ha)*
01.	Bhadhravathi	39,724 (93.36)	2,827 (6.64)	42,551
02.	Hosanagara	16,744 (93.68)	1,129 (6.32)	17,873
03.	Sagar	23,254 (88.55)	3,007 (11.45)	26,261
04.	Shikaripura	46,566 (93.18)	3,406 (6.82)	49,972
05.	Shimoga	39,650 (87.45)	5,688 (12.55)	45,338
06.	Soraba	39,591 (88.57)	5,108 (11.43)	44,699
07.	Thirthahalli	24,204 (94.28)	1,468 (5.72)	25,672
	Total	2,29,733 (91.03)	22,633 (8.97)	2,52,366 (100.00)

Source: Shimoga District–at a Glance 2001-02, District Statistical Office, Shimoga.

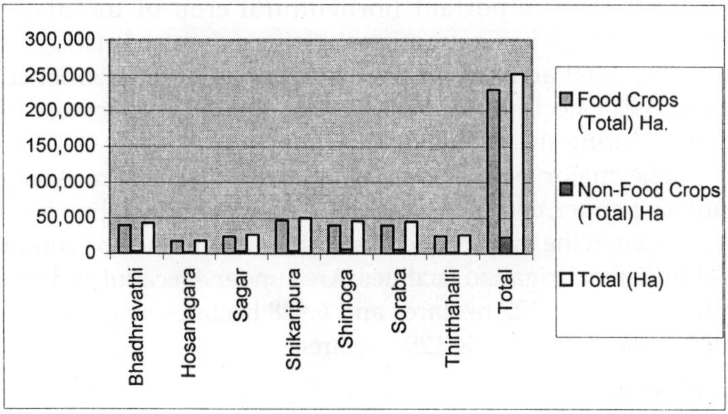

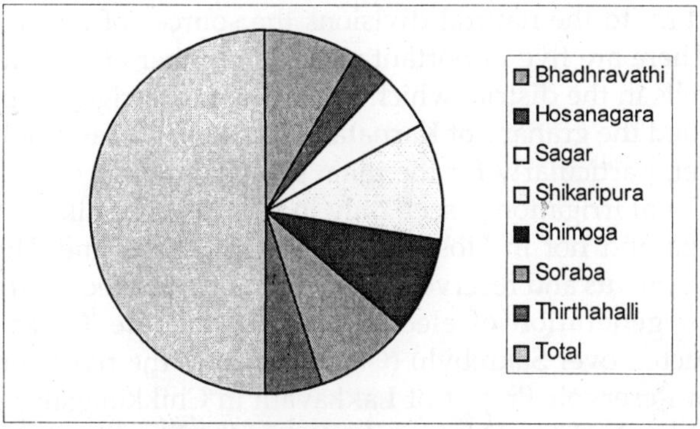

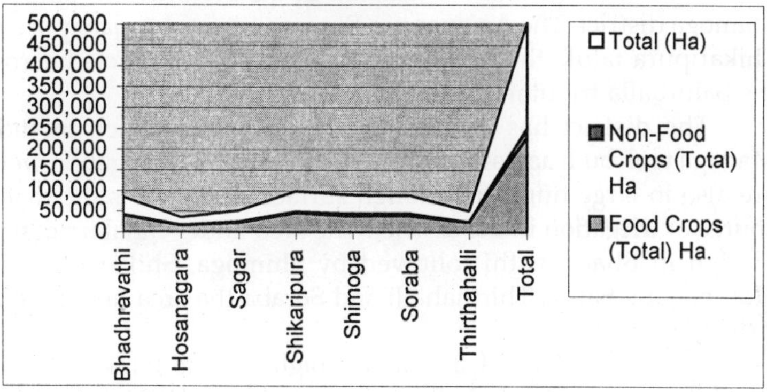

take the horticultural products to the people at their doorsteps. As a result the Department of Horticulture came into existence in the State in 1963 and its district office was opened at Shimoga during the same year.

The most important horticultural crop of the district is arecanut, which has a prominent place in the markets.

The total area under fruit production in the district covers about 8,214 hectares and vegetables about 704 hectares in the district during the year 2001-02.

The major plantation crops in the district are Arecanut, banana, pepper, cocoa. However the Arecanut plantation is highly prominent in the district due to suitable climate and soil conditions and sufficient irrigation facilities. Area under Arecanut and coconut cultivation is 23,927 hectares and 6,938 hectares respectively. The Area under betelvine is 129 hectares.

Irrigation

According to the natural divisions the sources of irrigation also vary. There are five important rivers, a number of streams, tanks and wells in the district which are utilised for irrigation purpose. It is called the granary of Karnataka as there is an assured supply of water, particularly for the main seasonal crops.

Canal irrigation is seen only in Bhadravati, Shikaripura and Shimoga and not in Hosanagara, Sagar, Soraba and Thirtahalli taluks. Anicuts and reservoirs have been constructed for irrigation and for generation of electricity. They include Tunga Anicut constructed over Sakrebylu (Gajanur) across the river Tunga, the Bhadra Reservoir Project of Lakkavalli in Chikkmagalur district, the left bank of the Dam is situated in the Bhadravathi taluk of Shimoga district. The Anjanapura Reservoir is near Anjanapura in Shikaripura taluk, the Ambligola Reservoir is constructed across the Salurballa tributary of the Kumadvathi River.

The district has a large number of tanks which include Madaga tank built across the Kumadvathi river. The irrigation wells are also in large numbers, though surface irrigation is the major source of irrigation in the district. The area under canal irrigation is high in Bhadravathi followed by Shimoga, Shikaripura. In Hosanagara, Sagar, Thirthahalli and Soraba the area under canal irrigation is nil.

The area under tank irrigation is high in Sorab Taluk, followed by Shikaripura, Thirthahalli, Sagar, Shimoga, Hosanagara and Bhadravathi taluks.

The area irrigated through wells and tubewells is high in Shikaripura taluk followed by Soraba, Shimoga,Sagar, Thirthahalli, Bhadravathi and Hosanagara taluks of Shimoga district.

Co-operatives, Banking, Trade and Commerce

In the year 2002, there were 131 commercial banks, 26 rural banks, 21 urban co-operative banks, 15 other co-operative banks, 8 Primary Land Development banks in Shimoga district. The Primary Land Development Banks have provided Rs. 1071 lakhs credit to agriculture.

In the year 2002, there were 890 co-operative societies. Out of them 155 were Agricultural co-operative banks, 286 milk co-operatives, 44 house building co-operative societies, 14 marketing co-operative societies. In the district 4,85,800 members belong to these co-operative societies.

In addition there were 18 regulated markets working in the district. During the year 2002, agricultural co-operative societies have provided Rs. 7,683 lakhs as a short term loan Rs. 156 lakhs as a medium term loans.

Industry

In the year 2001-02, there were 170 industries in sample district. Out of them one chemical industry, 36 engineering industries and 133 were other industries. Nearly 17,458 people were employed in these industries.

Climate, Rainfall and Soils

As the district is covered with mountains and hills it has a cool climate. All the taluks in the district receive rainfall from June to September from South-West monsoons and from October to December from North-East monsoons. The regular average rainfall of the district is 1813 mm for the year 2001-02. The rainfall is more in Thirthahalli followed by Hosanagara, Sagar, Soraba, Shikaripura, Bhadravathi and Shimoga respectively. The second wettest place in India i.e. 'Agumbe' is situated in this district.

The important varieties of soils in the district are Red Soil, Black Soil, Sandy Soil and Laterate Soil. Thus, the district has favourable agro-climatic conditions for growing of variety of food and non-food crops.

4 SOCIO-ECONOMIC CONDITIONS AND CULTIVATION PRACTICES OF THE SAMPLE FARMERS

In this chapter an attempt is made to examine the cultivation practices and the socio-economic conditions of the sample farmers in the study area. Such an analysis of the cultivation practices and the socio-economic background of the farmers will have an important bearing on the cultivation practices of the farmers such as the use of modern inputs, nature of technology, amount of investment, yield per hectare. Etc. With this view in mind the present analysis is made.

Size of Land holdings

The size of land holding is one of the determinants of productivity in agriculture. It is more so in case of plantation crops. The landholding should not be too small or too large instead it should be viable. If it is viable in size there will be intensive cultivation of land, which promotes productivity. In this context let us examine the average size of landholdings owned by sample small, medium and large farmers in the study area.

It is evident from the Table 1 that the average size of land owned by small farmers is 0.45 hectares for the entire study area. In Sagar taluk the average size of land held by small farmers is below the district average whereas in case of Shimoga taluk it is slightly above the overall average size. Almost same conditions exist even in case of medium and large farmers category between Sagar and Shimoga taluks as compared to the district average. From this it may be inferred that the average size of land holdings of small, medium and large farmers in Shimoga taluk is slightly bigger than that of Sagar taluk for all categories of farmers.

Housing Conditions

Better housing conditions speak of better economic position of the farmers. Majority of people in rural areas will be having bad

Table 1
Average Size of Land Holdings of Sample Respondents

(Area in hectares)

Farmer Category	*Sagar Taluk*	*Shimoga Taluk*	*Shimoga District*
Small	0.40	0.50	0.45
Medium	1.20	1.35	1.27
Large	3.25	3.50	3.37

Source: Survey Data.

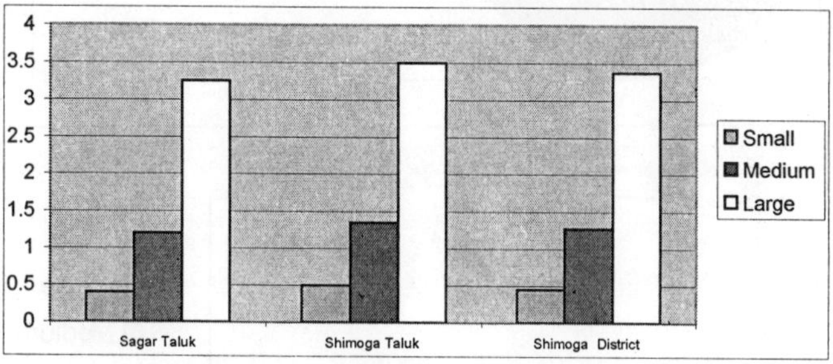

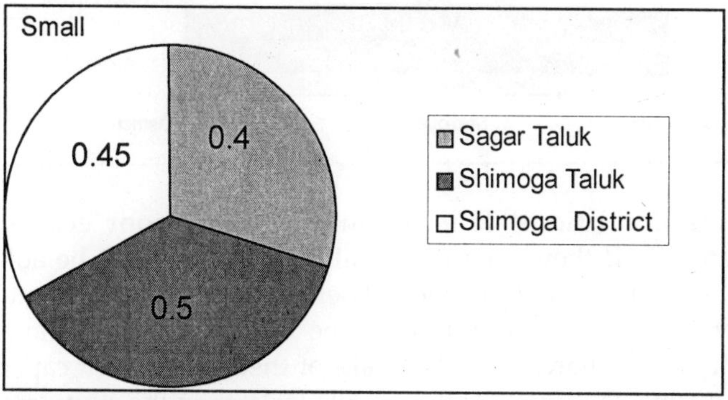

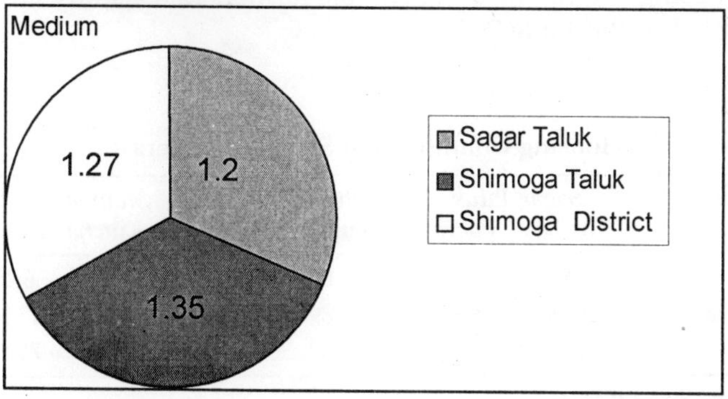

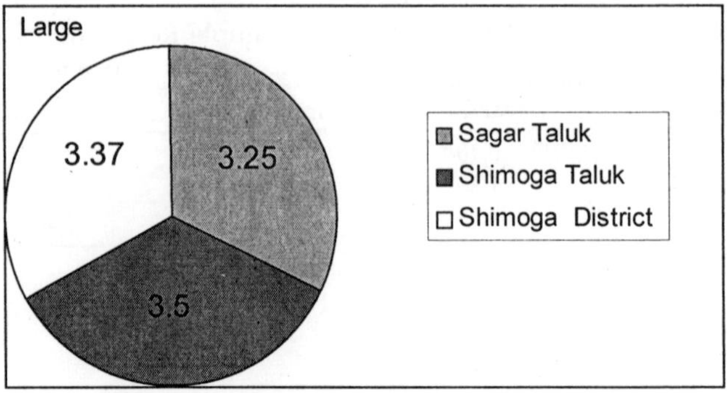

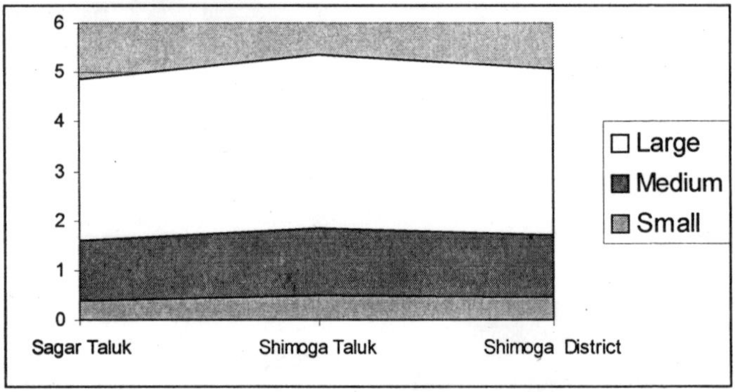

housing conditions. It is because of their poor economic background. If they are economically sound they will be able to invest more in agriculture and get better returns from agriculture. Therefore, it is necessary to examine the housing conditions of farmers in rural areas which speaks of their investment capacity. The housing conditions of the sample farmers in the study area is presented in the Table 2.

Table 2
Housing Conditions of Sample Farmers

Farmer category	*Sagar Taluk*		*Shimoga Taluk*		*Shimoga District*	
	Kutcha	*Pucca*	*Kutcha*	*Pucca*	*Kutcha*	*Pucca*
Small	91.67	8.33	95.83	4.17	93.75	6.25
Medium	83.33	16.67	88.89	11.11	86.11	13.88
Large	12.50	87.50	32.50	62.50	25.00	75.00

Source: Survey Data.

It is clear from the Table 2 that very large number of small and medium farmers in the study area own kutcha houses. It indicates their poor economic condition. In case of large category farmers it is quite opposite. That is, majority of them own pucca houses and very few will be owning kutcha houses. It is but natural that large farmers because of large size of land holdings earn better income and naturally possess better housing facilities.

The inter-taluka comparison of housing conditions of farmers reveal that in Sagar taluk all categories of farmers possess better

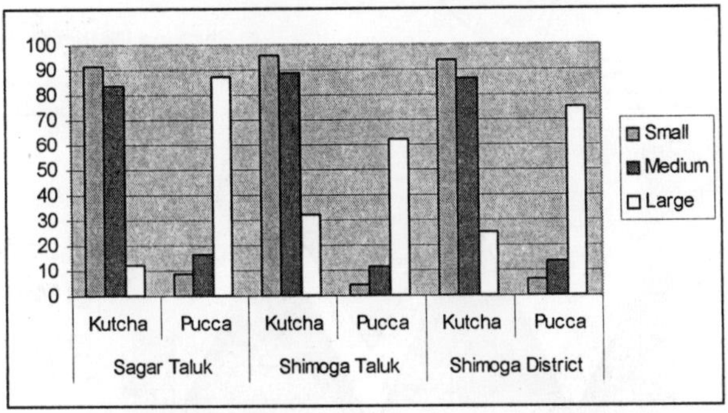

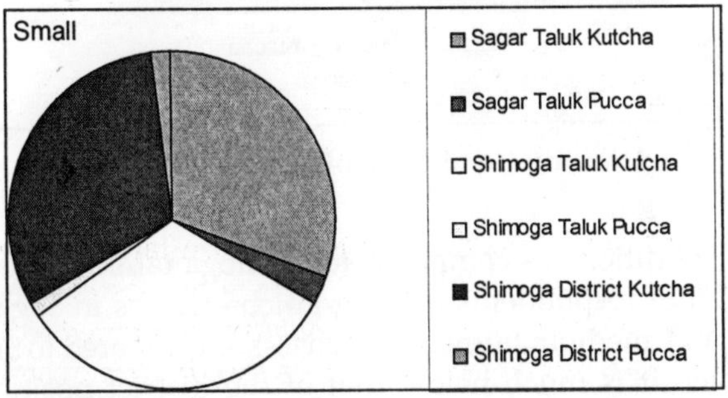

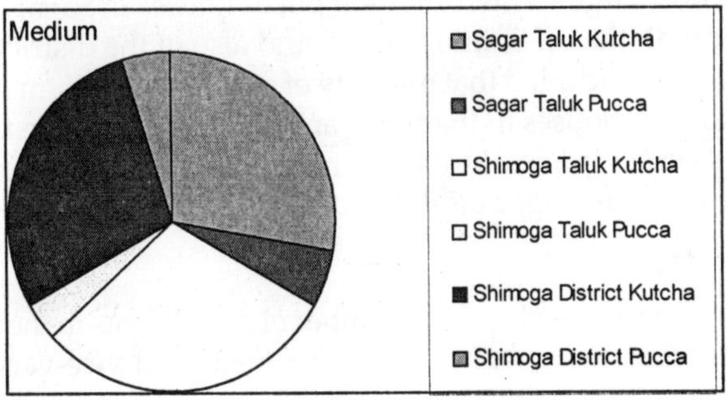

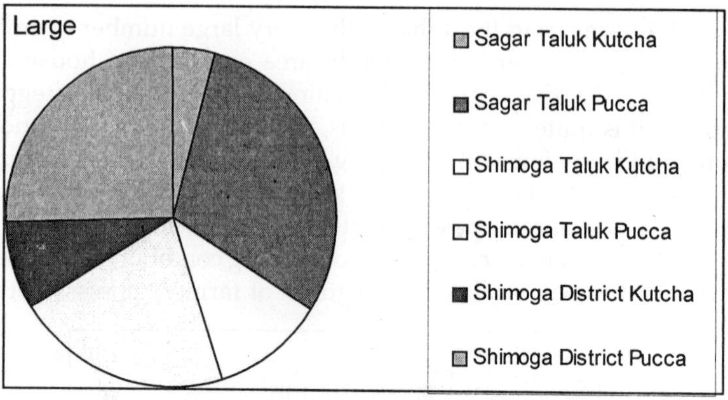

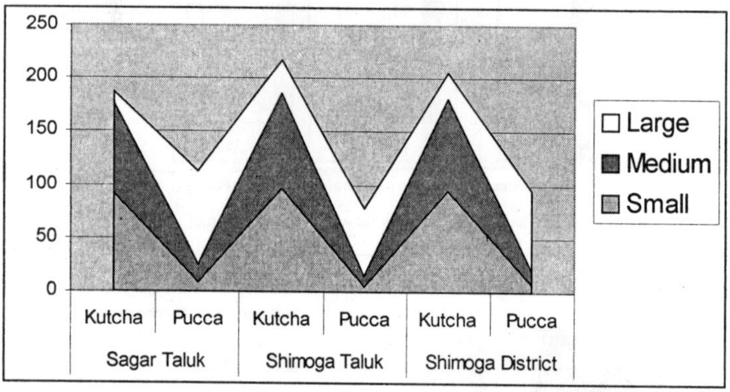

Housing Conditions of Sample Farmers

housing conditions as compared to Shimoga taluk. It means the proportion of respondents owning kutcha houses in Sagar taluk by small and medium farmer is much less as compared to Shimoga taluk. Even it is much below that of the district position. The proportion of large farmers owning pucca houses in Sagar taluk is far better than that of Shimoga taluk and also of the district. From this it may be concluded that majority of small and medium farmers possess kutcha houses in the study area whereas the large farmers mainly possess pucca houses. The respective conditions are certainly better in Sagar taluk as compared to the Shimoga taluk.

Family size

The size of family speaks of the number of dependents in the family. Larger the size, more will be the dependents and vice-versa. The high dependency ratio reduces the percapita income in the family. This in turn will affect adversely their savings, investment and consumption standards. It is generally observed that poor families will have large size families as compared to rich. The information regarding family size of the sample respondents in the study area is presented in the Table 3.

Table 3
Average Family Size of Sample Farmers

Farmer Category	*Sagar Taluk*	*Shimoga Taluk*	*Shimoga District*
Small	07	08	07
Medium	06	07	06
Large	05	06	05

Source: Survey Data.

It is clear from the Table 3 that the average size of family is large in case of small farmers category as compared to medium and large farmers. The average family size in case of all categories of farmers in Sagar taluk is exactly the same as that of the entire study area. In case of Shimoga taluk all categories of farmers have bigger size families compared to the district average. It means in Shimoga taluk there is high dependency ratio. From the analysis it may be concluded that there is inverse relationship between the size of land holdings and the family size. In other words the small farmers will have big size families and the vice-versa.

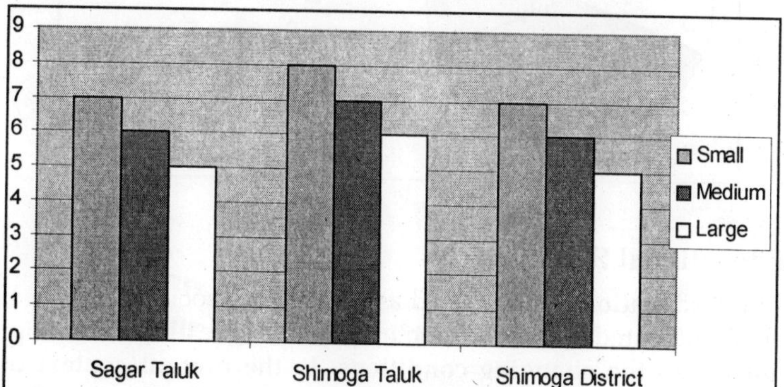

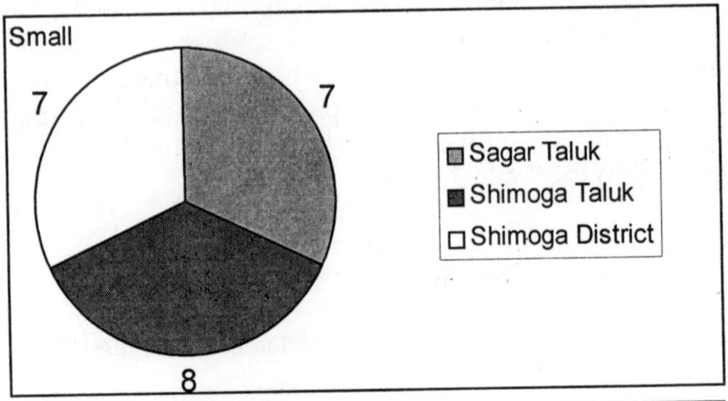

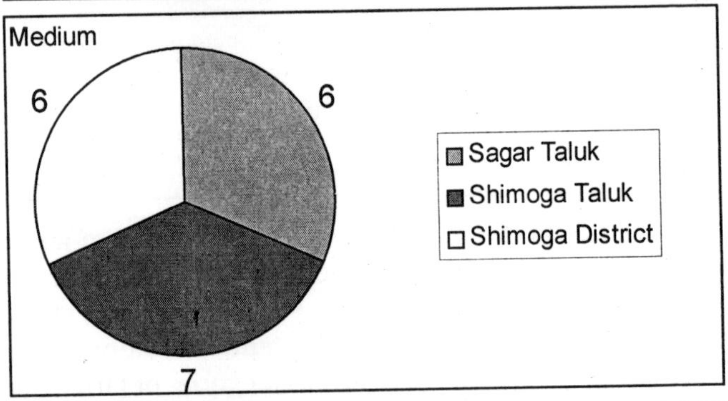

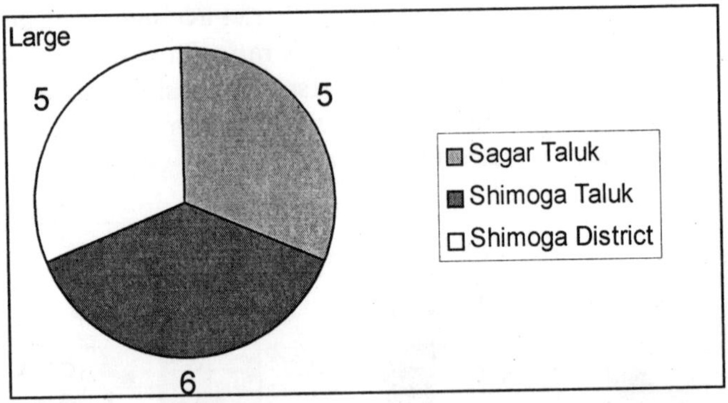

Educational Status

Today education is considered as a symbol of social progress. If one is educated he will be resourceful, dynamic alert and adopt himself to the changing conditions. In the present context of modernisation and commercialisation of agriculture, education

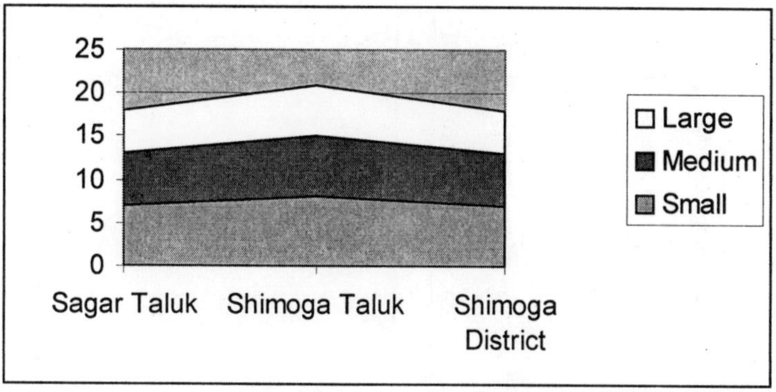

Average Family size of Sample Farmers

plays a vital role. Therefore, minimum education is necessary even for the farmers who are engaged in progressive agricultural practices. Such farmers can really reap the benefits of modernisation. In this context let us examine the educational status of the sample farmers in the study area. It is presented in the Table 4.

It is evident from the Table 4 that educational status of sample farmers seems to be better in the study area except 5 per cent of the total respondents, who are illiterate. It is quite negligible. It means the sample farmers in the study area are educated. However the level of education varies from category to category. In case of large farmers category they are found to be possessing high level of education as compared to medium and small farmers. Here we find the level of education varies positively with the size of land holding.

The inter-taluka comparison of the educational status of different categories of farmers shows that in Sagar taluk all categories of farmers have better education than that of Shimoga taluk. Therefore, it may be concluded that even educationally Shimoga taluk is lagging behind the Sagar taluk and it is even far below the district average.

Consumption Expenditure

The level of consumption expenditure determines the standard of living. Further, the item-wise allocation of expenditure shows priority given by particular category of farmers towards a particular consumption item. Let us examine the consumption

Table 4

Educational Status of Sample Farmers in the Study Area

Farmer Category	*Sagara Taluk*					*Shimoga Taluk*					*Shimoga District*				
	Illite-rate	*Read & Write*	*Upto SSLC*	*College*	*Total*	*Illite rate*	*Read & Write*	*Upto SSLC*	*College*	*Total*	*Illite rate*	*Read & Write*	*Upto SSLC*	*College*	*Total*
Small	—	20	15	13	48	05	22	12	09	48	5	42	27	22	96
		(41.67)	(31.25)	(27.08)	(100)	(10.42)	(45,83)	(25.00)	(18.75)	(100)	(5.21)	(43.75)	(28.12)	(22.92)	(100.00)
Medium	—	15	10	11	36		18	12	06	36	-	33	22	17	72
		(41.67)	(27.78)	(30.55)	(100.00)	—	(50.00)	(33.33)	(16.67)	(100)	—	(45.83)	(30.56)	(23.61)	(100)
Large	—	08	05	03	16		10	04	02	16		18	09	05	32
		(50.00)	(31.25)	(18.75)	(100.00)	—	(62.50)	(25.00)	(12.50)	(100)	—	(56.25)	(28.12)	(15.63)	(100)
				100					100						200

Source: Survey Data

Note: Figures in the parenthesis are percentages to the total

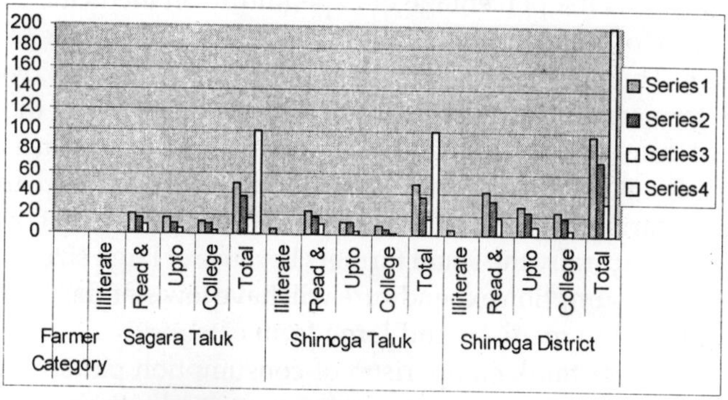

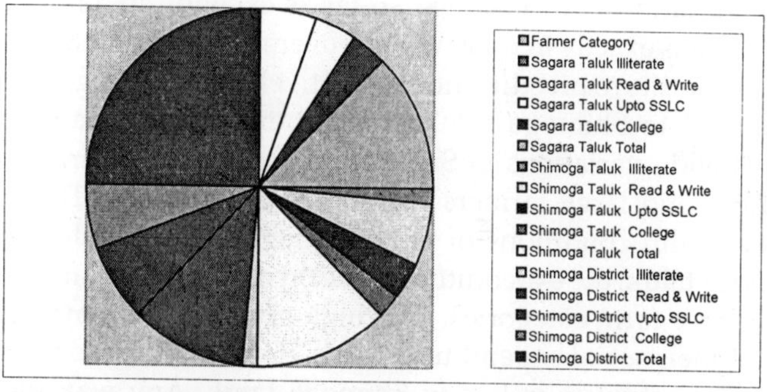

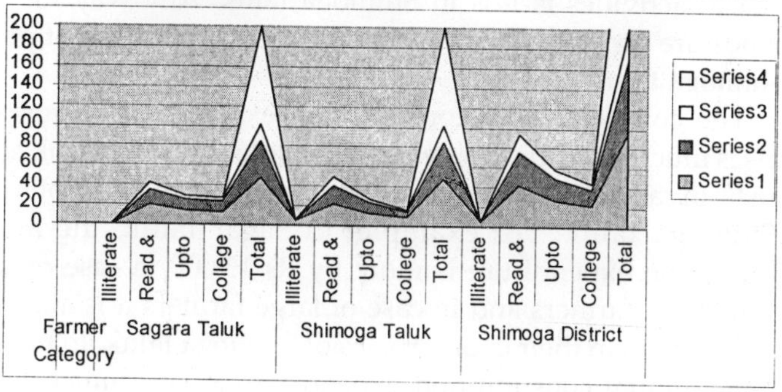

pattern of the sample farmers in the study area. This can be seen from the Table 5.

It is clear from the Table 5 that food and clothing account for nearly half of the total expenditure. This is in accordance with 'Engles Law' of consumption. The average Indian spends nearly more than half of the income on food and clothing, which is evident in the study area. The proportion of expenditure on education and social items is almost same in all categories of farmers in the study area, whereas the percentage of expenditure on medicine is more in the case of small and medium farmers, and less in case of large farmers. This may be due to better health conditions enjoyed by large farmers in the area. However, in absolute terms the total annual consumption expenditure incurred by large farmers is nearly Rs. 30,000 more than that of small farmers and that of medium farmers it is Rs.10,000 to Rs.15,000 more than that of small farmers. Naturally the small farmers because of large size families and low consumption expenditure will have low standard of living as compared to medium and large farm categories.

The inter taluk comparison of consumption pattern reveals some variations. For instance, so far as expenditure on food and clothing it is exactly in tune with the overall position for the district. The expenditure on education is relatively more in Sagar taluk as compared to Shimoga taluk. But the expenditure on medicine shows wide variations in Sagar taluk except small farmers. The medium and large farmers spend less on medicine. This shows better health conditions of these farmers in Sagar taluk. But in Shimoga taluk, the expenditure made on medicine is relatively high in all three farm categories. This high expenditure is made at the cost of their social expenditure. Thus, naturally their expenditure on social activities is less in Shimoga taluk. Any way the high expenditure on medicine shows poor health conditions of people in Shimoga taluk.

The comparison of consumption expenditure in absolute terms is much disturbing between the taluks. In Sagar taluk all the three farm categories spend relatively more than their counterparts in Shimoga taluk. For example, in Sagar taluk, the annual consumption expenditure is more by Rs 15,000 in case of small and medium farmers and in case of large farmers it is almost Rs 20,000 more than their counterparts of Shimoga taluk. In brief the average annual consumption expenditure is very much less in Shimoga taluk as compared to Sagar taluk. From this it may be concluded that people in Sagar taluk have better standard of living as compared to Shimoga taluk .

Consumer Durables and Agricultural Equipments of Sample Farmers

As regards the ownership of consumer durables like radio, TV, refrigerator, bicycle, motor cycle, cars and other agricultural

Table 5
Average Annual Consumption Expenditure of the Sample Farmers in the Study Area

Particulars	*Sagar Taluk*			*Shimoga Taluk*			*Shimoga District*		
	Small	*Medium*	*Large*	*Small*	*Medium*	*Large*	*Small*	*Medium*	*Large*
Food	30,000	35,000	40,000	25,000	30,000	36,000	27,500	32,500	38,000
	(32,43)	(33.02)	(32.79)	(32.47)	(33.71)	(35.64)	(32.84)	(32.99)	(34.08)
Clothing	15,000	16,000	20,000	12,000	14,000	16,000	13,500	15,000	18,000
	(16.22)	(15.09)	(16.39)	(15.58)	(15.73)	(15.85)	(16.12)	(15.23)	(16.14)
Education	12,000	15,000	18,000	10,000	12,000	14,000	11,000	13,500	16,000
	(12.97)	(14.16)	(14.75)	(12.99)	(13.48)	(13.86)	(13.13)	(13.70)	(14.35)
Medicines	10,500	10,000	9,000	15,000	13,000	10,000	11,750	11,500	9,500
	(11.35)	(9.43)	(7.38)	(19.48)	(14.61)	(9.90)	(14.03)	(11.68)	(8.52)
Other Social	25,000	30,000	35,000	15,000	20,000	25,000	20,000	26,000	30,000
Expenditures	(27.03)	(28.30)	(28.69)	(19.48)	(22.47)	(24.75)	(23.88)	(26.40)	(26.91)
Total	92,500	1,06,000	1,22,000	77,000	89,000	1,01,000	83,750	98,500	1,11,500
	(100.00)	(100.00)	(100.00)	(100.00)	(100.00)	(100.00)	(100.00)	(100.00)	(100.00)

Source: Survey Data.
Note: Figures in the parenthesis are percentages to the total.

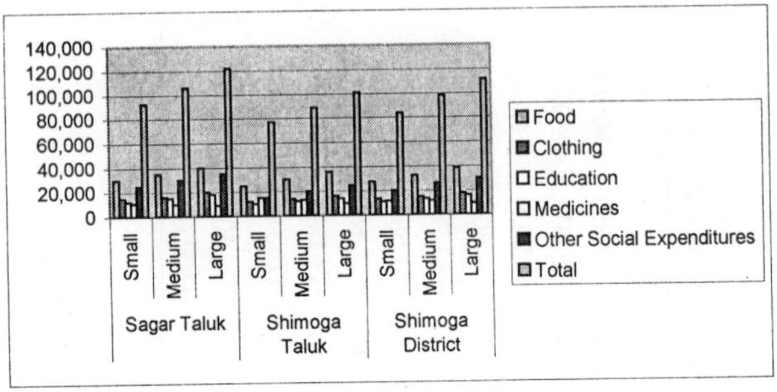

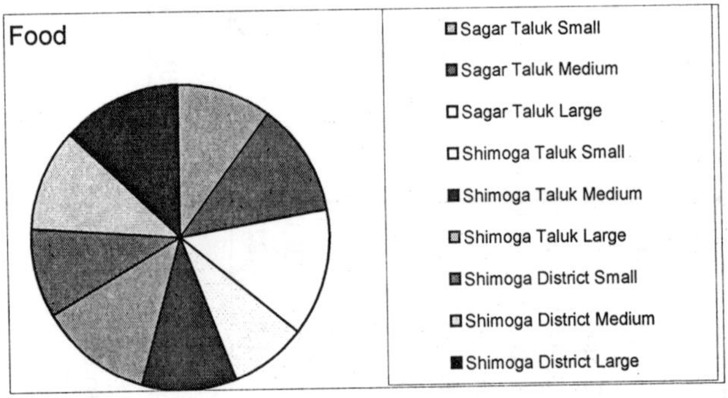

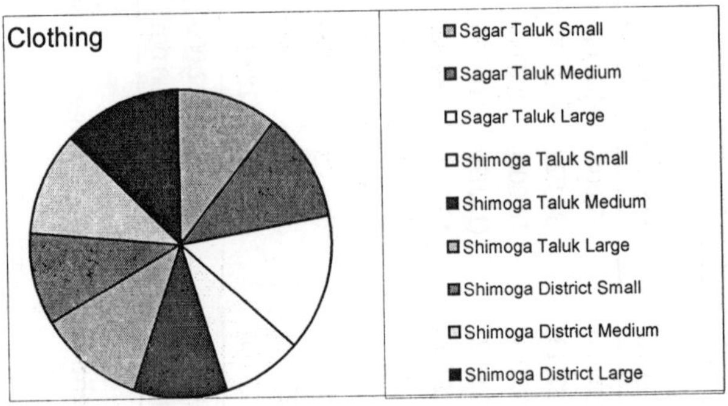

implements Sagar taluk is better placed as compared to the Shimoga taluk.

Accessibility to Mass-Media of Sample Farmers in the Study Area

In both the taluks the accessibility to mass-media is high among large farmers when compared to medium and small. Because large farmers in both the taluks have more leisure time as they only

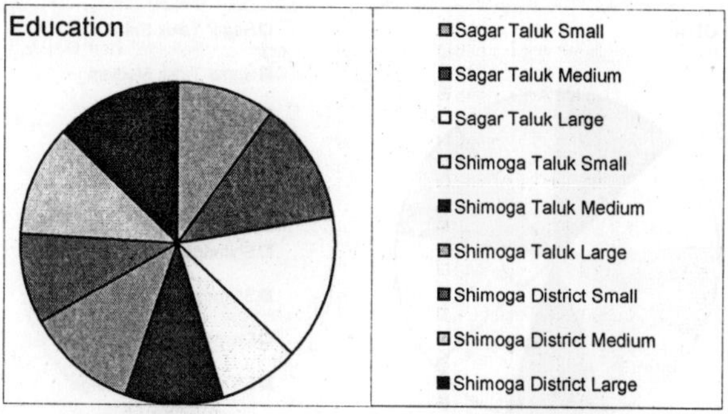

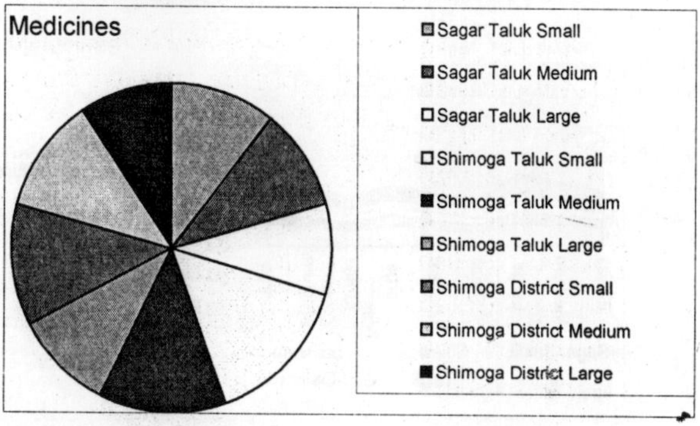

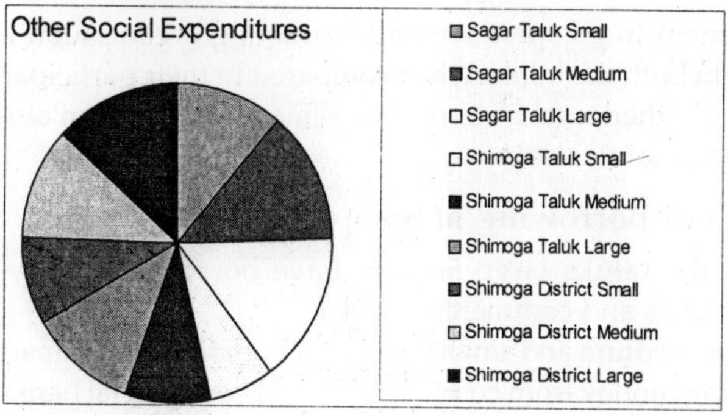

supervise their areca gardens, when compared to medium and small category of sample farmers.

Institutional Participation of Sample Farmers in the Study Area

In Sagar taluk the institutional participation is high among large farmers when compared to medium and small farmers. The

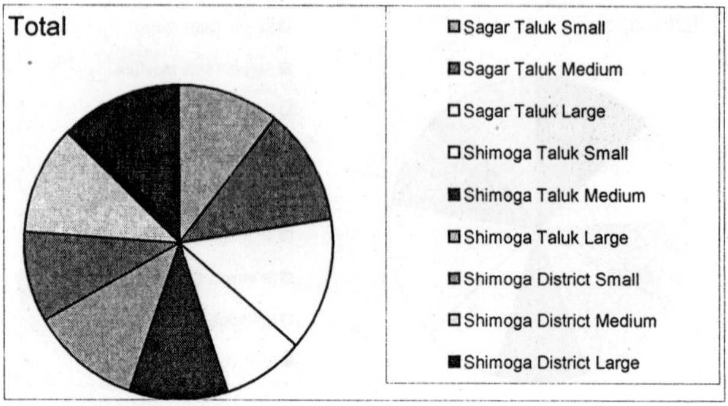

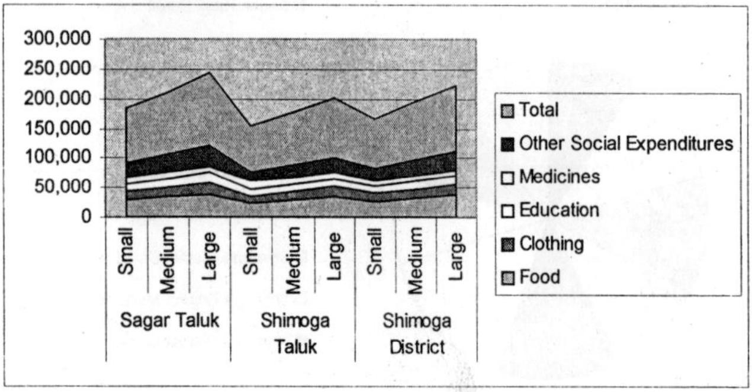

involvement in co-operative and marketing organisation is cent percent in both the taluks when compared to their participation in social and other organisations. The same thing has been observed in Shimoga taluk also.

Sources of Borrowing of Sample Farmers

In both the taluks large farmers have borrowed money from co-operatives and commercial banks.

The medium and small farmers of both the taluks, apart from borrowing money from co-operatives and commercial banks have also borrowed money from Areca merchants as they are easily accessible.

It is evident from the above analysis that the socio-economic status of the large farmers is better when compared to medium and small farmers in both the taluks.

The socio-economic status of the all categories of farmers in Sagar taluk is better when compared with the conditions of farmers of Shimoga taluk.

For the district as a whole the large farmers socio-economic status is better when compared to medium and small farmers.

Cultivation Practices of Sample farmers

The cultivation practices of sample areca cultivators in the study area exhibits the different methods of cultivation adopted, types of irrigation followed, variety of seedlings used, intercrops and mixed crops grown, method of marketing etc. All these will have their impact on cost of cultivation and yield. Therefore, an attempt is made here to present the cultivation practices of farmers in the study area.

Sagar Taluk

The method of cultivation followed in Sagar taluk (traditional areca growing area) is markedly different from the methods adopted in Shimoga taluk, (non -traditional areca growing area).

The heavy South-West monsoon and the broken hilly nature with steep and narrow valleys alternating with jungle-clad uphills and the slope are the special characteristics of the Malnad track, (Sagar taluk).

The site selected for areca garden is invariably the narrow width of the valley, almost from the head of the valley going on until the valley widens out. At the head of such narrow valley there is usually a small irrigation tank which furnishes irrigation water during summer months. Often banks of rivers are also selected for this crop. The steep hills on both the sides of the selected sites provide necessary protection from the monsoon winds and often the South-West afternoon sun.

Once a suitable length of valley bottoms is selected, it is levelled, and the next operations like the digging of the drains, irrigation channels and laying out of elevated ridges will be taken up. Along the natural drainage line, the main drain is dug, which is about a meter deep and 3/4 th of a meter wide, and is lead from the head of the garden to the outlet at the end of the garden.

Irrigation channels are laid higherups the valley sides along the margin of the garden on both the sides. The land between the irrigation channel and drainage channel is then divided into strips of about 5 meters width by narrow sub-drains about 30 cms wide which open into the maindrain.

The next operation is planting of banana as a shade crop, the supply of which is kept throughout the life of the banana garden

Table 6

Consumer Durable and Agricultural Equipments of Sample Farmers in the Study Area (in percentage)

Particulars	*Sagar Taluk*			*Shimoga Taluk*			*Shimoga District*		
	Small	*Medium*	*Large*	*Small*	*Medium*	*Large*	*Small*	*Medium*	*Large*
Radio	100	100	100	100	100	100	100	100	100
Television	100	100	100	100	100	100	100	100	100
Refrigerator	50	69.44	100	25	41.67	100	39.50	55.55	100
Bicycle	100	100	100	100	100	100	100	100	100
Motor Cycle	62.50	72.22	100	31.25	55.50	100	46.87	63.89	100
Motor Car	2.08	5.55	100	-	-	100	1.04	2.78	100
Power Tiller	4.17	8.33	100	-	-	100	3.12	6.94	100
Tractor	-	-	62.50	-	-	50	-	-	56.25
Other Agricultural implements	-	-	100	-	-	50	-	-	75.00
Total	48	36	16	48	36	46	96	72 200	32

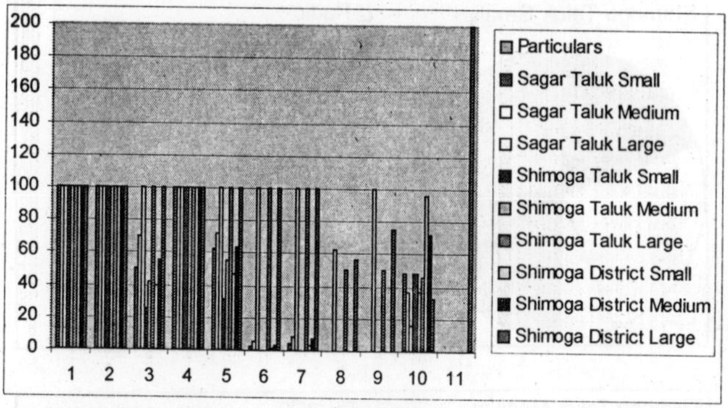
200
180
160
140
120
100
80
60
40
20
0
1 2 3 4 5 6 7 8 9 10 11
Particulars
Sagar Taluk Small
Sagar Taluk Medium
Sagar Taluk Large
Shimoga Taluk Small
Shimoga Taluk Medium
Shimoga Taluk Large
Shimoga District Small
Shimoga District Medium
Shimoga District Large

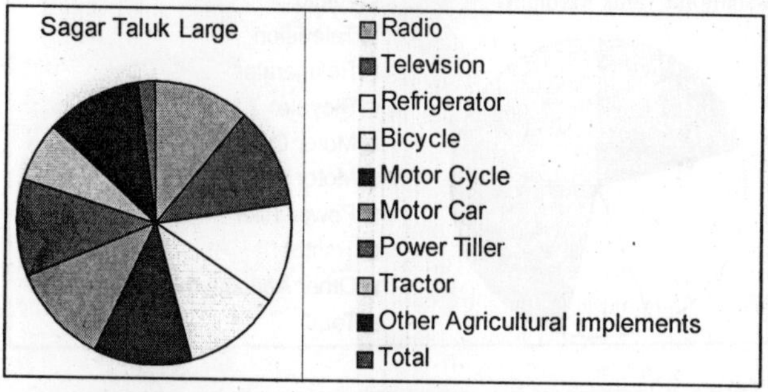
Sagar Taluk Large
Radio
Television
Refrigerator
Bicycle
Motor Cycle
Motor Car
Power Tiller
Tractor
Other Agricultural implements
Total

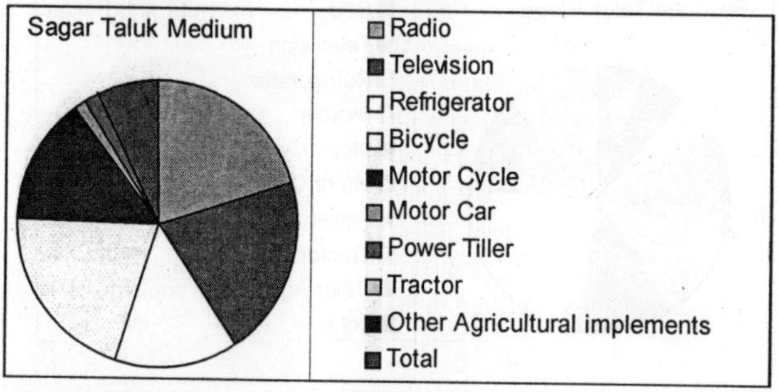
Sagar Taluk Medium
Radio
Television
Refrigerator
Bicycle
Motor Cycle
Motor Car
Power Tiller
Tractor
Other Agricultural implements
Total

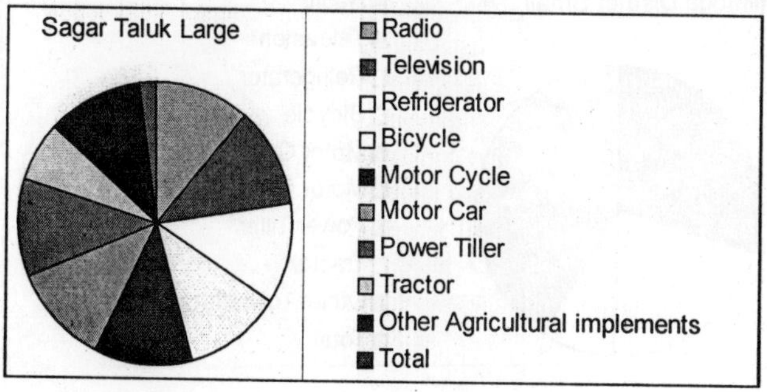
Sagar Taluk Large
Radio
Television
Refrigerator
Bicycle
Motor Cycle
Motor Car
Power Tiller
Tractor
Other Agricultural implements
Total

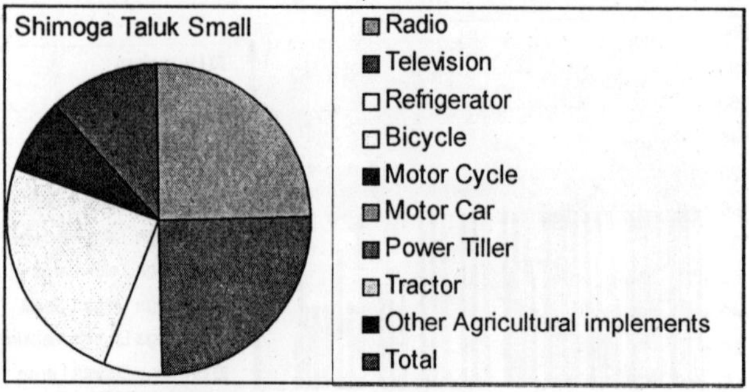
Shimoga Taluk Small
Radio
Television
Refrigerator
Bicycle
Motor Cycle
Motor Car
Power Tiller
Tractor
Other Agricultural implements
Total

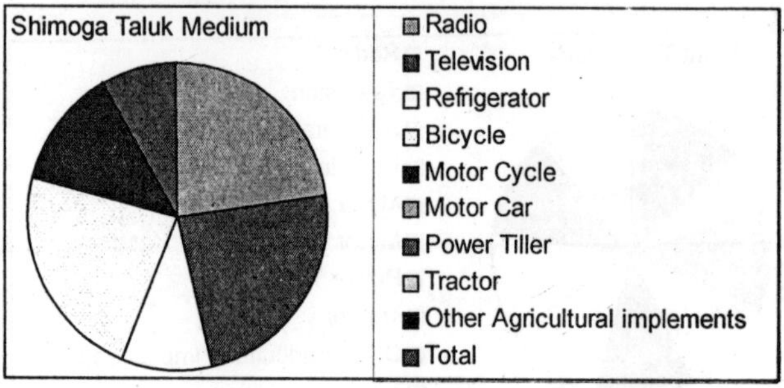
Shimoga Taluk Medium
Radio
Television
Refrigerator
Bicycle
Motor Cycle
Motor Car
Power Tiller
Tractor
Other Agricultural implements
Total

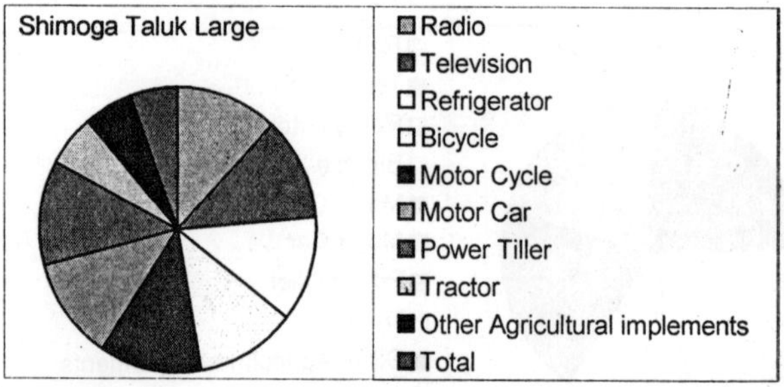
Shimoga Taluk Large
Radio
Television
Refrigerator
Bicycle
Motor Cycle
Motor Car
Power Tiller
Tractor
Other Agricultural implements
Total

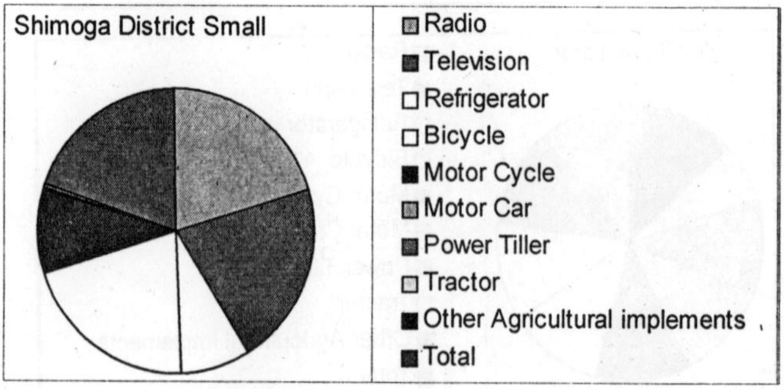
Shimoga District Small
Radio
Television
Refrigerator
Bicycle
Motor Cycle
Motor Car
Power Tiller
Tractor
Other Agricultural implements
Total

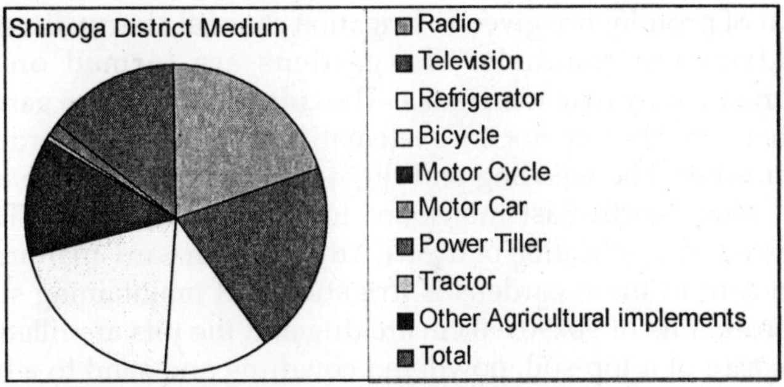

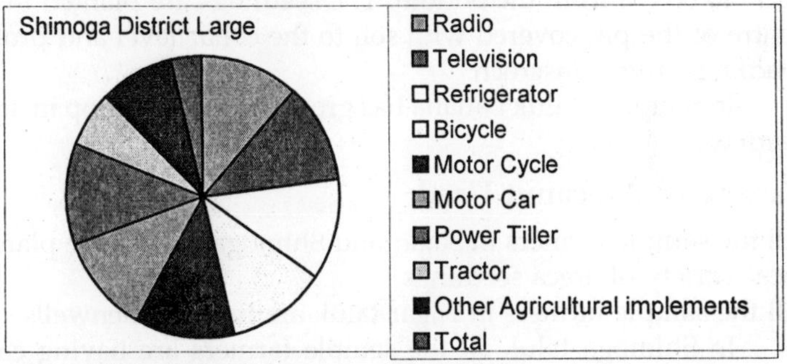

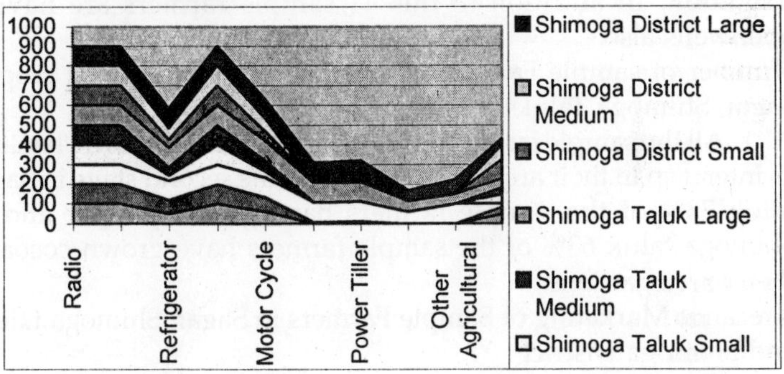

The banana suckers are planted in the months of May-June to be followed by the planting of areca seedlings in the month of September.

Shimoga Taluk

The arecanut gardens in the Shimoga taluk (non-traditional areca growing area) occupy large areas of levelled fields. Since the rainfall here is less than 50 cms, the important difference in the cultivation of areca gardens as compared to that of Malnad tracts (Sagar Taluk) is that of prominence given to irrigation channel almost discarding the drianage channels. The gardens are formed on land commanded by irrigation tanks . The cultivation of these garden is neither so elaborate nor so systematic as in the areca gardens in Sagar taluk. The weeding and light-digging is done once a year soon after North-East monsoon in December-January. This is followed by application of fresh earth and farm yard manure. The main care in these gardens is irrigation and maintaining subsoil moisture. Pits of 90x90x90 cm are dug and the pits are filled with a mixture of a top-soil, powdered cowdung and sand to a height of 50 to 60 cm from the bottom. The seedlings are planted in the centre of the pit, covered with soil to the collar level and protect seedlings from sunscroch.

In Shimoga taluk banana has grown as a shade crop in areca gardens.

Variety of Arecanut Used

All the sample farmers in Sagar and Shimoga taluk have planted local variety of areca seedlings.

All the sample farmers in Sagar taluk are having openwells.

In Shimoga taluk all the sample farmers are having canal irrigation. In addition to this 41 sample farmers are having openwells also.

Number of sample Farmers grown Intercrop and Mixed crop in Sagar, Shimoga Taluks and Shimoga District

All the sample farmers in both the taluks have grown 'banana' as intercrop in their areca gardens. But in the second stage in Sagar taluk 78% of the sample farmers have grown pepper and in Shimoga taluk 63% of the sample farmers have grown cocoa in their areca gardens.

Arecanut Marketing of Sample Farmers in Sagar, Shimoga taluks and Shimoga District

The majority of the sample farmers in both the taluks have marketed their produce through Agricultural Produce Marketing Committee (APMC), and very few of them have sold their produce in the local markets.

On the whole the sample farmers of Sagar taluk have more efficient in the adoption of cultivation practices and marketing of arecanut as compared to sample farmers of Shimoga taluk. Because of this reason, the sample farmers of Sagar taluk are getting higher yield per hectare and good price for their produce as compared to sample farmers of Shimoga taluk.

5 COST OF CULTIVATION OF ARECANUT–AN ANALYSIS

In agriculture cost of cultivation definitely has its impact on the yield from crop. Hence in this chapter an attempt has been made to estimate the cost of cultivation of arecanut garden in different stages with the help of information provided by the sample farmers in both the taluks i.e., Sagar and Shimoga taluks in Shimoga district.

To establish an arecanut garden it requires huge amount of investment as it is a perennial crop. Areca palm takes seven years to establish and start bearing economic yield. During this period (i., gestation period) Banana is grown as an inter crop mainly to provide shade to the young areca palm and to get some early returns in the study area. The banana suckers will be removed once the areca palm attain four years of age.

In the second stage of arecanut garden (i.e, 8-40 years) in the study area the farmers are found growing pepper and cocoa as mixed crops to get additional income.

Cost of Cultivation in the First Stage

As arecanut is a perennial crop the cost of cultivation consists of establishment cost and maintenance cost. In the first stage it is the establishment cost which constitute considerable proportion of cost and at later stages it will be maintenance cost which becomes important. But both of them will have a bearing on yield from the crop. Hence the relative role of establishment cost and maintenance cost need to be examined so as to see which cost is most influential in determining the yield. For this purpose the analysis of cost of cultivation among different categories of farmers in two taluks is considered in the present study.

The establishment cost is one time investment on arecanut garden. The amount of establishment cost some time determines the healthy growth of a plant and its yield. Thus it is necessary to examine it. In the present analysis establishment cost consists cost incurred on land levelling, fencing, open well and pumpsets, sprinkler, conveyor pipes, pumphouse, processing yard, interest on fixed capital, land revenue, seedlings, red earth etc.

The maintenance cost consists items like wages paid to labourers, hiring cost of bullocks, machines and cost of chemical fertilisers and manures, pesticides and insecticides, irrigation cost etc.

In the gestation period the total establishment cost of Sagar and Shimoga taluks and in the entire district, the share of the first year establishment cost is highest because investment made on irrigation infrastructure which includes openwells, pumpsets, sprinklers, conveyor pipes-pumphouse and for intensive labour is high.

The expenses made on labour cost which includes activities like land levelling, digging of pits-planting the seedling, irrigating the garden, application of manures and fertilizers etc.

In the first year the expenses incurred on hired machines is also high for the preparation of the land where in Sagar taluk it is still higher compared to Shimoga taluk because of the geographical conditions.

Expenses made on the nursery of seedlings is having considerable impact on the economic bearing of the areca garden.

Subsequently investment made on from second year to sixth year on irrigation of the garden, manuring, plant protection chemicels, which inevitably includes labour cost also.

In the life of areca palm the seventh year is considered as the penultimate year before which bears nuts, hence fertilizers will be applied more in quantity.

It is evident from the above analysis that in the gestation period, the share of the establishment as well as the maintenance cost is considerably high as compared to second and third stages among all the categories of farmers in the study area.

It is clear from the Table 1 that the average amount of investment per hectare in the study area is Rs. 2,11,969.80. More than half of this constitutes maintenance cost. The establishment cost accounts for hardly 37 per cent of the total investment. The amount of investment per hectare varies among different categories of farmers. For instance, in case of large farmers the per hectare investment is more than the overall average for the district. Even the percentage gap between establishment cost and maintenance cost is not as much as it is for the entire district. Whereas in case of medium and

Table 1
Average Per hectare Cost of Cultivation in the First Stage Among Different Farm Categories

	Sagar Taluk				*Shimoga Taluk*				*District*			
	Small	*Medium*	*Large*	*Average*	*Small*	*Medium*	*Large*	*Average*	*Small*	*Medium*	*Large*	*Average*
Establishment Cost	53,369.49	59,499.00	1,20,972.90	77,947.13	56,125.98	63,159.00	1,25,315.73	81,533.57	54,747.73	61,329.00	1,23,144.31	79,740.35
	(27.27)	(28.90)	(44.49)	(34.72)	(32.84)	(34.84)	(50.91)	(40.88)	(29.87)	(31.68)	(47.54)	(37.62)
Maintenance Cost	1,42,311.78	1,46,371.70	1,50,941.30	1,46,541.59	1,14,776.56	1,18,122.37	1,20,853.00	1,17,917.31	1,28,544.17	1,32,247.04	1,35,897.15	1,32,229.45
	(72.73)	(71.10)	(55.51)	(65.28)	(67.16)	(65.16)	(49.09)	(59.12)	(70.13)	(68.32)	(52.46)	(62.38)
Total Cost	1,95,681.27	2,05,870.70	2,71,914.20	2,24,488.72	1,70,902.54	1,81,281.37	2,46,168.73	1,99,450.88	1,83,291.90	1,93,576.04	2,59,041.46	2,11,969.80
	(100.00)	(100.00)	(100.00)	(100.00)	(100.00)	(100.00)	(100.00)	(100.00)	(100.00)	(100.00)	(100.00)	(100.00)

Source: Survey Data.
Note: Figures in parentheses are percentages to total cost.

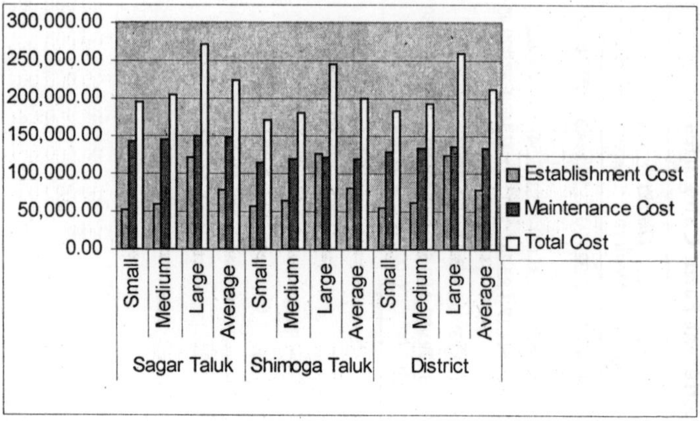

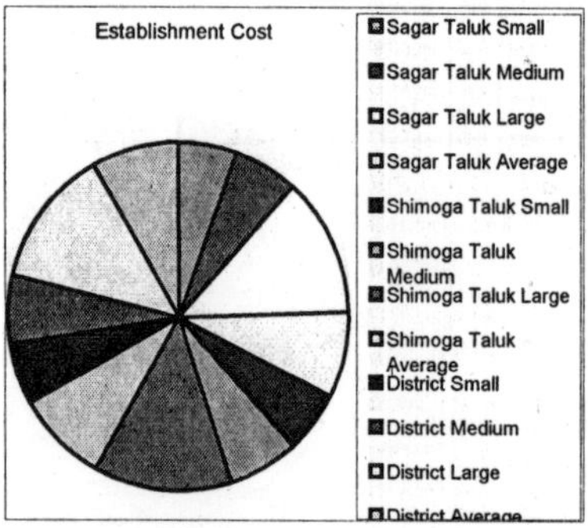

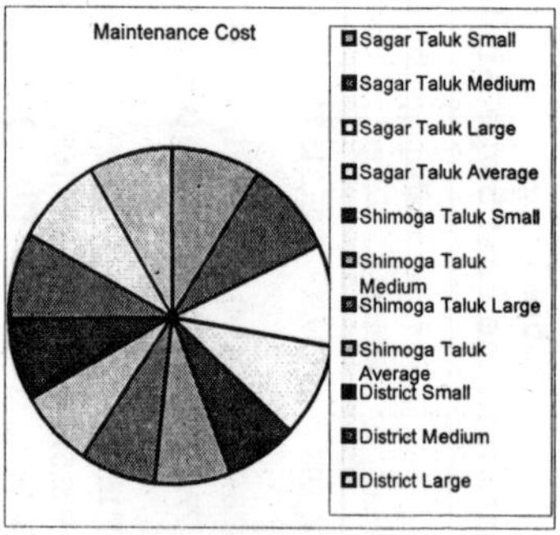

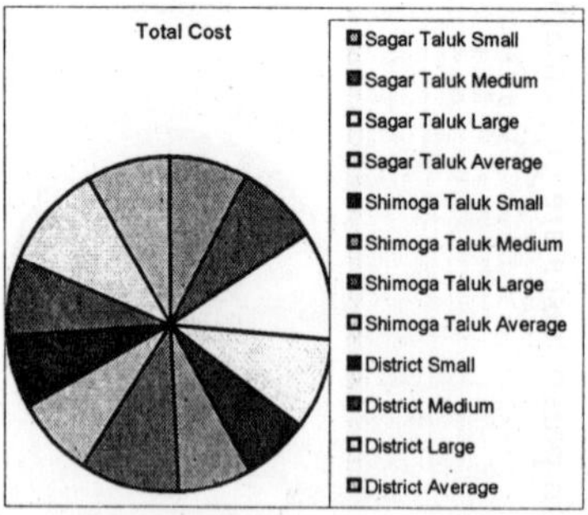

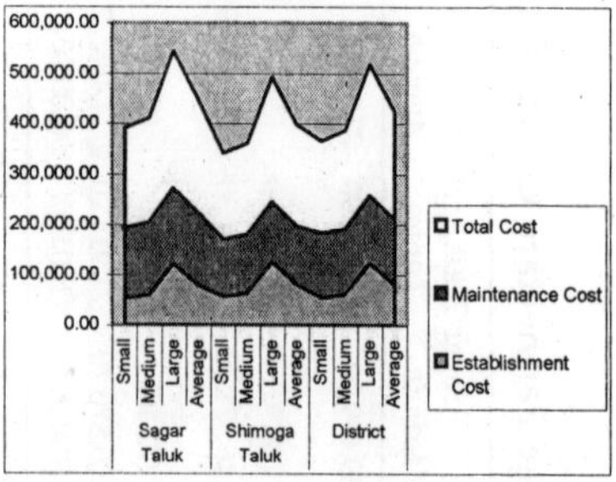

small farmers category the average investment per hectare is less than the overall average investment. However the investment made by medium farmers is slightly more than the small farmers. It is further clear from the data that the proportion of maintenance cost is found increasing as the size of holding decreases. In otherwords, in case of small farmers the proportion of maintenance cost is more the establishment cost. This ratio decreases with increasing size of holdings. It means maintenance cost is more and establishment cost is less in case of small farmers and this gap declines with increasing size of holdings.

The taluka-wise comparison of the volume of investment depicts a disturbing picture. In Sagar taluk the per hectare investment is much above the overall investment in the study area whereas in case of Shimoga taluk it is very much below the overall position. From this, it may be concluded that farmers in Sagar taluk are investing more as compared to farmers of Shimoga taluk. But in Shimoga taluk the percentage share of establishment cost is more than maintenance cost but this ratio is less in Sagar taluk. That is establishment cost is less than maintenance cost in Sagar taluk.

Within the taluk the percentage share of establishment Vs maintenance cost varies between different farm categories. For example, in Sagar taluk the share of maintenance cost is more than establishment cost. Further this share decreases as size of holdings increases. It is also evident from the data that there is not much difference between small and medium farmers as regards the share of establishment and maintenance cost. But it is totally different in case of large farmers. Where in the percentage share between the two costs is not much. From this it may be concluded that in Sagar taluk in case of small and medium farmers more money is spent on maintenance of areca farms than on establishment. Whereas large farmers in the same taluk spend relatively more on establishment of the areca farms. Such variation will have some impact on the yield from the palm.

In Shimoga taluk the investment picture is altogether different as compared to Sagar Taluk. In this taluk, the percentage share of establishment cost is more as compared to Sagar taluk in all categories of farms. It is still on higher side incase of large farm categories wherein the proportion of establishment cost is more than maintenance cost. This is the distinct feature of large farmer category in Shimoga taluk, which is not found in the entire study area.

From the above analysis it is clear that the average per hectare investment is highest in Sagar taluk and much less in Shimoga taluk when compared to entire study area. Another special feature of investment in the study area shows that the per hectare investment by large farmers is much above the overall average investment for the study area in both the taluks.

Among them it is found to be highest in Sagar taluk followed by the District and Shimoga taluk. Even the small and medium farmers in Sagar taluk are found investing more as compared to Shimoga taluk and the District.

Thus it may be concluded that investment by small, medium and large farmers in Sagar taluk is much more than the same in other taluk and the District as a whole. Such variation in investment will have definitely impact on yield from the crop.

It is clear from the foregoing discussion that with increase in the size of holding, there is an increase in the cost incurred in the first stage of Arecanut cultivation. This trend seems to be obvious as large farmers possess more resources and hence are able to invest more.

FIRST STAGE: AVERAGE COST OF CULTIVATION

Sagar Taluk

It is clear from the Table 2 that in the first stage, the large farmers in Sagar taluk are investing more as compared to medium and small farmers. Further the total maintenance cost is more as compared to total establishment cost among all the categories of farmers. Within the maintenance cost all the categories of farmers have made more investment on human labour followed by manures (organic manures) and chemical fertilisers, irrigation, interest on working capital, bullock power, hired machines and plant protection chemicals.

In the establishment cost the medium and large categories of farmers have made more investment on irrigation infrastructure followed by land levelling together with red earth and fencing, land revenue, interest on fixed capital and processing yard, seedlings etc. Where as in small farmers category in the total cost the share of seedlings is little bit higher than land revenue, interest on working capital and processing yard.

The expenditure made on total maintenance cost is high among large farmers as compared to other categories of farmers. And large farmers have made more expenditure on human labour chemical fertilisers, manures,0020irrigation with interest on working capital and ppc as compared to medium and small farmers.

Table 2
Average Per Hectare Cost of Cultivation of Various Farms Category in the First Stage in Sagar Taluk

A.	*Establishment Cost*	*Small*	*Medium*	*Large*	*Average*
I	Land Leveling, Red earth, Fencing	16,160.00	18,315.00	22,770.00	19,81.66
		(8.26)	(8.90)	(8.37)	(8.50)
II	Open well and pumpset Sprinkler,	23,900.00	27,000.00	80,080.00	43,660.00
	Conveyor Pipes, Pump House (Irrigation)	(12.21)	(13.11)	(29.45)	(19.45)
III	Seedlings	6,750.00	6,800.00	6,850.00	6,800.00
		(3.45)	(3.30)	(2.52)	(3.03)
IV	Land Revenue	6,559.49	7,384.00	11,272.90	8,405.47
	Interest on Fixed Capital and Processing Yard	(3.35)	(3.59)	(4.15)	(3.74)
	Total Establishment Cost	53,369.49	59,499.00	1,20,972.90	77,947.13
		(27.27)	(28.90)	(44.49)	(34.72)
B.	*Maintenance Cost*				
I	1. Human Labour	96,600.00	99,000.00	1,02,000.00	99,200.00
		(49.37)	(48.09)	(37.51)	(44.19)
II	Bullock PowerHired Machines	7,740.00	8,560.10	9,380.00	8,560.03
		(3.96)	(4.16)	(3.45)	(3.81)
III	Material Cost	24,858.50	25,316.50	25,725.40	25,300.13
	1. Manure's and Fertilizers (FYM,CF,GL)	(12.70)	(12.30)	(9.46)	(11.27)
	2. Plant Protection Chemicals	3,172.00	3,235.00	3,267.00	3,224.67
		(1.62)	(1.57)	(1.20)	(1.44)
	3. Irrigation Cost and Interest on Working Capital	9,941.28	10,260.10	10,568.90	10,256.76
		(5.08)	(4.98)	(3.89)	(4.57)
	Total Maintenance Cost	1,42,311.78	1,46,371.70	1,50,941.30	1,46,541.59
		(72.73)	(71.10)	(55.51)	(65.28)
C.	Total Cost (A+B)	1,95,681.27	2,05,870.70	2,71,914.20	2,24,488.72
		(100.00)	(100.00)	(100.00)	(100.00)

Source: Survey Data.
Note: Figures in parentheses are percentages to total cost.

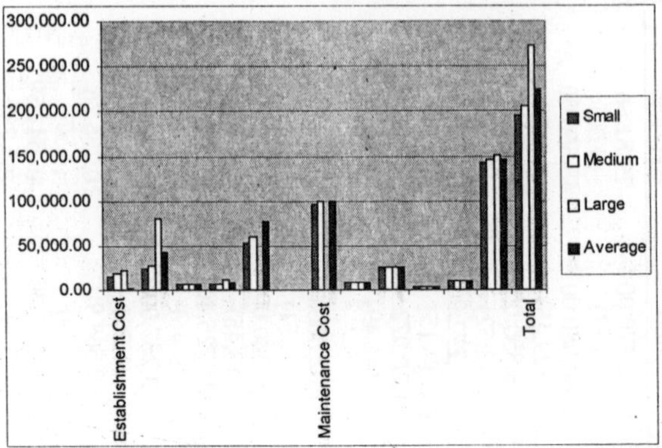
300,000.00
250,000.00
200,000.00
150,000.00
100,000.00
50,000.00
0.00
Establishment Cost
Maintenance Cost
Total
Small
Medium
Large
Average

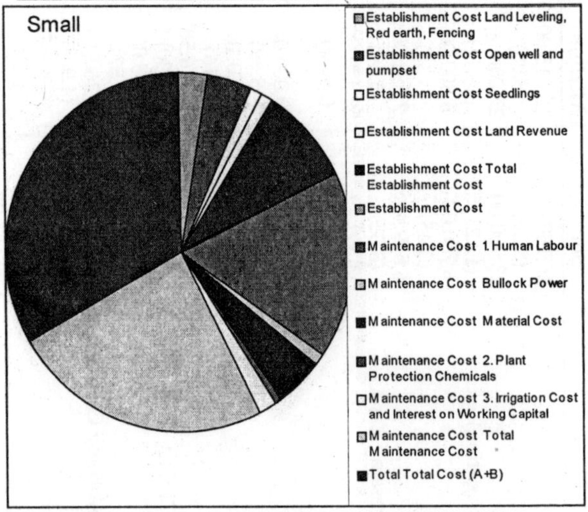
Small
Establishment Cost Land Leveling, Red earth, Fencing
Establishment Cost Open well and pumpset
Establishment Cost Seedlings
Establishment Cost Land Revenue
Establishment Cost Total Establishment Cost
Establishment Cost
Maintenance Cost 1. Human Labour
Maintenance Cost Bullock Power
Maintenance Cost Material Cost
Maintenance Cost 2. Plant Protection Chemicals
Maintenance Cost 3. Irrigation Cost and Interest on Working Capital
Maintenance Cost Total Maintenance Cost
Total Total Cost (A+B)

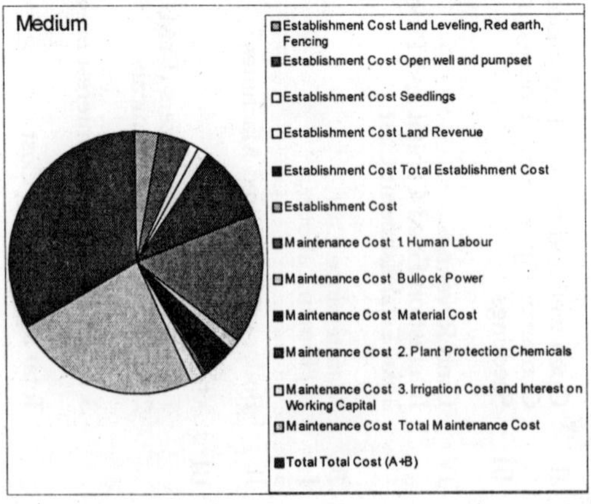
Medium
Establishment Cost Land Leveling, Red earth, Fencing
Establishment Cost Open well and pumpset
Establishment Cost Seedlings
Establishment Cost Land Revenue
Establishment Cost Total Establishment Cost
Establishment Cost
Maintenance Cost 1. Human Labour
Maintenance Cost Bullock Power
Maintenance Cost Material Cost
Maintenance Cost 2. Plant Protection Chemicals
Maintenance Cost 3. Irrigation Cost and Interest on Working Capital
Maintenance Cost Total Maintenance Cost
Total Total Cost (A+B)

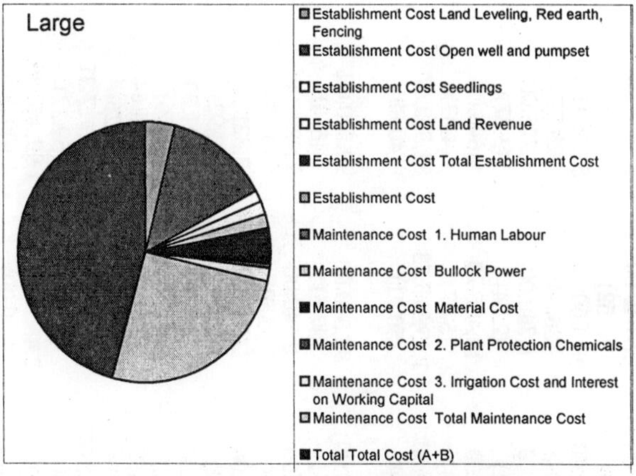
Large
Establishment Cost Land Leveling, Red earth, Fencing
Establishment Cost Open well and pumpset
Establishment Cost Seedlings
Establishment Cost Land Revenue
Establishment Cost Total Establishment Cost
Establishment Cost
Maintenance Cost 1. Human Labour
Maintenance Cost Bullock Power
Maintenance Cost Material Cost
Maintenance Cost 2. Plant Protection Chemicals
Maintenance Cost 3. Irrigation Cost and Interest on Working Capital
Maintenance Cost Total Maintenance Cost
Total Total Cost (A+B)

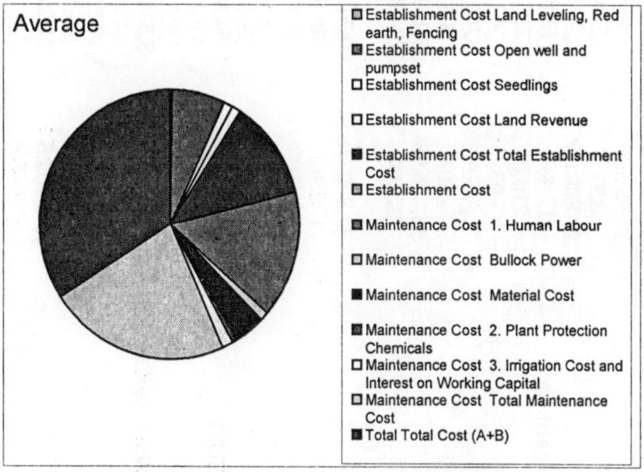
Average
Establishment Cost Land Leveling, Red earth, Fencing
Establishment Cost Open well and pumpset
Establishment Cost Seedlings
Establishment Cost Land Revenue
Establishment Cost Total Establishment Cost
Establishment Cost
Maintenance Cost 1. Human Labour
Maintenance Cost Bullock Power
Maintenance Cost Material Cost
Maintenance Cost 2. Plant Protection Chemicals
Maintenance Cost 3. Irrigation Cost and Interest on Working Capital
Maintenance Cost Total Maintenance Cost
Total Total Cost (A+B)

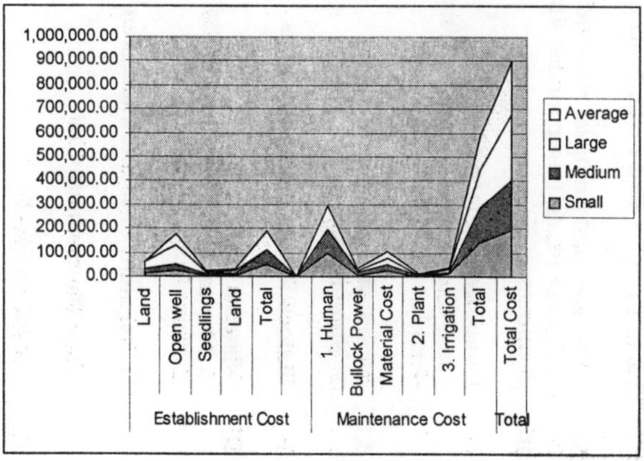
1,000,000.00
900,000.00
800,000.00
700,000.00
600,000.00
500,000.00
400,000.00
300,000.00
200,000.00
100,000.00
0.00
Average
Large
Medium
Small
Land
Open well
Seedlings
Land
Total
1. Human
Bullock Power
Material Cost
2. Plant
3. Irrigation
Total
Total Cost
Establishment Cost
Maintenance Cost
Total

Table 3
Average Per Hectare Cost of Cultivation of Various Farms Category in the First Stage in Shimoga Taluk

		Small	Medium	Large	Average
A.	*Establishment Cost*				
I	Land Leveling, Red earth, Fencing	11,930.00 (6.97)	13,485.00 (7.44)	16,040.00 (6.52)	13,818.33 (6.93)
II	Open well and pumpset Sprinkler, Conveyor Pipes, Pump House (Irrigation)	29,800.00 (17.44)	34,200.00 (18.86)	90,050.00 (36.58)	51,350.00 (25.75)
III	Seedlings	6,710.00 (3.93)	6,725.00 (3.71)	6,740.00 (2.74)	6,725.00 (3.37)
IV	Land Revenue Interest on Fixed Capital and Processing Yard	7,685.98 (4.50)	8,749.00 (4.83)	12,485.73 (5.07)	9,640.00 (4.83)
	Total Establishment Cost	56,125.98 (32.84)	63,159.00 (34.84)	1,25,315.73 (50.91)	81,533.57 (40.88)
B.	*Maintenance Cost*				
I	1. Human Labour	88,800.00 (51.96)	90,540.00 (49.94)	92,340.00 (37.51)	90,560.00 (45.40)
II	Bullock Power, Hired Machines	7,000.00 (4.10)	8,120.00 (4.48)	8,640.00 (3.50)	7,920..00 (3.98)
III	Material Cost 1. Manure's and Fertilizers (FYM,CF,GL)	7,695.00 (4.50)	7,823.00 (4.32)	7,946.00 (3.23)	7,821.33 (3.92)
	2. Plant Protection Chemicals	3.050.00 (1.78)	3,111.00 (1.72)	3,173.00 (1.29)	3,111.33 (1.56)
	3. Irrigation Cost and Interest on Working Capital	8,231.56 (4.82)	8,528.37 (4.70)	8,754.00 (3.56)	8,504.64 (4.26)
	Total Maintenance Cost	1,14,776.56 (67.16)	1,18,122.37 (65.16)	1,20,853.00 (49.09)	1,17,917.31 (59.12)
C.	Total Cost (A+B)	1,70,902.54 (100.00)	1,81,281.37 (100.00)	2,46,168.73 (100.00)	1,99,450.88 (100.00)

Source: Survey Data.
Note: Figures in parentheses are percentages to total cost.

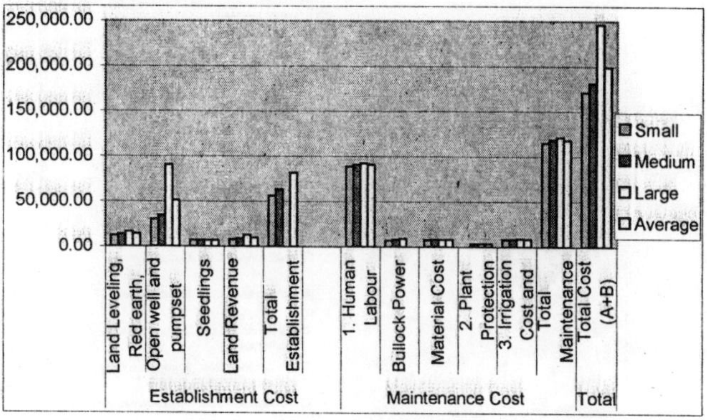
250,000.00
200,000.00
150,000.00
100,000.00
50,000.00
0.00
Small
Medium
Large
Average
Land Leveling, Red earth,
Open well and pumpset
Seedlings
Land Revenue
Total Establishment
1. Human Labour
Bullock Power
Material Cost
2. Plant Protection
3. Irrigation Cost and
Total Maintenance
Total Cost (A+B)
Establishment Cost
Maintenance Cost
Total

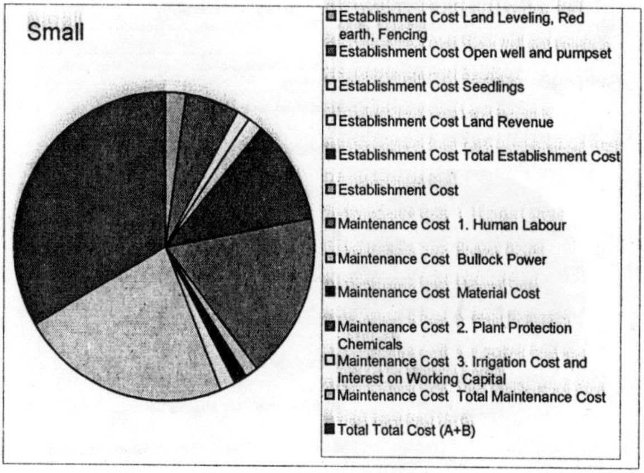
Small
Establishment Cost Land Leveling, Red earth, Fencing
Establishment Cost Open well and pumpset
Establishment Cost Seedlings
Establishment Cost Land Revenue
Establishment Cost Total Establishment Cost
Establishment Cost
Maintenance Cost 1. Human Labour
Maintenance Cost Bullock Power
Maintenance Cost Material Cost
Maintenance Cost 2. Plant Protection Chemicals
Maintenance Cost 3. Irrigation Cost and Interest on Working Capital
Maintenance Cost Total Maintenance Cost
Total Total Cost (A+B)

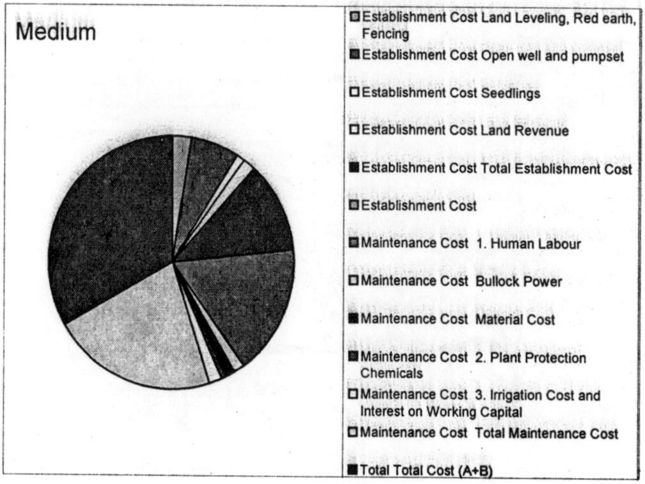
Medium
Establishment Cost Land Leveling, Red earth, Fencing
Establishment Cost Open well and pumpset
Establishment Cost Seedlings
Establishment Cost Land Revenue
Establishment Cost Total Establishment Cost
Establishment Cost
Maintenance Cost 1. Human Labour
Maintenance Cost Bullock Power
Maintenance Cost Material Cost
Maintenance Cost 2. Plant Protection Chemicals
Maintenance Cost 3. Irrigation Cost and Interest on Working Capital
Maintenance Cost Total Maintenance Cost
Total Total Cost (A+B)

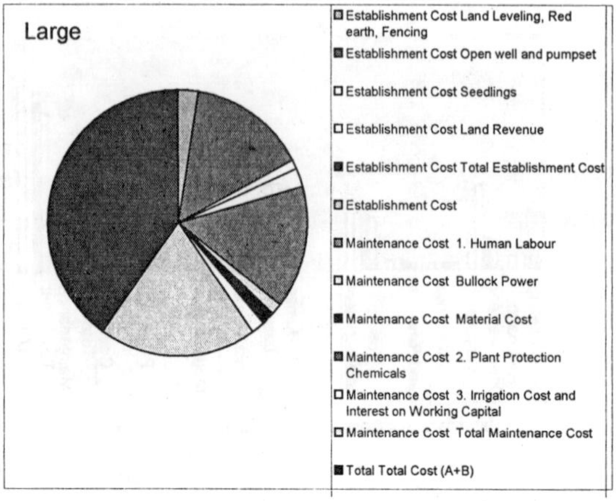
Large
Establishment Cost Land Leveling, Red earth, Fencing
Establishment Cost Open well and pumpset
Establishment Cost Seedlings
Establishment Cost Land Revenue
Establishment Cost Total Establishment Cost
Establishment Cost
Maintenance Cost 1. Human Labour
Maintenance Cost Bullock Power
Maintenance Cost Material Cost
Maintenance Cost 2. Plant Protection Chemicals
Maintenance Cost 3. Irrigation Cost and Interest on Working Capital
Maintenance Cost Total Maintenance Cost
Total Total Cost (A+B)

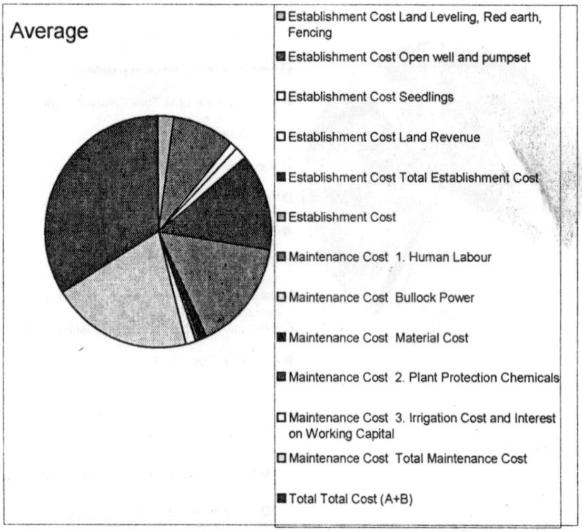
Average
Establishment Cost Land Leveling, Red earth, Fencing
Establishment Cost Open well and pumpset
Establishment Cost Seedlings
Establishment Cost Land Revenue
Establishment Cost Total Establishment Cost
Establishment Cost
Maintenance Cost 1. Human Labour
Maintenance Cost Bullock Power
Maintenance Cost Material Cost
Maintenance Cost 2. Plant Protection Chemicals
Maintenance Cost 3. Irrigation Cost and Interest on Working Capital
Maintenance Cost Total Maintenance Cost
Total Total Cost (A+B)

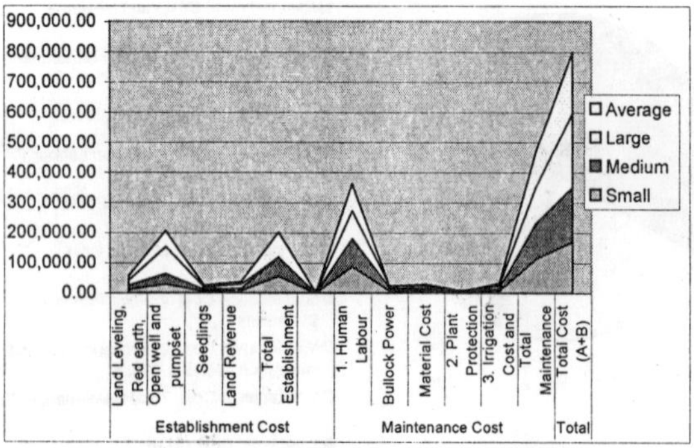
900,000.00
800,000.00
700,000.00
600,000.00
500,000.00
400,000.00
300,000.00
200,000.00
100,000.00
0.00
Average
Large
Medium
Small
Land Leveling, Red earth,
Open well and pumpset
Seedlings
Land Revenue
Total Establishment
1. Human Labour
Bullock Power
Material Cost
2. Plant Protection
3. Irrigation Cost and
Total Maintenance
Total Cost (A+B)
Establishment Cost
Maintenance Cost
Total

Table 4
Average Per Hectare Cost of Cultivation of Various Farms Category in the First Stage in Shimoga District

A.	*Establishment Cost*	*Small*	*Medium*	*Large*	*Average*
I	Land Leveling, Red earth, Fencing	14,045.00	15,900.00	19,405.00	16,450.00
		(7.66)	(8.21)	(7.49)	(7.76)
II	Open well and pumpset. Sprinkler, Conveyor Pipes, Pump House (Irrigation)	26,850.00	30,600.00	85,065.00	47,505.00
		(14.65)	(15.81)	(32.84)	(22.41)
III	Seedlings	6,730.00	6,762.50	6,795.00	6,762.50
		(3.67)	(3.49)	(2.62)	(3.19)
IV	Land Revenue	7,122.73	8,066.50	11,879.31	9,022.85
	Interest on Fixed Capital and Processing Yard	(3.89)	(4.17)	(4.59)	(4.26)
	Total Establishment Cost	54,747.73	61,239.00	1,23,144.31	79,740.35
		(29.87)	(31.68)	(47.54)	(37.62)
B.	*Maintenance Cost*				
I	1. Human Labour	92,700.00	94,770.00	97,170.00	94,880.00
		(50.58)	(48.96)	(37.51)	(44.76)
II	Bullock PowerHired Machines	7,370.00	8,340.05	9,010.00	8,240.02
		(4.01)	(4.31)	(3.48)	(3.89)
III	Material Cost1.	16,276.75	16,569.75	16,835.70	16,560.73
	Manure's and Fertilizers (FYM,CF,GL)	(8.88)	(8.56)	(6.50)	(7.81)
	2. Plant Protection Chemicals	3,111.00	3,173.00	3,220.00	3,168.00
		(1.70)	(1.64)	(1.24)	(1,49)
	3. Irrigation Cost and Interest on Working Capital	9,086.42	9,394.24	9,661.45	9,380.70
		(4.96)	(4.85)	(3.73)	(4.43)
	Total Maintenance Cost	1,28,544.17	1,32,247.04	1,35,897.15	1,32,229.45
		(70.13)	(68.32)	(52.46)	(62.38)
C.	Total Cost (A+B)	1,83,291.90	1,93,576.04	2,59,041.46	2,11,969.80
		(100.00)	(100.00)	(100.00)	(100.00)

Source: Survey Data.
Note : Figures in parentheses are percentages to total cost.

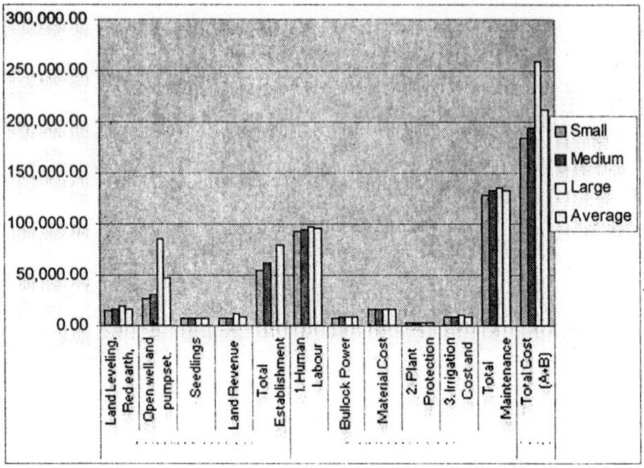
300,000.00
250,000.00
200,000.00
150,000.00
100,000.00
50,000.00
0.00
Small
Medium
Large
Average
Land Leveling, Red earth,
Open well and pumpset.
Seedlings
Land Revenue
Total Establishment
1. Human Labour
Bullock Power
Material Cost
2. Plant Protection
3. Irrigation Cost and
Total Maintenance
Total Cost (A+B)

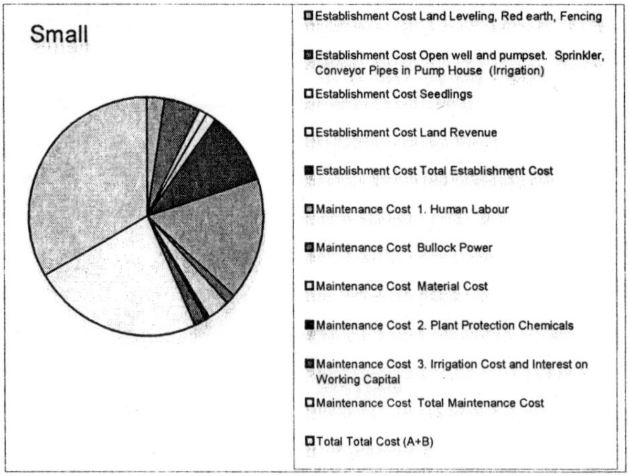
Small
Establishment Cost Land Leveling, Red earth, Fencing
Establishment Cost Open well and pumpset. Sprinkler, Conveyor Pipes in Pump House (Irrigation)
Establishment Cost Seedlings
Establishment Cost Land Revenue
Establishment Cost Total Establishment Cost
Maintenance Cost 1. Human Labour
Maintenance Cost Bullock Power
Maintenance Cost Material Cost
Maintenance Cost 2. Plant Protection Chemicals
Maintenance Cost 3. Irrigation Cost and Interest on Working Capital
Maintenance Cost Total Maintenance Cost
Total Total Cost (A+B)

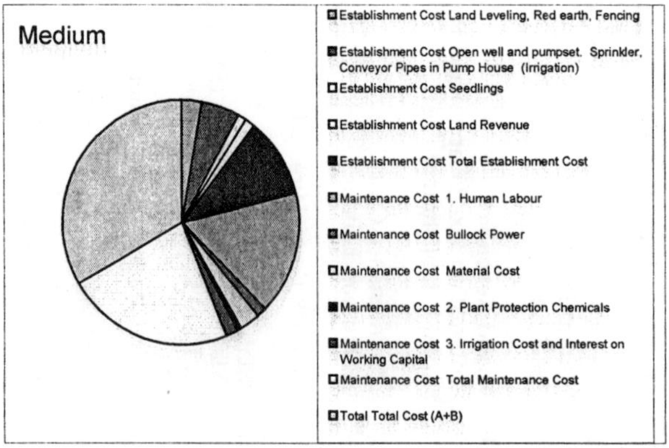
Medium
Establishment Cost Land Leveling, Red earth, Fencing
Establishment Cost Open well and pumpset. Sprinkler, Conveyor Pipes in Pump House (Irrigation)
Establishment Cost Seedlings
Establishment Cost Land Revenue
Establishment Cost Total Establishment Cost
Maintenance Cost 1. Human Labour
Maintenance Cost Bullock Power
Maintenance Cost Material Cost
Maintenance Cost 2. Plant Protection Chemicals
Maintenance Cost 3. Irrigation Cost and Interest on Working Capital
Maintenance Cost Total Maintenance Cost
Total Total Cost (A+B)

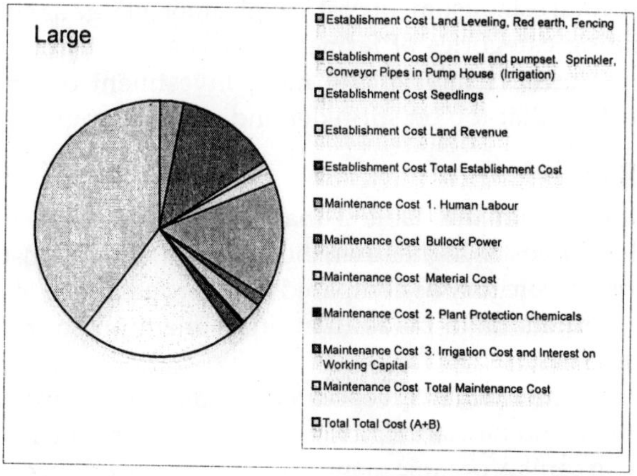
Large
Establishment Cost Land Leveling, Red earth, Fencing
Establishment Cost Open well and pumpset. Sprinkler, Conveyor Pipes in Pump House (Irrigation)
Establishment Cost Seedlings
Establishment Cost Land Revenue
Establishment Cost Total Establishment Cost
Maintenance Cost 1. Human Labour
Maintenance Cost Bullock Power
Maintenance Cost Material Cost
Maintenance Cost 2. Plant Protection Chemicals
Maintenance Cost 3. Irrigation Cost and Interest on Working Capital
Maintenance Cost Total Maintenance Cost
Total Total Cost (A+B)

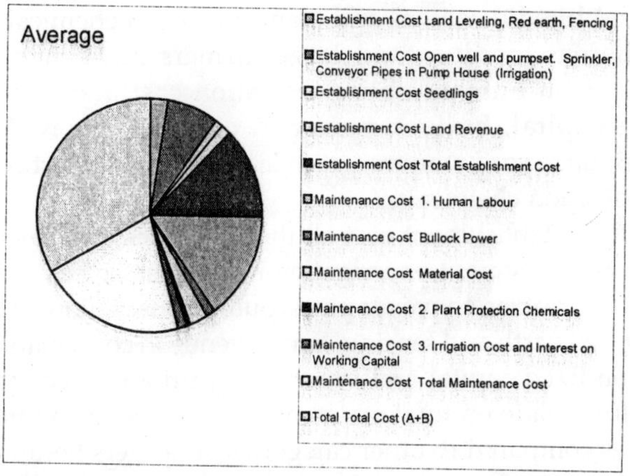
Average
Establishment Cost Land Leveling, Red earth, Fencing
Establishment Cost Open well and pumpset. Sprinkler, Conveyor Pipes in Pump House (Irrigation)
Establishment Cost Seedlings
Establishment Cost Land Revenue
Establishment Cost Total Establishment Cost
Maintenance Cost 1. Human Labour
Maintenance Cost Bullock Power
Maintenance Cost Material Cost
Maintenance Cost 2. Plant Protection Chemicals
Maintenance Cost 3. Irrigation Cost and Interest on Working Capital
Maintenance Cost Total Maintenance Cost
Total Total Cost (A+B)

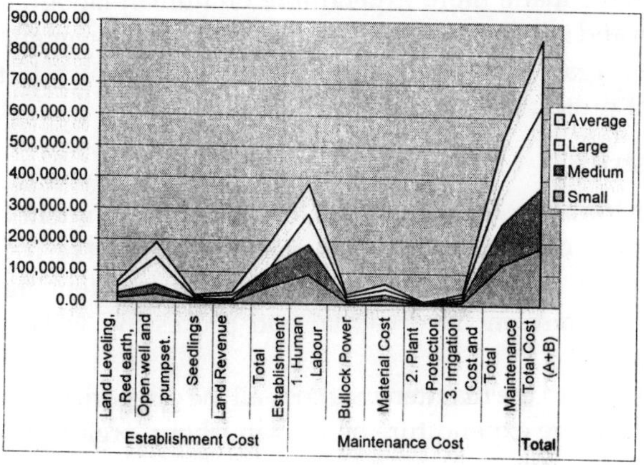
900,000.00
800,000.00
700,000.00
600,000.00
500,000.00
400,000.00
300,000.00
200,000.00
100,000.00
0.00
Average
Large
Medium
Small
Land Leveling, Red earth,
Open well and pumpset.
Seedlings
Land Revenue
Total Establishment
1. Human Labour
Bullock Power
Material Cost
2. Plant Protection
3. Irrigation Cost and
Total Maintenance
Total Cost (A+B)
Establishment Cost
Maintenance Cost
Total

The total establishment cost is high among large as compared to remaining categories of farmers as it is evident from the fact that large farmers have made more investment on irrigation infrastructure that too on sprinkler and conveyor pipes.

Shimoga taluk

It is evident from the Table 3 that, in Shimoga taluk the total establishment cost is higher than the total maintenance cost among large farmers category as compared to other categories of farmers as large farmers have made more investment on sprinkler and conveyor pipes.

In the maintenance cost small farmers have made more investment on human labour followed by irrigation and investment on working capital, organic manure with chemical fertilizer, bullock power and hired machines and plant protection chemicals.

Whereas medium and large farmers have made more investment on human labour, irrigation cost and interest on working capital, bullock power in combination with hired machines, farm yard manure, green leaves, chemical fertilizer and plant protection chemicals.

In the establishment cost all the categories of farmers have made more investment on irrigation infrastructure i.e., openwell, pumpsets, sprinkler, conveyor pipes, pump house followed by land levelling, red earth and fencing, land revenue in combination with interest on fixed capital and processing yard and seedlings. The expenditure made on total maintenance cost is high among large farmers as compared to other categories of farmers because large farmers have made more expenditure on human labour, cost on irrigation and interest on working capital, bullock power and hired machines, organic manures in combination with chemical fertilizers and plant protection chemicals.

The District

It is clear from the Table 4 that, in the total establishment cost all the categories of farmers have made more investment on irrigation infrastructure and land levelling, red earth and fencing, land revenue, interest on fixed capital and processing yard and on seedlings.

Whereas in the maintenance cost, all the categories of farmers have made more expenditure on human labour, organic manures and chemical fertilizers, irrigation cost and interest on working capital, bullock power, hired machine and plant protection chemicals.

Cost of Cultivation in Second Stage

The structure of cost of cultivation in the second stage gives altogether a different picture. In the second stage, the establishment cost becomes insignificant and the maintenance cost becomes dominant. Now let us examine how and to what extent it varies between different categories of farmers and in two taluks. This is presented in the Table 5.

It is clear from the Table 5 that the average amount of investment per hectare in the study area is Rs. 43,114.61. More than three-fourth of this constitutes maintenance cost and the establishment cost accounts for hardly 3.09 per cent of the total investment. Here also (in this stage) the amount of investment per hectare varies among different categories of farmers. For instance, in case of medium and large farmers the per hectare investment is slightly higher than overall average for the District. But in absolute terms cost incurred in all items are higher in large farms than medium and small. Whereas in case of small farmers category the average investment per hectare is less than the overall average investment.

It is further clear from the data that the proportion of maintenance cost is found increasing as the size of holding decreases. In other words, in case of small farmers the proportion of maintenance cost is more than the establishment cost. This rate decreases with increasing size of holdings. It means maintenance cost is more and establishment cost is less in case of small farmers and this gap slightly declines with increasing size of holdings.

Here also the taluk wise comparison of the volume of investment depicts a disturbing picture. In Sagar taluk the per hectare investment is much above the overall investment in the study area, whereas in case of Shimoga taluk it is very much below the overall position. From this it may be concluded that farmers in Sagar taluk are investing more as compared to Shimoga taluk. In both the taluks the percentage share of the maintenance cost is more than the establishment cost.

Within the taluk the percentage share of establishment Vs maintenance cost varies between different farm categories. For example, in both the taluks the share of maintenance cost is more

Table 5
Average Per hectare Cost of Cultivation in the Second Stage Among Different Farm Categories

	Sagar Talu				*Shimoga Taluk*				*District*			
	Small	*Medium*	*Large*	*Average*	*Small*	*Medium*	*Large*	*Average*	*Small*	*Medium*	*Large*	*Average*
Establishment	657.07	758.42	1,268.98	894.82	665.14	772.00	1,289.39	908.84	661.11	765.21	1,279.19	901.84
Cost	(1.39)	(1.55)	(2.51)	(1.83)	(1.87)	(2.05)	(3.33)	(2.43)	(1.60)	(1.76)	(2.36)	(3.09)
Maintenance	46,467.37	48,218.37	49,310.62	47,998.79	34,872.31	36,963.31	37,444.62	36,426.75	40.669.84	42,590.84	43,377.62	42,212.77
Cost	(98.61)	(98.45)	(97.49)	(98.17)	(98.13)	(97.95)	(96.67)	(97.57)	(98.40)	(98.24)	(97.14)	(97.91)
Total Cost	47,124.44	48, 976.79	50,579.60	48,893.61	35,537.45	37,735.31	38,734.01	37,335.59	41,330.95	43,356.05	44,656.81	43,114.61
	(100.00)	(100.00)	(100.00)	(100.00)	(100.00)	(100.00)	(100.00)	(100.00)	(100.00)	(100.00)	(100.00)	(100.00)

Source: Survey Data.

Note: Figures in parenthesis are percentages to total cost.

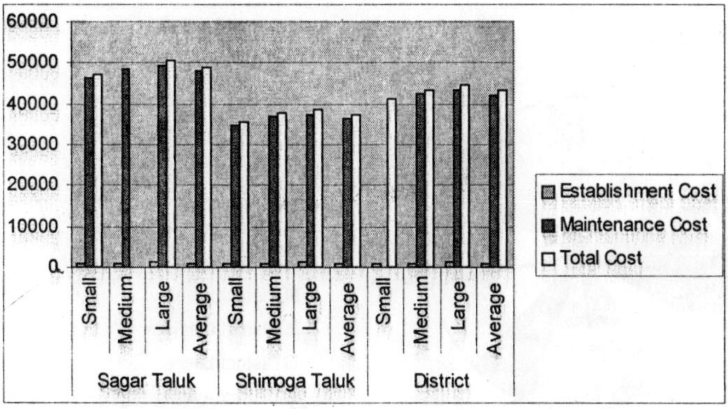
60000
50000
40000
30000
20000
10000
0
Small
Medium
Large
Average
Small
Medium
Large
Average
Small
Medium
Large
Average
Sagar Taluk
Shimoga Taluk
District
Establishment Cost
Maintenance Cost
Total Cost

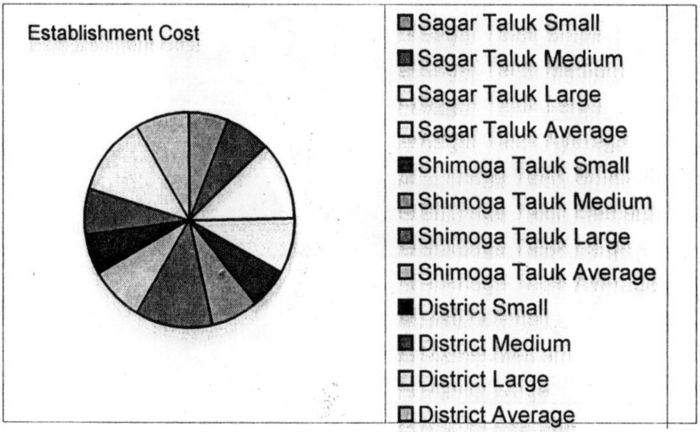
Establishment Cost
Sagar Taluk Small
Sagar Taluk Medium
Sagar Taluk Large
Sagar Taluk Average
Shimoga Taluk Small
Shimoga Taluk Medium
Shimoga Taluk Large
Shimoga Taluk Average
District Small
District Medium
District Large
District Average

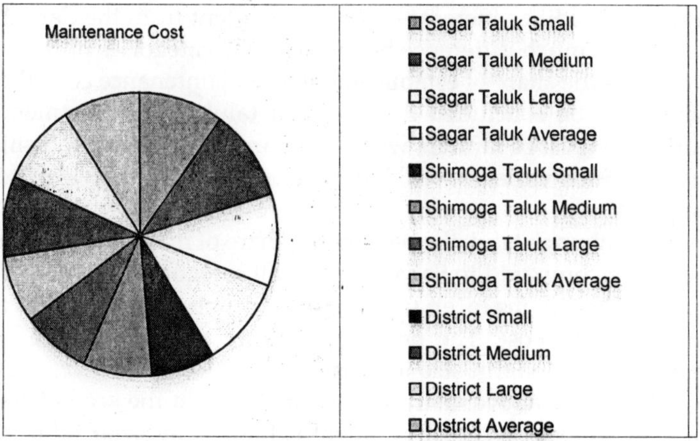
Maintenance Cost
Sagar Taluk Small
Sagar Taluk Medium
Sagar Taluk Large
Sagar Taluk Average
Shimoga Taluk Small
Shimoga Taluk Medium
Shimoga Taluk Large
Shimoga Taluk Average
District Small
District Medium
District Large
District Average

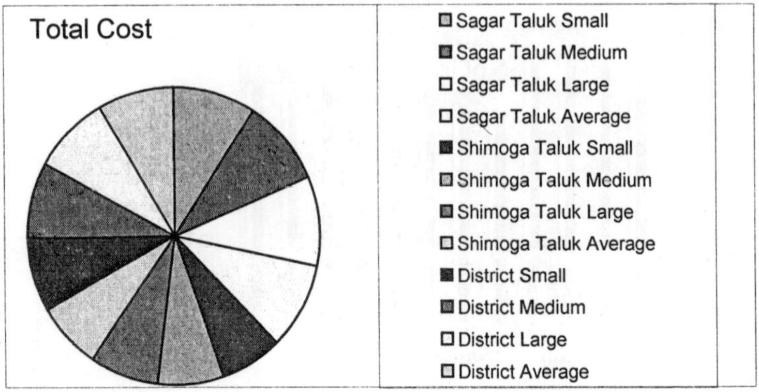

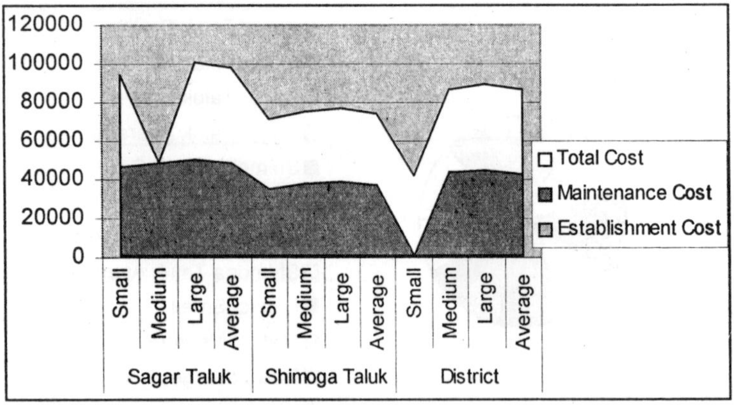

than the establishment cost. Further this share slightly decreases as size of holdings increases. It is also evident from the data that there is not much difference between all the categories of farmers as regards the share of establishment and maintenance cost. From this it may be concluded that in Sagar taluk total investment is more among large farmers when compared to medium and small farmers. Such variation will have some impact on the yield from the palm.

In Shimoga taluk the percentage share of maintenance cost is less when compared to Sagar taluk in all categories of farms. The proportion of maintenance cost is much higher than the establishment cost. The percentage share of maintenance cost decreases as the farm size increases.

From the above analysis it is clear that in the second stage the average per hectare investment is highest in Sagar taluk and much less in Shimoga taluk when compared to entire study area. Another special feature of investment in the study area shows that the per hectare investment by large farmers is much above the overall average investment for the study area. Here also among large farmers it is found to be highest in Sagar taluk followed by district and Shimoga taluk. Even the small and medium farmers in Sagar taluk are found investing more as compared to Shimoga taluk and the district.

Thus it may be concluded that as in the gestation period, here also the investment by small, medium and large farmers in Sagar taluk is much more than the same in other taluk and the district as a whole. Such variation in investment will have definite impact on yield from the crop.

SECOND STAGE: AVERAGE COST OF CULTIVATION

Sagar Taluk

It is clear from the Table 6 that in Sagar taluk in second stage the large farmers are investing more as compared to medium and small farmers.

Apart from this the total maintenance cost is more as compared to total establishment cost.

In the maintenance cost all the categories of farmers have made more investment on human labour followed by organic manures and chemical fertilizers, irrigation cost with interest on working capital and plant protection chemicals.

In the establishment cost all the categories of farmers have made more investment on red earth, interest on fixed capital and land revenue, which is comparatively negligible.

The expenditure made on total maintenance cost is high among large farmers as compared to other categories of farmers. Because large farmers have made more investment on human labour, organic mannures and chemical fertilizers, irrigation cost and interest on working capital and ppc.

The total establishment cost is high among large farmers as compared to other categories of farmers because the large category of farmers have made more investment on red earth in combination with interest on fixed capital and land revenue.

Shimoga Taluk

It is clear from the respective Table from 7. That the large farmers have invested more as compared to medium and small farmers.

Table 6
Average Per Hectare Cost of Cultivation of Various Farms Category in the Second Stage in Sagar Taluk

A.	*Maintenance Cost*	*Small*	*Medium*	*Large*	*Average*
I	Human Labour	35,100.00	36,000.00	36,240.00	35,780.00
		(74.48)	(73.50)	(71.65)	(73.18)
II	Material Cost1.	7,224.00	7,767.00	8,480.00	7,823.67
	Organic Manure's and Chemical Fertilizers	(15.33)	(15.86)	(16.77)	(16.00)
	(FYM, GL, CF)				
	2. Plant Protection Chemicals	1,050.00	1,076.00	1,090.00	1,071.67
		(2.23)	(2.20)	(2.15)	(2.19)
	3. Irrigation Cost and Interest on Working Capital	3,093.37	3,376.37	3,500.62	3,323.45
		(6.57)	(6.89)	(6.92)	(6.80)
	Total Maintenance Cost	46,467.37	48,218.37	49,310.62	47,998.79
		(98.61)	(98.45)	(97.49)	(98.17)
B.	Total Establishment Cost (Red earth,	657.07	758.42	1,268.98	894.82
	Interest on Fixed Capital, Land Revenue)	(1.39)	(1.55)	(2.51)	(1.83)
C.	Total Cost (A+B)	47,124.44	48,976.79	50,579.60	48,893.61
		(100.00)	(100.00)	(100.00)	(100.00)

Source: Survey Data.
Note: Figures in parenthesis are percentages to total cost.

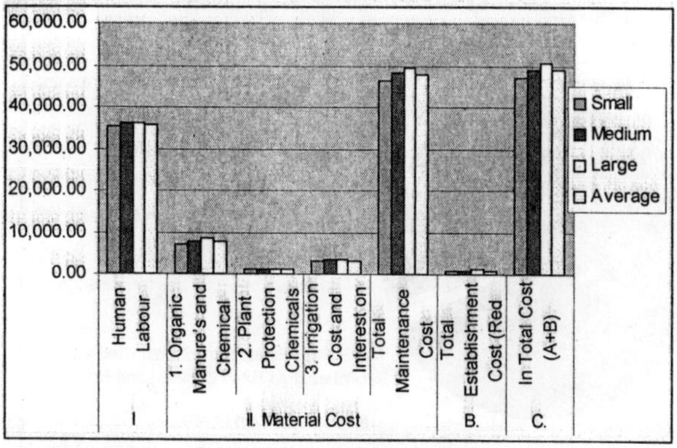
60,000.00
50,000.00
40,000.00
30,000.00
20,000.00
10,000.00
0.00
Small
Medium
Large
Average
Human Labour
1. Organic Manure's and Chemical
2. Plant Protection Chemicals
3. Irrigation Cost and Interest on
Total Maintenance Cost
Total Establishment Cost (Red
In Total Cost (A+B)
I
II. Material Cost
B.
C.

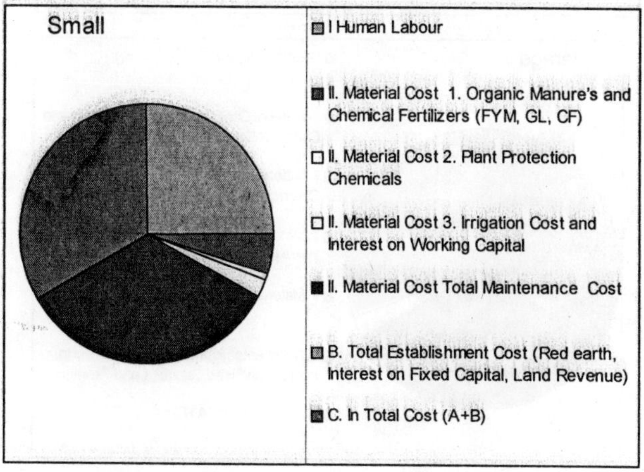
Small
I Human Labour
II. Material Cost 1. Organic Manure's and Chemical Fertilizers (FYM, GL, CF)
II. Material Cost 2. Plant Protection Chemicals
II. Material Cost 3. Irrigation Cost and Interest on Working Capital
II. Material Cost Total Maintenance Cost
B. Total Establishment Cost (Red earth, Interest on Fixed Capital, Land Revenue)
C. In Total Cost (A+B)

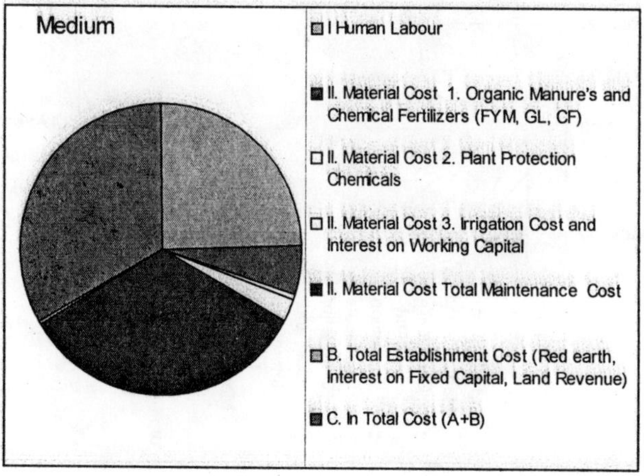
Medium
I Human Labour
II. Material Cost 1. Organic Manure's and Chemical Fertilizers (FYM, GL, CF)
II. Material Cost 2. Plant Protection Chemicals
II. Material Cost 3. Irrigation Cost and Interest on Working Capital
II. Material Cost Total Maintenance Cost
B. Total Establishment Cost (Red earth, Interest on Fixed Capital, Land Revenue)
C. In Total Cost (A+B)

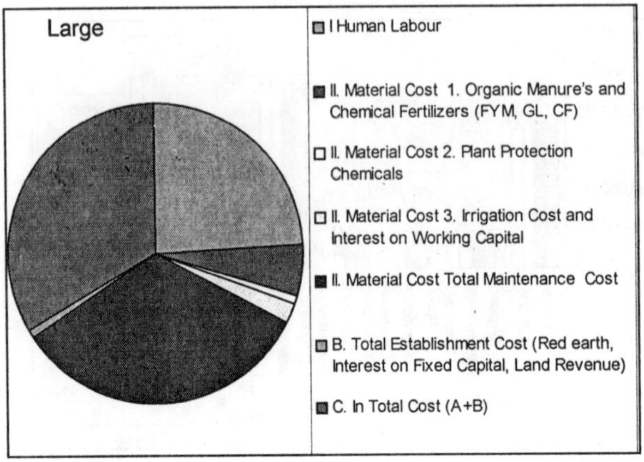
Large
I Human Labour
II. Material Cost 1. Organic Manure's and Chemical Fertilizers (FYM, GL, CF)
II. Material Cost 2. Plant Protection Chemicals
II. Material Cost 3. Irrigation Cost and Interest on Working Capital
II. Material Cost Total Maintenance Cost
B. Total Establishment Cost (Red earth, Interest on Fixed Capital, Land Revenue)
C. In Total Cost (A+B)

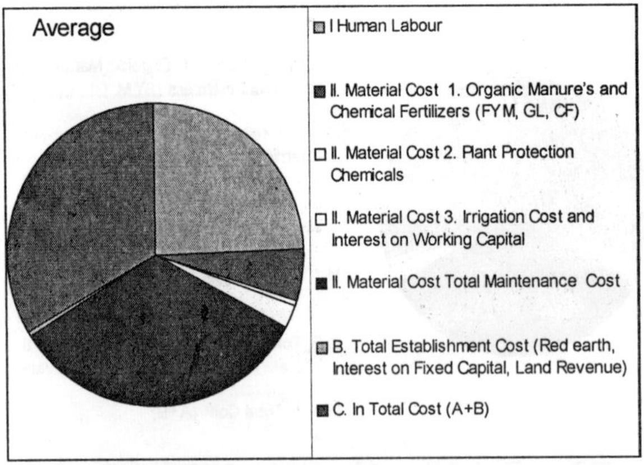
Average
I Human Labour
II. Material Cost 1. Organic Manure's and Chemical Fertilizers (FYM, GL, CF)
II. Material Cost 2. Plant Protection Chemicals
II. Material Cost 3. Irrigation Cost and Interest on Working Capital
II. Material Cost Total Maintenance Cost
B. Total Establishment Cost (Red earth, Interest on Fixed Capital, Land Revenue)
C. In Total Cost (A+B)

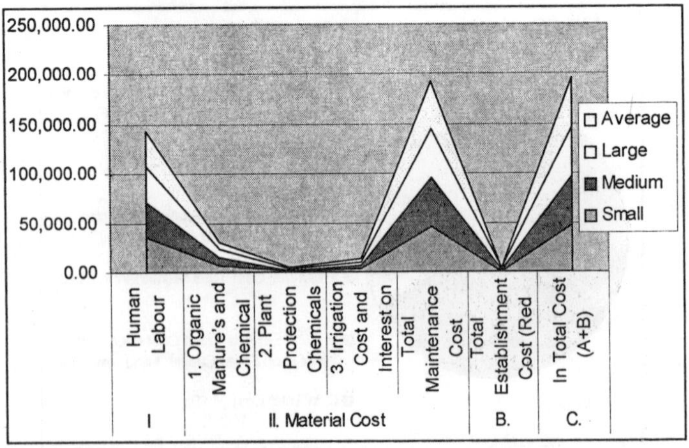
250,000.00
200,000.00
150,000.00
100,000.00
50,000.00
0.00
Average
Large
Medium
Small
Human Labour
1. Organic Manure's and Chemical
2. Plant Protection Chemicals
3. Irrigation Cost and Interest on
Total Maintenance Cost
Total Establishment Cost (Red
In Total Cost (A+B)
I
II. Material Cost
B.
C.

Table 7
Average Per Hectare Cost of Cultivation of Various Farms Category in the Second Stage in Shimoga Taluk

	Maintenance Cost	*Small*	*Medium*	*Large*	*Average*
A.					
I	Human Labour	29,400.00 (82.73)	30,900.00 (81.89)	31,080.00 (80.24)	30,460.00 (81.58)
II	Material Cost 1. Organic Manure's and Chemical Fertilizers (FYM, GL, CF)	2,121.00 (5.97)	2,249.00 (5.96)	2,457.00 (6.34)	2,275.67 (6.10)
	2. Plant Protection Chemicals	1,000.00 (2.81)	1,160.00 (3.07)	1,165.00 (3.01)	1,108.33 (2.97)
	3. Irrigation Cost and Interest on Working Capital	2,351.31 (6.62)	2,654.31 (7.03)	2,742.62 (7.08)	2,582.75 (6.92)
	Total Maintenance Cost	34,872.31 (98.13)	36,963.31 (97.95)	37,444.62 (96.67)	36,426.75 (97.57)
B.	Total Establishment Cost (Red earth, Interest on Fixed Capital, Land Revenue)	665.14 (1.87)	772.00 (2.05)	1,289.39 (3.33)	908.84 (2.43)
C.	Total Cost (A+B)	35,537.45 (100.00)	37,735.31 (100.00)	38,734.01 (100.00)	37,335.59 (100.00)

Source: Survey Data.
Note: Figures in parentheses are percentages to total cost.

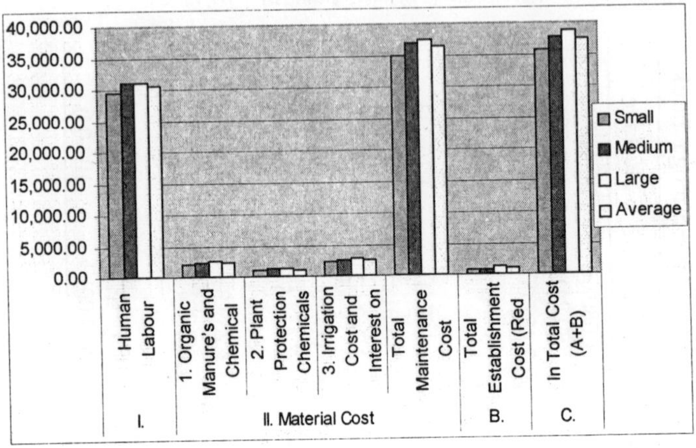
40,000.00
35,000.00
30,000.00
25,000.00
20,000.00
15,000.00
10,000.00
5,000.00
0.00
Small
Medium
Large
Average
Human Labour
1. Organic Manure's and Chemical
2. Plant Protection Chemicals
3. Irrigation Cost and Interest on
Total Maintenance Cost
Total Establishment Cost (Red
In Total Cost (A+B)
I.
II. Material Cost
B.
C.

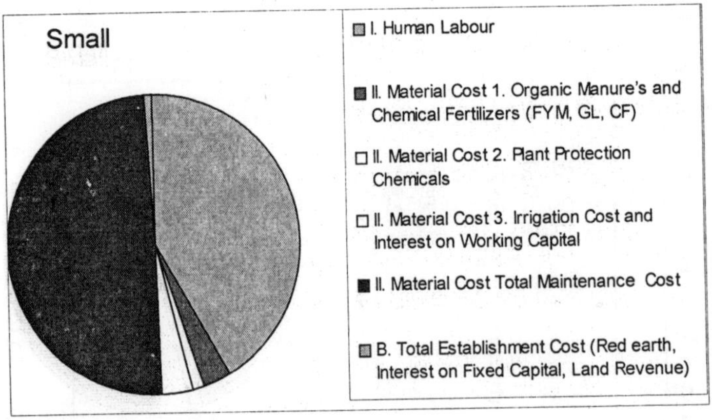
Small
I. Human Labour
II. Material Cost 1. Organic Manure's and Chemical Fertilizers (FYM, GL, CF)
II. Material Cost 2. Plant Protection Chemicals
II. Material Cost 3. Irrigation Cost and Interest on Working Capital
II. Material Cost Total Maintenance Cost
B. Total Establishment Cost (Red earth, Interest on Fixed Capital, Land Revenue)

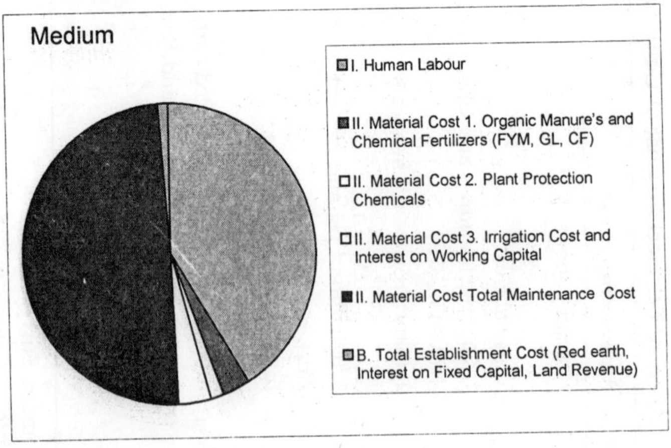
Medium
I. Human Labour
II. Material Cost 1. Organic Manure's and Chemical Fertilizers (FYM, GL, CF)
II. Material Cost 2. Plant Protection Chemicals
II. Material Cost 3. Irrigation Cost and Interest on Working Capital
II. Material Cost Total Maintenance Cost
B. Total Establishment Cost (Red earth, Interest on Fixed Capital, Land Revenue)

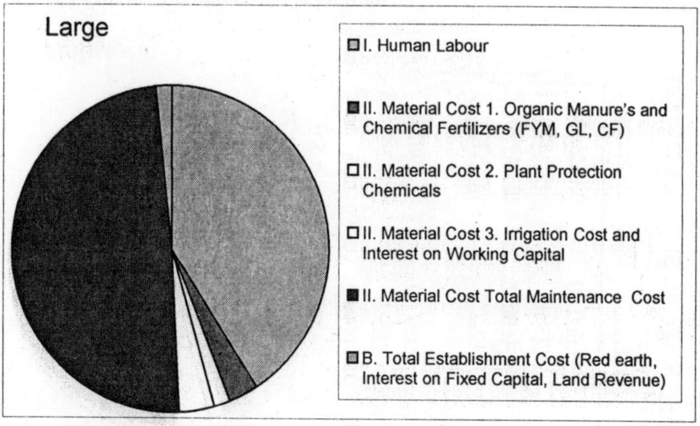
Large
I. Human Labour
II. Material Cost 1. Organic Manure's and Chemical Fertilizers (FYM, GL, CF)
II. Material Cost 2. Plant Protection Chemicals
II. Material Cost 3. Irrigation Cost and Interest on Working Capital
II. Material Cost Total Maintenance Cost
B. Total Establishment Cost (Red earth, Interest on Fixed Capital, Land Revenue)

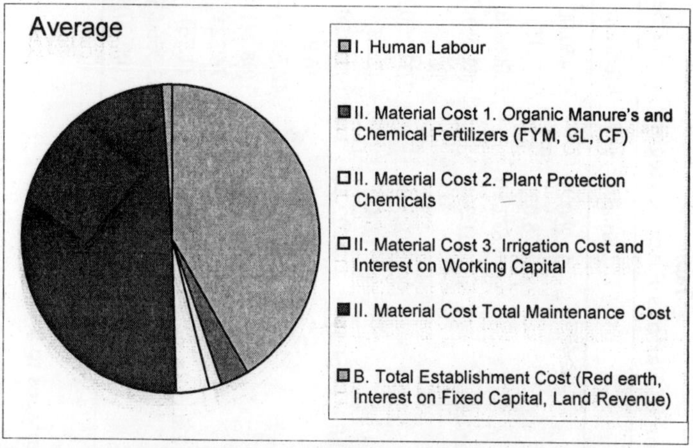
Average
I. Human Labour
II. Material Cost 1. Organic Manure's and Chemical Fertilizers (FYM, GL, CF)
II. Material Cost 2. Plant Protection Chemicals
II. Material Cost 3. Irrigation Cost and Interest on Working Capital
II. Material Cost Total Maintenance Cost
B. Total Establishment Cost (Red earth, Interest on Fixed Capital, Land Revenue)

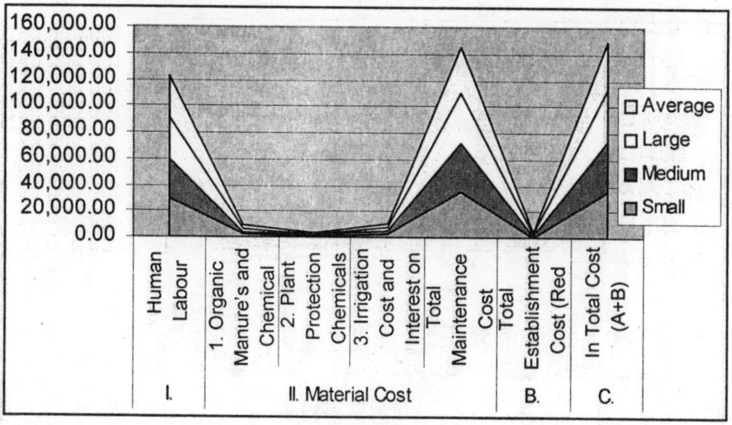
160,000.00
140,000.00
120,000.00
100,000.00
80,000.00
60,000.00
40,000.00
20,000.00
0.00
Average
Large
Medium
Small
Human Labour
1. Organic Manure's and Chemical
2. Plant Protection Chemicals
3. Irrigation Cost and Interest on
Total Maintenance Cost
Total Establishment Cost (Red
In Total Cost (A+B)
I.
II. Material Cost
B.
C.

Table 8

Average Per Hectare Cost of Cultivation of Various Farms Category in the Second Stage in Shimoga District

	Maintenance Cost	*Small*	*Medium*	*Large*	*Average*
A.					
I	Human Labour	32,250.00	33,450.00	33,660.00	33,120.00
		(78.03)	(77.15)	(75.8)	(76.82)
II	Material Cost	4,672.50	5,008.00	5,468.50	5,049.67
	1. Organic Manure's and Chemical Fertilizers (FYM, GL, CF)	(11.30)	(11.55)	(12.25)	(11.71)
	2. Plant Protection Chemicals	1,025.00	1,117.50	1,127.50	1,090.00
		(2.48)	(2.58)	(2.52)	(2.53)
	3. Irrigation Cost and Interest on Working Capital	2,722.34	3,015.34	3,121.62	2,953.10
		(6.59)	(6.96)	(6.99)	(6.85)
	Total Maintenance Cost	40,669.84	42,590.84	43,377.62	42,212.77
		(98.40)	(98.24)	(97.14)	(97.91)
B.	Total Establishment Cost	661.11	765.21	1,279.19	901.84
	(Red earth, Interest on Fixed Capital, Land Revenue)	(1.60)	(1.76)	(2.86)	(2.09)
C.	Total Cost (A+B)	41,330.95	43,356.05	44,656.81	43,114.61
		(100.00)	(100.00)	(100.00)	(100.00)

Source: Survey Data.

Note: Figures in parentheses are percentages to total cost.

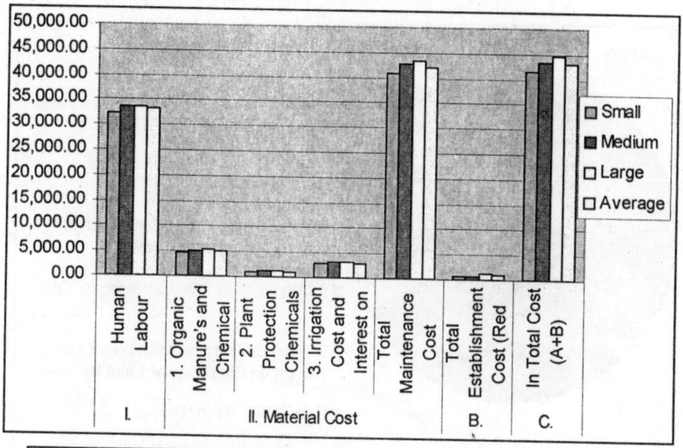
50,000.00
45,000.00
40,000.00
35,000.00
30,000.00
25,000.00
20,000.00
15,000.00
10,000.00
5,000.00
0.00
Small
Medium
Large
Average
Human Labour
1. Organic Manure's and Chemical
2. Plant Protection Chemicals
3. Irrigation Cost and Interest on
Total Maintenance Cost
Total Establishment Cost (Red
In Total Cost (A+B)
I.
II. Material Cost
B.
C.

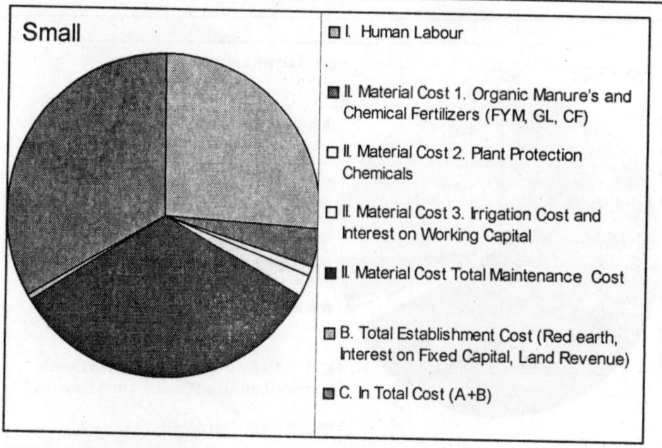
Small
I. Human Labour
II. Material Cost 1. Organic Manure's and Chemical Fertilizers (FYM, GL, CF)
II. Material Cost 2. Plant Protection Chemicals
II. Material Cost 3. Irrigation Cost and Interest on Working Capital
II. Material Cost Total Maintenance Cost
B. Total Establishment Cost (Red earth, Interest on Fixed Capital, Land Revenue)
C. In Total Cost (A+B)

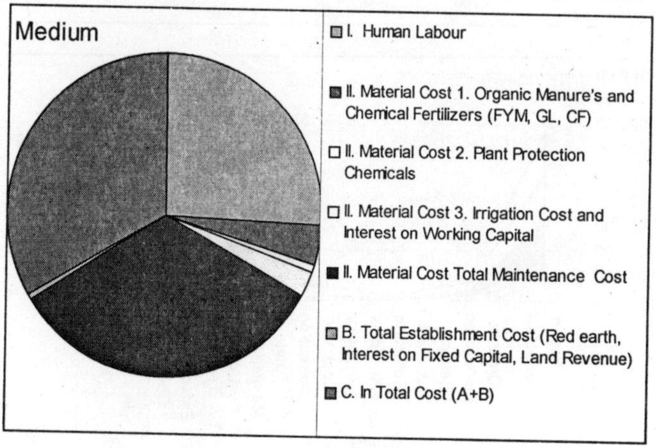
Medium
I. Human Labour
II. Material Cost 1. Organic Manure's and Chemical Fertilizers (FYM, GL, CF)
II. Material Cost 2. Plant Protection Chemicals
II. Material Cost 3. Irrigation Cost and Interest on Working Capital
II. Material Cost Total Maintenance Cost
B. Total Establishment Cost (Red earth, Interest on Fixed Capital, Land Revenue)
C. In Total Cost (A+B)

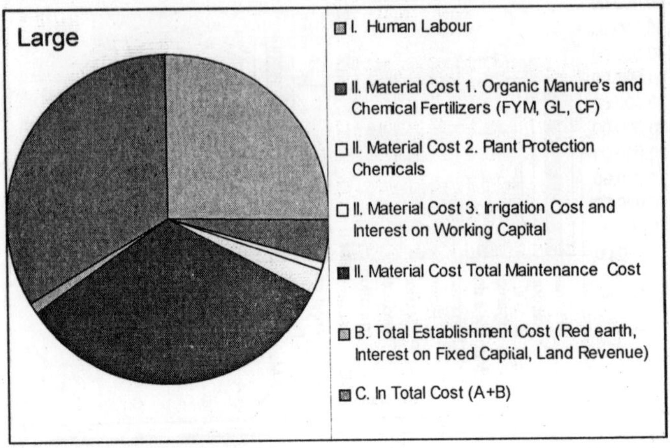
Large
I. Human Labour
II. Material Cost 1. Organic Manure's and Chemical Fertilizers (FYM, GL, CF)
II. Material Cost 2. Plant Protection Chemicals
II. Material Cost 3. Irrigation Cost and Interest on Working Capital
II. Material Cost Total Maintenance Cost
B. Total Establishment Cost (Red earth, Interest on Fixed Capital, Land Revenue)
C. In Total Cost (A+B)

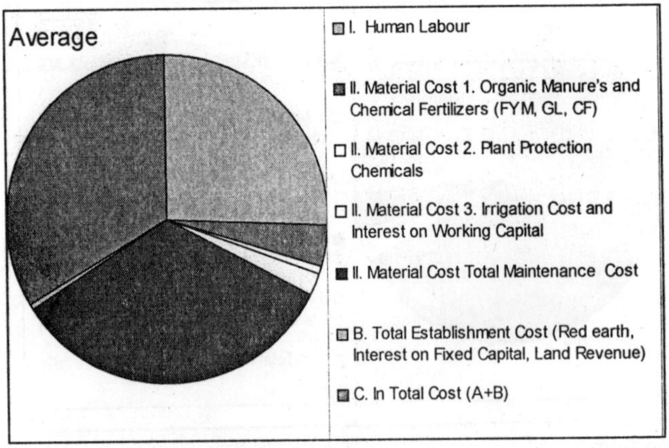
Average
I. Human Labour
II. Material Cost 1. Organic Manure's and Chemical Fertilizers (FYM, GL, CF)
II. Material Cost 2. Plant Protection Chemicals
II. Material Cost 3. Irrigation Cost and Interest on Working Capital
II. Material Cost Total Maintenance Cost
B. Total Establishment Cost (Red earth, Interest on Fixed Capital, Land Revenue)
C. In Total Cost (A+B)

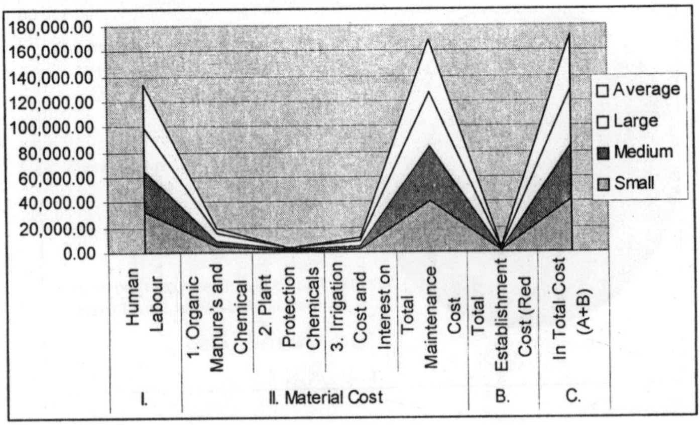
180,000.00
160,000.00
140,000.00
120,000.00
100,000.00
80,000.00
60,000.00
40,000.00
20,000.00
0.00
Average
Large
Medium
Small
Human Labour
1. Organic Manure's and Chemical
2. Plant Protection Chemicals
3. Irrigation Cost and Interest on
Total Maintenance Cost
Total Establishment Cost (Red
In Total Cost (A+B)
I.
II. Material Cost
B.
C.

Further comparison with the maintenance cost establishment cost is negligible among all the categories of farmers.

In the maintenance cost all the categories of farmers have made major investment on human labour followed by irrigation and interest on working capital, organic manure's and chemical fertilizers, ppc.

The expenditure made on total maintenance cost is high among large farmers as compared to other categories of farmers. As large farmers have made more investment on human labour, cost on irrigation, interest on working capital organic manure's and chemical fertilizers and plant protection chemicals.

The District

It is clear from the Table 8, for the entire study area within the maintenance cost among all the categories of farmers more expenditure is made on human labour, organic manures and chemical fertilizers, irrigation cost in combination with interest on working capital and plant protection chemicals in that order.

Cost of Cultivation in the Third Stage

As compared to the first and second stage, in the third stage the cost of cultivation shows totally a different picture. In this stage both the costs are found to be declining though the proportional share between the two remains same. It is because during this stage the yield from the plants start diminishing. Naturally farmers invest less on their areca gardens. In this context, let us see who will be investing how much in different farm categories in the study area. This is presented in the Table 9.

It is evident from the Table 9 that in the Third stage the average amount of investment per hectare in the study area is Rs. 32,476.37 more than three fourth of this constitutes maintenance cost and the establishment cost accounts for hardly 2.56 per cent of the total investment. Here also as seen in the first and second stages the amount of investment per hectare varies among different categories of farmers. For instance, in case of large farmers per hectare investment is slightly higher than overall average for the district whereas in case of small and medium farmers category the average investment per hectare is less than the overall average investment. It is further clear from the data that the proportion of maintenance cost is found slightly increasing as the size of holding decreases. In other words, in case of small farmers the proportion

Table 9
Average Per hectare Cost of Cultivation in the Third Stage Among Different Farm Categories

	Sagar Taluk				Shimoga Taluk				District			
	Small	*Medium*	*Large*	*Average*	*Small*	*Medium*	*Large*	*Average*	*Small*	*Medium*	*Large*	*Average*
Establishment Cost	602.07 (1.67)	659.42 (1.78)	1,125.98 (2.96)	795.82 (2.15)	665.14 (2.46)	728.00 (2.63)	1,201.39 (4.16)	864.84 (3.10)	633.61 (2.01)	693.71 (2.14)	1,163.69 (3.48)	830.34 (2.56)
Maintenance Cost	35,449.25 (98.33)	36,470.31 (98.22)	36,949.50 (97.04)	36,289.69 (97.85)	26,398.87 (97.54)	26,917.37 (97.37)	27,690.87 (95.84)	27,002.37 (96.90)	30,924.06 (97.99)	31,693.84 (97.86)	32,320.19 (96.52)	31,646.03 (97.44)
Total Cost	36,051.32 (100.00)	37,129.73 (100.00)	38,075.48 (100.00)	37,085.51 (100.00)	27,064.01 (100.00)	27,645.37 (100.00)	28,892.26 (100.00)	27,867.21 (100.00)	31,557.67 (100.00)	32,387.55 (100.00)	33,483.88 (100.00)	2,476.37 (100.00)

Source: Survey Data.
Note: Figures in parenthesis are percentages to total cost.

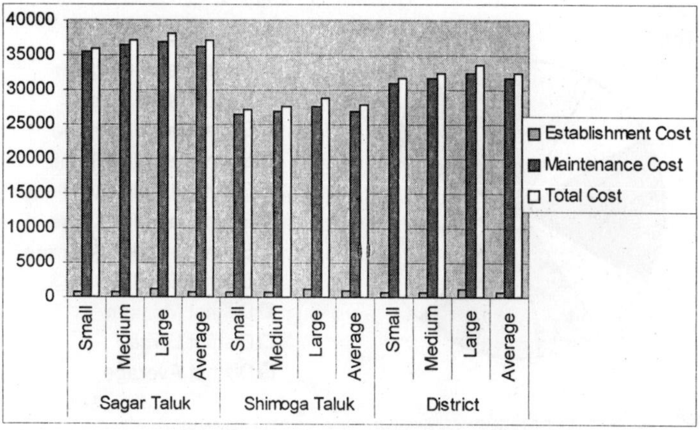
40000
35000
30000
25000
20000
15000
10000
5000
0
Establishment Cost
Maintenance Cost
Total Cost
Small
Medium
Large
Average
Sagar Taluk
Shimoga Taluk
District

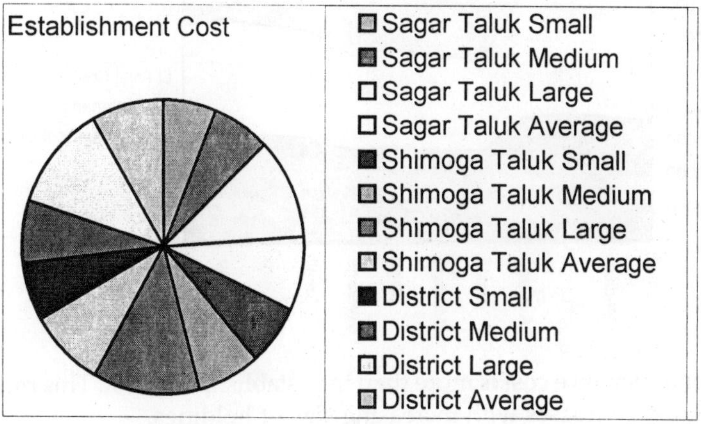
Establishment Cost
Sagar Taluk Small
Sagar Taluk Medium
Sagar Taluk Large
Sagar Taluk Average
Shimoga Taluk Small
Shimoga Taluk Medium
Shimoga Taluk Large
Shimoga Taluk Average
District Small
District Medium
District Large
District Average

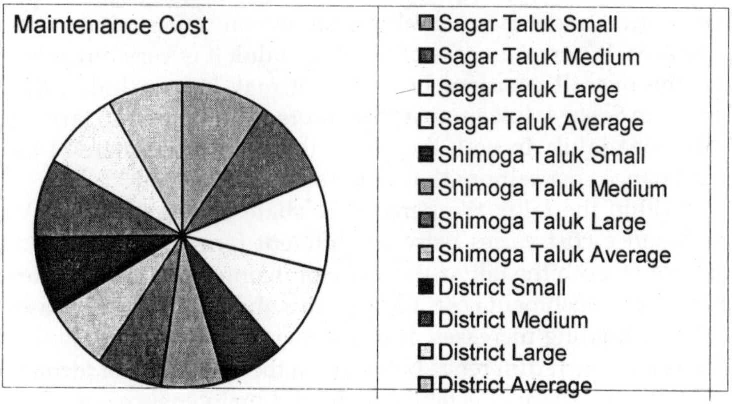
Maintenance Cost
Sagar Taluk Small
Sagar Taluk Medium
Sagar Taluk Large
Sagar Taluk Average
Shimoga Taluk Small
Shimoga Taluk Medium
Shimoga Taluk Large
Shimoga Taluk Average
District Small
District Medium
District Large
District Average

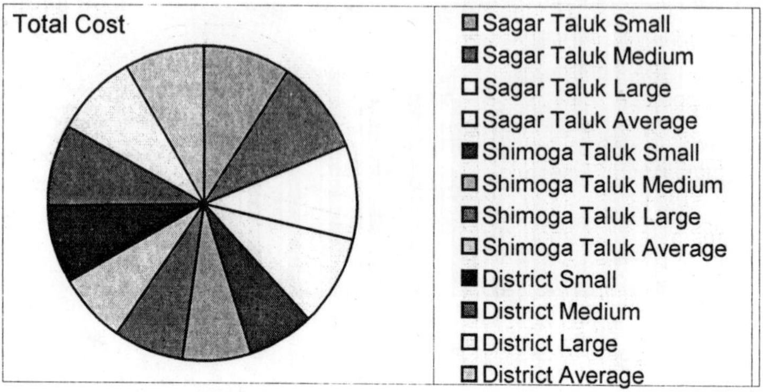

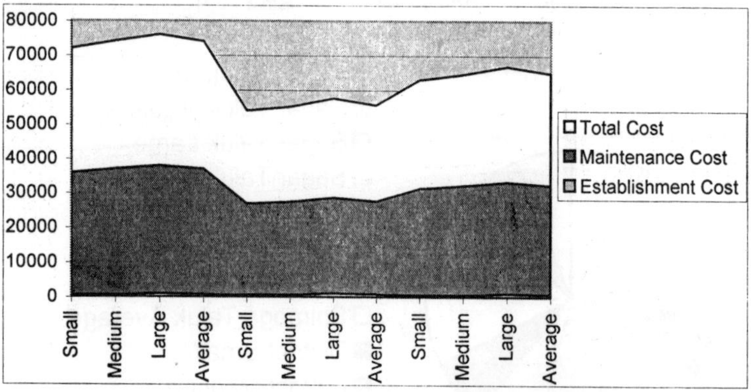

of maintenance cost is more than the establishment cost. This ratio slightly decreases with increasing size of holdings.

The taluk-wise comparison shows that in Sagar taluk the per hectare investment is much above the overall investment in the study area. Whereas in case of Shimoga taluk it is very much less than the overall position. From this it may be concluded that farmers in Sagar taluk are investing more as compared to farmers in Shimoga taluk. In both the taluks the percentage share of the maintenance cost is more than the establishment cost.

Within the taluk the percentage share of establishment Vs maintenance cost varies between different farm categories. For example, in both the taluks the share of maintenance cost is more than the establishment cost. Further, this share slightly decreases as size of holding increases. It is also evident from the data that there is not much difference between all the categories of farmers as regards the share of establishment and maintenance cost.

Table 10

Average Per Hectare Cost of Cultivation of Various Farms Category in the Third Stage in Sagar Taluk

A.	*Maintenance Cost*	*Small*	*Medium*	*Large*	*Average*
I	Human Labour	26.400.00	27.000.00	27,180.00	26,860.00
		(73.23)	(72.72)	(71.38)	(72.43)
II	Material Cost	5,869.00	6,157.00	6,360.00	6,128.67
	1. Organic Manure's and Chemical Fertilizers (FYM, GL, CF)	(16.28)	(16.58)	(16.70)	(16.52)
	2. Plant Protection Chemicals	795.00	808.00	816.00	806.33
		(2.20)	(2.18)	(2.15)	(2.17)
	3. Irrigation Cost and Interest on Working Capital	2,385.25	2,505.31	2,592.50	2,494.69
		(6.62)	(6.74)	(6.81)	(6.73)
	Total Maintenance Cost	35,449.25	36,470.31	36,949.50	36,289.69
		(98.33)	(98.22)	(97.04)	(97.85)
B.	Total Establishment Cost (Red earth,	602.07	659.42	1,125.98	795.82
	Interest on Fixed Capital, Land Revenue)	(1.67)	(1.78)	(2.96)	(2.15)
C.	Total Cost (A+B)	36,051.32	37.129.73	38,075.48	37,085.51
		(100.00)	(100.00)	(100.00)	(100.00)

Source: Survey Data.
Note : Figures in parentheses are percentages to total cost.

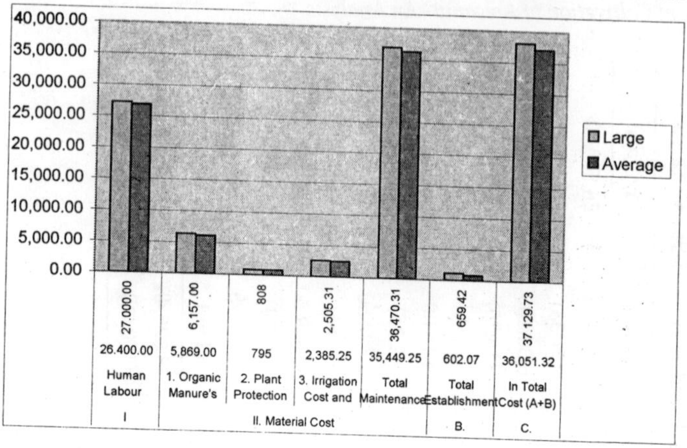
40,000.00
35,000.00
30,000.00
25,000.00
20,000.00
15,000.00
10,000.00
5,000.00
0.00
Large
Average
27,000.00
26,400.00
Human Labour
I
6,157.00
5,869.00
1. Organic Manure's
808
795
2. Plant Protection
2,505.31
2,385.25
3. Irrigation Cost and
36,470.31
35,449.25
Total Maintenance
II. Material Cost
659.42
602.07
Total Establishment
B.
37,129.73
36,051.32
In Total Cost (A+B)
C.

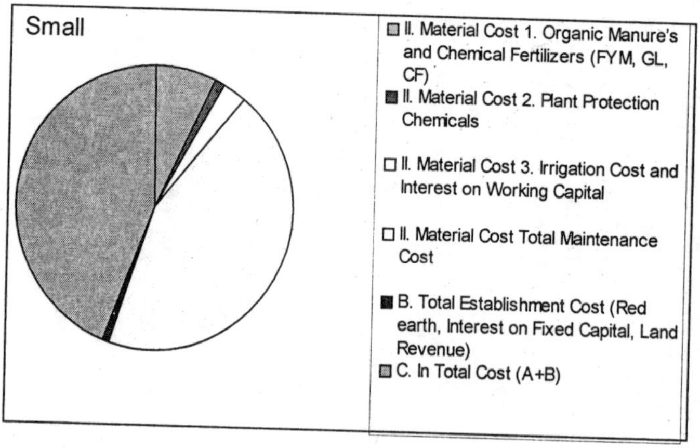
Small
II. Material Cost 1. Organic Manure's and Chemical Fertilizers (FYM, GL, CF)
II. Material Cost 2. Plant Protection Chemicals
II. Material Cost 3. Irrigation Cost and Interest on Working Capital
II. Material Cost Total Maintenance Cost
B. Total Establishment Cost (Red earth, Interest on Fixed Capital, Land Revenue)
C. In Total Cost (A+B)

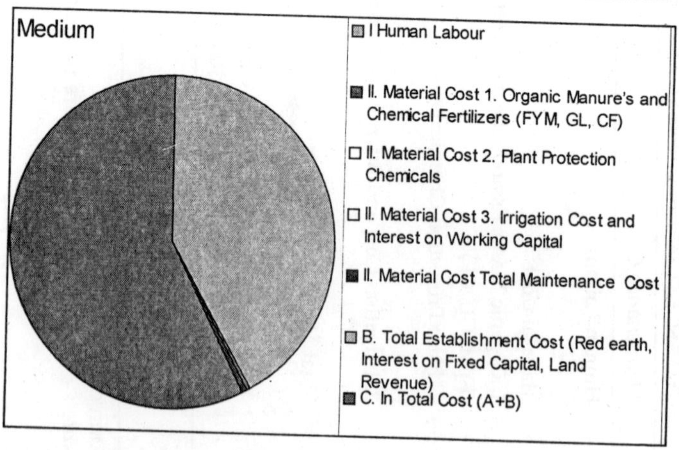
Medium
I Human Labour
II. Material Cost 1. Organic Manure's and Chemical Fertilizers (FYM, GL, CF)
II. Material Cost 2. Plant Protection Chemicals
II. Material Cost 3. Irrigation Cost and Interest on Working Capital
II. Material Cost Total Maintenance Cost
B. Total Establishment Cost (Red earth, Interest on Fixed Capital, Land Revenue)
C. In Total Cost (A+B)

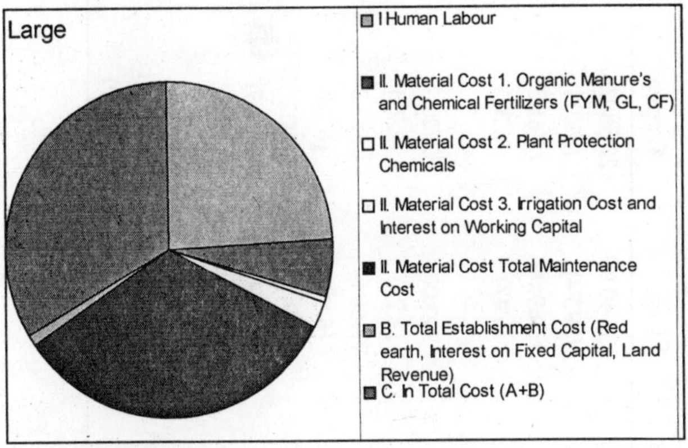
Large
I Human Labour
II. Material Cost 1. Organic Manure's and Chemical Fertilizers (FYM, GL, CF)
II. Material Cost 2. Plant Protection Chemicals
II. Material Cost 3. Irrigation Cost and Interest on Working Capital
II. Material Cost Total Maintenance Cost
B. Total Establishment Cost (Red earth, Interest on Fixed Capital, Land Revenue)
C. In Total Cost (A+B)

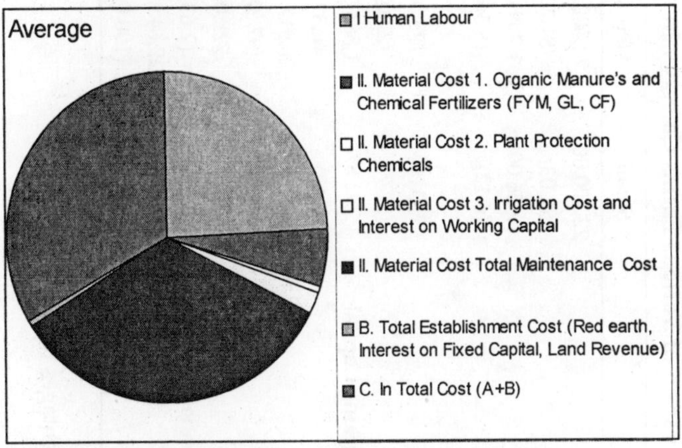
Average
I Human Labour
II. Material Cost 1. Organic Manure's and Chemical Fertilizers (FYM, GL, CF)
II. Material Cost 2. Plant Protection Chemicals
II. Material Cost 3. Irrigation Cost and Interest on Working Capital
II. Material Cost Total Maintenance Cost
B. Total Establishment Cost (Red earth, Interest on Fixed Capital, Land Revenue)
C. In Total Cost (A+B)

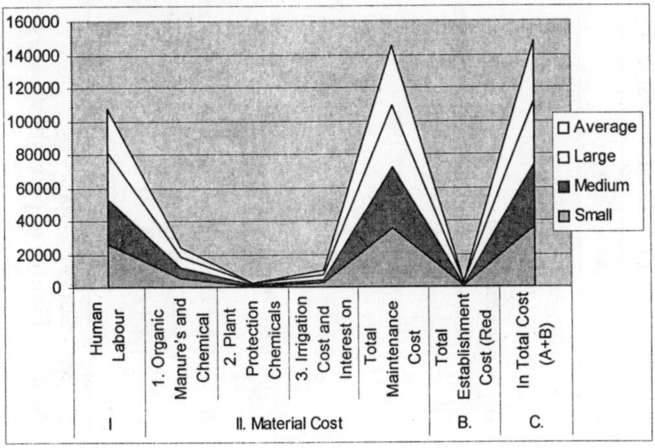
160000
140000
120000
100000
80000
60000
40000
20000
0
Average
Large
Medium
Small
Human Labour
1. Organic Manure's and Chemical
2. Plant Protection Chemicals
3. Irrigation Cost and Interest on
Total Maintenance Cost
Total Establishment Cost (Red
In Total Cost (A+B)
I
II. Material Cost
B.
C.

Table 11

Average Per Hectare Cost of Cultivation of Various Farms Category in the Third Stage in Shimoga Taluk

	Maintenance Cost	*Small*	*Medium*	*Large*	*Average*
A.					
I	Human Labour	22,200.00	22,500.00	23,040.00	22,580.00
		(82.03)	(81.39)	(79.74)	(81.03)
II	Material Cost	1,656.00	1,759.00	1,869.00	1,761.33
	1. Organic Manure's and Chemical	(6.12)	(6.36)	(6.47)	(6.32)
	Fertilizers (FYM, GL, CF)				
	2. Plant Protection Chemicals	750.00	775.00	793.00	772.67
		(2.77)	(2.80)	(2.74)	(2.77)
	3. Irrigation Cost and Interest on Working Capital	1,792.87	1,883.37	1,988.87	1,888.37
		(6.62)	(6.82)	(6.89)	(6.78)
	Total Maintenance Cost	26,398.87	26,917.37	27,690.87	27,002.37
		(97.54)	(97.37)	(95.84)	(96.90)
B.	Total Establishment Cost (Red earth,	665.14	728.00	1,201.39	864.84
	Interest on Fixed Capital, Land Revenue)	(2.46)	(2.63)	(4.16)	(3.10)
C.	Total Cost (A+B)	27,064.01	27,645.37	28,892.26	27,867.21
		(100.00)	(100.00)	(100.00)	(100.00)

Source: Survey Data.

Note : Figures in parentheses are percentages to total cost.

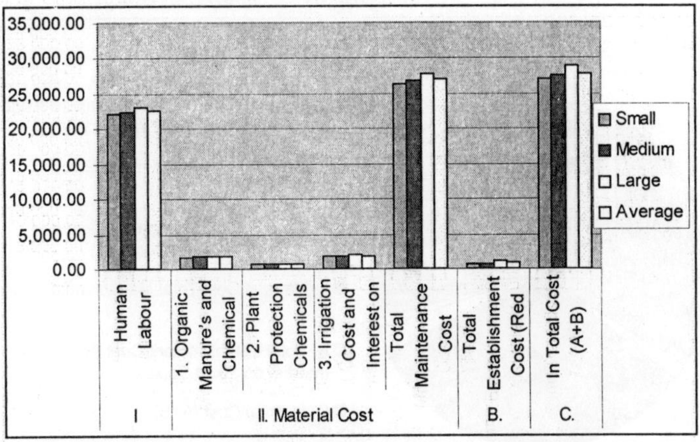
35,000.00
30,000.00
25,000.00
20,000.00
15,000.00
10,000.00
5,000.00
0.00
Small
Medium
Large
Average
Human Labour
1. Organic Manure's and Chemical
2. Plant Protection Chemicals
3. Irrigation Cost and Interest on
Total Maintenance Cost
Total Establishment Cost (Red
In Total Cost (A+B)
I
II. Material Cost
B.
C.

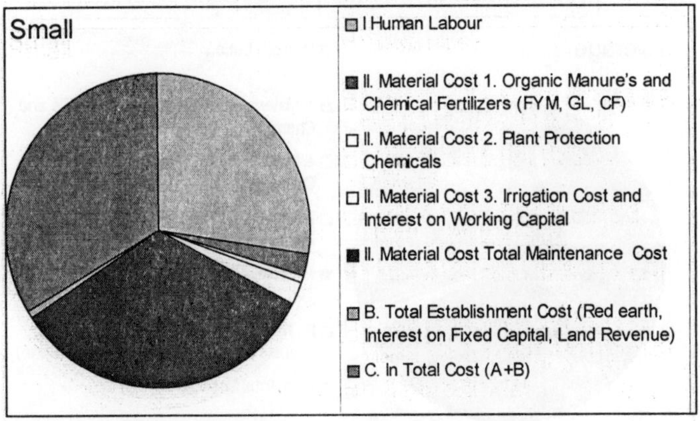
Small
I Human Labour
II. Material Cost 1. Organic Manure's and Chemical Fertilizers (FYM, GL, CF)
II. Material Cost 2. Plant Protection Chemicals
II. Material Cost 3. Irrigation Cost and Interest on Working Capital
II. Material Cost Total Maintenance Cost
B. Total Establishment Cost (Red earth, Interest on Fixed Capital, Land Revenue)
C. In Total Cost (A+B)

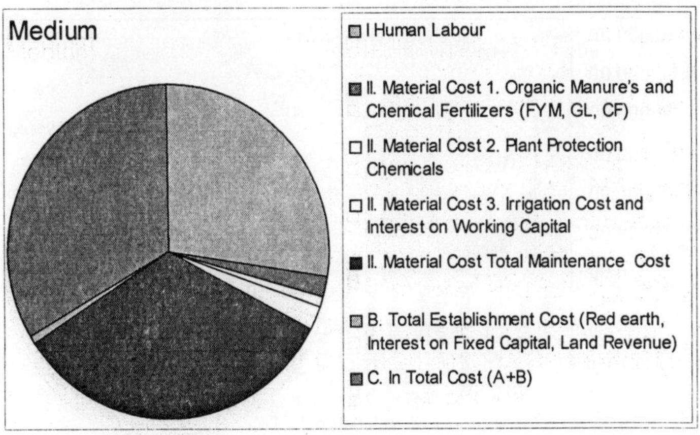
Medium
I Human Labour
II. Material Cost 1. Organic Manure's and Chemical Fertilizers (FYM, GL, CF)
II. Material Cost 2. Plant Protection Chemicals
II. Material Cost 3. Irrigation Cost and Interest on Working Capital
II. Material Cost Total Maintenance Cost
B. Total Establishment Cost (Red earth, Interest on Fixed Capital, Land Revenue)
C. In Total Cost (A+B)

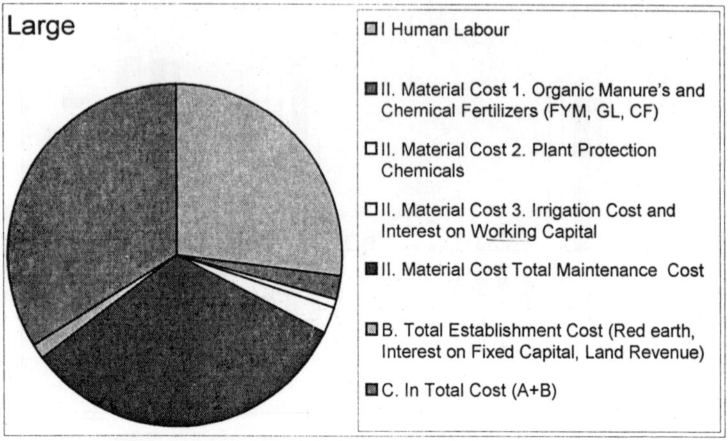
Large
I Human Labour
II. Material Cost 1. Organic Manure's and Chemical Fertilizers (FYM, GL, CF)
II. Material Cost 2. Plant Protection Chemicals
II. Material Cost 3. Irrigation Cost and Interest on Working Capital
II. Material Cost Total Maintenance Cost
B. Total Establishment Cost (Red earth, Interest on Fixed Capital, Land Revenue)
C. In Total Cost (A+B)

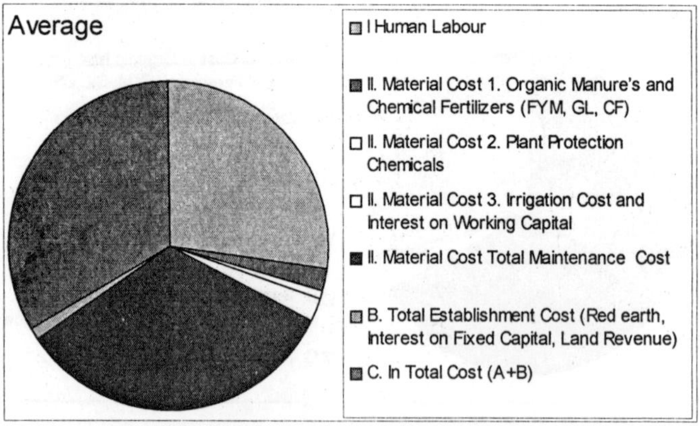
Average
I Human Labour
II. Material Cost 1. Organic Manure's and Chemical Fertilizers (FYM, GL, CF)
II. Material Cost 2. Plant Protection Chemicals
II. Material Cost 3. Irrigation Cost and Interest on Working Capital
II. Material Cost Total Maintenance Cost
B. Total Establishment Cost (Red earth, Interest on Fixed Capital, Land Revenue)
C. In Total Cost (A+B)

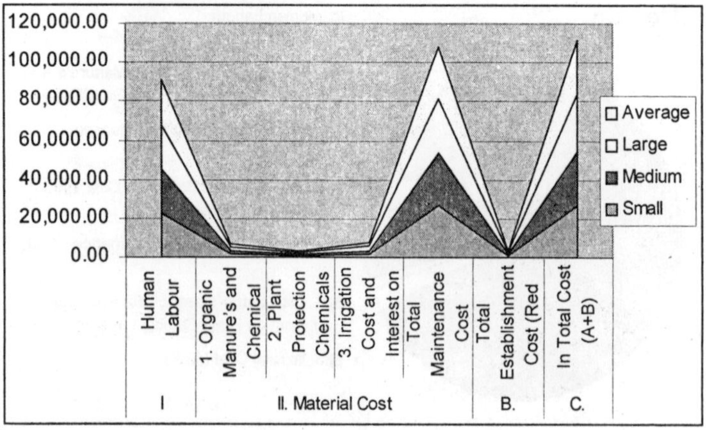
120,000.00
100,000.00
80,000.00
60,000.00
40,000.00
20,000.00
0.00
Average
Large
Medium
Small
Human Labour
1. Organic Manure's and Chemical
2. Plant Protection Chemicals
3. Irrigation Cost and Interest on
Total Maintenance Cost
Total Establishment Cost (Red
In Total Cost (A+B)
I
II. Material Cost
B.
C.

Table 12
Average Per Hectare Cost of Cultivation of Various Farms Category in the Third Stage in Shimoga District

A.	*Maintenance Cost*	*Small*	*Medium*	*Large*	*Average*
I	Human Labour	24,300.00	24,750.00	25,110.00	24,720.00
		(77.00)	(76.42)	(74.99)	(76.12)
II	Material Cost	3,762.50	3,958.00	4,114.50	3,945.00
	1. Organic Manure's and Chemical Fertilizers (FYM, GL, CF)	(11.92)	(12.22)	(12.29)	(12.15)
	2. Plant Protection Chemicals	772.50	791.50	804.50	789.50
		(2.45)	(2.44)	(2.40)	(2.42)
	3. Irrigation Cost and Interest on Working Capital	2,089.06	2,194.34	2,291.19	2,191.53
		(6.62)	(6.78)	(6.84)	(6.75)
	Total Maintenance Cost	20,924.06	31,693.84	32,320.19	31,646.03
		(97.99)	(97.86)	(96.52)	(97.44)
B.	Total Establishment Cost (Red earth,	633.61	693.71	1,163.69	830.34
	Interest on Fixed Capital, Land Revenue)	(2.01)	(2.14)	(3.48)	(2.56)
C.	Total Cost (A+B)	31,557.67	32,387.55	33,483.88	32,476.37
		(100.00)	(100.00)	(100.00)	(100.00)

Source: Survey Data.
Note: Figures in parentheses are percentages to total cost.

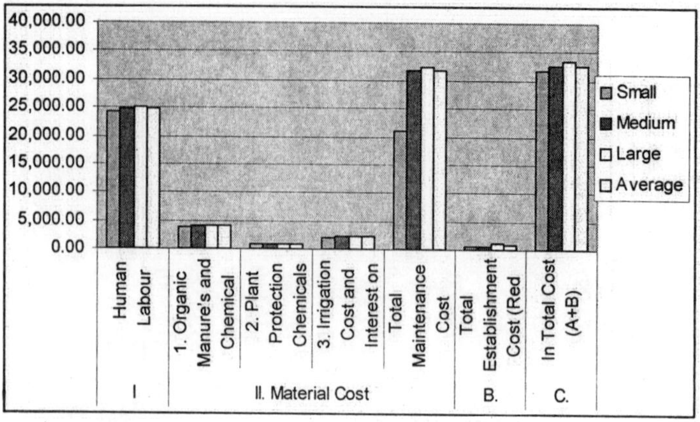
40,000.00
35,000.00
30,000.00
25,000.00
20,000.00
15,000.00
10,000.00
5,000.00
0.00
Small
Medium
Large
Average
Human Labour
1. Organic Manure's and Chemical
2. Plant Protection Chemicals
3. Irrigation Cost and Interest on
Total Maintenance Cost
Total Establishment Cost (Red
In Total Cost (A+B)
I
II. Material Cost
B.
C.

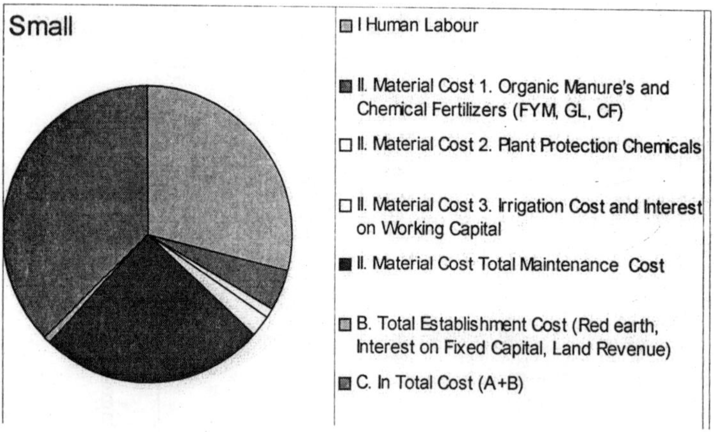
Small
I Human Labour
II. Material Cost 1. Organic Manure's and Chemical Fertilizers (FYM, GL, CF)
II. Material Cost 2. Plant Protection Chemicals
II. Material Cost 3. Irrigation Cost and Interest on Working Capital
II. Material Cost Total Maintenance Cost
B. Total Establishment Cost (Red earth, Interest on Fixed Capital, Land Revenue)
C. In Total Cost (A+B)

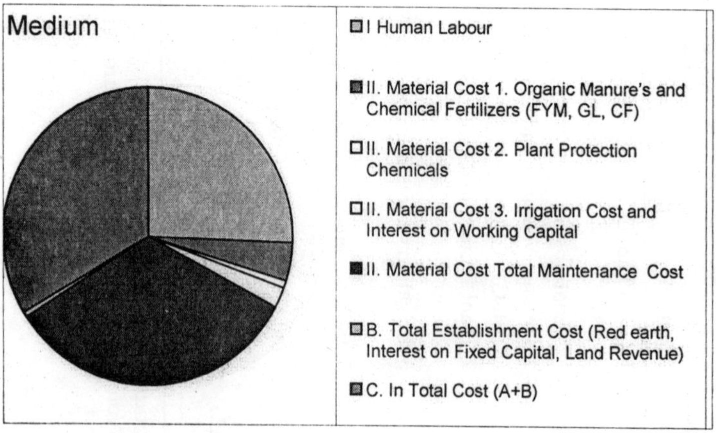
Medium
I Human Labour
II. Material Cost 1. Organic Manure's and Chemical Fertilizers (FYM, GL, CF)
II. Material Cost 2. Plant Protection Chemicals
II. Material Cost 3. Irrigation Cost and Interest on Working Capital
II. Material Cost Total Maintenance Cost
B. Total Establishment Cost (Red earth, Interest on Fixed Capital, Land Revenue)
C. In Total Cost (A+B)

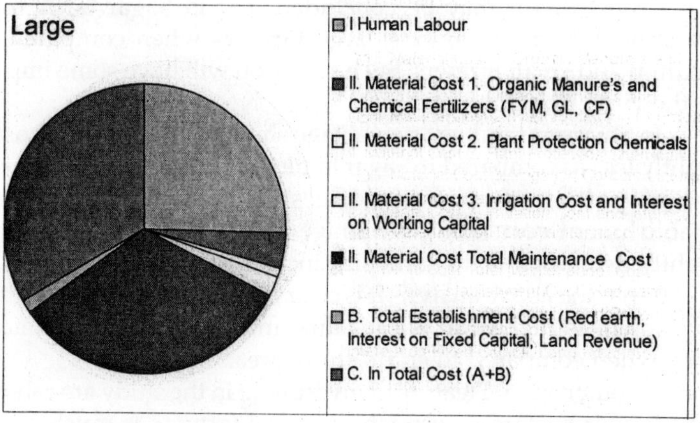
Large
I Human Labour
II. Material Cost 1. Organic Manure's and Chemical Fertilizers (FYM, GL, CF)
II. Material Cost 2. Plant Protection Chemicals
II. Material Cost 3. Irrigation Cost and Interest on Working Capital
II. Material Cost Total Maintenance Cost
B. Total Establishment Cost (Red earth, Interest on Fixed Capital, Land Revenue)
C. In Total Cost (A+B)

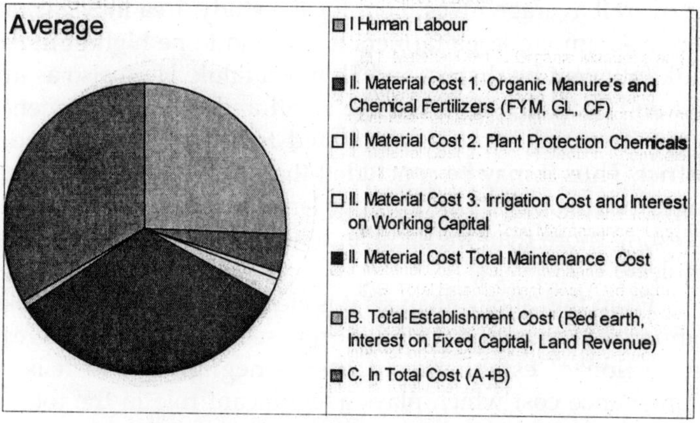
Average
I Human Labour
II. Material Cost 1. Organic Manure's and Chemical Fertilizers (FYM, GL, CF)
II. Material Cost 2. Plant Protection Chemicals
II. Material Cost 3. Irrigation Cost and Interest on Working Capital
II. Material Cost Total Maintenance Cost
B. Total Establishment Cost (Red earth, Interest on Fixed Capital, Land Revenue)
C. In Total Cost (A+B)

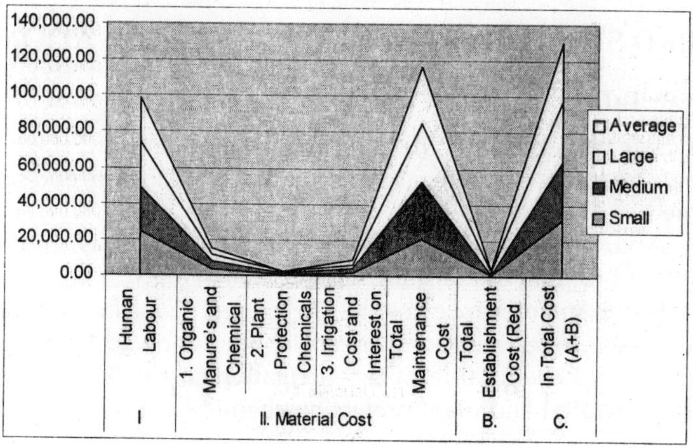
140,000.00
120,000.00
100,000.00
80,000.00
60,000.00
40,000.00
20,000.00
0.00
Average
Large
Medium
Small
Human Labour
1. Organic Manure's and Chemical
2. Plant Protection Chemicals
3. Irrigation Cost and Interest on
Total Maintenance Cost
Total Establishment Cost (Red
In Total Cost (A+B)
I
II. Material Cost
B.
C.

From this it may be concluded that in Sagar taluk total investment is more among large farmers when compared to medium and small farmers. Such variation will have some impact on the yield from the palm.

In Shimoga taluk the percentage share of maintenance cost is slightly less as compared to Sagar taluk in all categories of farmers. The proportion of maintenance cost is much higher than the establishment cost. The percentage share of maintenance cost slightly decreases as the farm size increases.

From the above analysis it is clear that the average per hectare investment is highest in Sagar taluk and much less in Shimoga taluk when compared to entire study area.

Another special feature of investment in the study area shows that the per hectare investment by large farmers is much above the overall average investment for the study area in Sagar taluk. Here also among large farmers it is found to be highest in Sagar taluk followed by district and Shimoga taluk. Here also as in the first and second stage even the small and medium farmers are found investing more as compared to Shimoga taluk and the district. Thus it may be concluded that as in the first and second stages the small; medium and large farmers in Sagar taluk are found investing more than the same in other taluk and the district as a whole.

From the above analysis it is clear that in both the taluks as compared to gestation period, during second and third stages the proportion of establishment cost is negligible and it is only maintenance cost which plays a significant role in the total cost because in the long run all costs become variable.

THIRD STAGE: AVERAGE COST OF CULTIVATION

Sagar Taluk

It is clear from the Table 10 that in Sagar taluk in third stage the large farmers are investing more as compared to medium and small farmers.

Apart from this the total maintenance cost is more as compared to total establishment cost.

In the maintenance cost all the categories of farmers have made more investment on human labour followed by organic manures and chemical fertilizers, irrigation cost with interest on working capital and plant protection chemicals.

In the establishment cost all the categories of farmers have made more investment on red earth, interest on fixed capital and land revenue which is comparatively negligible.

The expenditure made on total maintenance cost is high among large farmers as compared to other categories of farmers. Because large farmers have made more investment on human labour, organic manure's and chemical fertilizers, irrigation cost and interest on working capital and plant protection chemicals.

The total establishment cost is high among large farmers as compared to other categories of farmers because the large category of farmers have made more investment on red earth in combination with interest on fixed capital and land revenue.

Shimoga Taluk

It is clear from the respective Table from 11 that the large farmers have invested more as compared to medium and small farmers. Further comparison with the maintenance cost establishment cost is negligible among all the categories of farmers.

In the maintenance cost all the categories of farmers have made major investment on human labour followed by irrigation and interest on working capital, organic manure's and chemical fertilizers, ppc.

The expenditure made on total maintenance cost is high among large farmers as compared to other categories of farmers. As large farmers have made more investment on human labour, cost on irrigation, interest on working capital organic manure's and chemical fertilizers and plant protection chemicals.

The District

It is clear from the Table 12, for the entire study area within the maintenance cost among all the categories of farmers more expenditure is made on human labour, organic manures and chemical fertilizers, irrigation cost in combination with interest on working capital and plant protection chemicals in that order.

The overall investment in both taluks and entire district declined considerably from second to third stage among all the categories of farmers.

Cost of Cultivation of Intercrop

Farmers in the study area are found growing inter-crop in the gestation period. It is because in the gestation period the areca nut plants are in the growing stage and they will not yield any income till they attain the age of 5-6 years. During this period the farmers have to simply go on investing on the garden. Therefore, to supplement their investment most of the farmers grow inter-crop. Such inter-crop not only bring some income to farmers but also act as shade to the areca plants.

Therefore, it is necessary to see how much money they invest on such inter-crops and what is the return from such crops. Such an analysis will enable us to know how far the inter-crop will help farmers economically. This is presented in the Table 13.

It is clear from the Table 13 that the average amount of investment on inter-crop per hectare in the study area is Rs. 44,760.83. The amount of investment per hectare varies among different categories of farmers. For instance, in case of large farmers the per hectare investment is more than the overall average for the district.

The taluk-wise comparison shows that in Sagar taluk the per hectare investment is much above the overall investment in the study area whereas in case of Shimoga taluk it is very much below the overall position. From this it may be concluded that farmers in Sagar taluk are investing more as compared to Shimoga taluk.

From the above analysis it is clear that the average per hectare investment is highest in Sagar taluk and much less in Shimoga taluk when compared to entire study area.

Another special feature of investment in the study area is that, the per one hectare investment by large farmers is much above the overall average investment for the study area in both the taluks. Among large farmers it is found to be highest in Sagar taluk followed by district and Shimoga taluk. Even the small and medium farmers in Sagar taluk are found investing more as compared to Shimoga taluk and the district. Thus it may be concluded that investment by small medium and large farmers in Sagar taluk is much more than the same in other taluk and the district as a whole.

In Sagar taluk the investment per hectare made by small farmers is almost equal to the investment made by large farmers in Shimoga taluk. It clearly shows the average investment by all categories of farmers in Sagar taluk is much more than in Shimoga taluk.

It is also evident from the data that small farmers in Shimoga taluk are found investing least on intercrop as compared to others,

Table 13
Average Per hectare Cost of Cultivation of Intercrop in the First Stage Among Various Farmer's Category

	Sagar Taluk				*Shimoga Taluk*				*District*			
	Small	*Medium*	*Large*	*Average*	*Small*	*Medium*	*Large*	*Average*	*Small*	*Medium*	*Large*	*Average*
Cost of Cultivation of Inter crop	44,975	47,545	51,400	47,973.33	38,550	41,120	44,975	41,548.33	41,762.50	44,332.50	48,187.50	44,760.83

Source: Survey Data.

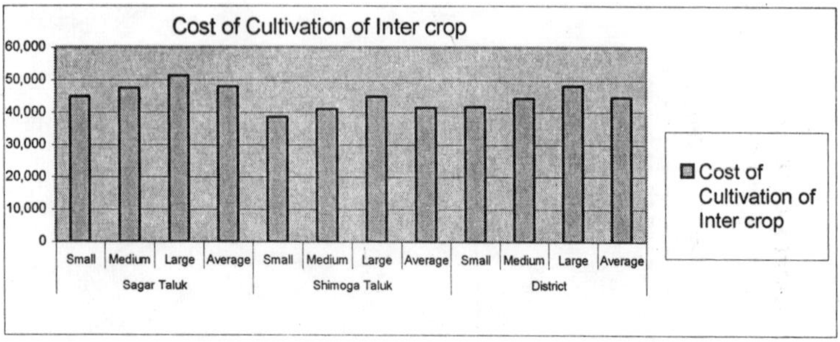

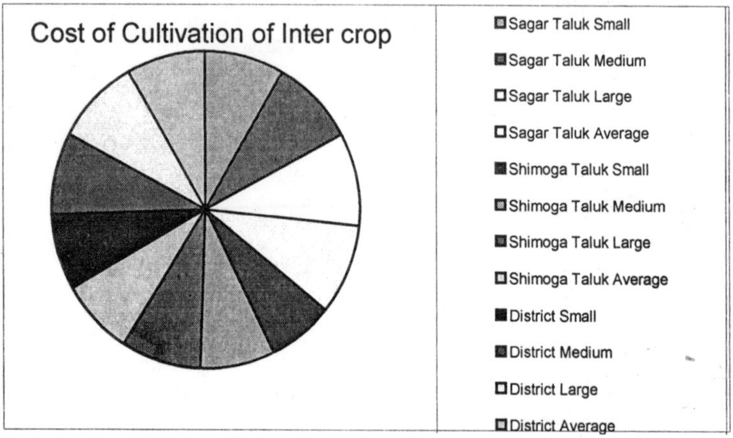

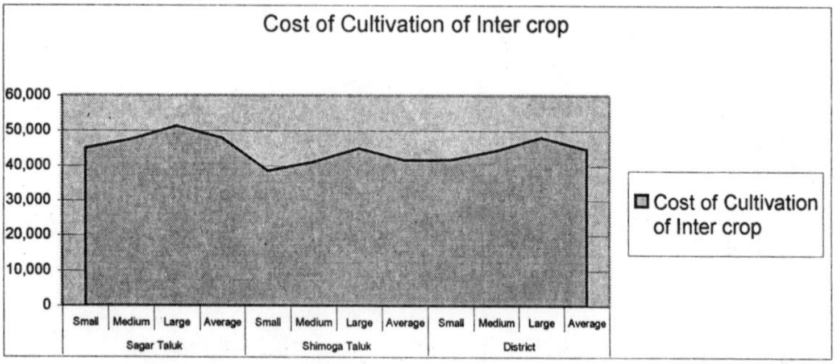

and further cost of cultivation of intercrop showed increasing trend with the increase in the size of holding.

Cost of Cultivation of Mixed Crop

Mixed crop is grown in the second stage in the study area. This crop is grown under the shade of arecanut palm. For this farmers spend some extra amount but it will also bring additional income to farmers. Thus it is necessary to examine the cost on these crops and also the yield from this crop so as to see the benefit of cultivating arecanut by farmers. The cost of cultivation of mixed crop in the study area is presented in the Table 14.

It is clear from the Table 14 that the average amount of investment per hectare in the study area is Rs. 31,405.83. The amount of investment per hectare varies among different categories of farmers. For instance, in case of large farmers the per hectare investment is more than the overall average for the District. It is clear from the above analysis that the investment increases as the size of holding increases.

The taluk-wise comparison shows that in Sagar taluk the per hectare investment is much above the overall investment in the study area whereas in case of Shimoga taluk it is very much below the overall position. From this it may be concluded that farmers in Sagar taluk are investing more as compared to Shimoga taluk.

From the above analysis it is clear that the average per hectare investment is highest in Sagar taluk and much less in Shimoga taluk when compared to entire study area. A special feature of investment in the study area is that the per hectare investment by large farmers is much less in Shimoga taluk when compared to entire study area. Another special feature of investment in the study area is that the per hectare investment by large farmers is much above the overall average investment for the entire study area in both the taluks. Among large farmers it is found to be highest in Sagar taluk followed by the district. The medium farmers are found investing more as compared to small category of farmers in Shimoga taluk and the district. Thus it may be concluded that investment by small, medium and large farmers in Sagar taluk is much more than the same in other taluk and the district as a whole.

In Sagar taluk the per hectare investment made by small farmers is almost equal to the investment made by medium farmers in Shimoga taluk. It clearly shows the average investment by all categories of farmers in Sagar taluk is much more than Shimoga taluk.

It is also clear from the data that small farmers in Shimoga taluk are found investing least on mixed crop as compared to others.

Table 14
Average Per hectare Cost of Cultivation of Mixed Crop in the Second Stage Among Various Farmer's Category

	Sagar Taluk				*Shimoga Taluk*				*District*			
	Small	*Medium*	*Large*	*Average*	*Small*	*Medium*	*Large*	*Average*	*Small*	*Medium*	*Large*	*Average*
Cost of Cultivation of Mixed Crop	28,400	33,935	39,960	34,098 .33	20,720	28,400	37,020	28,713.33	24,560	31,167.50	38,490	31,405.83

Source: Survey Data.

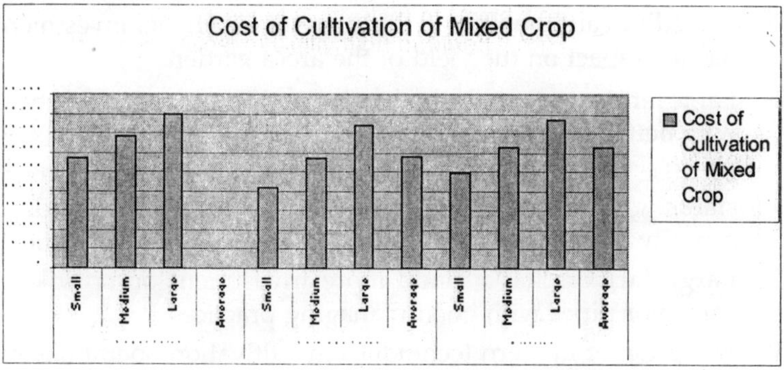

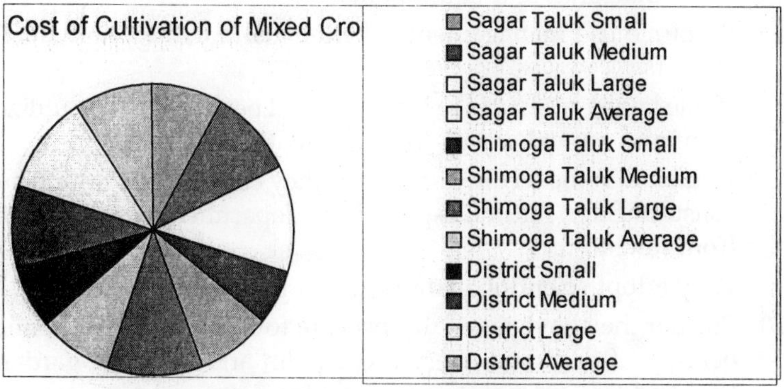

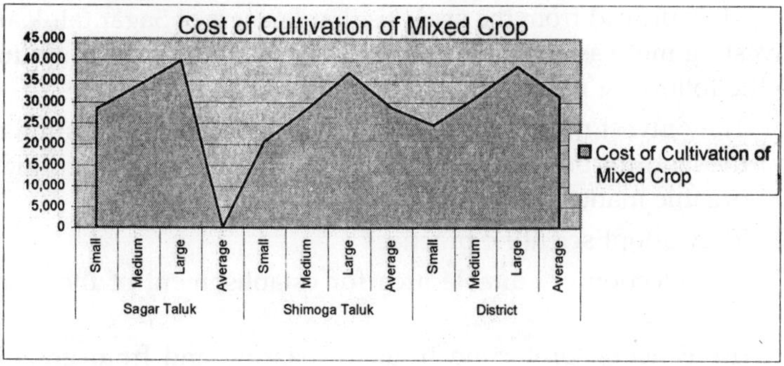

In all the three stages large farmers in the study area of both the taluks are investing more as compared to medium and small category of farmers due to the following reasons:

1. Cost of cultivation depends upon the method of cultivation. Cost of cultivation is high among large farmers as compared

to medium and small in all the three stages. Higher investment has its impact on the yield of the areca garden.

2. Large farmers adopt planned and scientific cultivation practices with better management
3. Because of higher socio-economic status, higher educational status. good mass media participation, better withstanding capacity in adverse conditions and in times of price fluctuations
4. Large farmers have made more investment on sprinkler, conveyor pipes with good managing practices
5. Adoption of modern techniques in cultivation operations by using machines and equipments
6. Resource use management is better than medium and small farmers.
7. While taking measures to increase yield per hectare they utilize plant and animal wastes very efficiently
8. To maintain the fertility of the soil they conduct soil testing by consulting agricultural experts from department of agriculture from time to time.
9. They adopt scientific manuring and irrigation practices
10. Further they have taken utmost care to increase the economic bearing of each and every areca palm and keep the garden cool and tidy by maintaining soppina betta and gomala

It is proved from the analysis that farmers of Sagar taluk are investing more as compared to the farmers of Shimoga taluk due to the following reasons

1. They invest more on irrigation infrastructure, preparation of the land for the establishment of the areca garden, seedlings, organic manuring and labour cost
2. They adopt scientific practices
   - (i) selection of suitable area for establishment of the areca garden
   - (ii) Fencing, protection from trespassing and from grazing animals
   - (iii) Selection of better quality seedlings and rising up of the nursery
   - (iv) Preparation of pits as required
   - (v) Having trenches, drainages in and around the garden for the free flow of excess sepage and rain water.

(vi) Planned and scientific water management infrastructure

(vii) De-weeding, periodical manuring, mulching and giving red earth etc.

(viii) Slurry will be used as a liquid manure to the areca garden through sprinklers.

(ix) Plant and animal wastes will be used in the form of manure

(x) Proper economic usage of land area by adopting inter cropping and mixed cropping for economic feasibility.

(xi) They will take preventive measure against pests and diseases with proper supervision and care.

(xii) For the periodical manuring of the garden farmers of Sagar taluk maintain soppina betta and gomala for the benefit of green leaves and farm yard manure.

3. Involvement of labourers is high because of the following manual works:

(i) land levelling, fencing.

(ii) Trench work, drainage for the free flow of excess sepage and rain water.

(iii) To maintain the seedlings nursery.

(iv) Planting the saplings.

(v) Irrigation of the garden, application of manures, fertilizers, plant protection chemicals likewise cultivation activities and supervision etc.

4. Areca cultivation is the way of life for farmers of Sagar taluk because they are cultivating areca since a long time. There is no alternative crop to grow apart from areca except inter and mixed crop due to geographical and climatic condition. They are taking proper care regarding the crop.

5. Areca grown in Sagar taluk fetches fairly good and remunerative price in the market due to its good quality and consistency.

Here is an attempt is made to bring out the salient features for the low investment made by farmers of Shimoga taluk as compared to the farmers of Sagar taluk.

1. Farmers of Shimoga taluk basically are not traditional growers they have not adopted systematic and planned cultivation practices.

(i) In the selection of site for the areca garden paddy and sugarcane fields will be presently converted into areca garden in the recent decades.

(ii) There is no proper fencing around the garden for protection from trespassing and cattle grazing

(iii) Selection of nut variety and in raising of the nursery

As arecanut is exclusively seed propogated crop. Being a perennial it is essential that adequate care is bestowed in the selection of proper planting material. There are four important stage to be observed in selection and raising of arecanut seedlings, which includes

(a) selection of mother palm

(b) selection of seed nuts

(c) selection of proper technique in germinating and raising seedlings

(d) selection of seedlings

The above procedure is not followed systematically

(iv) Digging of pits depends upon,

(a) loose soil with lower water table

(b) Heavy soil with higher water table

(c) specification for the size of the pit *l* x b x ht is not followed properly

(v) Drainages and trenches.

The successful establishment of the seedlings and the performance of young palms depend on two important factors viz, perfect drainage and protection from sunscorch. In order to ensure the adequate drainage it is essential that one drainage channel is dug for every two rows of palms. The channel should be at least 15-30 cm deeper than the depth at which the seedling were planted. At the beginning of monsoon each year these drains are to be clean to have an easy flow to stagnant water. Even the planted pit are to be provided with outlets and emptied to the drains.

The above specification is not followed properly

(vi) Periodical deweeding mulching, proper manuring and giving red earth is not at all done properly.

(vii) Plant, animal and bio-degradable wastes are not properly used.

(viii) There is no planned usage of land for inter cultivation practices.

(ix) Though organic manuring is thought provoking. Soppinabetta and gomala is not in vogue and there is no land in Shimoga taluk for soppinabetta.

(x) Preventive measure have not been followed against the pests and diseases.

2. As owners of the land are absentee land lords, the supervision and other agricultural activities will be done by their managers or by local farmers etc.
3. Subdivision and fragmentation of the areca land is more. Hence they cannot implement the intensive and scientific methods of cultivation practices
4. Crop is not that much suitable to local soil and climatic condition

Because of fluctuation in areca prices they do not give sole attention towards the establishment and maintenance cost as they are having main income from other sources. Because as they are professionals like doctors, engineers, contractors, merchants, lecturers and retired officials, hence the main income is from their profession and areca cultivation is secondary to them.

STATISTICAL ANALYSIS

Correlation Co-efficient

In the present study correlation co-efficient is carried out to check for multicolliniarity among the independent variables.

(i) Whether there is any correlation between the variables.

(ii) Whether the correlation is positive or negative.

Correlation Co-efficient of Maintenance Cost Among Various Farmers' Category in Sagar Taluk

The data presented in the Tables 15, 16 and 17 reveals that all the variable in the equation are highly positively correlated with the total maintenance cost. This indicates that, all the variables influences the total maintenance cost.

Table 15

Correlation Co-efficient of Dependent Variables (maintenance cost) Among Small Farmers in Sagar Taluk

Sl.No.		*MC*	*BP*	*CF*	*FYM*	*GL*	*HL*	*IC*	*IWC*	*HM*	*PPC*
1.	MC	1.00									
2.	BP	0.99**	1.00								
3.	CF	0.99**	0.99**	1.00							
4.	FYM	0.57**	0.52**	0.49**	1.00						
5.	GL	0.99**	0.99**	0.99**	0.48**	1.00					
6.	HL	0.99**	0.99**	0.99**	0.52**	0.99**	1.00				
7.	IC	0.99**	0.99**	0.97**	0.99**	0.98**	0.99**	1.00			
8.	IWC	0.99**	0.99**	0.99**	0.99**	0.99**	0.98**	0.98**	1.00		
9.	HM	0.98**	0.96**	0.98**	0.52**	0.98**	0.98**	0.98**	0.97**	1.00	
10.	PPC	0.57**	0.62**	0.65**	0.33**	0.66**	0.62**	0.97**	0.99**	0.60**	1.00

Source: Tables 5.1, 5.2, 5.5, 5.6, 5.9 & 5.10.

** indicate significant at 1%.

Table 16

Correlation Co-efficient of Dependent Variables (maintenance cost) Among Medium Farmers in Sagar Taluk

Sl.No.		MC	BP	CF	FYM	GL	HL	IC	IWC	HM	PPC
1.	MC	1.00									
2.	BP	0.99**	1.00								
3.	CF	0.99**	0.99**	1.00							
4.	FYM	0.95**	0.95**	0.96**	1.00						
5.	GL	0.83**	0.85**	0.85**	0.81**	1.00					
6.	HL	0.99**	0.99**	1.00**	0.96**	0.86**	1.00				
7.	IC	0.99**	0.99**	0.97**	0.99**	0.97**	0.99**	1.00			
8.	IWC	0.84**	0.81**	0.82**	0.77**	0.44**	0.80**	0.99**	1.00		
9.	HM	0.98**	0.89**	0.99**	0.96**	0.88**	0.99**	0.99**	0.77**	1.00	
10.	PPC	0.84**	0.80**	0.81**	0.76**	0.43**	0.79**	0.99**	1.00**	0.76**	1.00

Source: Tables 5.1, 5.2, 5.5, 5.6, 5.9 & 5.10.

** indicate significant at 1%.

Table 17
Correlation Co-efficient of Dependent Variables (maintenance cost) Among Large Farmers in Sagar Taluk

Sl.No.		MC	BP	CF	FYM	GL	HL	IC	IWC	HM	PPC
1.	MC	1.00									
2.	BP	0.99**	1.00								
3.	CF	0.99**	0.99**	1.00							
4.	FYM	0.99**	0.99**	0.99**	1.00						
5.	GL	0.99**	0.99**	0.99**	0.99**	1.00					
6.	HL	0.99**	0.99**	0.99**	0.99**	0.99**	1.00				
7.	IC	0.99**	0.99**	0.99**	0.99**	0.99**	0.99**	1.00			
8.	IWC	0.60**	0.63**	0.63**	0.58**	0.60**	0.61**	0.99**	1.00		
9.	HM	0.99**	0.99**	0.99**	0.99**	0.99**	0.99**	1.00**	0.55**	1.00	
10.	PPC	1.00**	0.99**	0.99**	0.99**	0.99**	0.99**	0.80**	0.61**	0.99**	1.00

Source: Tables 5.1, 5.2, 5.5, 5.6, 5.9 & 5.10.

** indicate significant at 1%.

Within the total maintenance cost all the variable are positively correlated with each other at 1% level of significance.

All categories of farmers in Sagar taluk have made more investment on total maintenance cost. In the total maintenance cost the dominant variables are human labour, farm yard manure, green leaves, chemical fertilizer, cost on irrigation, interest on working capital, bullock power, hired machines and plant protection chemicals.

The large farmers in Sagar taluk have made more investment on farm yard manure, green leaves, chemical fertilizer as compared to medium and small farmers in the study area.

Application of farm yard manure, green leaves, chemical fertilizers, plant protection chemicals requires more labour. As a result of this human labour is highly dominant in the maintenance cost, among all the categories of farmers.

Correlation Co-efficient of Maintenance Cost among Various Farmers' Category in Shimoga Taluk

The data presented in Tables 18, 19 and 20 shows that the total maintenance cost is the total maintenance cost is positively correlated with all the variables in the equation at 1% level of significance.

Within the maintenance cost all the variables are positively correlated with each other at 1% level of significance.

Among all the categories of farmers there is little variation in the application of chemical fertilizers, farmyard manure and green leaves. Because farmers of Shimoga taluk have used more chemical fertilizers and farm yard manures as compared to Green leaves due to non-availability of green leaves in Shimoga taluk.

In Shimoga taluk in the maintenance cost the dominant variables are human labour, irrigation cost, organic manures chemical fertilizer, bullock power, machines hired, Plant protection chemicals respectively.

In Shimoga taluk also human labour is the dominant variable in the maintenance cost.

In organic manuring the non-availability of green leaves is one of the major problem faced by sample farmers of Shimoga taluk. They depend more on farm yard manures and chemical fertilizer, Because Shimoga taluk is a semi-malnad region. The non-availability of green leaves has its effect on yield. It is because of

Table 18

Correlation Co-efficient of Dependent Variables (maintenance cost) Among Small Farmers in Shimoga Taluk

Sl.No.		*MC*	*BP*	*CF*	*FYM*	*GL*	*HL*	*IC*	*IWC*	*HM*	*PPC*
1.	MC	1.00									
2.	BP	0.99**	1.00								
3.	CF	0.99**	0.99**	1.00							
4.	FYM	0.99**	0.99**	0.99**	1.00						
5.	GL	0.99**	0.99**	0.99**	0.99**	1.00					
6.	HL	0.99**	0.99**	0.99**	0.99**	0.99**	1.00				
7.	IC	0.99**	0.99**	0.99**	0.99**	0.99**	0.99**	1.00			
8.	IWC	0.99**	0.99**	0.99**	0.99**	0.99**	0.99**	0.99**	1.00		
9.	HM	0.98**	0.98**	0.99**	0.98**	0.99**	0.99**	0.99**	0.98**	1.00	
10.	PPC	0.99**	0.99**	0.99**	0.99**	0.99**	0.99**	0.99**	0.99**	0.99**	1.00

Source: Tables 5.1, 5.3, 5.5, 5.7, 5.9, 5.11.

** indicate significant at 1%.

Table 19

Correlation Co-efficient of Dependent Variables (maintenance cost) Among Medium Farmers in Shimoga Taluk

Sl.No.		*MC*	*BP*	*CF*	*FYM*	*GL*	*HL*	*IC*	*IWC*	*HM*	*PPC*
1.	MC	1.00									
2.	BP	0.96**	1.00								
3.	CF	0.99**	0.96**	1.00							
4.	FYM	0.99**	0.96**	0.99**	1.00						
5.	GL	0.76**	0.51**	0.51**	0.51**	1.00					
6.	HL	0.99**	0.98**	0.99**	0.98**	1.00**	1.00				
7.	IC	0.95**	0.90**	0.99**	0.99**	0.46**	0.99**	1.00			
8.	IWC	0.99**	0.99**	0.99**	0.99**	0.99**	0.99**	0.99**	1.00		
9.	HM	0.99**	0.96**	0.99**	0.99**	0.99**	0.98**	0.30**	0.99**	1.00	
10.	PPC	0.75**	0.61**	0.75**	0.77**	0.03**	0.79**	0.54*	0.80**	0.75**	1.00

Source: Tables 5.1, 5.3, 5.5,5.7,5.9, 5.11.
** indicate significant at 1%.

Table 20
Correlation Co-efficient of Dependent Variables (maintenance cost) Among Large Farmers in Shimoga Taluk

Sl.No.		*MC*	*BP*	*CF*	*FYM*	*GL*	*HL*	*IC*	*IWC*	*HM*	*PPC*
1.	MC	1.00									
2.	BP	0.74**	1.00								
3.	CF	0.74**	0.99**	1.00							
4.	FYM	0.88**	0.57**	0.63**	1.00						
5.	GL	0.74**	0.99**	0.99**	0.59**	1.00					
6.	HL	0.87**	0.89**	0.89**	0.58**	0.88**	1.00				
7.	IC	0.72**	0.96**	0.62**	0.99**	0.99**	0.99**	1.00			
8.	IWC	0.99**	0.97**	0.95**	0.99**	0.96**	0.99**	0.99**	1.00		
9.	HM	0.75**	0.99**	0.99**	0.64**	0.99**	0.89**	0.99**	0.97*	1.00	
10.	PPC	0.74**	0.99**	0.99**	0.60**	0.99**	0.98**	0.99**	0.96**	0.98**	1.00

Source: Tables (5.1, 5.3, 5.5,5.7,5.9, 5.11.)

** indicate significant at 1%.

this reason the farmers of Shimoga taluk are unable to do proper mulching procedure in cultivation operation every time. As a result of this the manuring cannot be properly done. This will have a definite impact on yield.

Correlation Co-efficient of Maintenance Cost among Various Farmers Category in Shimoga District

The data presented in the Tables 21, 22 and 23 reveals that the maintenance cost is positively correlated with all the variables in the equation at 1% level of significance.

The intercost comparision of the variables shows that they are positively correlated with each other at 1% level of significance.

There is little variation in the application of chemical fertilizer, farm yard manure and green leaves. Because of the non-availability of green leaves in Shimoga taluk and government is acquiring soppina betta in malnad region (Sagar taluk) as a result the farmers have opted for the application of farm yard manure in order to get high returns and disease free areca garden.

They believe that application of more chemical fertilizers will lead to diseases to the garden and as a result yield will decline over a period of time and also it will affect the lifespan of areca garden.

In Shimoga district human labour is the most dominant variable in the maintenance cost. The next dominant variables are organic manures, chemical fertilizers, irrigation cost, bullock power and machines hired in that order.

In conclusion, it is evident from the above statistical analysis that, there is significant correlation between the variables among the various farmers categories in both the taluks in the study area and highly positive correlation is existing between the variables in the maintenance cost.

The results indicate that there is significant correlation between the variables among the various farmers category in both the taluks in the study area.

There is positive correlation between the variables in the maintenance cost.

Multiple Regression

The multiple regression is applied to analyse the significance of different variables in the present context and how these variables influence the total maintenance cost. At the same time it will enable

Table 21

Correlation Co-efficient of Dependent variables (maintenance cost) among small farmers in Shimoga District

Sl.No.		*MC*	*BP*	*CF*	*FYM*	*GL*	*HL*	*IC*	*IWC*	*HM*	*PPC*
1.	MC	1.00									
2.	BP	0.80**	1.00								
3.	CF	0.80**	0.99**	1.00							
4.	FYM	0.38**	0.73**	0.71**	1.00						
5.	GL	0.36**	0.47**	0.47**	0.48**	1.00					
6.	HL	0.79**	0.99**	0.99**	0.74**	0.53**	1.00				
7.	IC	0.55**	0.51**	0.51**	0.50**	0.49**	0.44**	1.00			
8.	IWC	0.66**	0.85**	0.86**	0.67**	0.81**	0.87**	0.03**	1.00		
9.	HM	0.34**	0.48**	0.47**	0.39**	0.50**	0.42**	0.93**	0.01**	1.00	
10.	PPC	0.76**	0.54**	0.90**	0.29**	0.96**	0.99**	0.99**	0.99**	0.92**	1.00

Source: Tables 5.1, 5.4, 5.5, 5.8, 5.9, 5.12.

** indicate significant at 1%.

Table 22

Correlation Co-efficient of Dependent Variable (maintenance cost) Among Medium Farmers in Shimoga District

Sl.No.		MC	BP	CF	FYM	GL	HL	IC	IWC	HM	PPC
1.	MC	1.00									
2.	BP	0.97**	1.00								
3.	CF	0.99**	0.98**	1.00							
4.	FYM	0.99**	0.97**	0.97**	1.00						
5.	GL	0.56**	0.23**	0.20**	0.15**	1.00					
6.	HL	0.99**	0.99**	0.99**	0.97**	0.40**	1.00				
7.	IC	0.76**	0.47**	0.48**	0.44**	0.41**	0.42**	1.00			
8.	IWC	0.75**	0.99**	0.99**	0.97**	0.07**	0.99**	0.41**	1.00		
9.	HM	0.55**	0.77**	0.78**	0.76**	0.11**	0.79**	0.58**	0.75**	1.00	
10.	PPC	0.95**	0.97**	0.99**	0.99**	0.99**	0.99**	0.99*	0.99**	0.90**	1.00

Source: Tables 5.1, 5.4, 5.5, 5.8, 5.9, 5.12.

** indicate significant at 1%.

Table 23

Correlation Co-efficient of Dependent Variables (maintenance cost) Among Large Farmers in Shimoga District

Sl.No.		*MC*	*BP*	*CF*	*FYM*	*GL*	*HL*	*IC*	*IWC*	*HM*	*PPC*
1.	MC	1.00									
2.	BP	0.84**	1.00								
3.	CF	0.82**	0.99**	1.00							
4.	FYM	0.78**	0.78**	0.80**	1.00						
5.	GL	0.76**	0.46**	0.44**	0.27**	1.00					
6.	HL	0.91**	0.94**	0.93**	0.75**	0.56**	1.00				
7.	IC	0.33**	0.41**	0.41**	0.49**	0.39**	0.36**	1.00			
8.	IWC	0.88**	0.98**	0.98**	0.78**	0.57**	0.95**	0.32**	1.00		
9.	HM	0.83**	0.99**	0.99**	0.80**	0.45**	0.93**	0.40**	0.98**	1.00	
10.	PPC	0.80**	0.86**	0.99**	0.99**	0.99**	0.98**	0.99**	0.99**	0.96**	1.00

Source: Tables 5.1, 5.4, 5.5, 5.8, 5.9, 5.12.
** indicate significant at 1%.

us to understand as to which is the dominant variable in determining the yield of areca and intercrop as well as mixed crop.

Multiple Regression of Maintenance Cost Among Various Farmers' Category in Sagar Taluk

In the present context the multiple regression is applied to study the importance of different variables and how these variables influence on the total cost.

The analysis of the data presented in the Table 24 reveals that among small, medium and large farmers category all the variables are dominant at 5% level of significance in the maintenance cost.

The R sequare value of small and medium farmers is 99% each and for large farmers 100%.

In the maintenance cost dominant variables are human labour, organic manures, chemical fertilizers, cost on irrigation, interest

Table 24
Multiple Regression of Dependent Variables (MC) Among Various Category of Farmers in Sagar Taluk

Sl.No	*Variable*	*Standardized Beta of Regression Coefficient*		
		Small	*Medium*	*Large*
1.	Bullock Power	-0.01 (-0.68*)	0.02 (1.40*)	0.03 (1.89*)
2.	Chemical Fertilizer	-0.03 (-0.47*)	0.43 (2.10*)	0.35 (6.94*)
3.	Farm Yard Manure	0.004 (0.15*)	-0.01 (-0.24*)	0.01 (1.36*)
4.	Green Leaves	0.36 (8.71*)	6.36 (-0.24*)	0.46 (12.94*)
5.	Human labour	0.55 (16.28*)	0.86 (40.29*)	0.58 (44.51*)
6.	Interest on working capitalIrrigation Cost	0.60 (1.11*)	0.11 (1.55*)	0.61 (9.97*)
7.	Hired Machines	0.005 (0.40*)	0.004 (0.39*)	-0.03 (-3.75*)
8.	Plant protection Chemicals	-0.12 (-2.16*)	-0.01 (-0.17*)	0.64 (10.50*)
	R Square	0.99	0.99	1.00

Source: Tables 5.1, 5.2, 5.5, 5.6, 5.9,5.10.
Figures in the parenthesis indicate calculated t values.
*- indicates significance at 5 per cent.

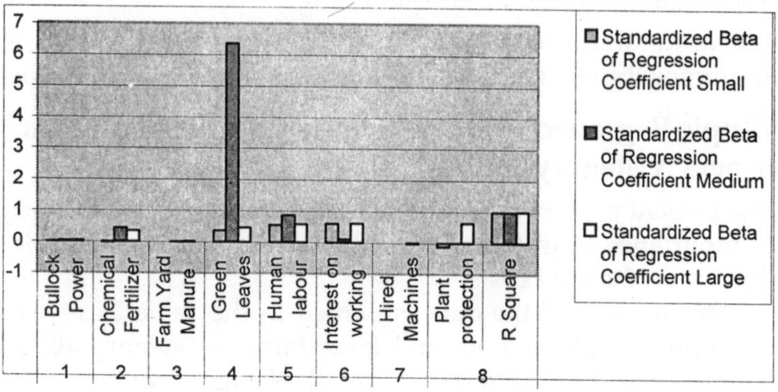

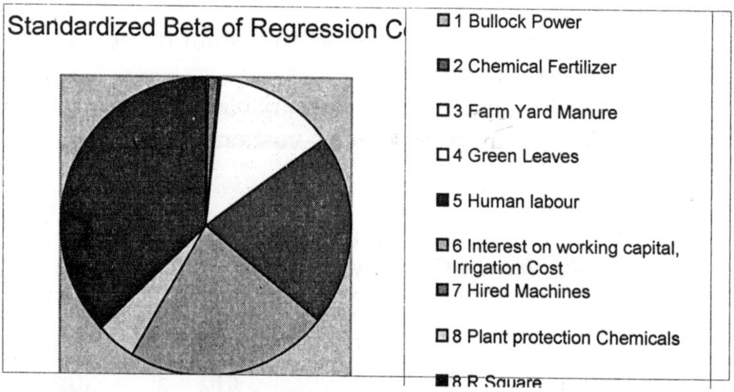

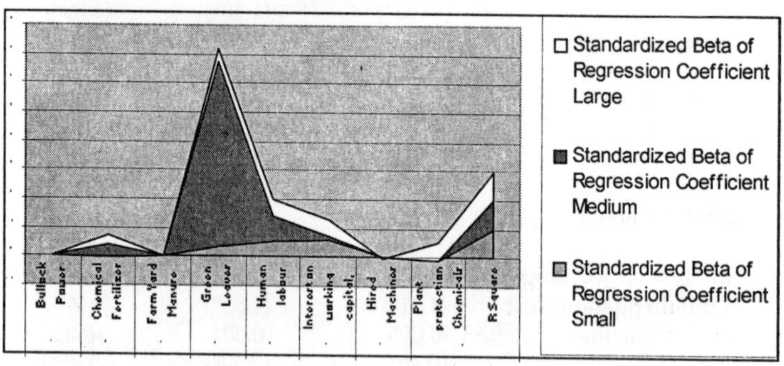

on working capital bullock power, hired machines and plant protection chemicals. It implies that the expenditure incurred on each component in the maintenance cost has influenced significantly in enhancing returns of arecanut as well as returns of intercrop/mixed crop.

Human labour is remarkably significant in the maintenance cost. Because human labour is involved in all the maintenance activities of the areca garden in all the three stages.

Multiple Regression of Maintenance Cost Among Various Farmer's Category in Shimoga Taluk

It is evident from the data presented in the Table 25 that among small, medium and large category of farmers all the variables are dominant at 5% level of significance.

The R square value of small and medium farmers is 99% each and for large farmers 100%.

The dominant variables in the total maintenance cost are human labour, farm yard manure, green leaves, chemical fertilizers, cost

Table 25
Multiple Regression of Dependent Variables (MC) Among Various Category of Farmers in Shimoga Taluk

Sl.No.	*Variable*	*Standardized Beta of Regression Coefficient*		
		Small	*Medium*	*Large*
1.	Bullock Power	0.03	0.08	0.04
		(0.71*)	(0.72*)	(4.49*)
2.	Chemical Fertilizer	0.08	0.01	0.59
		(1.38*)	(0.17*)	(594.95*)
3.	Farm Yard Manure	0.05	0.13	0.04
		(2.09*)	(4.33*)	(-0.47*)
4.	Green Leaves	-0.16	0.01	0.01
		(-1.90*)	(2.66)	(0.42*)
5.	Human labour	0.68	1.39	0.99
		(6.99*)	(8.46*)	(637.23*)
6.	Interest on working	0.16	0.08	0.60
	capitalIrrigation Cost	(2.69*)	(3.12*)	(1.10*)
7.	Hired Machines	-0.01	0.08	0.03
		(-0.76*)	(3.32*)	(-0.93*)
8.	Plant protection	0.16	0.69	-0.55
	Chemicals	(2.31*)	(4.38*)	(-13.11*)
	R Square	0.99	0.99	1.00

Source: Tables 5.1, 5.3, 5.5, 5.7,5.9, 5.11.

Figures in the parenthesis indicate calculated t values

*- indicates significance at 5 per cent.

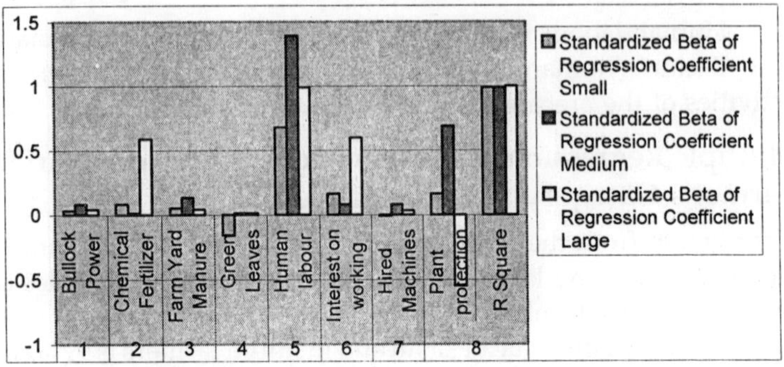

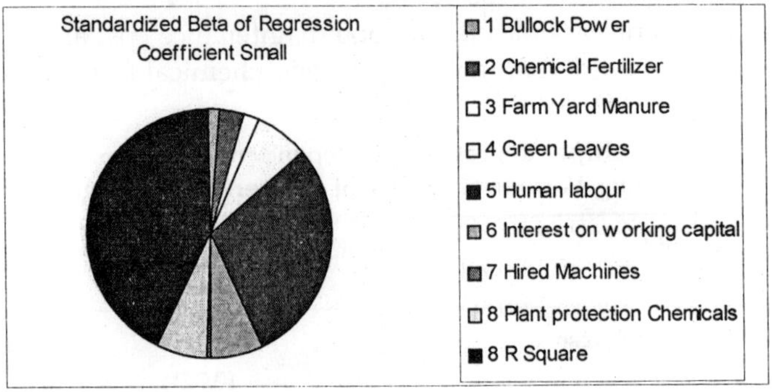

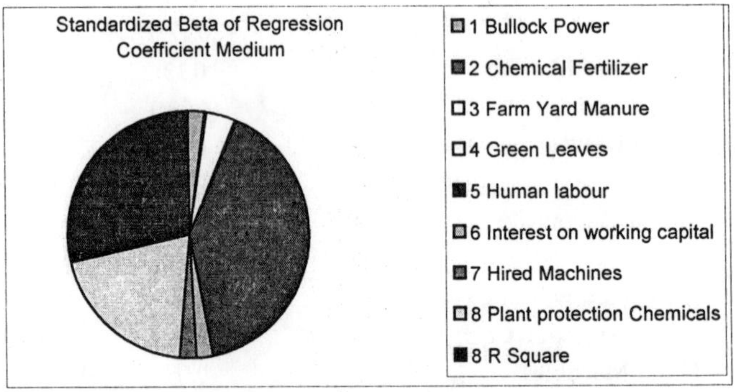

on irrigation, interest on working capital, bullock power, hired machines and plant protection chemicals.

As in Sagar taluk, here also human labour is the highly dominant variable in the maintenance cost.

It evidently shows that the expenses incurred on each components in the maintenance cost has a significant bearing on the returns of areca.

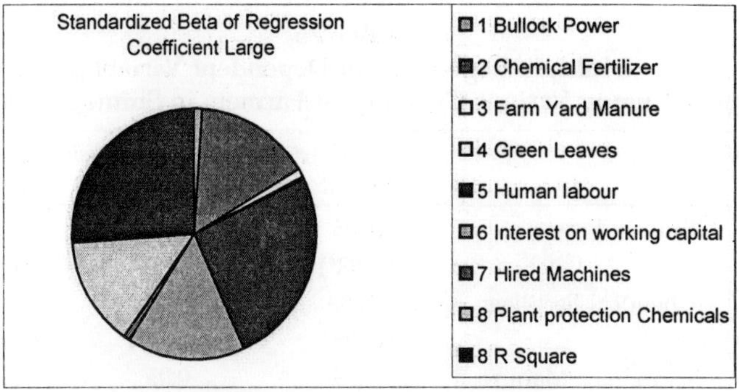

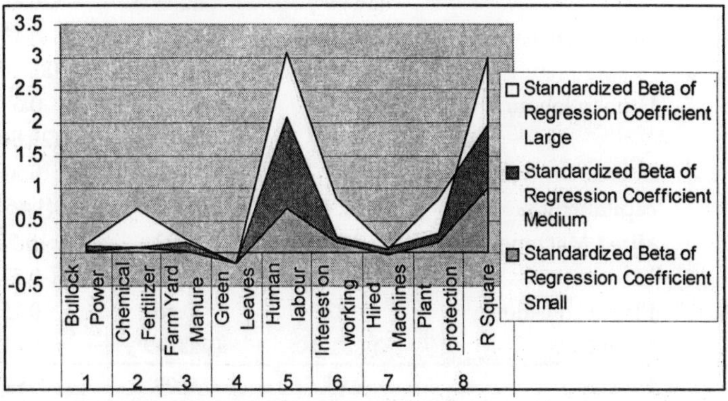

Multiple Regression of Maintenance Cost Among Various Farmers' Category in the District

It is evident from the data presented in the Table 26 that among small, medium and large category of farmers all the variables are dominant at 5% level of significance.

The R square value is 99% each for all the categories of farmers.

The dominant variables in the total maintenance cost are human labour, farm yard manure, green leaves, chemical fertilizers, irrigation cost, bullock power, machines hired and plant protection chemicals.

In conclusion, it is clear from the above statistical analysis that all the variables are dominant in the maintenance cost. Within the maintenance cost human labour is proved to be highly significant variable. Because human labour is involved in all the maintenance activities of the areca garden in all the three stages.

Table 26
Multiple Regression of Dependent Variables (MC) Among Various Category of Farmers in Shimoga District

Sl.No.	*Variable*	*Standardized Beta of Regression Coefficient*		
		Small	*Medium*	*Large*
1.	Bullock Power	0.06	0.08	-0.21
		(0.82*)	(3.83*)	(-1.93*)
2.	Chemical Fertilizer	-0.33	-0.01	-0.21
		(-0.28*)	(-0.49*)	(-0.68*)
3.	Farm Yard Manure	0.39	0.05	0.41
		(16.69*)	(-12.99*)	(26.68*)
4.	Green Leaves	0.79	0.27	0.43
		(4.37*)	(105.01*)	(26.18*)
5.	Human labour	0.21	0.79	0.67
		(-0.67*)	(28.54*)	(29.86*)
6.	Interest on working capitalIrrigation cost	0.03	0.93	0.01
		(-0.29*)	(-493.17*)	(1.45*)
7.	Hired Machines	0.03	0.02	-0.05
		(1.01*)	(2.26*)	(-0.57*)
8.	Plant protection Chemicals	0.37	0.45	0.15
		(4.51*)	(-200.49*)	(-0.41*)
	R Square	0.99	0.99	0.99

Source: Tables 5.1, 5.4, 5.5, 5.8, 5.9, 5.12
Figures in the paranthesis indicate calculated t values
* indicates significance at 5 per cent

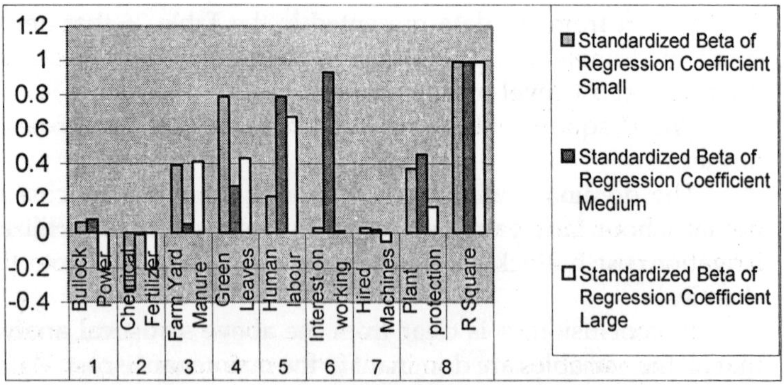

In both the taluks among all the categories of sample farmers human labour is the most dominant variable as compared to other variables in the maintenance cost.

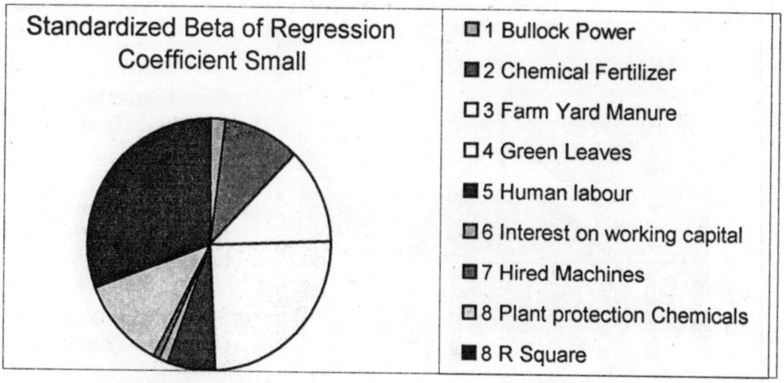

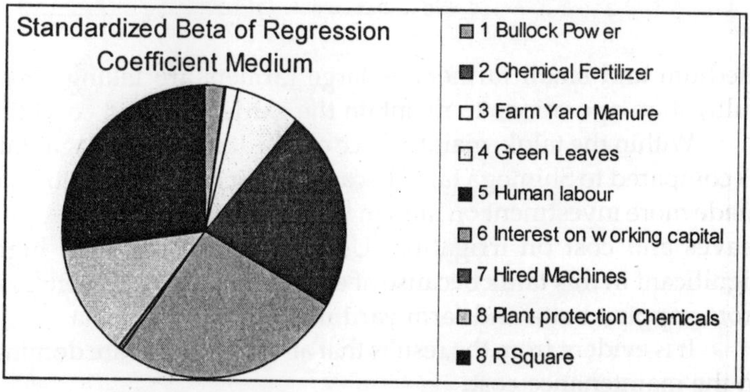

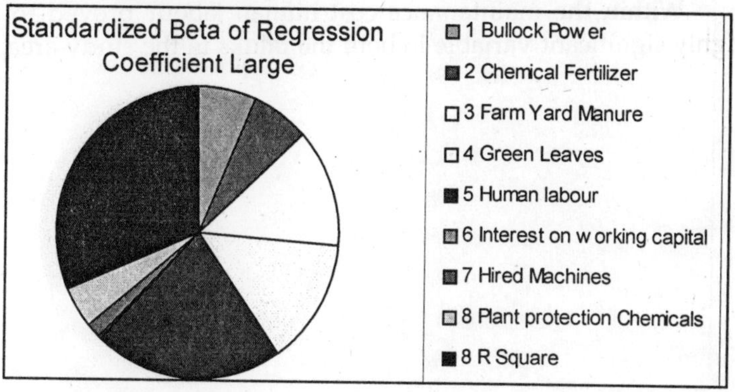

The dominant variables in succession are farm yard manure, green leaves, chemical fertilizers, irrigation cost, bullock power, machines hired and plant protection chemicals respectively.

Within the farmers' category the investment per hectare is more among large farmers in both the taluks as compared to

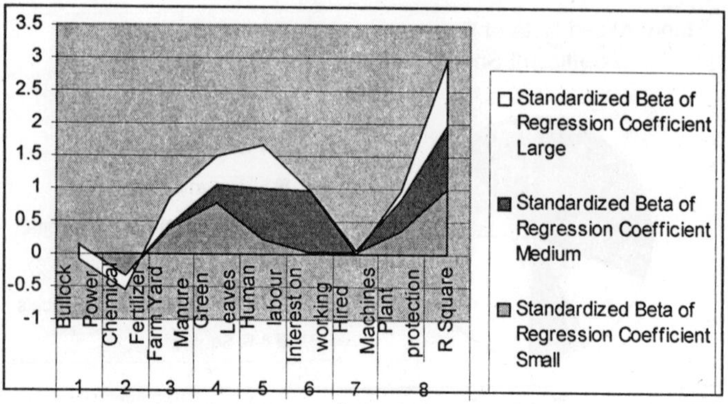

medium and small farmers as large farmers are taking several cultivation operations to maintain the garden in good condition.

Within the taluk, maintenance cost is dominant in Sagar taluk as compared to Shimoga taluk because farmers of Sagar taluk have made more investment on human labour, farm yard manure, green leaves and cost on irrigation. Usage of green leaves is highly significant in this taluk because of easy availability of green leaves from soppina betta and farm yard manure from Gomala.

It is evident from the results that all the variables are dominant in the maintenance cost.

Within the maintenance cost human labour proved to be highly significant variable in both the taluks in the study area.

6 RETURNS OF ARECANUT– AN ANALYSIS

In this chapter an attempt is made to bring out the yield and returns of arecanut in the study area.

Yield of any field crop which is the average amount of produce per unit area is simple and definite in conception but biologically is very complex and is influenced by many factors. Normally, type of soil, crop husbandry, season, quality of seed materials and incidence of pests and diseases are the important factors that affect the yield of crops. Arecanut being a perennial crop unlike annuals, the yield is further subjected to the influence of the age of the tree.

"Returns on investment is a calculation used to determine whether a proposed investment is wise and how well it will repay the investor. It is calculated as the ratio of the amount gained, which is taken as positive or lost which is taken as negative relative to the investment made"[1]

In other words, the value of output realised in any of the enterprise is called as returns.

Successful cultivation operation is an individual problem involves many physical and economic factors. The success of any particular farmer is determined largely by the resources available, his willingness to work industriously and his ability to manage the farm in such a manner so as to get maximum returns. A farmer must be skilled in numerous and varied physical jobs required in the farm and must involve himself diligently to his work, to be a successful farmer. In addition he must be a skilled manager.

Farm management principles serve to organise production skills and technical knowledge in such a way to apply each one in its proper place in the complete farming programme so that the highest possible returns can be earned.

The most important factors which effects returns in farming are as follows:

1. Application of the farm to the available source.
2. Size of the farm.
3. Efficiency in the use of labour and equipment.
4. Efficiency in the work and farm management.
5. Marking Practices.

The above factors include the relationship of farm returns and the ways in which the farmer can adjust his management practice to best advantage in getting maximum returns.[2]

With this background, the evaluation of returns of arecanut per hectare with respect to various stages in traditional as well as non-traditional areas of Shimoga district is made.

In the study area, irrespective of category of farmers will prepare three different grades of arecanut in 3:2:1 ratio respectively out of their respective yields. The price of each grade in both the taluks is mentioned as below.

Varieties	*Sagar Taluk*	*Shimoga Taluk*
Grade 1.	Rs.11,300/qtl.	Rs.11,100/qtl.
Grade 2.	Rs. 9,900/qtl.	Rs. 9,300/qtl.
Grade 3.	Rs. 4,300/qtl.	Rs. 3,400/qtl.

It is clear from the above data that the farmers of Sagar taluk get slightly better price as compared to farmers of Shimoga taluk.

In the present study during the gestation period i.e. at the end of 6th and 7th year areca palm starts yielding and in the second stage yield will go on increasing year after year and in the third stage yield will slightly decline.

Returns of Arecanut in the First Stage

In the present study the yield and returns of arecanut in the first stage is represented in the Table 1.

In the entire district the percentage variation of yield between small and medium farmers is 21.36% while it is 61% between medium and large farmers.

In Sagar taluk the percentage variation of yield between small and medium farmers is 20% whereas in between medium and large farmers it is 35%.

In Shimoga taluk between small and medium farmers the percentage variation of yield is about 23.08% while in between medium and large farmers it is 100%.

Table 1
Average Per Hectare Returns of Arecanut in the First Stage in the Study Area

Particulars	*Sagar Taluk Farmers Category*				*Shimoga Taluk Farmers Category*				*District Farmers Category*			
	Small	*Medium*	*Large*	*Average*	*Small*	*Medium*	*Large*	*Average*	*Small*	*Medium*	*Large*	*average*
Yield Per Ha (in Quintals)	5.00	6.00	8.10	6.37	3.25	4.0	8. 00	5.08	4.12	5.00	8.05	5.72
Total Returns (in Rs.)	48,352	58,000	78,300	61,550.67	29,973	36,847	73,753	46,857.67	39,162.50	47,423.50	76,026.50	54,204.17

Source: Survey Data.

Between Sagar and Shimoga taluk percentage variation of yield is 25.39%.

In the entire district the percentage variation of returns between small and medium is 21.09% while between medium and large it is 60.31%.

In Sagar taluk the percentage variation of returns between small and medium farmers is 19.95% but between medium and large farmers it is 35%.

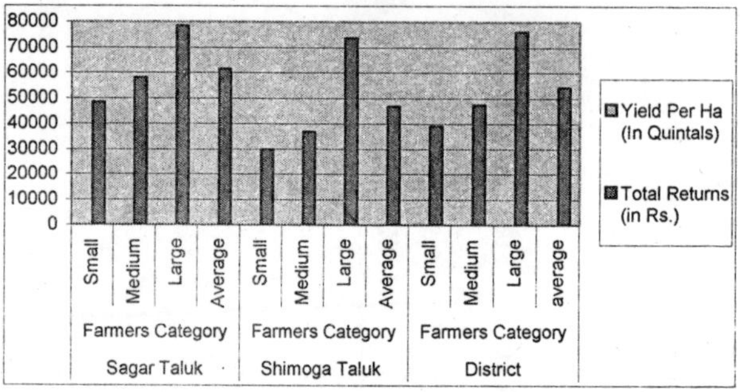

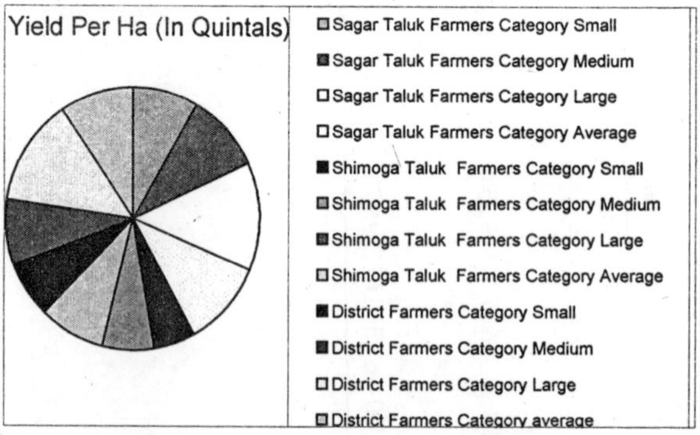

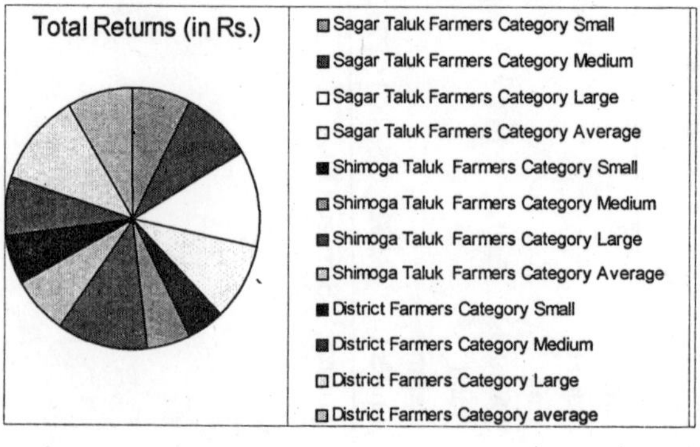

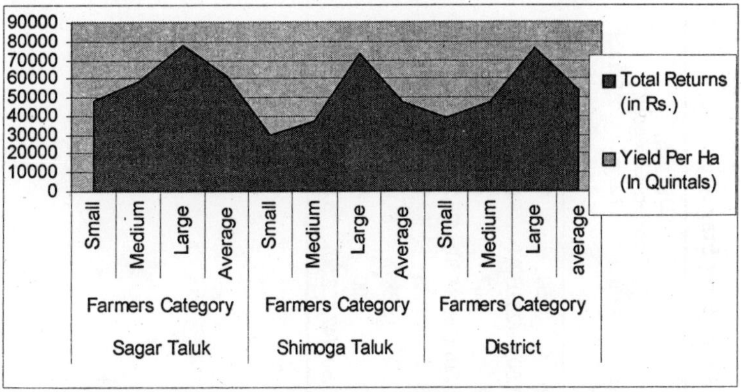

In Shimoga taluk between small and medium category the percentage variation of returns is 22.93% whereas between medium and large farmers it is 100.16%.

Between Sagar and Shimoga taluks percentage variation of returns is 31.36 %. It is clear from the above analysis in the entire study area and in both the taluks large category of farmers are getting better yield and returns as compared to medium and small farmers.

With respect to Sagar and Shimoga taluk here also large farmers are in better position compared to medium and small.

In taluk-wise comparison in the study area farmers of Sagar taluk are getting better yield and returns as compared to farmers of Shimoga taluk.

It is evident from the Table 1 that in the study area the returns per hectare is Rs. 54204.17. The total returns of the arecanut per hectare in the district varies among all the three categories of farmers.

For instance, in case of large farmers' the returns of arecanut per hectare is more than the overall for the district. While in the case of medium and small farmers category of the average returns of arecanut per hectare is less than the total returns of the district.

However in comparison the total returns of arecanut is slightly higher among medium farmers category than the small farmers' category.

In the study area the taluk-wise comparison of total returns shows that in Sagar taluk it is much above the district average whereas in Shimoga taluk it is very much below the district average total returns. When both the taluks are taken into account on an

Table .2
Different Grades of Arecanut Produced by Farmers in the Study Area (First Stage)

Particulars	*Sagar Taluk Farmers Category*				*Shimoga Taluk Farmers Category*				*Dictrict Farmers Category*			
Qty. (in Quintals)	*Small*	*Medium*	*Large*	*Average*	*Small*	*Medium*	*Large*	*Average*	*Small*	*Medium*	*Large*	*Average*
Grade 1	2.50	3.00	4.05	3.18	1.63	2.00	4.00	2.54	2.06	2.50	4.02	2.86
	(28,250)	(33,900)	(45,765)	(35,971.67)	(18,093)	(22,200)	(44,400)	(28,231)	(23,171.50)	(28,050)	(45,082.50)	(32,101.33)
Grade 2	1.67	2.00	2.70	2.12	1.08	1.33	2.67	1.69	1.38	1.67	2.69	1.91
	(16,533)	(19,800)	(26,730)	(21,021)	(10,044)	(12,369)	(24,831)	(15,748)	(13,288.50)	(16,084.50)	(25,780.50)	(18,384.50)
Grade 3	0.83	1.00	1.35	1.06	0.54	0.67	1.33	0.85	0.68	0.83	1.34	0.95
	(3,569)	(4,300)	(5,805)	(4,558)	(1,836)	(2,278)	(4,522)	(2,878.67)	(2,702.50)	(3,289)	(5,163.50)	(3,718.33)
Total	5.00	6.00	8.10	6.37	3.25	4.00	8.00	5.08	4.12	5.00	8.05	5.72
	(48,352	(58,00)	(78,300)	(61,550.67)	(29,973)	(36,847)	(73,753)	(46,857.67)	(39,162.50)	(47,423.50)	(76,026.50)	(54,204.17)

Source: Survey Data.
Note: Figures in the brackets indicate value in Rupees.

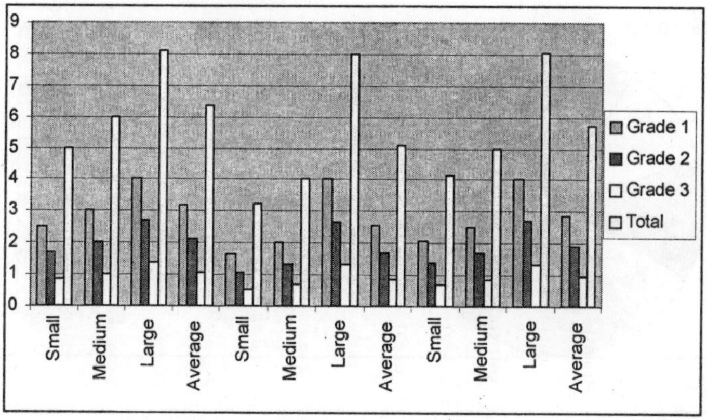

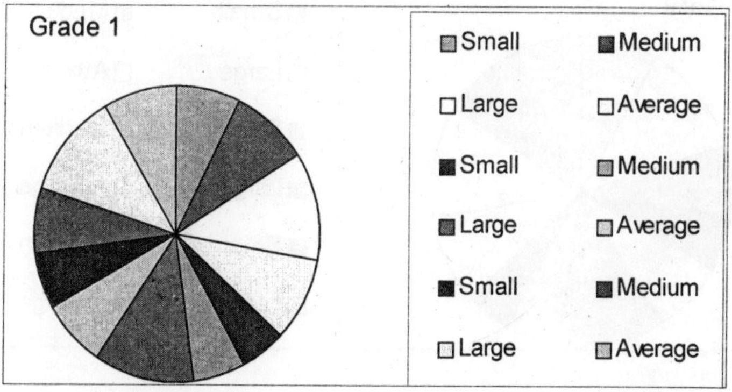

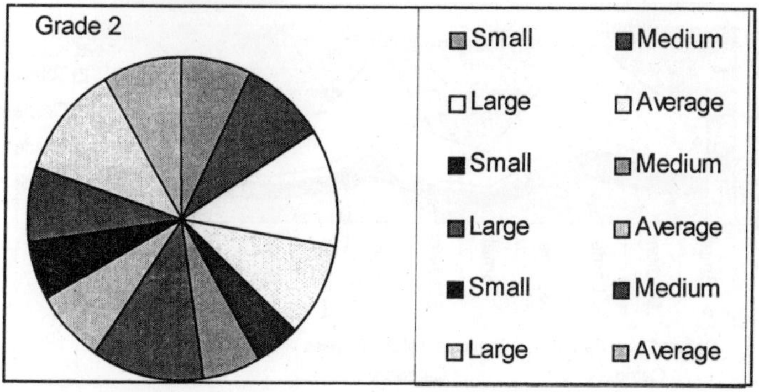

average the total returns per hectare is more among large farmers than medium and small farmers.

Further large farmers are getting more returns in comparison with the overall average of the district.

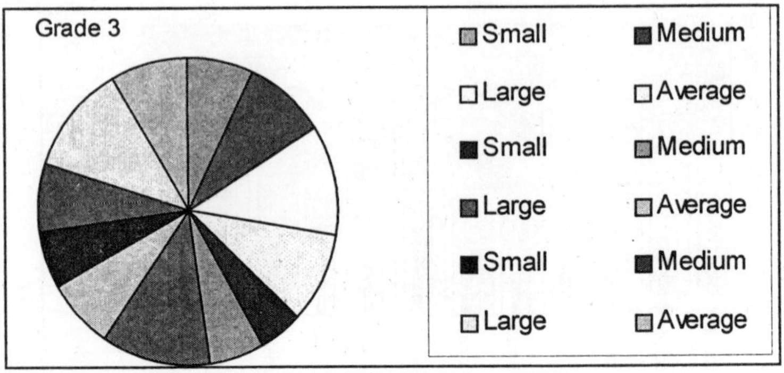

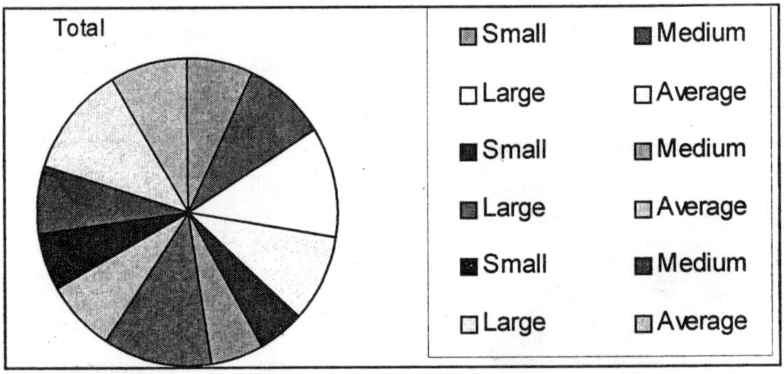

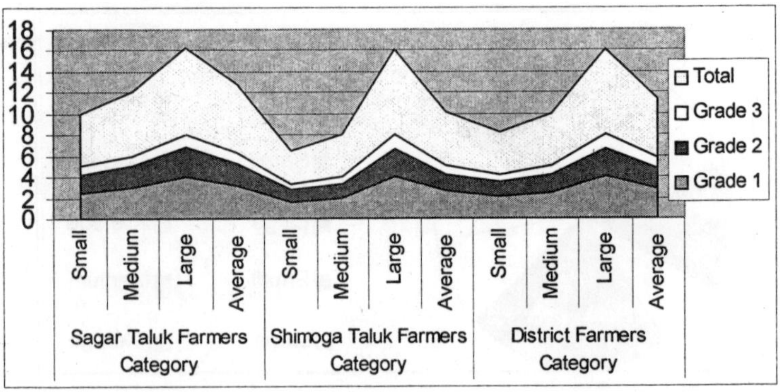

While in the case of medium and small farmers on an average the total returns is less than the overall average total returns.

The above analysis reveals that on an average the total returns is highest in Sagar taluk as compared to Shimoga taluk and also the entire study area due to the higher investment made by the farmers of Sagar taluk as compared to the farmers of Shimoga taluk. In addition, farmers in Sagar taluk adopt scientific methods of cultivation as compared to farmers in Shimoga taluk. Further the soil and climatic condition in Sagar taluk are more favourable to arecanut cultivation. That is the reason as to why farmers in Sagar taluk get better returns.

Mulching in the inter spaces of arecanut gardens with green leaves or dry leaves is a common practice in Malnad specially in Sagar taluk. The practice of mulching prevents evaporation of the water from the ground, protects loose soils from erosion during heavy rains and forms humus and manure to the soil.[4]

Moreover application of green leaves as an organic manure increases organic carbon and nitrogen contents of soil[5] in turn the yield per hectare in Sagar taluk.

Whereas in Shimoga taluk because of the low investment, unsuitability of the crop to the local soil and climatic conditions, poor management practice, lack of planned and scientific cultivation practices the returns per hectare is relatively low.

Further the successful establishment of the seedlings and the performance of young palms depends on two important factors. Viz., perfect drainage and protection from the sun scorch. But in Shimoga taluk farmers have not made drainage channel for every two rows of palms.

Moreover protecting the stems of young palms from sun-scorch is also important, if the young palms get damaged it cannot be recovered. Sun-scorch is mostly seen during the months of October to May. Hence from the beginning of October the exposed stems of individual palms are to be protected by covering with materials like dry leaves of arecanut or white opaque polythene. When there is no natural protection, the exposure of palms to direct sun can be avoided by raising a belt of quick growing trees on the western and southern aspects of the garden.[6]

The above measures have not at all followed vigorously by the farmers of Shimoga taluk leading to low returns per hectare as compared to farmers of Sagar taluk.

In addition in both the taluks the per hectare total returns is high among large farmers as compared to medium and small due to establishment and maintenance cost being high among large farmers. It may be because of their better economic condition, good-educational background, planned and scientific cultivation practices etc.

Further, adaption of modern techniques in cultivation operations, efficient resource use management, maintaining the fertility of the soil, adopting preventive measures to protect the crop against the pests and diseases etc. will result in higher returns as compared to medium and small farmers.

It is also clear from the Table 2 that large farmers are getting more returns in the entire district and in both the taluks. Between the taluks farmers of Sagar taluk are getting higher returns as compared to Shimoga taluk.

Returns of Arecanut in the Second Stage

As compared to the first stage returns from areca palm will go on increasing steadily year after year during the second stage. In other words, it is only in the second stage the farmers can get maximum returns from arecanut garden and make some profits. Therefore, the analysis of returns in the second stage will throw light on the economic feasibility of arecanut cultivation. With this view in mind the present analysis is made.

The yield and returns of arecanut in the second stage is presented in the Table 3.

An insight is given pertaining to the yield of arecanut among various category of farmers in the study area.

In the entire district the percentage variation of yield between small and medium farmers is 12.35% while it is 19.46% between medium and large farmers.

In Sagar taluk the percentage variation between small and medium farmers is 11.11% and between medium and large farmers it is 20%.

In Shimoga taluk between small and medium farmers the percentage variation of yield is about 13.94% while in between medium and large it is 18.78%.

Between Sagar and Shimoga taluk percentage variation of yield is 26.78 %.

In the entire district the percentage variation of returns per hectare between small and medium farmers is 12.35% while between medium and large farmers it is 19.42 per cent.

Table 3
Average Per Hectare Returns of Arecanut in the Second Stage in the Study Area

Particulars	*Sagar Taluk Farmers Category*				*Shimoga Taluk Farmers Category*				*District Farmers Category*			
	Small	*Medium*	*Large*	*Average*	*Small*	*Medium*	*Large*	*Average*	*Small*	*Medium*	*Large*	*Average*
Yield per ha (in Quintals)	22.23	24.70	29.64	25.52	17.29	19.70	23.40	20.13	19.76	22.20	26.52	22.83
Total Returns (in Rs.)	2,14,925	2,38,946	2,86,520	2,46,797	1,59,375	1,81,588	2,15,670	1,85,544.33	1,87,150	2,10,267	2,51,095	2,16,170.66

Source: Survey Data.

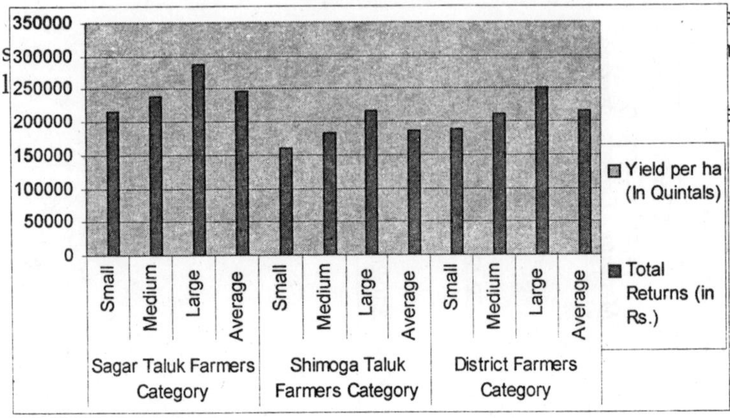
350000
300000
250000
200000
150000
100000
50000
0
Small
Medium
Large
Average
Small
Medium
Large
Average
Small
Medium
Large
Average
Sagar Taluk Farmers Category
Shimoga Taluk Farmers Category
District Farmers Category
Yield per ha (In Quintals)
Total Returns (in Rs.)

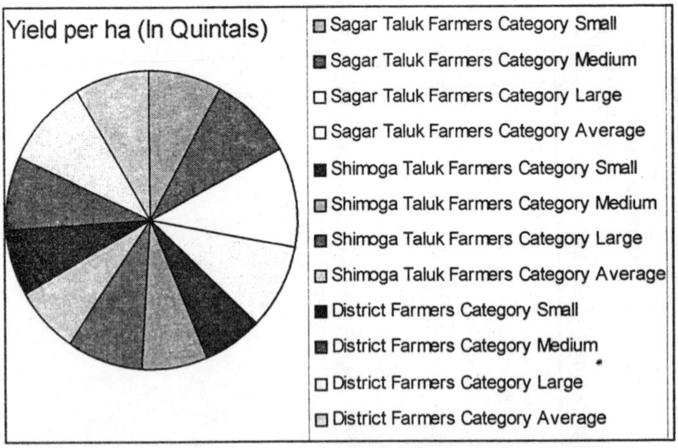
Yield per ha (In Quintals)
Sagar Taluk Farmers Category Small
Sagar Taluk Farmers Category Medium
Sagar Taluk Farmers Category Large
Sagar Taluk Farmers Category Average
Shimoga Taluk Farmers Category Small
Shimoga Taluk Farmers Category Medium
Shimoga Taluk Farmers Category Large
Shimoga Taluk Farmers Category Average
District Farmers Category Small
District Farmers Category Medium
District Farmers Category Large
District Farmers Category Average

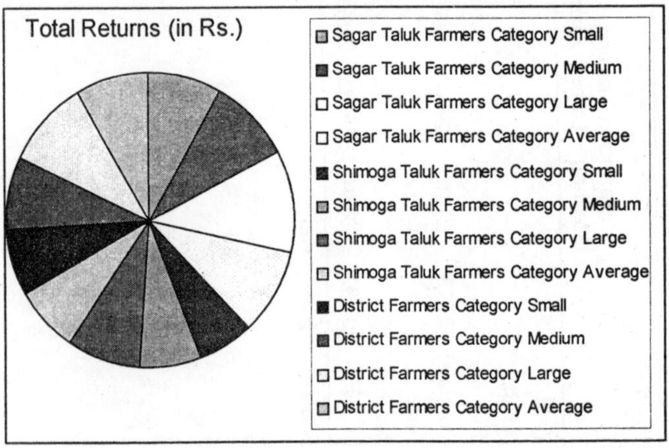
Total Returns (in Rs.)
Sagar Taluk Farmers Category Small
Sagar Taluk Farmers Category Medium
Sagar Taluk Farmers Category Large
Sagar Taluk Farmers Category Average
Shimoga Taluk Farmers Category Small
Shimoga Taluk Farmers Category Medium
Shimoga Taluk Farmers Category Large
Shimoga Taluk Farmers Category Average
District Farmers Category Small
District Farmers Category Medium
District Farmers Category Large
District Farmers Category Average

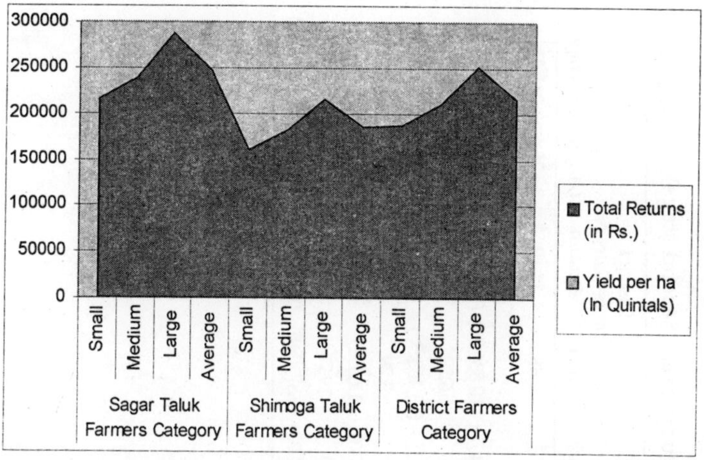

small and medium farmers is 13.94% whereas between medium and large farmers it is 18.77%.

Between Sagar and Shimoga taluk rate of increase in the returns is 33.01%.

It is clear from the above analysis that large farmers category in the study area are getting higher yield and returns in comparon with the medium and small farmers.

When compared to the farmers of Shimoga taluk and the district the farmers of Sagar taluk are getting higher yields and returns.

It is customary among the farmers in the study area that irrespective of farmers category they produce 50% of grade 1, 34% of grade 2 and 16% of grade 3 arecanut out of their total yields. Accordingly the returns are calculated.

It is also evident from the Table 4 that large farmers are getting more returns in the entire district and in both the taluks. Between the taluks farmers of Sagar taluk are getting higher returns as compared to Shimoga taluk.

The Table 3 reveals that the returns per hectare in the study area is Rs. 2,16,170.66. The total returns of the district of arecanut per hectare varies among different categories of farmers. For instance in case of large farmers the per hectare total returns of the arecanut is more than the overall average for the district-whereas in case of medium and small farmer's categories the average returns of the arecanut per hectare is less than the overall average.

Table 4
Different Grades of Arecanut Produced in Farmers in the Study Area (Second stage)

Particulars	Sagar Taluk Farmers Category				Shimoga Taluk Farmers Category				District Farmers Category			
	Small	Medium	Large	Average	Small	Medium	Large	Average	Small	Medium	Large	Average
Grade 1	11.12	12.35	14.82	12.76	8.65	9.85	11.70	10.07	9.88	11.10	13.26	11.41
Qty. (in qtls)	(1,25,656)	(1,39,555)	(1,67,466)	(1,44,225.67)	(96,015)	(1,09,335)	(1,29,870)	(1,11,740)	(1,10,835.50)	(1,24,445)	(1,48,668)	(1,27,982.83)
Grade 2	7.41	8.23	9.88	8.51	5.76	6.57	7.80	6.71	6.59	7.40	8.84	7.61
	(73,359)	(81,675)	(97,812)	(84,282)	(53,568)	(61,101)	(72,540)	(62,403)	(63,463.50)	(71,388)	(85,176)	(73,342.50)
Grade 3	3.70	4.12	4.94	4.25	2.88	3.28	3.90	3.35	3.29	3.70	4.42	3.80
	(15,910)	(17,716)	(21,242)	(18,289.33)	(9,792)	(11,152)	(13,260)	(11,401.33)	(12,851)	(14,434)	(17,251)	(14,845.33)
Total	22.23	24.70	29.64	25.52	17.29	19.70	23.40	20.13	19.76	22.20	26.52	22.83
	(2,14,925)	(2,38,946)	(2,86,520)	(2,46,797)	(1,59,375)	(1,81,588)	(2,15,670)	(1,85,544.33)	(1,87,150)	(2,10,267)	(2,51,095)	(2,16,170.66)

Source: Survey Data.
Note: Figures in brackets indicate value in Rs.

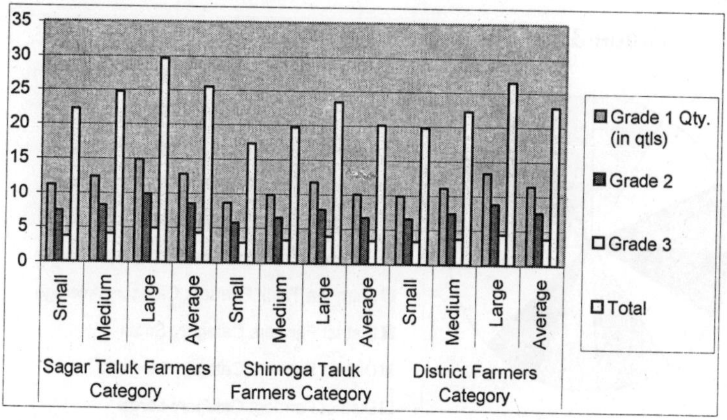
35
30
25
20
15
10
5
0
Small
Medium
Large
Average
Small
Medium
Large
Average
Small
Medium
Large
Average
Sagar Taluk Farmers Category
Shimoga Taluk Farmers Category
District Farmers Category
Grade 1 Qty. (in qtls)
Grade 2
Grade 3
Total

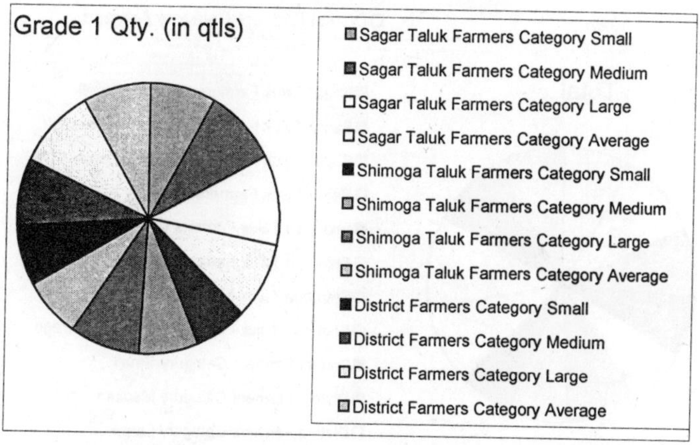
Grade 1 Qty. (in qtls)
Sagar Taluk Farmers Category Small
Sagar Taluk Farmers Category Medium
Sagar Taluk Farmers Category Large
Sagar Taluk Farmers Category Average
Shimoga Taluk Farmers Category Small
Shimoga Taluk Farmers Category Medium
Shimoga Taluk Farmers Category Large
Shimoga Taluk Farmers Category Average
District Farmers Category Small
District Farmers Category Medium
District Farmers Category Large
District Farmers Category Average

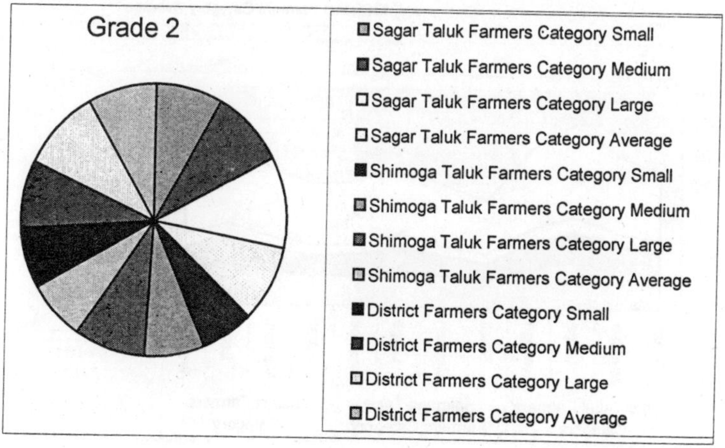
Grade 2
Sagar Taluk Farmers Category Small
Sagar Taluk Farmers Category Medium
Sagar Taluk Farmers Category Large
Sagar Taluk Farmers Category Average
Shimoga Taluk Farmers Category Small
Shimoga Taluk Farmers Category Medium
Shimoga Taluk Farmers Category Large
Shimoga Taluk Farmers Category Average
District Farmers Category Small
District Farmers Category Medium
District Farmers Category Large
District Farmers Category Average

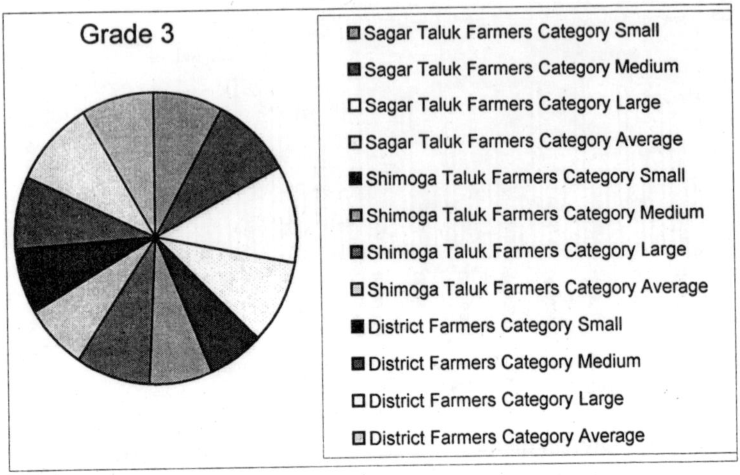
Grade 3
Sagar Taluk Farmers Category Small
Sagar Taluk Farmers Category Medium
Sagar Taluk Farmers Category Large
Sagar Taluk Farmers Category Average
Shimoga Taluk Farmers Category Small
Shimoga Taluk Farmers Category Medium
Shimoga Taluk Farmers Category Large
Shimoga Taluk Farmers Category Average
District Farmers Category Small
District Farmers Category Medium
District Farmers Category Large
District Farmers Category Average

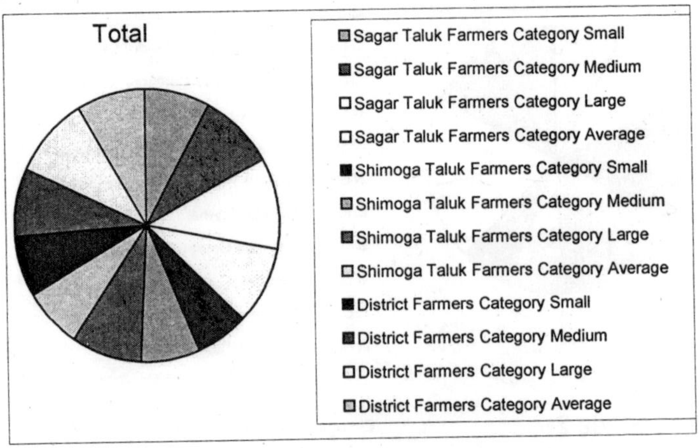
Total
Sagar Taluk Farmers Category Small
Sagar Taluk Farmers Category Medium
Sagar Taluk Farmers Category Large
Sagar Taluk Farmers Category Average
Shimoga Taluk Farmers Category Small
Shimoga Taluk Farmers Category Medium
Shimoga Taluk Farmers Category Large
Shimoga Taluk Farmers Category Average
District Farmers Category Small
District Farmers Category Medium
District Farmers Category Large
District Farmers Category Average

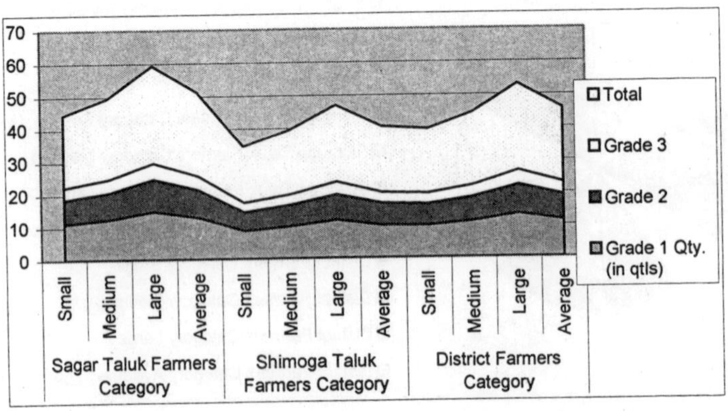
70
60
50
40
30
20
10
0
Small
Medium
Large
Average
Small
Medium
Large
Average
Small
Medium
Large
Average
Sagar Taluk Farmers Category
Shimoga Taluk Farmers Category
District Farmers Category
Total
Grade 3
Grade 2
Grade 1 Qty. (in qtls)

However, the total returns of the arecanut of medium farmers category is slightly more than the small farmers category. It is further evident from the data that the total returns is found increasing as the size of land holding increases.

The talukwise comparison of the total returns depicts a disturbing picture. In Sagar taluk the per hectare total returns is much above the overall total returns in the study area, whereas in case of Shimoga taluk it is very much below the overall position.

From this it may be concluded that farmers in Sagar taluk are getting more total returns as compared to farmers of Shimoga taluk.

Within the district in both the taluks the total returns per hectare is Rs. 2,46,797 and Rs. 1,85,544.33 respectively. For instance, in case of large farmers the per hectare total returns is more than the overall average for the respective taluks. Whereas, in case of medium and small farmers' category the average total returns per hectare is less than the overall average total returns.

However, the total returns of medium farmers is slightly more than the small farmers. From the above analysis it is clear that the average per hectare total returns is highest in Sagar taluk and much less in Shimoga taluk as compared to the entire study area.
Large farmers in both the taluks, are getting more returns as compared to medium and small farmers due to,

I. Higher investment per hectare.

II. Planned and Scientific Cultivation Practices.

III. Deweeding, periodical manuring with red earth, proper irrigation management with sprinklers, mulching, proper maintenance of drainage's and trenches periodically, diseased palms will be removed completely the open pit will be left for natural sunlight for few months after soil testing and consulting agricultural experts after proper processing new sapling will be planted in that place.

Efficient Management is Done Routinely

All these operations will be carried out properly in Sagar taluk whereas in Shimoga taluk the above mentioned operations are not strictly followed, hence returns is comparatively low among large farmers of Shimoga taluk when compared to the large farmers of Sagar taluk.

Returns of Arecanut in the Third Stage

As compared to the second stage the yield of the areca palm shows, a declining trend after 40 years, due to the age of the palm and soil conditions.

The returns of the areca garden in the third stage is taken into account for the evaluation of total yield from the arecanut cultivation so as to bring about the economic feasibility of the areca garden in the study area. The yield and returns of arecanut presented in the Table 5.

In the entire district the percentage variation of yield between small and medium farmers is 19.60%, while between medium and large farmers it is 33.78%.

In Sagar taluk the percentage of variation of yield between small and medium farmers is 16.06%, while between medium and large farmers it is 29.24%.

In Shimoga taluk the percentage of variation of yield between small and medium farmers is 25%, where between medium and large farmers it is 40%.

Between Sagar and Shimoga taluks the percentage variation of yield is 37.28%.

In the entire district the percentage variation of returns between small and medium farmers is 19.53% while in between medium and large farmers it is 33.65%.

In Sagar taluk the percentage variation of returns between small and medium farmers is 16.05% whereas between medium and large farmers it is 29.28%.

In Shimoga taluk the percentage variation of returns between small and medium farmers is 25.01% whereas between medium and large farmers it is 40.04%.

Between Sagar and Shimoga taluk the percentage variation of returns is 43.99%.

It is evident from the analysis that in the district as a whole and in both the taluks large farmers are in better position with respect to yield and returns when compared to medium and small farmers category.

While in taluk wise comparison the farmers of Sagar taluk are getting higher yield as compared to farmers of Shimoga taluk. Another special feature to be noted in this stage is that, the yield is comparatively less among all the categories of farmers in the study area.

Table 5

Average Per Hectare Returns of Arecanut in the Third Stage in The Study Area

Particulars	*Sagar Taluk Farmers Category*				*Shimoga Taluk Farmers Category*				*District Farmers Category*			
	Small	*Medium*	*Large*	*Average*	*Small*	*Medium*	*Large*	*Average*	*Small*	*Medium*	*Large*	*Average*
Yield per ha (in Quintals)	14.82	17.20	22.23	18.08	9.88	12.35	17.29	13.17	12.35	14.77	19.76	15.62
Total Returns (in Rs.)	1,43,260	1,66,248	2,14,925	1,74,811	91,041	1,13,807	1,59,375	1,21,407.67	1,17,150.50	1,40,027.50	1,87,150	1,48,109.33

Source : Survey Data

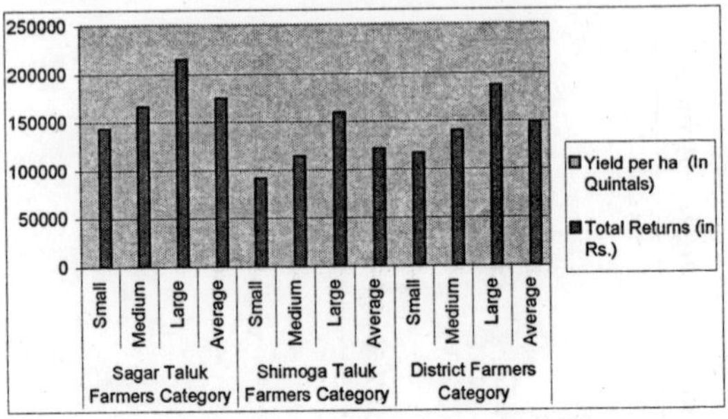
250000
200000
150000
100000
50000
0
Small
Medium
Large
Average
Sagar Taluk Farmers Category
Shimoga Taluk Farmers Category
District Farmers Category
Yield per ha (In Quintals)
Total Returns (in Rs.)

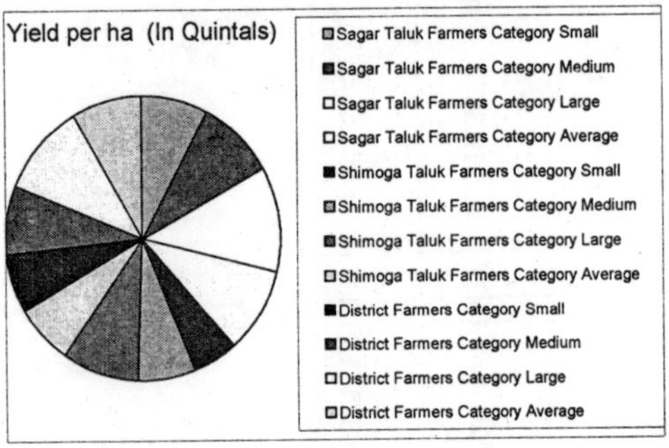
Yield per ha (In Quintals)
Sagar Taluk Farmers Category Small
Sagar Taluk Farmers Category Medium
Sagar Taluk Farmers Category Large
Sagar Taluk Farmers Category Average
Shimoga Taluk Farmers Category Small
Shimoga Taluk Farmers Category Medium
Shimoga Taluk Farmers Category Large
Shimoga Taluk Farmers Category Average
District Farmers Category Small
District Farmers Category Medium
District Farmers Category Large
District Farmers Category Average

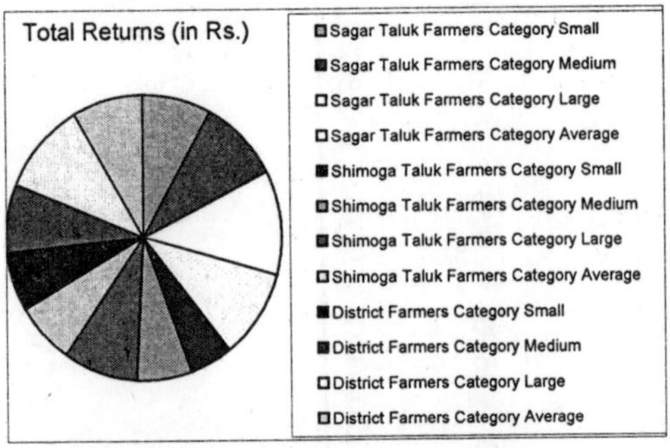
Total Returns (in Rs.)
Sagar Taluk Farmers Category Small
Sagar Taluk Farmers Category Medium
Sagar Taluk Farmers Category Large
Sagar Taluk Farmers Category Average
Shimoga Taluk Farmers Category Small
Shimoga Taluk Farmers Category Medium
Shimoga Taluk Farmers Category Large
Shimoga Taluk Farmers Category Average
District Farmers Category Small
District Farmers Category Medium
District Farmers Category Large
District Farmers Category Average

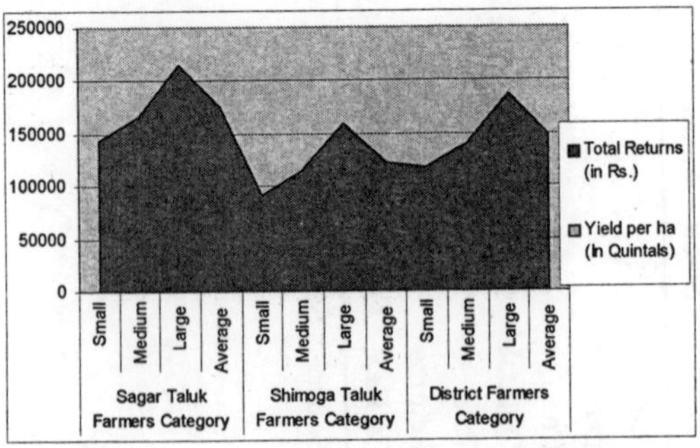
250000
200000
150000
100000
50000
0
Small
Medium
Large
Average
Sagar Taluk Farmers Category
Shimoga Taluk Farmers Category
District Farmers Category
Total Returns (in Rs.)
Yield per ha (In Quintals)

Table 6
Different Grades of Arecanut Produced by Farmers in the Study Area (Third Stage)

Particulars	*Sagar Taluk Farmers Category*				*Shimoga Taluk Farmers Category*				*Dictrict Farmers Category*			
Qty (in Qtls)	*Small*	*Medium*	*Large*	*Average*	*Small*	*Medium*	*Large*	*Average*	*Small*	*Medium*	*Large*	*Average*
Grade 1	7.41	8.60	11.12	9.04	4.94	6.17	8.65	6.59	6.17	7.38	9.88	7.81
	(83,733)	(97,180)	(1,25,656)	(1,02,189.67)	(54,834)	(68,487)	(96,015)	(73,112)	(69,283.50)	(82,833.50)	(1,10,835.50)	(87,650.83)
Grade 2	4.94	5.73	7.41	6.03	3.29	4.12	5.76	4.38	4.12	4.93	6.59	5.21
	(48,906)	(56,727)	(73,359)	(59,664)	(30,597)	(38,316)	(53,568)	(40,827)	(39,751.50)	(47,521.50)	(63,463.50)	(50,245.50)
Grade 3	2.47	2.87	3.70	3.01	1.65	2.06	2.88	2.20	2.06	2.46	3.29	2.60
	(10,621)	(12,641)	(15,910)	(12,957.33)	(5,610)	(7,004)	(9,792)	(7,468.67)	(8,115.50)	(9,672.50)	(12,851)	(10,213)
Total	14.82	17.20	22.23	18.08	9.88	12.35	17.29	13.17	12.35	14.77	19.76	15.63
	(1,43,260)	(1,66,248)	(2,14,925)	(1,74,811)	(91,041)	(1,13,807)	(1,59,375)	(1,21,407.67)	(1,17,150.50)	(1,40,027.50)	1,87,150)	(1,48,109.33)

Source: Survey Data.
Note: Figures in brackets indicate value in Rs.

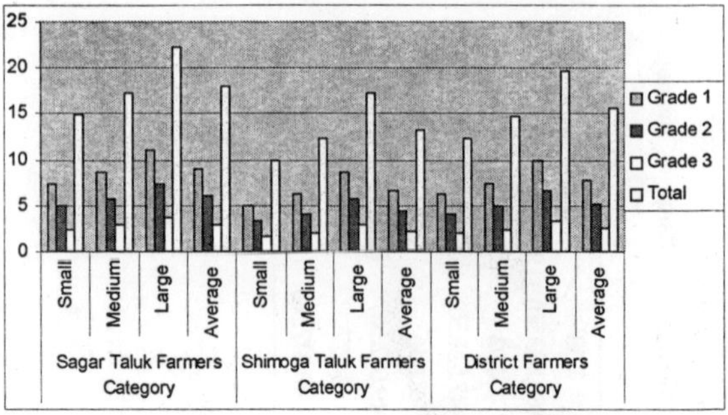
25
20
15
10
5
0
Grade 1
Grade 2
Grade 3
Total
Small
Medium
Large
Average
Small
Medium
Large
Average
Small
Medium
Large
Average
Sagar Taluk Farmers Category
Shimoga Taluk Farmers Category
District Farmers Category

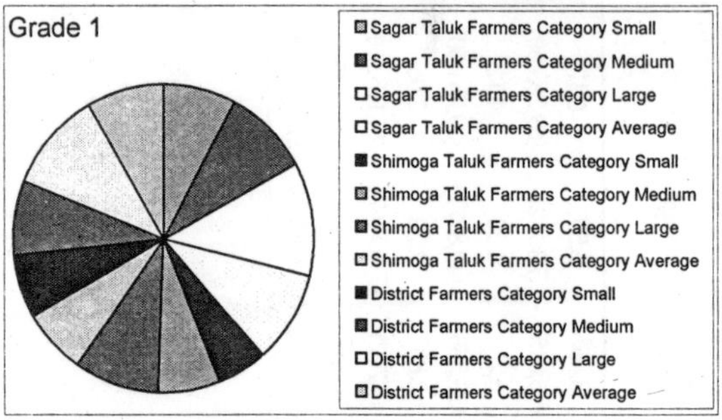
Grade 1
Sagar Taluk Farmers Category Small
Sagar Taluk Farmers Category Medium
Sagar Taluk Farmers Category Large
Sagar Taluk Farmers Category Average
Shimoga Taluk Farmers Category Small
Shimoga Taluk Farmers Category Medium
Shimoga Taluk Farmers Category Large
Shimoga Taluk Farmers Category Average
District Farmers Category Small
District Farmers Category Medium
District Farmers Category Large
District Farmers Category Average

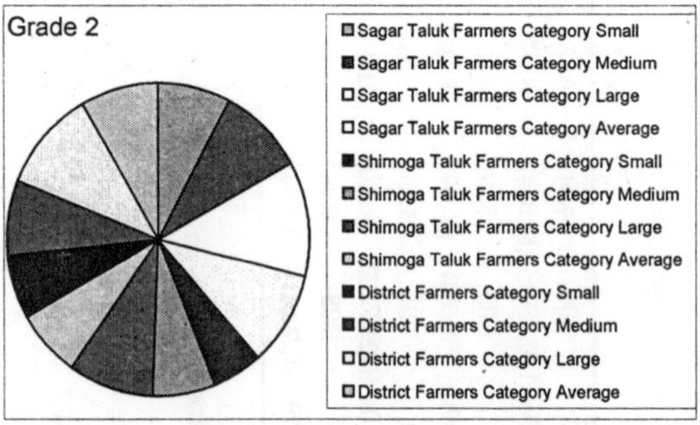
Grade 2
Sagar Taluk Farmers Category Small
Sagar Taluk Farmers Category Medium
Sagar Taluk Farmers Category Large
Sagar Taluk Farmers Category Average
Shimoga Taluk Farmers Category Small
Shimoga Taluk Farmers Category Medium
Shimoga Taluk Farmers Category Large
Shimoga Taluk Farmers Category Average
District Farmers Category Small
District Farmers Category Medium
District Farmers Category Large
District Farmers Category Average

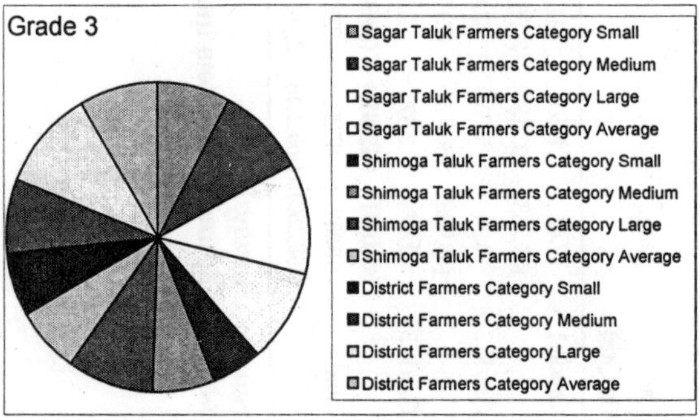
Grade 3
Sagar Taluk Farmers Category Small
Sagar Taluk Farmers Category Medium
Sagar Taluk Farmers Category Large
Sagar Taluk Farmers Category Average
Shimoga Taluk Farmers Category Small
Shimoga Taluk Farmers Category Medium
Shimoga Taluk Farmers Category Large
Shimoga Taluk Farmers Category Average
District Farmers Category Small
District Farmers Category Medium
District Farmers Category Large
District Farmers Category Average

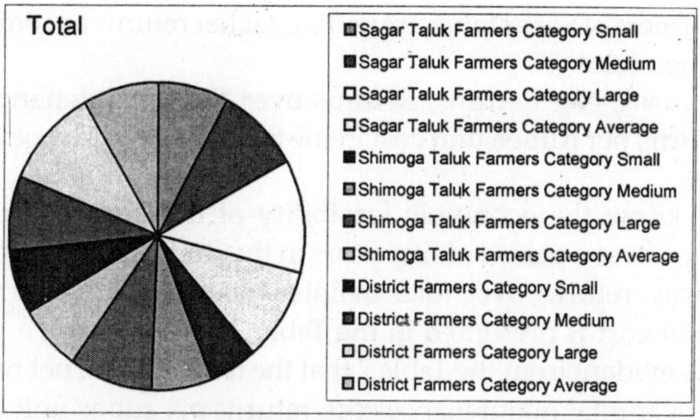

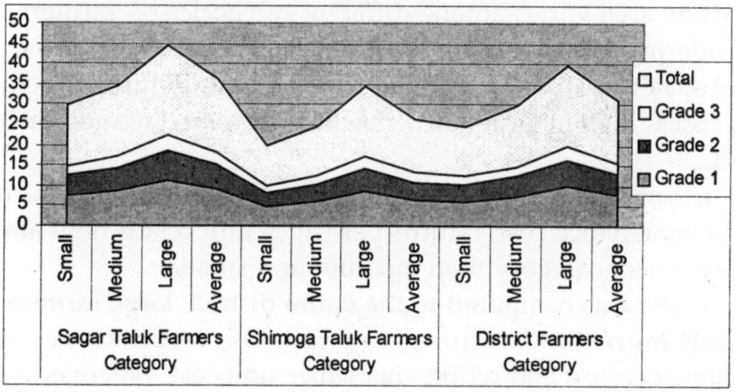

Inspite of declining returns in the third stage as usual the large farmers are getting comparatively higher returns than the medium and small farmers in the study area, because of their high investment and better farm management.

In both the taluks large farmers are getting more returns for hectare as compared to the medium and small category of farmers.

The talukwise comparison as observed in the first and second stages here also the farmers of Sagar taluk are getting more returns as compared to Shimoga taluk and overall for the study area. It is due to high investment, better management, eco-friendly nature of the crop and systematic and planned cultivation practices adopted.

The taluk wise comparison shows that the Sagar taluk has proved to be more efficient in areca cultivation as compared to Shimoga taluk and even the district.

It is also clear from the Table 6 that large farmers are getting more returns in the entire district and in both the taluks. Between the taluks farmers of Sagar taluk are getting higher returns as compared to Shimoga taluk.

Total Returns, Net Returns, Returns over Total maintenance cost and Returns per Rupee unit cost in the Study area over a period of 50 years

To know the economic feasibility of investment arecanut cultivation over a period of fifty years in the study area, total return, net returns, returns over total maintenance cost and returns per rupee unit cost is presented in the Table 7.

It is evident from the Table 7 that the total returns, net returns, returns over total maintenance cost, returns per rupee unit cost in the study area varies among different categories of farmers.

Considering the district as a whole, that the Total returns, Net returns,. Returns over total maintenance cost, Returns per rupee unit cost is high in large farmers when compared to medium and small.

In both the taluks, the total returns, net returns, returns over total maintenance cost, returns per rupee unit cost is high among large farmers category than medium and small.

Further as compared to the entire district, large farmers are getting more total returns, net returns, returns over total maintenance cost and returns per rupee unit cost. Whereas in case of the medium and small farmer's category the total returns, net returns, returns over total maintenance cost and returns per rupee unit cost is less.

The talukwise comparison shows that in Sagar taluk total returns, net returns, returns over total maintenance cost and returns per rupee unit cost is much above the overall position in the study area, whereas in Shimoga taluk it is very much less than the overall district average.The above analysis reveals that total returns, net returns, returns over total maintenance cost, returns per rupee unit cost is highest in Sagar taluk as compared to Shimoga taluk and also for the entire study area.

Returns of Inter crop in the First Stage.

Considering the long pre-bearing age of 6 to 7 years (i.e.,the gestation period) the farmers in the study area will grow intercrop to get some subsidiary income from intercrop and also as a shade to the tender areca palm which will improve the quality and condition of sub-soil-moisture.

Table 7
Average Annual Per Ha Total Returns, Net Returns, Returns Over Total Maintenance Cost and Returns per Rupee unit Cost in the Study Area Over a Period of 50 Years (in Rs.)

Particulars	*Sagar Taluk Farmers Category*				*Shimoga Taluk Farmers Category*				*District Farmers Category*			
	Small	*Medium*	*Large*	*Average*	*Small*	*Medium*	*Large*	*Average*	*Small*	*Medium*	*Large*	*Average*
Total Returns	4,06,537	4,63,194	5,79,745	4,83,158.67	2,80,389	3,32,242	4,48,798	3,53,809.67	3.43.463	3.97.718	5,14,271.50	4,18,484.17
Net Returns	1,27,679.97	1,71,216.78	2,19,175.72	1,72,690.89	46,885	85,579.95	1,35,003	89,155.99	87,282.49	1,28,398.27	1,77089.36	1,30923.41
Returns over TMC	1,82,308.60	2,32,133.62	3,42,543.58	2,52,328.60	1,04,341.26	1,50,238.95	2,62,809.51	1,72,463.24	1,43,324.93	1,91,186.28	3,02,676.54	2,12,395.92
Returns per Re unit cost	1.46	1.59	1.61	1.56	1.20	1.35	1.43	1.33	1.34	1.48	1.53	1.45

Source: Survey Data .

Hence, it is worth to analyse the returns of intercrop to know how far the intercrop will help farmers economically. The returns of intercrop in the study area is presented in the Table 8.

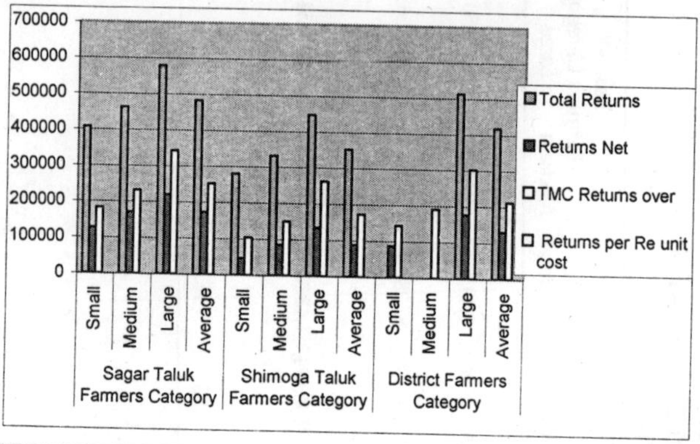

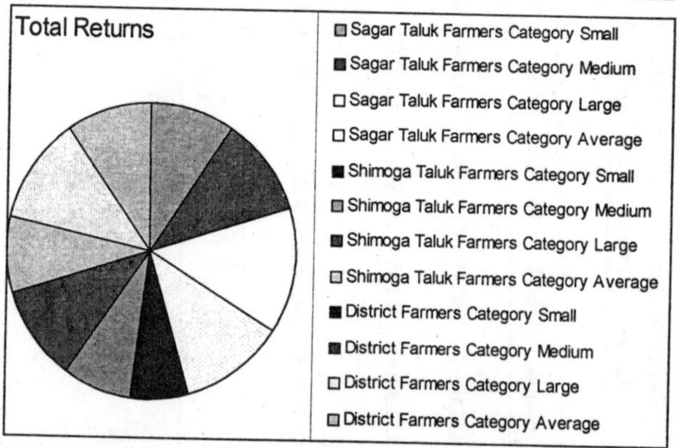

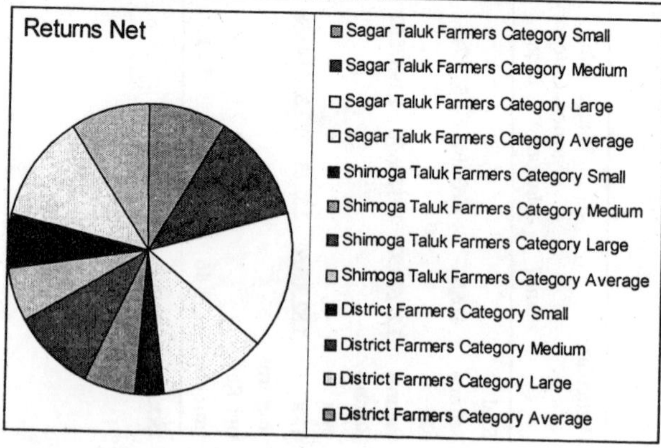

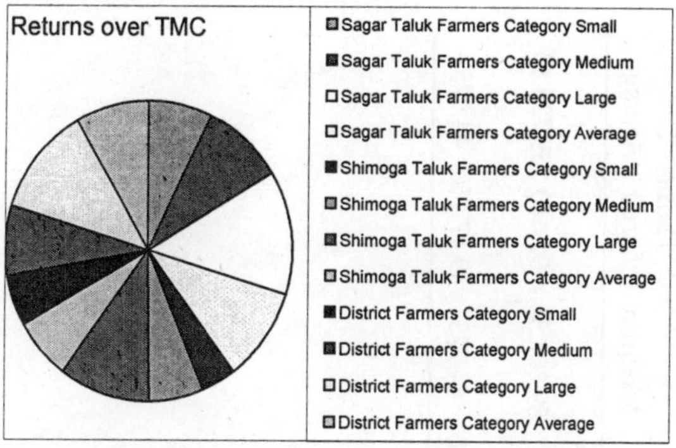

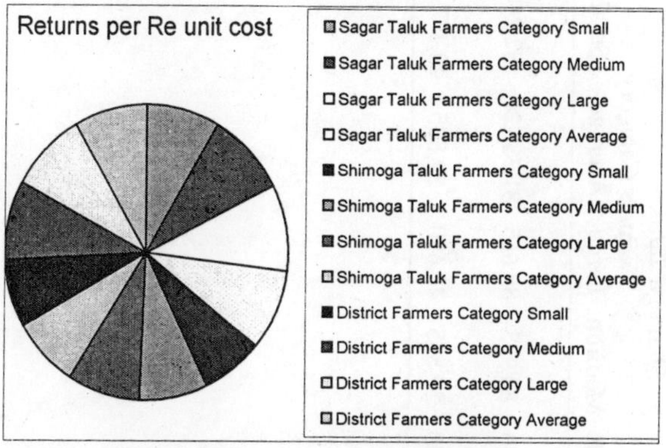

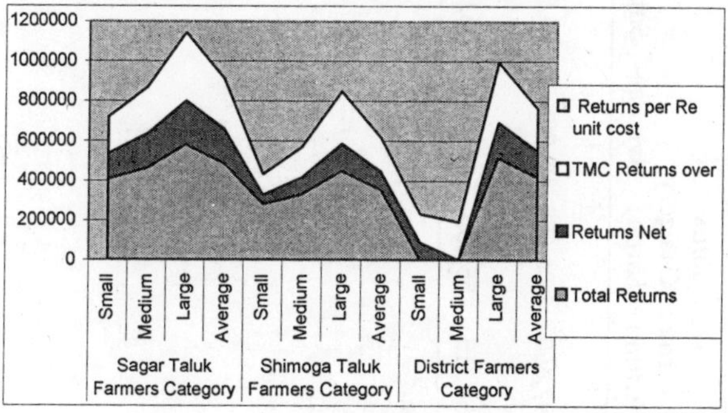

In the entire district the percentage variation of the returns from intercrop in between small and medium farmers is 8.59% while between medium and large farmers it is 9.35%.

In Sagar taluk the percentage variation of returns from intercrop between small and medium farmers is 8.57% where between medium and large farmers it is 9.21%.

Table 8
Average Per Hectare Returns of Intercrop (Banana) in the First Stage in the Study Area

Particulars	Sagar Taluk Farmers Category				Shimoga Taluk Farmers Category				District Farmers Category			
	Small	Medium	Large	Average	Small	Medium	Large	Average	Small	Medium	Large	Average
Total Returns	89,950	97,660	1,06,655	98,088.33	74,530	80,955	88,665	81,383.33	82,240	89,307.50	97,660	89,735.83
Net Returns	44,975	50,115	55,255	50,115	35,980	39,835	43,690	39,835	40,477.50	44,975	49,472.50	44,975

Source: Survey Data.

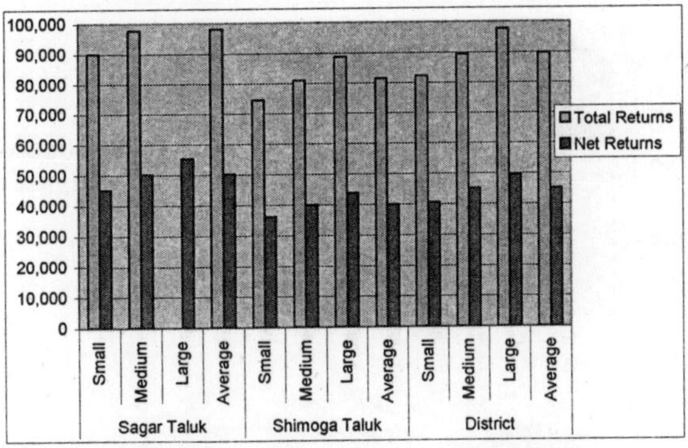

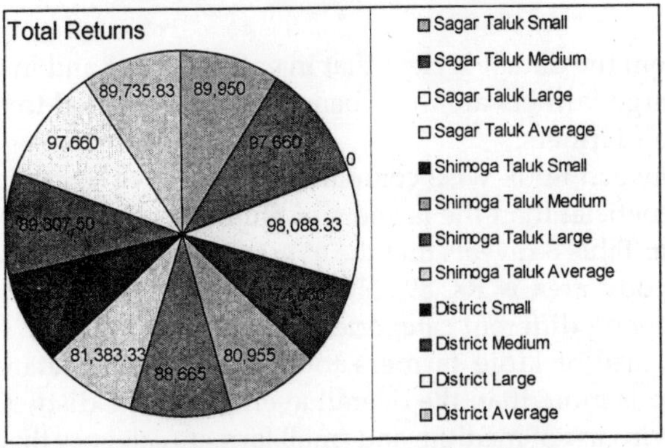

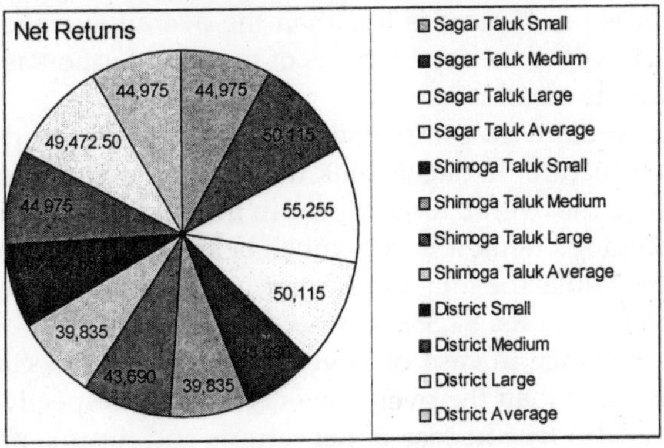

In Shimoga taluk the percentage variation of returns from intercrop between small and medium farmers is 8.62% while between medium and large farmers it is 9.52%.

Between Sagar and Shimoga taluks the percentage variation is 20.53%.

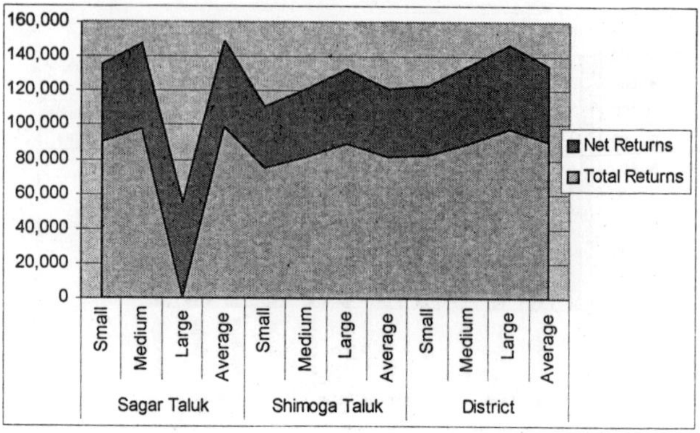

From the data it is clear that in entire district and in both the taluks large farmers are more beneficial as compared to medium and small farmers.

Between taluk wise comparison farmers of Sagar taluk are more beneficial than the farmers of Shimoga taluk.

The Table 8 reveals that the average total returns per hectare in the study area is Rs. 89,735.83. The total returns per hectare varies among different categories of farmers.

In case of large farmers total returns per hectare of the intercrop is more than the overall average for the district. Whereas in case of medium and small farmers category the average total returns per hectare is less than the overall average of total returns. However the total returns of medium farmers is slightly more than the small farmers.

The talukawise comparison of the total returns depicts a disturbing picture. In Sagar taluk the per hectare total returns is much above the overall total returns in the study area, whereas in case of Shimoga taluk it is very much below the overall position. In both the taluks the total returns per hectare in the study area is Rs. 98,088.33 and Rs. 81,383.33 respectively.

For instance in case of large farmers the per hectare total returns is more than the overall average for the respective taluks and this is also true in case of net returns and returns per rupee unit cost because of the higher investment, adaption of systematic cultivation of banana supplemented with better management.

Further it is clear from the data that the average per hectare total returns is highest in Sagar taluk and much less in Shimoga taluk as compared to entire study area due to higher

Table 9
Average Per Hectare Returns of Mixedcrop (Pepper/Cocoa) in the Second Stage in the Study Area

Particulars	Sagar Taluk Farmers Category				Shimoga Taluk Farmers Category				District Farmers Category			
	Small	Medium	Large	Average	Small	Medium	Large	Average	Small	Medium	Large	Average
Total Returns	68,160	86,380	1,05,560	87,033.33	45,500	63,900	87,000	65,466.67	56,830	75,140	96,780	76,250
Net Returns	39,760	52,445	66,600	52,935	24,780	35,500	49,980	36,753.33	32,270	43,972.50	58,290	44,844.17

Source: Survey Data

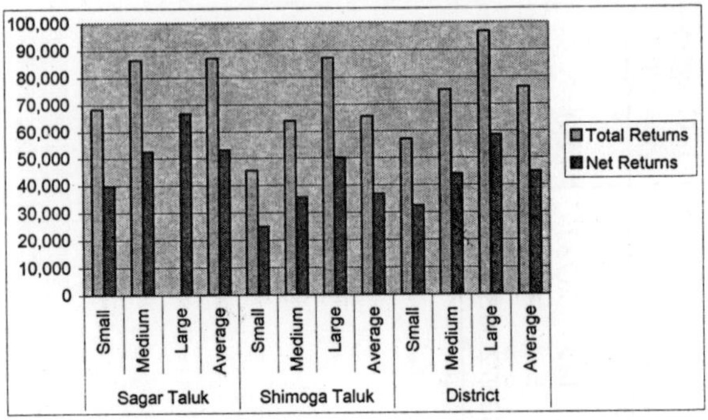

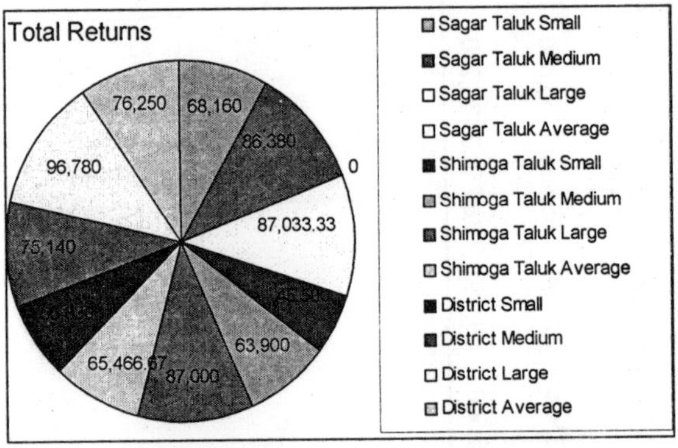

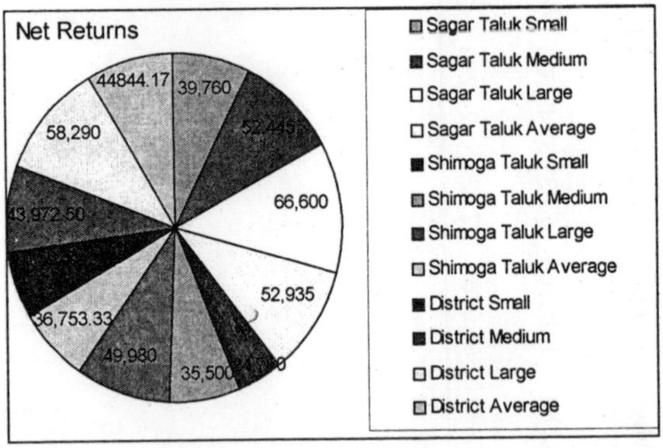

investment, planned and scientific cultivation practices with better management.

If the small and medium farmers in the study area in both the taluks invest little more and adopt scientific cultivation practices and vigilent farm management and proper marketing they can get substantial returns from intercrop.

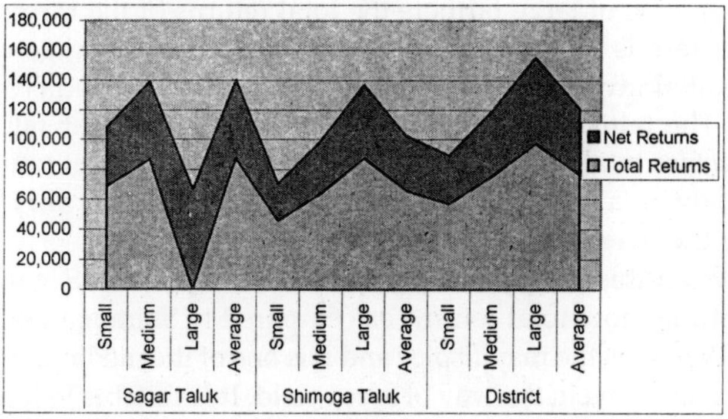

Returns of Mixed Crop in The Second Stage

Mixed crop is grown in the second stage in the study area. The farmers of Sagar taluk cultivate pepper while farmers of Shimoga taluk cultivate cocoa as mixed crops respectively.

Mixed crop brings additional income to farmers and it is necessary to examine the returns from this crop so as to see which farmers' category and also which taluk is more benefited in the study area.

The Returns of mixed crop in the study area is presented in the Table 9.

In the entire district the percentage variation of the returns between small and medium farmers is 32.22% while between medium and large farmers it is 28.80%.

In Sagar taluk the percentage variation of the returns between small and medium farmers is 26.73% while between medium and large farmers it is 22.20%.

In Shimoga taluk the percentage variation of returns between small and medium farmers is 40.44% while between medium and large farmers is 36.15%.

Between Sagar and Shimoga taluks percentage variation is 32.94%.

It is evident from the above analysis that large farmers are more beneficial in mixed crop cultivation as compared to medium and small in the entire district as well as in both the taluks.

Between the taluks farmers of Sagar taluk are more beneficial as compared to farmers of Shimoga taluks.

It is clear from the Table 9 that the average returns per hectare in the study area is Rs. 76,250. The total returns per hectare varies among different categories of farmers.

In case of large farmers the total returns of the mixed crop per hectare is more as compared to the district average due to substantial investment and management on the mixed crop.

The taluk-wise comparison shows that in Sagar taluk the per hectare total returns is much above the overall total returns in the study area. Whereas in case of Shimoga taluk it is very much below the overall position.

From this it may be concluded that farmers in Sagar taluk are getting more total returns as compared to Shimoga taluk.

Pepper is the major spice and it is one of the medicinal crops. It does not come in the way of areca yield. It is suitable to local soil and climatic conditions, that is why farmers of Sagar taluk are giving equal importance to the cultivation of pepper and because of efficient management they are getting remunerative price as compared to farmers of Shimoga taluk.

Mixed crop is generally grown in the second stage. Hence, it is worth analysing the income received from mixed crop so as to see to what extent it helps the farmers in recovering the cost of cultivation incurred on areca garden during that stage. In other words, to what extent the income from mixed crop can subsidise the cost of cultivation on areca garden during second stage. This kind of analysis will throw light in the economic benefit of cultivating mixed crop in the study area.

The District

For the district as a whole the net returns received from mixed crop among small farmers is Rs.32,270 which is about 78.08 percent of the total cost incurred on arecanut cultivation in the second stage.

In the case of medium farmers category the net returns received from the mixed crop is Rs.43,972.50 which is more than the total cost of cultivation incurred on arecanut cultivation in the second stage.

In case of large farmers category the net returns received from the mixed crop is Rs. 58,290.00 which is very much higher than the cost of cultivation of arecanut.

The overall position for the district shows that the net returns received from the mixed crop is Rs. 44,844.17 which fully covers the entire cost of cultivation during second stage.

From this it may be concluded that the income received from mixed crop gives lot of relief to farmers in the study area. Therefore, we suggest that the farmers should be encouraged to go in for mixed crop in areca gardens.

Sagar Taluk

Likewise is Sagar taluk the net returns received from the mixed crop among small farmers category is Rs. 39,780.00 which is about 84.41 percent of the total cost incurred on areca cultivation in the second stage.

In case of medium farmers category the net returns received from the mixed crop is Rs. 52,445 which is more than the total cost of cultivation incurred on arecanut cultivation in the second stage.

In case of large farmers category the net returns received from the mixed crop is Rs. 66,600.00 which is very much higher than the cost of cultivation of arecanut.

The overall position for Sagar taluk shows that the net returns received from the mixed crop is Rs. 52,935 which fully covers the entire cost of cultivation during the second stage.

From this it may be concluded that the income from mixed crop gives a lot of relief to farmers in the study area.

Shimoga Taluk

While in Shimoga taluk among small farmers category the net returns received from the mixed crop is Rs. 24,780.00 which is about 69.73 per cent of the total cost incurred on arecanut cultivation, in the second stage.

In case of medium farmers category the net returns received from the mixed crop is Rs. 35,500.00, which is about 94.08 per cent of the total cost incurred on arecanut cultivation in the second stage.

In case of large farmers category the net returns received from the mixed crop is Rs. 49,980.00 which is very much higher than the total cost of cultivation of arecanut in the second stage.

The overall position for Shimoga taluk shows that the net returns received from the mixed crop is Rs. 36,753.33 which is about 98.44 per cent of the total cost incurred on the arecanut cultivation in the second stage.

From this it may be concluded that, the income received from the mixed crop gives relief to farmers in the study area. Hence we suggest that small and medium farmers category should be encourage to go for intensive cultivation of mixed crop so as to meet the expenses incurred on areca cultivation in the second stage.

Table 10

Evaluation of Investments in Areca Garden in the Study Area

Particulars	Sagar Taluk Farmers Category				Shimoga Taluk Farmers Category				District Farmers Category			
	Small	Medium	Large	Average	Small	Medium	Large	Average	Small	Medium	Large	Average
NPV	4,11,251.5	4,44,593.3	5,20,944.7	4,58,928.83	3,32,882.8	3,74,049.4	4.65190.9	3.90,707.7	3,72,067.15	4,09,321.35	4,93,067.80	4,24,818.77
IRR	29.78	30.06	31.78	30.54	26.48	27.06	27.70	27.08	28.13	28.56	29.74	28.81
BCR	2.50	2.66	2.76	2.64	2.27	2.37	2.42	2.35	2.38	2.51	2.59	2.49
PBP	8.3	8	7.9	8.06	8.6	8.5	8.1	8.4	8.4	8.2	8	8.2

Source: Survey Data.

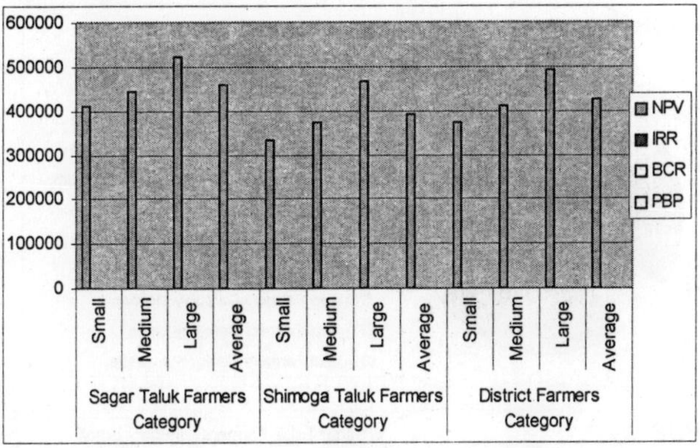

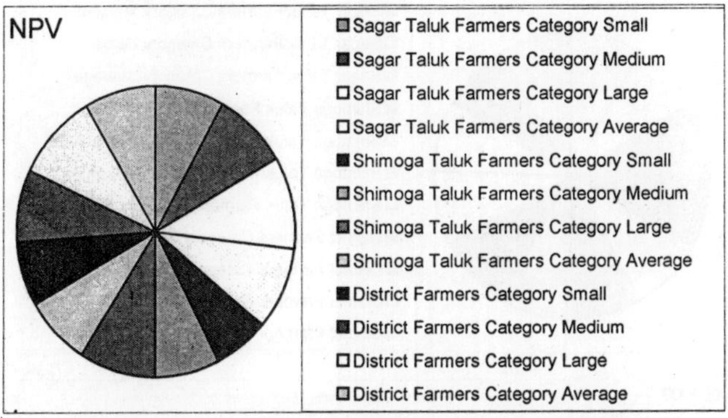

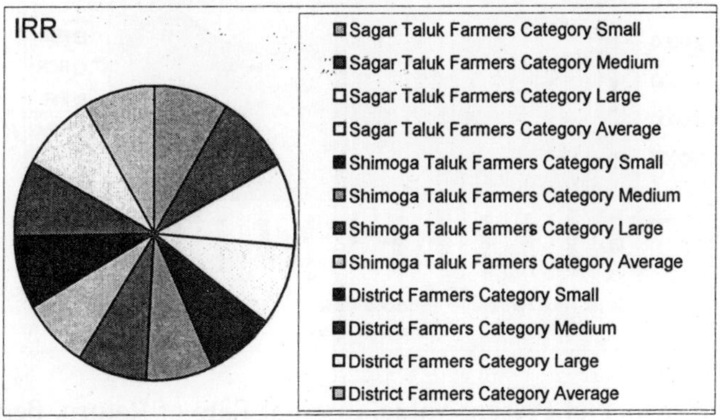

Evaluation of Investment in Areca Gardens

To know the economic feasibility of investment in areca gardens among various categories of farmers in the study area it is necessary to evaluate the returns on investment made on areca gardens.

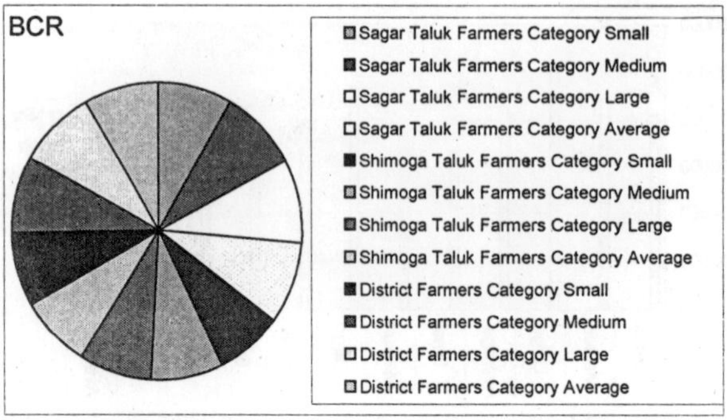

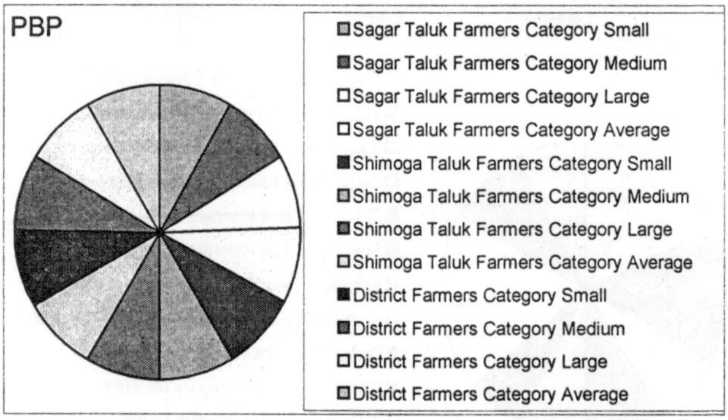

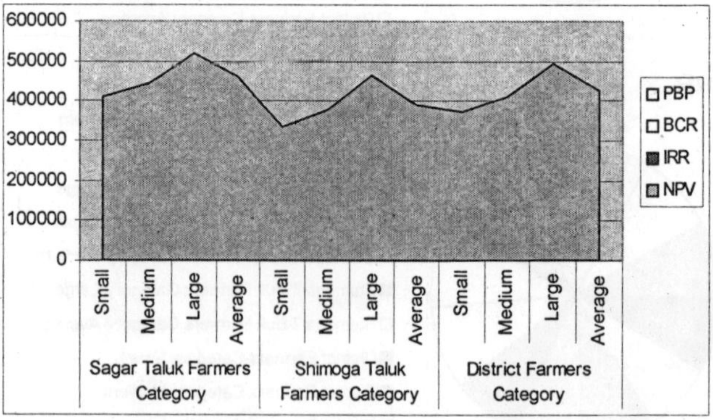

Hence, Net Present Value, Internal Rate of Return, Benefit-Cost Ratio (B:C ratio) and pay back period etc. were calculated. For calculating NPV, IRR, B: C Ratio and Pay back period etc. the establishment and maintenance costs, cost of cultivation of intercrop/mixed crop and total returns of areca and returns of intercrop/mixed crop are taken into account.

The analysis is made on per hectare basis for each size groups, this is represented in the Table 10.

Net Present Value (NPV)

It is the present value of net benefits of a project discounted at the opportunity cost of capital. The criterian is to assess the present net worth of accrued benefits over costs.

The NPV varies among different categories of farmers.

Within the farmer's category large farmers ranked first followed by medium and small in both the taluks, in the study area which proves objectives and the hypothesis made in the present study.

Between Sagar and Shimoga taluks NPV is more among farmers of Sagar taluk as compared to farmers of Shimoga taluk and even more than the overall average for the district.

The NPV is positive in all the categories of farmers which clearly indicates the investment in areca garden is feasible proposition.

Internal Rate of Return (IRR)

This criterion measures the rate of return that can be earned by investing in areca gardens. The investment and consequent returns are considered in this criterion. This technique has been indicated as important and scores on other techniques of evaluation since it considers the reinvestment opportunities which are absent in other techniques.

In the present study the internal rate of return from areca garden from the 6th and 7th year of the first stage till the end of the second stage is increasing year by year but it is declining in the third stage. IRR has proved that investment made on areca garden is worth irrespective of the category of farmers and found to be still better for large farmers.

However, in all the size group of areca gardens in both the taluks of the study area investment is found to be feasible since the internal rate is more than 15% which is the rate of return expected in agriculture as per the specification of the world bank.[7]

Thus the investment in areca gardens is found feasible with priority to large gardens as compared to medium and small gardens. In the study area which proves the objectives and hypothesis of the present study.

Table 11
Mandays of Employment generated in Arecanut Gardens in Various Categories of Farmers in Shimoga District

Particulars	*Sagar Taluk* Farmers Category				*Shimoga Taluk* Farmers Category				*District* Farmers Category			
	Small	*Medium*	*Large*	*Average*	*Small*	*Medium*	*Large*	*Average*	*Small*	*Medium*	*Large*	*Average*
First Stage												
Emplyment												
in Mandays	1,610	1,650	1,700	1,653.33	1,480	1,509	1,539	1,509.33	1,545	1,579.50	1,619.50	1,581.33
Value (Rs)	96,600	99,00	1,02,000	99,200	88,800	90,540	92,340	90,560	92,700	94,770	97,170	94,879.80
Second Stage												
Emplyment												
in Mandays	585	600	604	596.33	490	515	518	507.67	537.50	557.50	561	552
Value (Rs)	35,100	36,000	36,240	35,780	29,400	30,900	31,080	30,460	32,250	33,450	33,660	33,120
Third Stage												
Emplyment												
in Mandays	440	450	453	447.67	370	375	384	375	405	412.50	418.50	412
Value (Rs)	26,400	27,000	27,180	26,860	22,200	22,500	23,040	22,580	24,300	24,750	25,110	24,720

Source : Survey Data

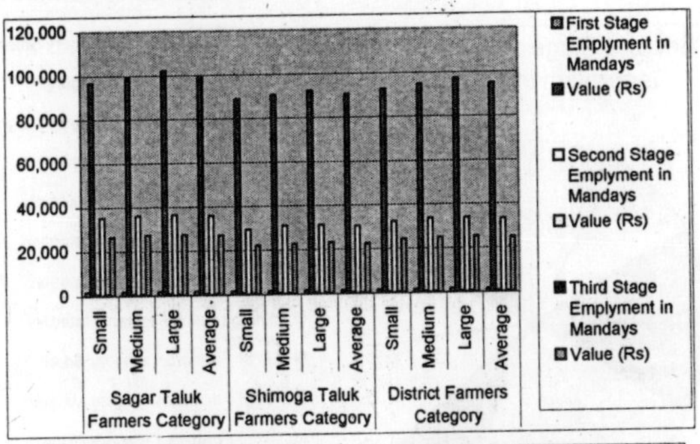

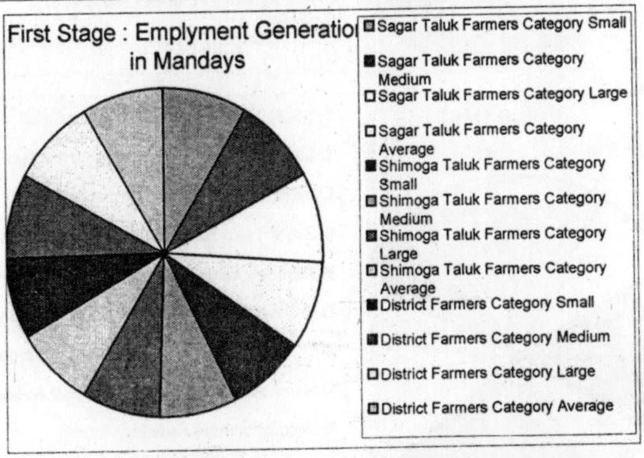

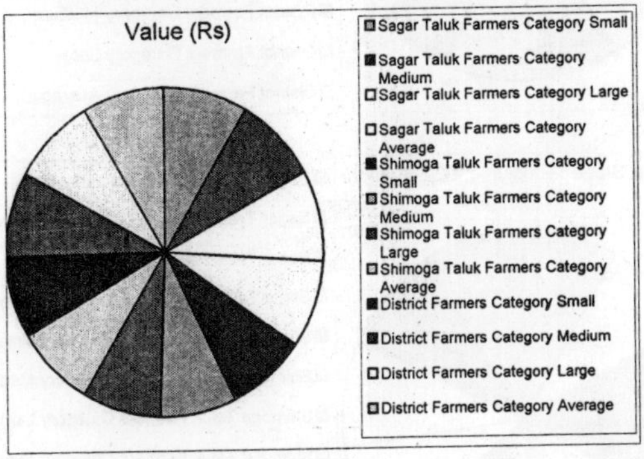

Benefit-Cost Ratio (B:C Ratio)

This criterion indicates the returns per-rupee invested in the areca garden. The benefit cost ratio is high for large farmers as compared to other categories of farmers in both the taluks in the study area.

This clearly shows that investment on large gardens is more profitable than the remaining size groups, which proves the objectives and hypothesis of the present study.

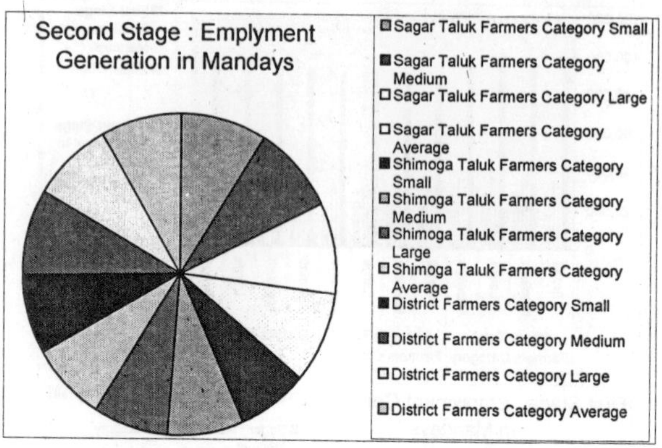

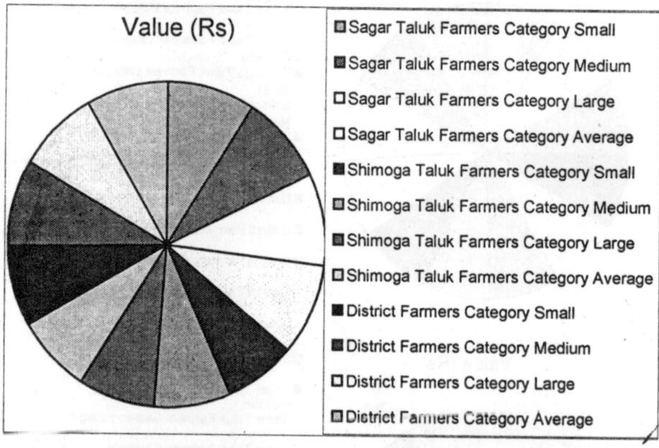

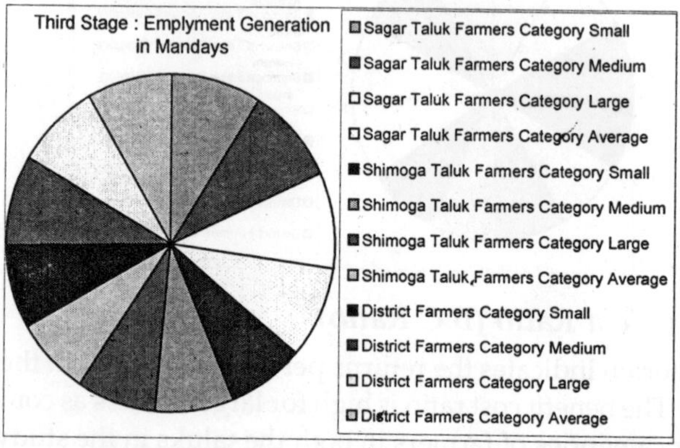

However since all the size groups had a benefit cost ratio of more than unity it can be concluded that the investment in areca gardens is financially sound and economically feasible.

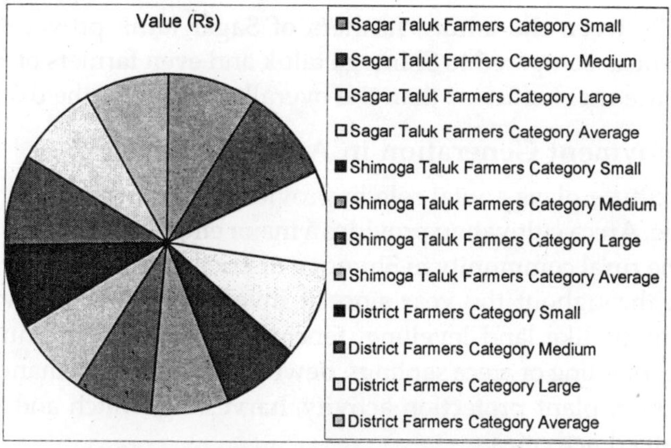

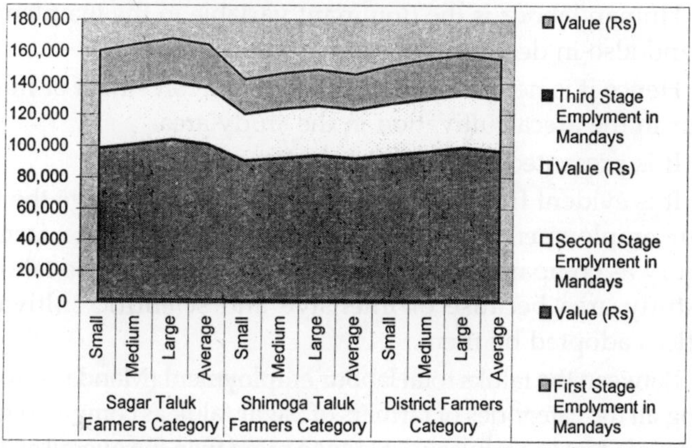

Between the taluks, Sagar taluk has proved to be more beneficial as compared to Shimoga taluk and it is more than the overall average for the district.

Pay-back Period (PBP)

The period taken to repay the initial investment in establishment of the areca garden.

It is evident from the data presented in the Table 10 that large farmers in both the taluks proved to be more efficient as compared to medium and small farmers in the study area as regards getting back the cash benefits from the initial investment made on the areca garden, evidently it proves the objectives and the hypothesis made in the present study.

Between the taluks, farmers of Sagar taluk proved to be efficient as compared to Shimoga taluk and even farmers of Sagar taluk are more efficient than the overall average for the district.

Employment Generation in Areca Gardens

Agriculture plays a vital role in providing employment for rural people. Areca cultivation provides a major employment generation for the rural community in Shimoga district. The garden provides work throughout the year since it involves various cultivation operations like land levelling, fencing, pit preparation, nursery rising, planting of areca saplings, deweeding, mulching, manuring, irrigation, plant protection activity, harvesting, watch and ward and allied activities.

Human labour is the dominant variable in the maintenance cost and also in determining the returns of arecanut.

Hence it is necessary to evaluate the involvement of human labour in the areca cultivation in the study area.

It is presented in the Table 11.

It is evident from the Table 11 that in the first stage the total labour employment in mandays is more among large farmer's category as compared to medium and small in both the taluks of the study area because of intensive and scientific cultivation practices adopted by them.

Between the taluks total labour employment (Mandays) is high among all the categories of farmers of Sagar taluk as compared to the farmers of Shimoga taluk and it is even more than the overall average of the district due to intensive and planned cultivation activities.

As compared to the first stage in second and third stages in the study area human labour employed is less because only maintenance of the areca garden will be followed. By and large it may be concluded that arecanut cultivation is more labour intensive in nature. This will help in solving the problem of rural unemployment in the study area. Hence, encouraging the farmers in arecanut cultivation will serve as an effective step in solving the problem of unemployment in the study area.

Correlation co-efficient of Dependent variables (Returns of Areca, Intercrop/Mixed crop, Establishment and Maintenance Cost, Cost of Cultivation of Intercrop/Mixed crop among various farmers' category in Sagar Taluk.

Statistical Analysis

Table 12
Correlation Coefficient of Dependent Variables (Returns of Areca, Inter Crop/mixed Crop, EC, MC, CCIC/CCMC of Small Farmers of Sagar Taluk)

Sl. No.	*Small farmers*	*Returns of intercrop/ mixed crop*	*Returns of Arecanut*	*Cost of Cultivation of intercrop/ mixed crop*	*Establishment cost*	*Maintenance cost*
1.	Returns of inter crop	1.00				
2.	Returns of Arecanut	0.55	1.00			
3.	Cost of Cultivation of intercrop/ mixed crop	-0.47**	-0.78**	1.00		
4.	Establishment cost	-0.84**	-0.91**	-	1.00	
5.	Maintenance cost	-0.98**	-0.42**	-	0.75**	1.00

** Indicate significant at 1%.
Source: Tables 5.1,5.5,5.9,5.13,5.14,6.1,6.3,6.5,6.8,6.9.

Table 13
Correlation Coefficient of Dependent Variables (Returns of Areca, Inter Crop/mixed Crop, EC, MC, CCIC/CCMC of Medium Farmers of Sagar Taluk)

Sl. No.	*Medium farmers*	*Returns of intercrop/ mixed crop*	*Returns of Arecanut*	*Cost of Cultivation of intercrop/ mixed crop*	*Establishment cost*	*Maintenance cost*
1	Returns of inter crop	1.00				
2	Returns of Arecanut	0.50	1.00			
3	Cost of Cultivation of intercrop/ mixed crop	-0.97**	-0.72**	1.00		
4	Establishment cost	-0.50**	-0.98**	-	1.00	
5	Maintenance cost	-0.52**	-0.39**	-	0.26**	1.00

** Indicate significant at 1%.
Source: Tables 5.1,5.5,5.9,5.13,5.14,6.1,6.3,6.5,6.8,6.9.

Table 14
Correlation Coefficient of Dependent Variables (Returns of Areca, Inter Crop/mixed Crop, EC, MC, CCIC/CCMC of Large Farmers of Sagar Taluk)

Sl. No.	*Large farmers*	*Returns of intercrop/ mixed crop*	*Returns of Arecanut*	*Cost of Cultivation of intercrop/ mixed crop*	*Establishment cost*	*Maintenance cost*
1.	Returns of inter crop	1.00				
2.	Returns of Arecanut	1.00**	1.00			
3.	Cost of Cultivation of intercrop/ mixed crop	-0.80**	-0.53**	1.00		
4.	Establishment cost	-0.99**	-0.96**	-	1.00	
5.	Maintenance cost	-1.00**	-0.93**	-	0.99**	1.00

** Indicate significant at 1%.
Source: Tables 5.1,5.5,5.9,5.13,5.14,6.1,6.3,6.5,6.8,6.9.

It is evident from the data presented in the Tables 12, 13 and 14 that, in all the categories of farmers the cost of cultivation of intercrop/mixed crop is highly negatively correlated with returns of intercrop/mixed crop and also with the returns of arecanut at 1% level of significance. This indicates that over a period of time cost of cultivation declines as the returns increase.

In all the categories of farmers the returns of intercrop/mixed crop is highly negatively correlated with all the variables in the equation with 1 % level of significance except returns of arecanut. Because, banana as an intercrop increases the returns of arecanut as it will improve the sub soil moisture and also helpful to increase the pH level of the soil.

Among all the categories of farmers returns of arecanut is highly negatively correlated with all the variables in the equation at 1% level of significance except maintenance cost for small and medium farmers their correlation is low negative. Because, over a period of time cost of cultivation of arecanut declines but at the same time returns of areca increase.

Establishment cost is highly negatively correlated with returns of intercrop/mixed crop and also with returns of arecanut at 1%

level of significance among all the categories of farmers. Because, in the areca gardens initial investment is high but in the second and third stage the component of establishment cost is very much negligible in the total cost. Establishment cost declines substantially over a period of time.

Among all the categories of farmers, maintenance cost is highly negatively correlated with returns of intercrop/mixed crop and also with the returns of arecanut at 1 % level of significance. The reason is, over a period of time maintenance cost declines substantially stage by stage but the returns of intercrop/mixed crop and returns of arecanut increases considerably upto the end of second stage. In the third stage returns of arecanut slightly declines. Due to this reason maintenance cost is perfectly negatively correlated with returns of intercrop/mixed crop and also with returns of arecanut.

Among all the categories of farmers the maintenance cost is also highly positively correlated with establishment cost at 1 %

Table 15

Correlation Coefficient of Dependent variables (returns of areca, intercrop/mixed crop, EC, MC, CCIC/CCMC of Small farmers of Shimoga taluk)

Sl. No.	*Small farmers*	*Returns of intercrop/ mixed crop*	*Returns of Arecanut*	*Cost of Cultivation of intercrop/ mixed crop*	*Establi-shment cost*	*Main-tenance cost*
1.	Returns of inter crop	1.00				
2.	Returns of Arecanut	0.22**	1.00			
3.	Cost of Cultivation of intercrop/ mixed crop	-0.99**	-1.00**	1.00		
4.	Establish-ment cost	-0.99**	-0.08**	-	1.00	
5.	Maintenance cost	-0.99**	-0.66**	-	0.80**	1.00

** Significant at 1%.

Source: Tables 5.1, 5.5, 5.9, 5.13, 5.14, 6.1, 6.3, 6.5, 6.8, 6.9

Table 16
Correlation Coefficient of Dependent Variables (Returns of Areca, Intercrop/mixed Crop), EC, MC, CCIC/CCMC of Medium Farmers of Shimoga Taluk

Sl. No.	*Medium farmers*	*Returns of intercrop/ mixed crop*	*Returns of Arecanut*	*Cost of Cultivation of intercrop/ mixed crop*	*Establi- shment cost*	*Main- tenance cost*
1.	Returns of inter crop	1.00				
2.	Returns of Arecanut	0.99**	1.00			
3.	Cost of Cultivation of intercrop/ mixed crop	-0.98**	-0.99**	1.00		
4.	Establish- ment cost	-0.99**	-0.28**	-	1.00	
5.	Maintenance cost	-0.99**	-0.15**	-	0.78**	1.00

** Significant at 1%.
Source: Tables 5.1, 5.5, 5.9, 5.13, 5.14, 6.1, 6.3, 6.5, 6.8, 6.9.

Table 17
Correlation Coefficient of Dependent variables (Returns of Areca, Intercrop/mixed Crop), EC, MC, CCIC/CCMC of Large Farmers of Shimoga Taluk

Sl. No.	*Large farmers*	*Returns of intercrop/ mixed crop*	*Returns of Arecanut*	*Cost of Cultivation of intercrop/ mixed crop*	*Establi- shment cost*	*Main- tenance cost*
1.	Returns of inter crop	1.00				
2.	Returns of Arecanut	1.00**	1.00			
3.	Cost of Cultivation of intercrop/ mixed crop	-1.00**	-0.98**	1.00		
4.	Establish- ment cost	-1.00**	-1.00**	-	1.00	
5.	Maintenance cost	-0.56**	-0.50	-	0.49	1.00

** Significant at 1%.
Source: Tables 5.1, 5.5, 5.9, 5.13, 5.14, 6.1, 6.3, 6.5, 6.8, 6.9.

level of significance. Hence maintenance cost has direct relationship with establishment cost but the relation is inverse with respect to returns of intercrop/mixed crop and also with the returns of arecanut.

Correlation co-efficient of Dependent variable (Returns of Arecanut, Returns of Intercrop/mixed crop) Maintenance cost and Establishment cost, cost of cultivation of intercrop/mixed crop of various farmers' categories in Shimoga taluk.

It is evident from the data presented in the Tables 15, 16 and 17 that the returns of intercrop/mixed crop is highly negatively correlated with all the variables in the equation at 1 % level of significance (among all the categories of farmers) except for returns of arecanut, which has highly positive correlation in case of medium and large farmers but low positive correlation for small farmers.

As the intercrop/mixed crop helps to increase the yield of areca palm, it is positively correlated with returns of arecanut at 1 % level of significance.

Among all the categories of farmers cost of cultivation of intercrop/mixed crop is negatively correlated with returns of intercrop/mixed crop and with returns of arecanut at 1 % level of significance because over a period of time cost declines and simultaneously returns increase.

Among all the categories of farmers returns of arecanut is negatively correlated with all the variables in the equation at 1 % level of significance because, over a period of time the cost declines at the same time returns increase.

Whereas establishment cost is positively correlated with the maintenance cost at 1% level of significance among all the categories of farmers because in each and every stage there is direct relation between the establishment and maintenance cost.

Among all the categories of farmers maintenance cost is negatively correlated with returns of intercrop/mixed crop and also with returns of arecanut at 1 % level of significance. Because, the cost of maintenance made on areca garden declines gradually at the same time areca yield per hectare increases.

Correlation coefficient of Dependent variables, Returns of Arecanut, Returns of Intercrop/Mixed crop, Maintenance cost and Establishment cost and Cost of Cultivation of Intercrop/ Mixed crop in Shimoga District.

Table 18
Correlation Coefficient of Dependent Variables (Returns of Areca, Intercrop/mixed crop), EC, MC, CCIC/CCMC of Small Farmers of Shimoga District

Sl. No.	*Small farmers*	*Returns of intercrop/ mixed crop*	*Returns of Arecanut*	*Cost of Cultivation of intercrop/ mixed crop*	*Establi-shment cost*	*Main-tenance cost*
1.	Returns of inter crop	1.00				
2.	Returns of Arecanut	0.67**	1.00			
3.	Cost of Cultivation of intercrop/ mixed crop	-0.47**	-0.53**	1.00		
4.	Establish-ment cost	-0.82**	-0.21*	-	1.00	
5.	Maintenance cost	-0.48**	-0.58**	-	0.58**	1.00

** Significant at 1%.
Source: Tables 5.1, 5.5, 5.9, 5.13, 5.14, 6.1, 6.3, 6.5, 6.8, 6.9)

Table 19
Correlation Coefficient of Dependent variables (Returns of Areca, Intercrop/mixed Crop), EC, MC, CCIC/CCMC of Medium Farmers of Shimoga District

Sl. No.	*Medium farmers*	*Returns of intercrop/ mixed crop*	*Returns of Arecanut*	*Cost of Cultivation of intercrop/ mixed crop*	*Establi-shment cost*	*Main-tenance cost*
1.	Returns of inter crop	1.00				
2.	Returns of Arecanut	0.20**	1.00			
3.	Cost of Cultivation of intercrop/ mixedcrop	-0.97**	-0.72**	1.00		
4.	Establish-ment cost	-0.67**	-0.50**	-	1.00	
5.	Maintenance cost	-0.49**	-0.52**	-	0.36**	1.00

** Significant at 1%.
Source: Tables 5.1, 5.5, 5.9, 5.13, 5.14, 6.1, 6.3, 6.5, 6.8, 6.9.

Table 20
Correlation Coefficient of Dependent variables (Returns of Areca, Intercrop/mixed Crop), EC, MC, CCIC/CCMC of Large farmers of Shimoga District

Sl. No.	*Large farmers*	*Returns of intercrop/ mixed crop*	*Returns of Arecanut*	*Cost of Cultivation of intercrop/ mixed crop*	*Establi-shment cost*	*Main-tenance cost*
1.	Returns of inter crop	1.00				
2.	Returns of Arecanut	0.57**	1.00			
3.	Cost of Cultivation of intercrop/ mixedcrop	-0.80**	-0.78**	1.00		
4.	Establish-ment cost	-0.14**	-0.51**	-	1.00	
5.	Maintenance cost	-0.49*	-0.68**	-	0.32	1.00

** Significant at 1%.
Source: Tables 5.1, 5.5, 5.9, 5.13, 5.14, 6.1, 6.3, 6.5, 6.8, 6.9

It is evident from the data presented in the Tables 18, 19 and 20 that among all the categories of farmers the returns of intercrop /mixed crop is negatively correlated with all the variables at 1% level of significance except returns of arecanut. Because, banana which is grown as an intercrop, will improve the sub soil moisture and also helps to maintain the pH level of the soil thereby, improve returns of areca.

Likewise mixed crop like pepper will also influence on the yield of areca and does not compete with the nutrients of the manure given to the areca palm.

The additional income received from intercrop/mixed cropping gives relief to the farmers in the study area.

Whereas cost of cultivation of intercrop/mixed crop is negatively correlated with returns of intercrop/mixed crop and also with returns of arecanut at 1% level of significance among all the categories of farmers. This indicates that over a period of time cost of cultivation declines and the returns increase.

Returns of arecanut is negatively correlated with all the variables at 1% level of significance. Because, over a period of time cost of cultivation of arecanut declines and at the same time returns increase, but in case of small and medium farmers their correlation is low negative.

Establishment and maintenance costs are negatively correlated with the returns of intercrop/mixed crop and also with returns of arecanut at 1% level of significance. Whereas, establishment and maintenance cost are positively correlated with each other at 1% level of significance among all the categories of farmers.

In conclusion, in the entire district and also in both the taluks in large farmers' category returns of arecanut, returns of intercrop /mixed crop is highly negatively correlated with the maintenance and establishment cost and cost of cultivation of intercrop/mixed crop as compared to medium and small farmers which indicates large farmers are more beneficial.

Between the taluks in Sagar taluk returns of intercrop/mixed crop and returns of arecanut is highly negatively correlated with the maintenance cost and establishment cost and with cost of cultivation of intercrop/mixed crop which implies that farmers of Sagar taluk are more beneficial as compared to farmers of Shimoga taluk and the entire district.

Multiple Regression

The results of correlation co efficient further subjected for verification by the multiple regression with respect to returns of arecanut and liner regression with respect to returns of intercrop/ mixed crop.

Multiple Regression of Returns of Arecanut among Various Farmers' Category in Sagar Taluk

It is evident from the data presented in the Table 21 that among all the categories of farmers the establishment and maintenance costs are dominant at 5% level of significance in determining returns of arecanut, which shows the expenditure incurred on establishment and maintenance costs are significant in enhancing returns of areca.

Within the maintenance cost, dominant variables are human labour farm yard manure, green leaves, chemical fertilizer, cost on irrigation.

R square value for medium and large farmers is 98% each and for small farmers it is 96%. This indicates the R square is found

Table 21
Multiple Regressions of Dependent Variables (Returns of Arecanut) of Various Farmer's Category in Sagar Taluk

Sl. No.	*Cost*	*Standardized Beta of Regression Coefficient*		
		Small	*Medium*	*Large*
1.	Establishment Cost	-2.59 (-5.86)*	-48.60 (0.630*)	-11.33 (-45.98*)
2.	Maintenance Cost	2.64 (4.32)*	0.99 (-39.61*)	10.80 (43.86*)
	R square	0.96	0.98	0.98

Source: Tables 5.1, 5.5, 5.9, 6.1, 6.3, 6.5.
Figures in the paranthesis indicate calculated t values.
* Significant at 5%.

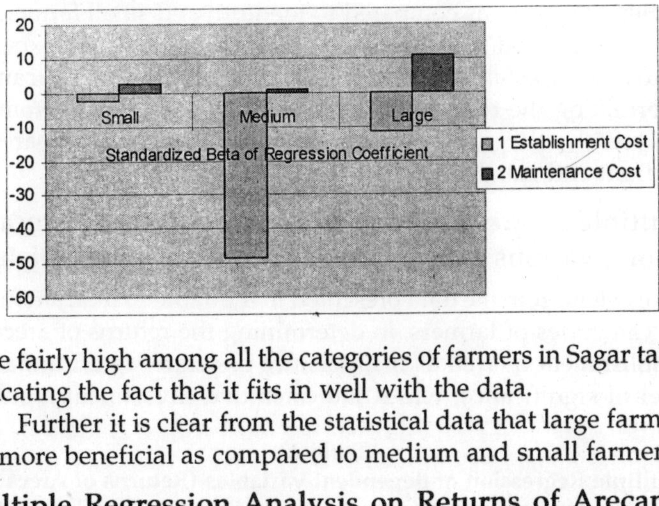

to be fairly high among all the categories of farmers in Sagar taluk indicating the fact that it fits in well with the data.

Further it is clear from the statistical data that large farmers are more beneficial as compared to medium and small farmers.

Multiple Regression Analysis on Returns of Arecanut among Various Farmers Categories in Shimoga Taluk

It is evident from the data presented in the Table 22 that among all the categories of farmers, in determining the returns of arecanut, establishment and maintenance costs are significant at 5% level of significance.

In the maintenance cost human labour, farm yard manure, chemical fertilizers and irrigation cost are dominant variables.

R square value for small, medium and large farmers is 11%, 39% and 71% respectively.

Table 22
Multiple Regression of Dependent Variables (Returns of Arecanut) of Various Farmer's Category in Shimoga Taluk

Sl. No.		*Standardized Beta of Regression Coefficient*		
		Small	*Medium*	*Large*
1.	Establishment	-0.35	0.09	-0.83
	Cost	(-1.37*)	(0.77)**	(-4.36*)
2.	Maintenance	0.03	-0.59]	0.02
	Cost	(-0.11**)	(-4.95)*	(0.12*)
	R square	0.11	0.39	0.71

Source: Tables 5.1, 5.5, 5.9, 6.1, 6.3, 6.5.
Figures in the paranthesis indicate calculated t values.
* Significant at 5%.

The R square value is found to be fairly high among large farmer's category as compared to medium and small farmers.

It is proved from the statistical analysis, that the expenses incurred on establishment and maintenance is significant in determining the returns of areca and also it is evident from the analysis that large farmers are more beneficial as compared to medium and small farmers.

Multiple Regression Analysis of Returns of Arecanut among various farmer's categories in Shimoga District.

It is evident from the data presented in the Table 23 that, among all the categories of farmers, in determining the returns of arecanut establishment as well as maintenance costs are significant at 5% level of significance, which indicates that investment made on

Table 23
Multiple Regression of dependent variables (Returns of Arecanut) of various farmer's category in Shimoga District

Sl. No.		*Standardized Beta of Regression Coefficient*		
		Small	*Medium*	*Large*
1.	Establishment	-1.89	0.27	-0.88
	Cost	(-1.48)*	(2.91*)	(-5.92*)
2.	Maintenance	1.59	0.59	0.01
	Cost	(1.25)*	(-6.25*)	(0.06*)
	R square	0.11	0.30	0.76

Source: Tables 5.1, 5.5, 5.9, 6.1, 6.3, 6.5.
Figures in the paranthesis indicate calculated t values.
* Significant at 5%.

establishment cost and maintenance cost has a significant influence on the areca yield.

The maintenance cost is dominant in all the three stages, within the maintenance cost the dominant variables are human labour, farm yard manure, green leaves, chemical fertilizers, cost on irrigation.

R square value for small, medium and large farmers category is 11%, 30% and 76% respectively. The R sequare value is fairly high among large farmers as compared to medium and small farmers.

In the gestation period large farmers made more investment on irrigation infrastructure that too on sprinklers and conveyor pipes as compared to medium and small farmers category.

Large farmers made more investment on maintenance cost in all the three stages as compared to medium and small farmers.

In conclusion it is clear from the above statistical analysis that in the entire district and also in both the taluks large farmers are more beneficial as compared to medium and small farmers.

Between the taluks, the farmers of Sagar taluk proved to be more beneficial as compared to farmers of Shimoga taluk.

Linear Regression of Dependent Variable (Returns of Intercrop/mixed crop) Among Various Farmers' Categories in Sagar Taluk

It is clear from the data presented in the Table 24 that among all the categories of farmers cost of cultivation of intercrop/mixed crop is significant at 5% level of significance with the returns of intercrop/mixed crop.

Table 24

Linear Regression of Dependent Variable (Returns of Intercrop/ mixed crop) of Various Farmer's Category in Sagar Taluk

Sl. No.		*Standardized Beta of Regression Coefficient*		
		Small	*Medium*	*Large*
1	Cost of cultivation of intercrop/ mixedcrop	0.99 -(-76.98*)	-0.99 (-937.50*)	-0.99 (-933.87*)
	R square	0.99	0.99	0.99

Source: Tables 5.13, 5.14, 6.8, 6.9.

Figures in the paranthesis indicate calculated t values.

* Significant at 5%.

It implies that, cost of cultivation of intercrop/mixed crop influence, significantly in determining the returns of intercrop/ mixed crop.

Further, among all the categories of farmers there is 99% of variation is existing between the variables. (R square value is 99%) which implies that all the categories of farmers in Sagar taluk is proved to be beneficial in intercrop/mixed crop cultivation.

Linear Regression of Returns of Intercrop/Mixed Crop among Various Farmer's Category in Shimoga Taluk

It is clear from the data presented in the Table 25 that in Shimoga taluk also among small, medium and large farmers' category the cost of cultivation of intercrop/mixed crop is significant at 5% level of significance, with returns of intercrop/mixedcrop, which implies that the cost of cultivation of intercrop/mixed crop influences, significantly in enhancing the returns of intercrop/mixed crop.

The R square value for medium and large farmers is 99% each whereas for small farmers it is 97%.

Linear Regression of Returns of Intercrop/Mixed Crop among various Farmers' Categories in the District

It is clear from the data presented in the Table 26 that the cost of cultivation of intercrop/mixed crop is significant with the returns of intercrop/mixed crop at 5% level of significance. Because farmers in Sagar taluk are giving equal prominence to the cultivation of intercrop/mixed crop. As a result returns are more.

Table 25

Linear Regression of Dependent Variable (Returns of Intercrop/ mixedcrop) of various farmer's Category in Shimoga Taluk

Sl. No.	*Variable*	*Standardized Beta of Regression Coefficient*		
		Small	*Medium*	*Large*
1.	Cost of cultivation of intercrop/ mixedcrop	-0.99 (-24.39*)	-0.98 (-63.40*)	-0.99 (-483.22*)
	R square	0.97	0.99	0.99

Source: Tables 5.13, 5.14, 6.8, 6.9.
Figures in the paranthesis indicate calculated t values.
* Significant at 5%.

Table 26

Linear Regression of Dependent Variable (Returns of intercrop/ mixedcrop) of Various Farmer's Category in Shimoga District

Sl. No.	*Variable*	*Standardized Beta of Regression Coefficient*		
		Small	*Medium*	*Large*
1.	Cost of cultivation of intercrop/ mixedcrop	-0.47 (-4.71*)	-0.80 (-6.44*)	-0.97 (-29.28*)
	R square	0.22	0.64	0.94

Source: Tables 5.13, 5.14, 6.8, 6.9.
Figures in the paranthesis indicate calculated t values.
* Significant at 5%.

The R square value is 22%, 64% and 94% for small, medium and large farmers respectively, which indicates clearly that large farmers are more beneficial as compared to medium and small farmers in the study area.

From the above statistical analysis made it is clear that in the entire district and in both the taluks large farmers evidently more beneficial than medium and small farmers category.

Between the taluks, farmers of Sagar taluk proved to be more remunerative in intercrop/ mixed crop cultivation as compared to farmers of Shimoga taluk and the entire district.

NOTES AND REFERENCES

1. Wikipedia: The Free Encyclopedia, page 1 of 1
2. J. Narman Efferson : 'Cost and Returns in farming', Principles of farm management 1953, p.81 to 85.
3. Preethi N. S.: Economic Analysis of Arecanut Cultivation And its Impact on Farm Economy in Shimoga District, Karnataka, 1998 MscAg Dissertation.
4. Coleman and Rao, 1918: The Arecanut Palm, CPCRI, Kasaragod, Kerala, 1982. P.122.
5. Anonymous 1969: The Arecanut Palm, CPCRI, Kasaragod, Kerala, 1982, P.100.
6. Bhat and Leela, 1968: The Arecanut Palm, CPCRI, Kasaragod, Kerala, 1982, P.117-118.
7. Krishnaraja E: An Evaluation of Investment in Arecanut Gardens in Dakshina Kannada District, Karnataka, 1981, MSCAg dissertation, UAS, Bangalore, P.89.

7 MARKETING OF ARECANUT

The market is the opportunity to buy or sell.

"A market is the sphere within which price making forces act"– *Hibbard*

"Markets may be properly described as the entire area within which the forces of demand for and supply of a given commodity or service interact in effecting exchanges and establishing prices. Wherever and whenever buyers and sellers are brought together, whatever the means for achieving communication, markets exist"– Kiekhofer.

In other words, marketing is a comprehensive function, which includes activities like assembling, storing, financing, grading and standardisation, insuring, transporting and selling.

The ultimate objective of any marketing system is to ensure a reasonable rate of return, which represents a fair remuneration to the producers and is within the consumer's ability to pay.

Price movement and Growth in Plantation

"Price" is a matter of vital importance to both the seller and the buyer in a market place. Price denotes the value of a product or service expressed in monetary terms. The exchange activity gets completed only when the buyers and sellers mutually agree upon a price for the produce to be transacted. In a competitive market economy, price is determined by supply and demand.

Price has multifaceted function namely, it regulates business profits, allocates the economic resources, influences consumer's purchase, decisions, reflects the purchasing power of currency and determines the general living standards. In essence, by and large every facet of our economic life is directly or indirectly governed by pricing.

There exists high co-relation between plantation and price. With prices picking up arecanut gained importance as a cash crop in the study area. Increasing prices attracted farmers. Lot of paddy and sugarcane growing areas were converted to arecanut gardens. When prices suddenly picked up, people other than traditional growers also started investing in arecanut plantation. Such price co-relation with crop area and plantation is found in all agricultural commodities. Whenever price increases for any commodity farmers shift to that crop.

Arecanut is a crop whose production is concentrated in a few states but consumption spreads throughout the country. The produce will be brought to the producing centres and is distributed to other areas. The arecanut is marketed in the primary, secondary market and at consuming centres or at terminal markets like any other agricultural commodity.

The primary markets are situated at village level and secondary markets are generally situated at taluk level or at district headquarters. Both assembling and distributing take place in three markets.

Consuming centres/terminal markets are those where arecanut is assembled for further marketing within the state, or outside the state or even for export.

In the present marketing system of arecanut, the intermediaries play a predominant role. In marketing chain of areca upto secondary market the intermediaries like commission agents, primary traders at village level, marketing society, processors and secondary traders are involved.

In distribution chain at consuming centre market commission agent, wholesalers, traders and retailers are involved.

The following major institutions play an important role in marketing of Areca.

1. Agricultural Produce Marketing Committee, Shimoga,
2. Agricultural Produce Marketing Committee, Sagar,
3. Co-operative Marketing Societies.
   - (i) Malnad Areca Marketing Co-operative Society Ltd. (MAMCOS)
   - (ii) Central Areca and Cocoa Marketing and processing co-operative Society, Ltd. (CAMPCO)
   - (iii) Arecanut Processing and Sales Co-operative Society Ltd. (APSCOS) Sagar.

   A brief note of each of the marketing society is mentioned below.

Agricultural Produce Marketing Committee (APMC) Shimoga

All the marketing activities are controlled by the APMC. Committee established in 1980 under the provisions of the Mysore Agricultural Prodnce Market Act 1939 (No XVI of 1939) with Shimoga and Thirthahalli taluks, Koppa, Sringeri taluks of Chickmagalur district as its functional areas.

The administrative office is situated in Shimoga city. The committee has three sub-market yards at Thirthahalli, Koppa and Sringeri.

These sub-markets performing all the marketing functions under the supervision of a head in each yard.

The interest of the farmers are duly represented in the marketing committee.

Agricultural Produce Marketing Committee (APMC), Sagar

APMC at Sagar was established during 1959-60 under the Mysore Agricultural Produce Marketing Act 1939. This market has Sorab and Hosanagar taluks as its functional areas and its administrative office is situated at Sagar. In this centre all trading interests are given due representation.

Co-operative marketing societies play an important role in the marketing of arecanut. These societies deal with market arrivals in bulk and assist their members in selling their produce whenever they wish. These societies provide other services also to its members like provision of the credit facilities, storage facilities. They have gained importance in recent years.

Maland Areca Marketing Co-operative Society (MAMCOS)

Growers in the sample district (Shimoga) were facing various problems in marketing by mediators, in weighing, in pricing, in finance, in storage and in credit facilities. All these deprived areca growers from getting a remunerative price for their produce and with the help of deputy commissioner of Shimoga resulted in the establishment of MAMCOS Ltd in 1939.

The administrative office is situated at Shimoga. It covers Sagar, Koppa, Tarikere, Thirthahalli, Sringeri, Birur.

The objectives of the MAMCOS are.

1. To provide good market for arecanut growing members.
2. Financial facilities to its members.
3. Storage facilities.
4. Export of arecanut to other states.
5. Provide financial assistance to control pests and diseases of areca palm to its growers.
6. To inculcate saving habits and cooperation among its members.
7. To open new branches and sales centres for the benefit of the areca growers.

Central Areca and Cocoa Marketing and Processing Co-operative Society Ltd. (CAMPCO)

It is a joint venture of state governments Karnataka and Kerala established in July 1973. When the restrictions imposed on imports of arecanut during the early 60's and withdrawl of excise duty on arecanut helped the growers to getting remunerative prices for their produce. This resulted in further increase both in area and production.

At the end of 1971, the price of arecanut fell drastically because of increased supply. In order to protect the interest of the growers both Governments of Karnataka and Kerala created *'The Central Arecanut and Cocoa Marketing and Processing Co-operative Society Ltd;* and this is popularly known as CAMPCO.

The head office is located at Mangalore, South Canara district. It has many procuring centres and sales depots, established and spread in various states in the Country. Such a procuring centre is established in the sample district at Shimoga. First processing centre was established in Sagar in 1973 followed at Shimoga during 1974.

The main objectives of the CAMPCO are,

1. To procure arecanut from members and if necessary from other growers, on outright purchase basis.
2. To arrange for the sale of arecanut to the best advantage of its members.
3. To provide credit facilities to its members.
4. To undertake processing of arecanut.
5. To export the produce.
6. To open branches, depots, godowns, showrooms and factories.

7. To arrange for the procurement and distribution of pesticides, fungicides, fertilisers, seed, implements etc.
8. To render technical guidance and advice to its members.
9. To promote scientific research on planting, growing, harvesting, processing, fermentation, preservation and manufacture of semi-finished and finished products of arecanut.

Arecanut Processing and Sales Co-operative Society Ltd. (APSCOS, Sagar)

It was established during 1973 at Sagar, Sagar and Sorab taluk growers as its members. It has a branch at Nittur at Hosanagar taluk established in 1975. The objectives of APSCOS is as same as MAMCOS and CAMPCO.

Marketing of White Variety

White variety of arecanut is processed from ripe arecanut after sun-drying it for 40-45 days. In almost all regions growers are bringing their produce in de-husked condition (nuts) to the market.

Three or four types of primary grading will be done depending on the arecanut by the growers.

The secondary traders who are involved in the business of inter-state marketing does further grading by size.

The marketing channels of white variety is presented below.

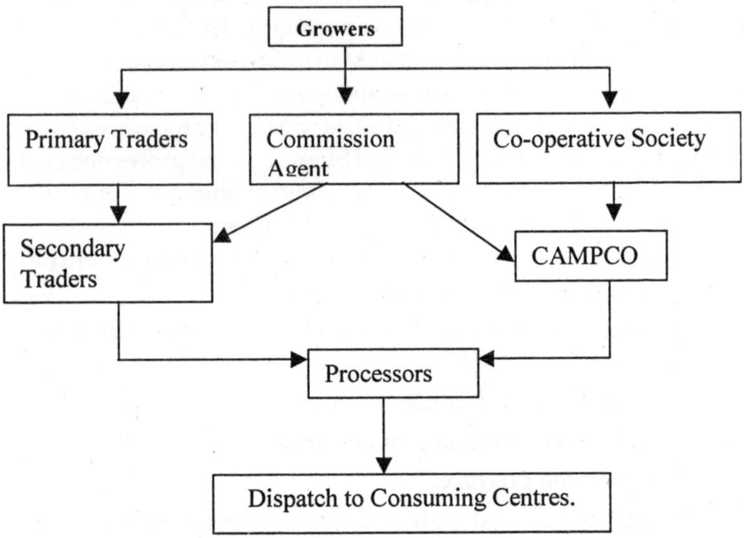

Marketing of Red Variety

Red variety of arecanut is produced by boiling tender nuts. Sometime growers themselves do the processing or sell the tender nuts to the primary traders or processors. Growers bring their produce to the market and sell it through commission agents or marketing societies.

Saraku, Bette, Api, Edi and Gorabalu are the types of grading done by the processors while bringing the produce to the market.

Traders do further grading based on quality, size and demand of the markets. Traders in turn sell it to the institutional and consumer markets. Red variety of areca is mainly used for preparation of Gutkha, Panmasala and Scented Supari. Very few quantity is consumed for direct chewing. Direct chewing of red variety is mainly in North Karnataka, part of Andra Pradesh and Tamil Nadu.

The marketing channels of Red variety is presented below:

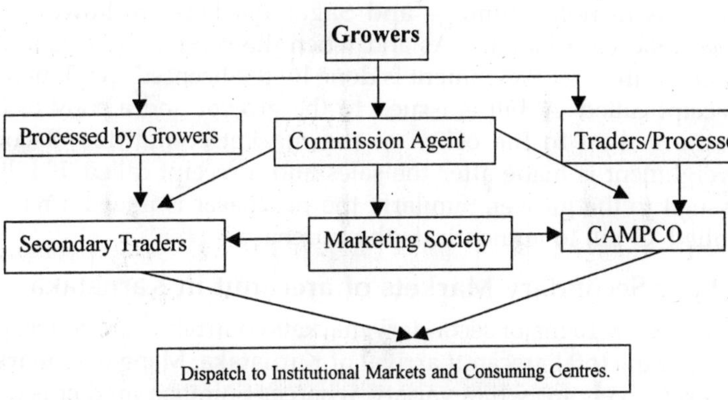

Procedure of Sales and its Proceedings in APMC Yard

As both the markets at Shimoga and Sagar are governed by the same act, there is no difference in the system of sale between two markets. Until the regulation of arecanut market in the district, the market used to follow a traditional closed tender system. The dealers used to cover their hands by cloth and symbolically quote the prices where the growers stood as mute witness without knowing what actually happens under the closed Tender. The growers were totally under the mercy of the mandi owners who used to extend their loans during pre-harvest period. This practice faded when the Agricultural Produce Market Act. came into existence. The Closed Tender system has given way to open Tender system.

Under the new system, if the growers wish to sell their produce to the commission agents of the marketing society, the produce is displayed in the market yard. The traders and agents go round the market yard and inspect the arecanuts filled gunny bags displayed in rows and quote prices for each variety in tender slips and insert them in the tender boxes kept in the yard. The market committee opens the tender boxes and announces the highest tender prices openly. The highest price for each variety of the day which will be broad casted through All India Radio to enable the farmers to know the day to day prices.

Weighing Procedure

The arecanut arrives in the market in the month of November every year and continues upto the month of February. The peak arrival periods in both Shimoga and Sagar markets are however in December and January. As and when the produce arrives in the market, the first Weighment is done by the licensed weighmen. A receipt called 'A' bill is issued to the grower and a copy of the same is sent to the office of the market committee. Second weighment is made after the sales and a receipt called 'B' bill is issued to the grower. Similarly the purchaser is issued a receipt called 'C' bill to authenticate the purchase.

Major Secondary Markets of arecanut in Karnataka

There are 8-10 major secondary markets controlling around 80 per cent of the total arecanut arrival of Karnataka. Mangalore market is exclusively for white variety, whereas Shimoga market is only for red variety. In the year 2000-01, estimated arecanut quantity handled in the Mangalore and Shimoga market is around 36 thousand tonnes and 29 thousand tonnes respectively.

Other markets such as Puttur, Sullia, Belthangadi, Sirsi, Siddapur, Kumta, Yellapur, Sagar, Channagiri and Bhimasamudra are also handling arecanut at marginal quantity.

Agricultural Produce Marketing Committee (APMC)

Arecanut is a listed commodity in APMC in Karnataka. APMCs are located at regional levels. In Karnataka APMC is playing a vital role handling about 75 percent of the total Karnataka's arecanut production.

Table 1
Arrivals of Arecanut to Major Markets of Karnataka

(in Tons)

Sl.No.	*Markets*	*Arrival*	*APMC Reporting*	*Campco's procurement.*
1.	Mangalore	35,900	23,350 (65%)	4,177 (12%)
2.	Shimoga	29,470	27,047 (95%)	915 (03%)
3.	Sagar	14,150	12,730 (90%)	973 (07%)
4.	Puttur	12,560	8,160(65%)	3,600(27%)
5.	Sirsi	11,700	11,140 (95%)	2,530 (22%)
6.	Sullia	7,460	3,730 (50%)	1,222 (16%)
7.	Bhimasamdra	6,000	3,180 (53%)	882 (15%)
8.	Channagiri	5,790	4,050 (70%)	998 (17%)
9.	Kumta	5,520	3,860 (70%)	350 (06%)
10.	Siddapura	5,400	3,760(70%)	835 (15%)
	All Karnataka	1,71,000	1,29,490 (75%)	22,030 (13%)

Mangalore and Puttur branch figures also include purchases by the sub-centres.

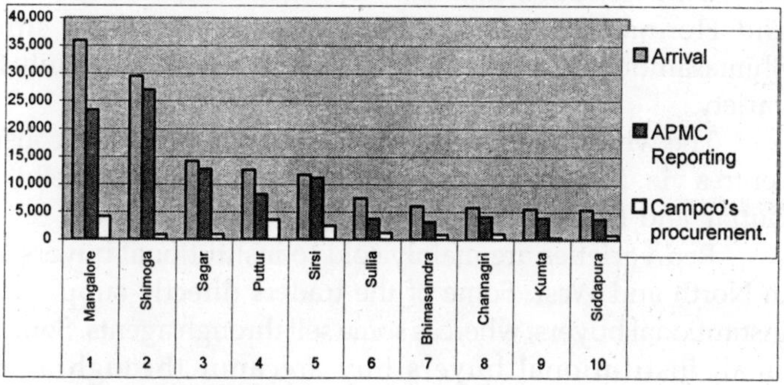

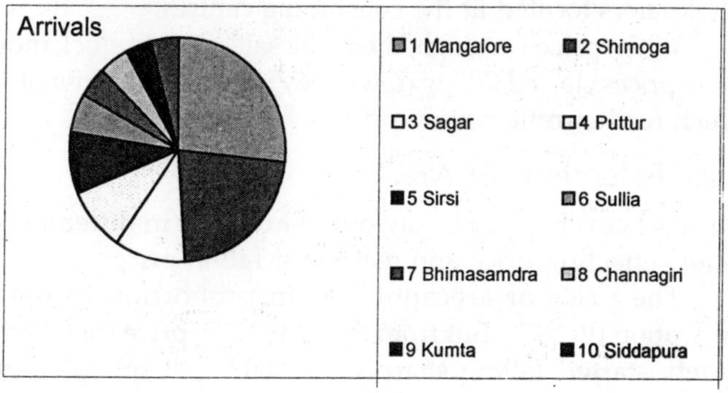

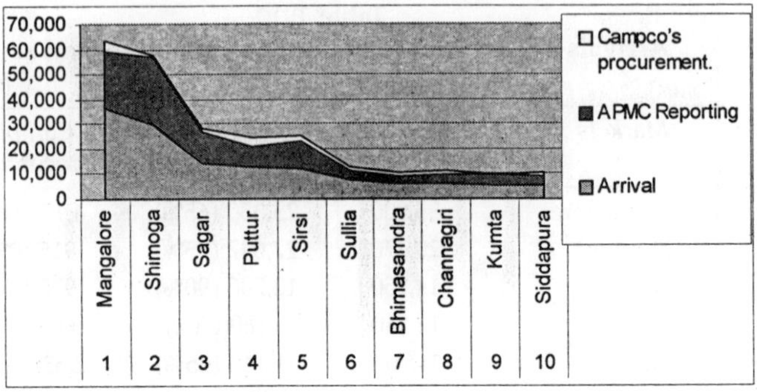

Production, APMC reporting and share of Campco.

In 1996-97, APMC arrival was around 63 per cent of the total production and has reached up to 75 percent in 2000-01, Campco's share is between 11-13 per cent and has come down to 10 percent in 1999-2000.

Mangalore, Puttur, Sullia and Belthangadi are the exclusive markets for white variety. Similarly Shimoga is an exclusive market for red variety other markets viz, Sagar, Sirsi, Siddapura, Kumta and Honnavara markets both the varieties, like shimoga, Bhimasamudra, Channagari and Birur markets are mainly for red variety.

The white varieties are mainly dispatched to the consuming centres viz, Mumbai, Ahmedabad, Nagpur, Indore, Delhi, Patna, Cuttak and Kolkata.

Red varieties are mainly sold to institutional buyers located in North and West. Some of the traders directly supply it to the institutional buyers, whereas some sell through agents. Some times, small institutional buyers buy arecanut through agents or wholesalers located at the consuming centres.

When price was high, the wholesalers use to stock more. Later when prices started falling down they reduced their inventory level, which further reflected on price.

Price Behaviour of Arecanut

This part covers price behaviour of arecanut in different markets, factors effecting price and reason for fall in price.

The price of arecanut was in proportion to the cost of cultivation till 1970. But from the year 1970, price for Chali (white) variety started falling sharply Rs. 600/- per qtl (price refers to

Mangalore Supari) to Rs 300/- per qtl by 1973. The arecanut farmers and their dependents were in panic and many of the traders in different parts of the country went bankrupt. Most of the traders withdraw from the market and the situation worsened further.

In order to stabilise the price, the Govt of Karnataka and Kerala jointly formed a marketing organization named Campco, In the co-operative sector. With starting of Campco's operation reasonable growth was observed for the arecanut prices.

During 90's the gutkha and panmasala industry entered the scene. Lot of small unorganised manufacturers started manufacturing gutkha and panmasala in northern and western region of India. By advertising intensively, this industry grown up suddenly. They got very good response from the consumers because of attractive packing and taste. This sudden growth of industry ultimately reflected on the demand for arecanut, as a consequence the prices started rising. At this time, lot of people invested money in this trade and market improved. During 1998-99, prices of arecanut started picking up and reached the peak level of Rs. 17,100/-per qtl by 1999-2000.

Factors effecting Prices of Arecanut

Prices of arecanut are fluctuating similar to other commodities as per the demand and supply. The various factors including demand, supply affecting prices of arecanut are summarized in following paragraphs.

1. Demand from consuming centres and institutional markets.
2. Supply from the production centres. If supply is in excess to the demand, price automatically falls down.
3. Price is governed by the quality of arecanut supplied, better the quality higher is the price.
4. Availability of money in the market which improves buying power of traders and the institutional buyers.
5. Stocking or holding capacity of growers, primary traders, secondary traders, consuming centres, traders and wholesalers.
6. Demand and support for the value added arecanut products manufacturing industry.
7. Consumption and chewing habits of Indian people.
8. Export demand from other countries.

9. Import of arecanut at cheaper rates.
10. Festival seasons, marriages etc.
11. Political situation and stability in the country.

Demand

Demand from consuming centres and institutional market. The demand for white variety for direct chewing has decreased due to the change in chewing habits of the people. They prefer ready products such as gutka, panmasala, mawa and scented supari etc ultimately this has effected the demand for white supari.

Increased demand and popularity of value added products have resulted into increased demand for arecanut and mainly the red variety. When prices of arecanut picked up suddenly and indigenous arecanut became unaffordable, institutional users started using imported arecanut.

Also these institutional buyers prefer inferior quality of arecanut which was available at cheaper rate. Ultimately this buying practices of institutional buyers affected the demand and hence the price of both the varieties of arecanut has fallen.

Govt. Policy Pertaining to Value Added Products

Ban by certain state govts for value added products such as gutkha has adversely affected the demand for arecanut in turn reflected on the price.

Increased Production

There is a surplus production of arecanut in the country. Production has been increasing steadily during the past several years, as compared to production demand for arecanut is not increasing at the same rate.

Stable Supply

Growers are holding stock at home or at society and sell it in the market as per their need and price movement. Growers are stocking arecanut with husked in packed room. Growers can stock arecanut more than a year. Hence supply has stabilized throughout the year except rainy seasons.

Stocking pattern at Procurement Centre

After sudden fall in price in 2000, traders at procurement centres also behave similar to traders at the consuming centres. To hold the stock they have to invest more money and have to take proper care of their warehouse. They have to do sulphur fumigation. This is a troublesome exercise for them.

Some of the traders hold stock with growers and buy as per the demand. Considering all the factors have reduced their inventory level. The inventory level maintained by them is based on the order in hand and their expectation of the demand.

Stocking Pattern at Consuming Centres

Earlier days, traders at the consuming centres use to stock more because of non-stability in the prices over a longer period of time. Nowadays prices are stable for longer period of time. Thus traders have reduced their inventory level and place orders according to market demand.

Update on Price Trends Makes it a Buyers Market

Traders at consuming centres are updated on the current arrival, prices and holding of stocks through modern means of communication such as telephone, fax, E-mail, Internet. Since they are updated on these issues they are in position to quote the prices accordingly while placing their requirement.

Lack of Financial Facility

When the prices for arecanut were high, people from other than areca business invested money in this trade through short-term loans to the traders in arecanut business. But after the sudden drop in prices of arecanut, many traders lost their confidence and they were scared to invest money in arecanut trade.

Also the overall economic condition is not healthy. Thus, due to the uncertainty involved in arecanut business investors are not willing to invest their money.

Export Demand from other Countries

Higher the export potential, more would be the market for the arecanut produced in the country. Higher export potential could result into balance between the local demand and supply, thus affecting price.

In reality the present export of arecanut from India is meagre. Thus the entire production is available mostly for local supply.

Import of Arecanut

Arecanut imports though negligible in comparison to total production of arecanut in India affects the prices of arecanut.

Natural Calamities, Political Situation and Instability

Uncertain political situation always affect any trade including arecanut trade. Eg. Gujrat is a major consuming centre and over the last two years, natural calamities (Drought, earthquake) unstable situation (riots) has effected arecanut trade.

Price Behaviour of Chali Variety

In July 1998, prices of arecanut started increasing. In a span of 15 months, it reached upto Rs, 17,100/- from Rs. 7700/ per qtl.

However from then onwards, it has been declining sharply and at present, (in March 2002) the average price of New Chali Supari and old Chali supari is Rs.4,700 and Rs. 5,740/-per qtl respectively. In last 6-7 months prices are almost fluctuating between Rs. 5,500/- to Rs.7,200/- for old and Rs.3,000/- to Rs. 6,000/- per qtl for the new.

Only in December 2001, price reached upto Rs. 10,050/- for old and Rs. 6,006/- per qtl for the new. This price rise was only for a short period. The reasons for the rise and fall of prices is summarised below:

Reasons for Sudden Rise in Price

1. During 1998-99 there was a rumor of short fall in the production. Due to scarcity of supply, traders at secondary market as well as consuming markets started stocking more. Ultimately demand for arecanut increased as a result of this, prices started picking up.
2. Day by day, increase in demand and the price of areca attracted more growers. The growers also started holding the produce at their level.
3. At the same time demand increased from north-eastern states. This was mainly due to the fall in production of Areca in Assam because of natural calamities. The eastern region had to depend on the Southern centres to meet its demand. The other regions, dependent on Assam were also affected by the fall in production of Arecanut in Assam.
4. To attract more and more price traders and growers created an artificial shortage and high demand from consuming end.

Reason for Sudden Fall in Price

1. After prices reached upto certain level, consumers could not afford the price, which reflected on demand for arecanut.

2. Institutional buyers and traders shifted to imports (official and clandestine)
3. Demand started falling down.
4. The traders who had purchased arecanut for high price were not ready to sell their goods for lower price. Inventory at secondary market with traders also piled up. Traders could not purchase more than their holding capacity.
5. At the same time the harvested new areca started arriving into the market.
6. After watching the price behaviour of the market, everybody realized that there would not be further increase in demand. Therefore they started releasing their stocks.
7. The arrival of arecanut increased suddenly and supply exceeded the demand.
8. Increased supply with respect to the demand finally resulted in down fall of the prices.
9. Pre-Kargil, lot of clandestine exports were taking place to Pakistan. However post-Kargil, this activity has almost stopped which has resulted in fall in prices.

Price Behaviour of Red Variety

Red variety of arecanut is mainly used by institutional market to manufacture. Gutkha, panmasala and scented supari. The Gutkha manufacturing industry in the northern region has developed since last 5-6 years. Lot of small, unorganised manufacturers entered into Gutkha manufacturing. Thus demand for red variety continuously went on increasing.

1996-97 saw a peak in prices due to short supply in the market. Nowadays prices for red variety is also witnessing down fall. Some of the reasons given below:

1. Ban on Gutkha in Andhra Pradesh and Tamil Nadu and threat of ban in others states.
2. Increase in production of arecanut.
3. Non willingness of traders at the production centres and consuming centres to increase their inventory level due to fall in demand from institutional buyers and price fluctuation in the market.

4. Non willingness of the manufacturers to increase their inventory level due to threat from Gutkha ban, policy by the various state level and also the price fluctuation.
5. Unstable political situation.

The difference between the price ultimately paid by the consumer and the price received by the grower referred as the price spread.

The price paid by the consumer includes the respective share of grower, trader and the retailer.

At Sagar and Shimoga markets the grower receives 88.21% and 87.79% respectively out of the price paid by the consumer and the rest includes traders, retailers profits and their respective marketing costs.

It is evident from the table that the price spread from grower to consumer is less in Sagar market as compared to Shimoga market because the profit margin quoted by traders and retailers is lower than the Shimoga counterparts.

Farmers Opinion on the Marketing system in the Study Area

Majority of the farmers sell their produce to APMC's of the respective taluks in the study area. Some small farmers will sell to the big farmers or some intermediaries.

Almost all farmers have good opinion about present co-operative marketing societies.

As the system is good and price will be fixed by tenders hence there is no problem regarding price fixation. The procedure adopted for price fixation is good.

Farmers informed at the time of survey that they will get all information regarding marketing arrivals, sales, stocks, loan facility, warehousing facility.

If the price of areca falls below certain level the farmers of Sagar informed that they will wait as there is no alternative way for them as it is their livelihood crop and they will go for mixed cropping whereas the farmers of Shimoga has informed that as the majority of the farmers are absentee landlords and they are having one or the other business. They told that at the time of survey that they donot go for further expansion of area, and they will give more prominence for intercropping.

Table 2
Price Spread Effect on Growers, Intermediaries and Consumers of the Study Area

(per Quintal)

Sl. No.	*Item*	*Sagar Market* Cost and Margin	*Sagar Market* Market Price (Per Qtl)	*Shimoga market* Cost and Margin	*Shimoga market* Market Price (Per Qtl)
	Net Price Received by the Grower		11,300 (88.21)		11,100 (87.79)
	Cost of Transportation	12.00 (0.09)		12.00 (0.09)	
	Weighment Charges	1.25 (9.76)		1.25 (9.89)	
	Handling Charges	4.00 (0.03)		4.00 (0.03)	
	Price to the Trader	17.25 (0.13)	11,317.25 (88.34)	17.25 (0.14)	11,117.25 (87.93)
	Sales Tax at 6% on Traders Price	679.03 (5.30)		667.03 (5.27)	
	Turn over Tax at 1.25% on Traders Price	141.46 (1.10)		138.96 (1.10)	
	Market Cess at Re 1 per Rs. 100	113.17 (0.88)		111.17 (0.88)	
	Handling Charges at Rs.0.30 per Qtl	0.30 (2.34)		0.30 (2.37)	
0.	Commission at Rs 2 per Rs.100	226.35 (1.77)		222.34 (1.36)	
1.	Transportation Cost	3.00 (0.02)		3.00 (0.02)	
2.	Profit Margin	175 (1.37)		200 (1.58)	
3.	Price to the Retailer	1338.31 (10.45)	12,665.87 (98.87)	1342.80 (10.62)	12,460.05 (98.56)
4.	Transportation Cost	3.00 (0.02)	3.00 (0.02)		
5.	Profit Margin	142 (1.11)	18	180 (1.42)	
6.	Consumers Price	145 (1.13)	12,810.56	183 (1.45)	12,643.05
	Price Spread	1510.56			1543.05

Note: Figures in parentheses are percentage share of intermediaries and the Grower in the Consumer's Rupee.

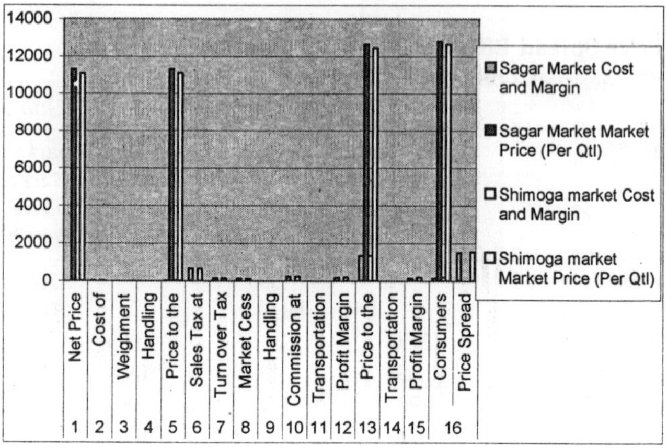
14000
12000
10000
8000
6000
4000
2000
0
Net Price
Cost of
Weighment
Handling
Price to the
Sales Tax at
Turn over Tax
Market Cess
Handling
Commission at
Transportation
Profit Margin
Price to the
Transportation
Profit Margin
Consumers
Price Spread
1 2 3 4 5 6 7 8 9 10 11 12 13 14 15 16
Sagar Market Cost and Margin
Sagar Market Market Price (Per Qtl)
Shimoga market Cost and Margin
Shimoga market Market Price (Per Qtl)

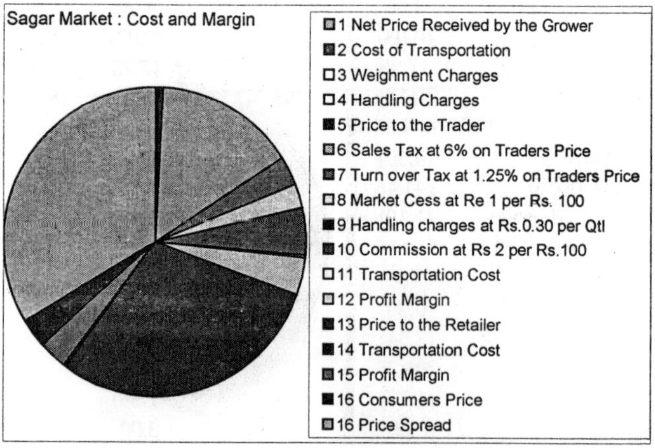
Sagar Market : Cost and Margin
1 Net Price Received by the Grower
2 Cost of Transportation
3 Weighment Charges
4 Handling Charges
5 Price to the Trader
6 Sales Tax at 6% on Traders Price
7 Turn over Tax at 1.25% on Traders Price
8 Market Cess at Re 1 per Rs. 100
9 Handling charges at Rs.0.30 per Qtl
10 Commission at Rs 2 per Rs.100
11 Transportation Cost
12 Profit Margin
13 Price to the Retailer
14 Transportation Cost
15 Profit Margin
16 Consumers Price
16 Price Spread

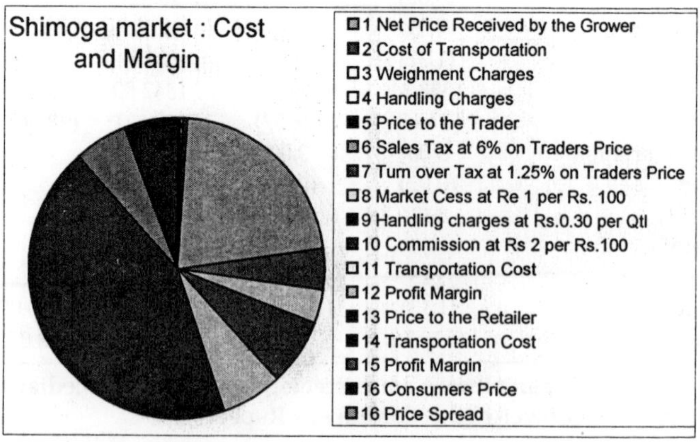
Shimoga market : Cost and Margin
1 Net Price Received by the Grower
2 Cost of Transportation
3 Weighment Charges
4 Handling Charges
5 Price to the Trader
6 Sales Tax at 6% on Traders Price
7 Turn over Tax at 1.25% on Traders Price
8 Market Cess at Re 1 per Rs. 100
9 Handling charges at Rs.0.30 per Qtl
10 Commission at Rs 2 per Rs.100
11 Transportation Cost
12 Profit Margin
13 Price to the Retailer
14 Transportation Cost
15 Profit Margin
16 Consumers Price
16 Price Spread

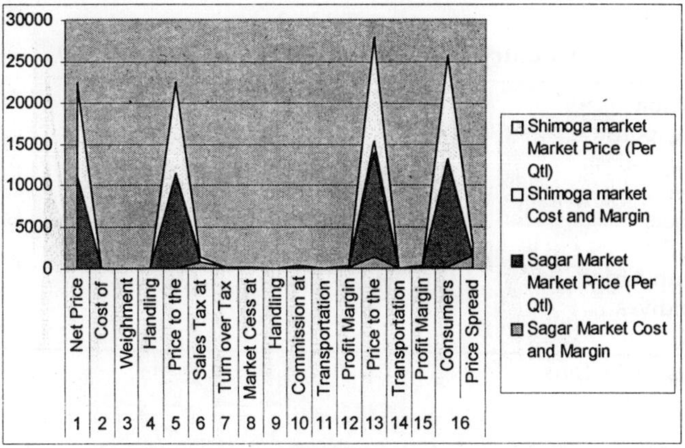

About the Govt. policy the farmers of Sagar taluk informed that the govt should make an amendment regarding the expansion of area under arecanut in non-traditional canal irrigated area. Because irrigation facility given to non-traditional farmers is basically to help paddy and sugarcane cultivation and the crop loan is misused by farmers of non-traditional area.
Regarding this farmers of Shimoga taluk no comments.

The farmers of the study area informed that there is an urgent need for the research related to:

(i) Least cost cultivation with profit maximization.

(ii) Innovative equipments in the arecanut cultivation as well as in processing.

(iii) On Diseases control measures,

(iv) On Alternative uses of Arecanut,

(v) By products of Arecanut.

Export of Arecanut

The bulk of production of arecanut in India is consumed within the country. However small quantity of arecanut is exported, mainly meant for the Indian settlers abroad. As per the DGCIS statistics export is ranging between 100 to 800 tons over the span of 50 years. During 2000-01, India exported about 639 tons (Rs 62.9 million) of arecanut, mainly to the UAE, UK, Maldives, South Africa and Canada, Afganistan, Australia, Pakistan etc.

Table 3
Country-wise Exports of Arecanut (2000-01)

Canada	5%
Singapore	2%
Bangaladesh	2%
USA	2%
Others	5%
UAE	46%
South Africa	6%
Maldives	15%
UK	17%

Base: 639 Tons

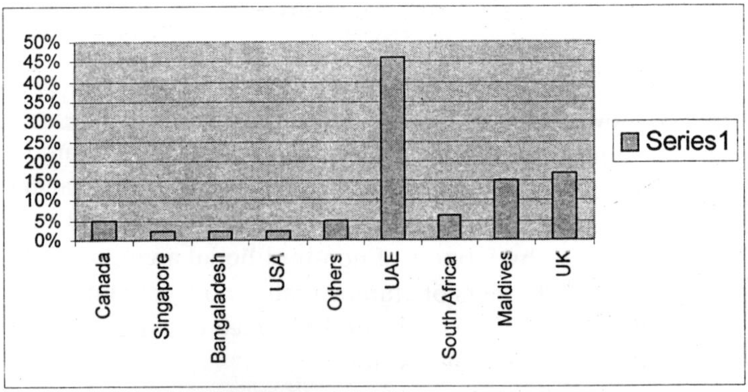

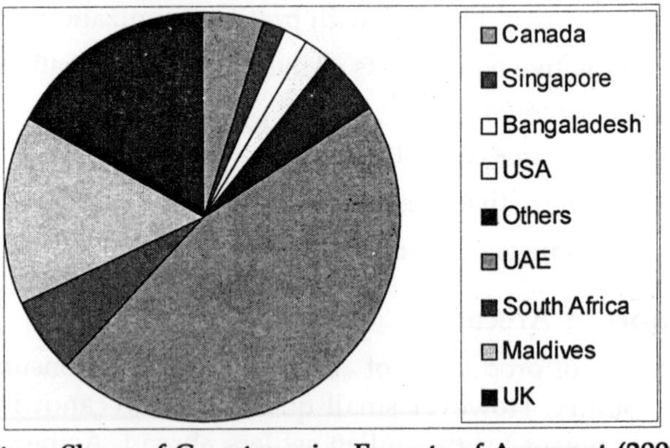

Percentage Share of Country-wise Exports of Arecanut (2000-01)

The survey conducted by DGCIS, and reported that arecanut is exported to Bhutan and Bangladesh from Fuentsholing town, a border town of West Bengal and Assam. Considering this export

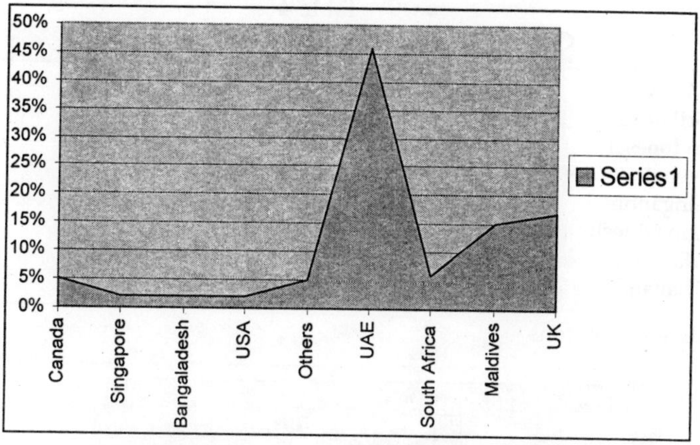

the estimated export of arecanut from India during 2000-01 was about 4000 tons (Rs. 390 million).

Imports of Arecanut

During the 50's arecanut production in the country was not sufficient to meet the internal requirement. This is reflected in the huge quantities that were imported during the fifties. The imported arecanut were in the form of betelnut whole or betelnut split. Thereafter the import gradually began to decline year after year due to the decision of the Indian Govt to restrict the import to protect the interest of domestic industry and farmers.

From 1974-75 there was no official import of arecanut. Since 1994-95, India started imported arecanut due to the increase in domestic consumption. However, compared to the total Indian production, arecanut import is negligible. As per the DGCIS statistics about 29,227 tons (Rs. 850 millions) of arecanut was imported during the year 2000-01.

Imports are taking place mainly from Indonesia, Thailnad and Mayanmar. Based on the survey conducted by DGCIS, estimated imports (Official and clandestine) in the year 2000-01 is around 44,290 tons (Rs. 1330 million) which is 12% of the total Production of India.

About 17 thousand tons of arecanut has been imported from Indonesia during the year 2000-01. Nepal is second major country after Indonesia due to re-export of arecanut to India through unofficial routes.

Table 4
Country-wise Imports of Arecanut (2000-01)

Malaysia	1%
SriLanka	1%
Indonesia	39%
Nepal	33%
Singapore	1%
Bangaldesh	1%
Mayanmar	9%
Thailand	15%

Base 44,290 tons

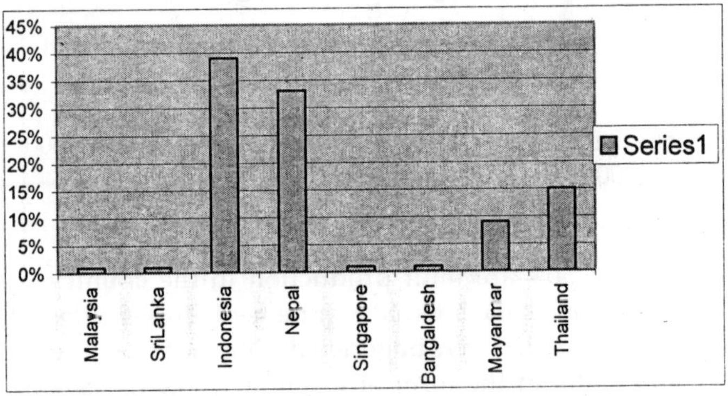

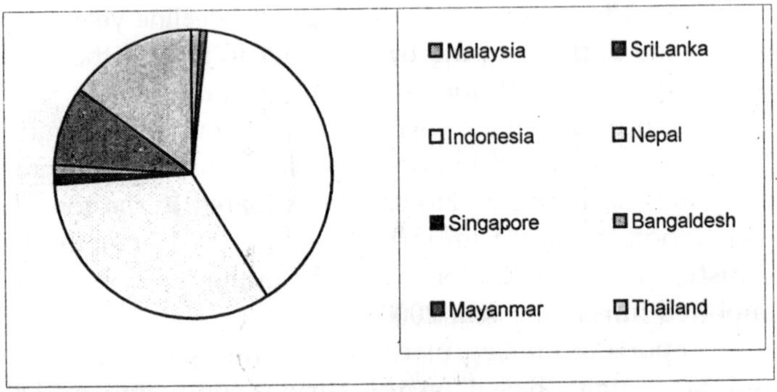

Percentage Share of Country-wise Imports of Arecanut (2000-01)

It has been observed that quality of the imported arecanut is inferior and tasteless therefore it is mainly used by gutkha and panmasala manufacturers. Also some of the traders mix the inferior imported arecanut in chali white variety and sell it in the open market.

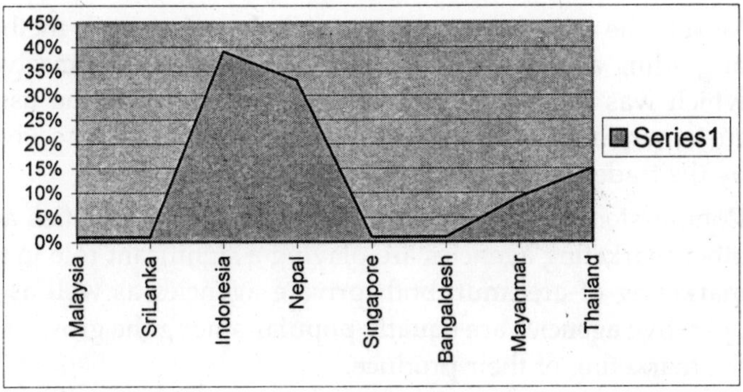

Increased import duty has reduced the price difference between the indigenous and imported arecanut. However clandestine imports still would continue. When prices suddenly picked up in 1999-2000, prices become unaffordable to the Indian consumers and mainly for the price sensitive value added products manufacturers. This was the start of clandestine imports. Though the imported arecanut is inferior compared to Indian quality it is very cheap and is mainly used for manufacturing gutkha. To protect the interest of domestic industry the Govt of India took major initiatives by rising duty on arecanut from 35% to 100% Thus the traders are using unofficial ways of import.

Imported arecanut from Indonesia, Malaysia, Mayanmar, Singapore arrives at the Kolkota port for exports to Nepal. During last 2-3 years, this arecanut is moved to Nepal by road and is again brought to Kolkata market or siliguri market through Dhalbari border. The estimated imports from Nepal bordar for the year 2000-01 is around 14,500 tons. The imported arecanut is supplied to Kolkota, Uttar Pradesh, Bihar and Siliguri market.

Conclusions

The major conclusions of this study are outlined below:

1. Arecanut is an important cash crop in Shimoga district and the livelihood of the growers is entirely dependent on this crop in Sagar taluk.
2. As most of the areca cultivators are small and medium category of farmers with limited resources and holding power, they are forced to market the produce immediately after the harvest because of urgency for money.

3. Most of the areca growers do not follow any scientific method of grading and as such they will do grading by themselves, which was followed by their ancestors and it is the usual customary method, hence the benefits of grading are received by the traders only.
4. Commission agents, wholesalers, co-operative societies and other marketing agencies are playing a significant role in the marketing of arecanut, both private agencies as well as co operative agencies are equally popular among the growers in the marketing of their produce.
5. Though arecanut prices are increasing in recent years they are subject to wide fluctuation, and there is no stability and certainty in the market.
6. Majority of the farmers will sell their produce to the marketing agencies and some of the farmers will sell their produce in the villages to the village traders.
7. Mainly two varieties of arecanut i.e., red areca and white areca is marketed in Sagar and exclusively red variety of areca is marketed in Shimoga market, the main consuming centres for both varieties are northern parts of Karnataka and northern parts of India.
8. After the establishment of APMC, MAMCOS, CAMPCO, APSCOS, malpractices and exploitation by local traders, commission agents and other intermediaries are reduced significantly.
9. The problem faced by the farmers of the study area are lack of skilled workers for plucking the arecanut, lack of knowledge about scientific method of cultivation and also about scientific grading, substantial loss due to diseases, pests and forest animals, difficulty in transporting facility and uncertainty in prices.
10. It can be concluded that the overall marketing system of arecanut is well organised and the market functionaries are operating well.

Suggestions

In the present study the overall marketing system of arecanut is well organised. Some concrete and practical suggestions are made to improve still further, the existing marketing system for the benefit of areca growers and to all concerned.

1. Alternative uses of arecanut and its by products,
2. Since self sufficiency is achieved in arecanut production, the lack of any alternative uses of arecanut at present tends to bring down the market price down to some extent. Hence the alternative uses of arecanut and its by products is to be taken up by the marketing societies. It will help the areca growers substantially.

For Eg.

- Use of chogaru for tanning of leather (the liquid obtained while boiling the tender arecanuts).
- Use of arecanut for the preparation of a suitable beverage.
- Extraction of fat from arecanut
- Extraction of alchohol.
- Use of arecanut in manufacturing of toothpaste and chewing gums.
- Use of arecanut in medicines.
- Use of arecanut husk in the manufacture of hard board, wrapping paper etc.
- Use of arecanut husk as poultry litter
- Use of arecanut leaf sheath for various industrial purpose etc.

3. Provision of knowledge about scientific method of cultivation.

   Most of the arecanut growers are ignorant about scientific and planned method of cultivation. It reflects on the yield and returns. Hence, it is advisable to provide knowledge about the scientific and planned method of cultivation through proper institutions.

4. More research work should be done in plant protection and the diseases.

   There will be substantial loss of production of arecanut due to diseases pertaining to areca palm, hence research work on damage causing diseases should be intensified and proper remedial measures to be important to the areca cultivators. It will promote the yield and returns.

5. Due to irregular monsoons the productivity is decreasing therefore financing agencies should provide liberal financial assistance for all categories of farmers for irrigation infrastructure like digging of open wells, pumpsets, sprinklers etc.
6. Designing mechanical equipment for plucking of arecanut in harvesting.

   The arecanut growers are facing problem of skilled labourers for the plucking of arecanut in the harvesting season, therefore it is necessary to design a suitable mechanical appliance for harvesting the arecanut. It will save time and precious life.
7. Due to drought, pests and diseases etc it will affect on the yield of the crop and also returns. Hence, it is desirable to introduce and popularise the crop insurance scheme.
8. Areca growers are facing difficulty in transportation of their produce from their village to the market place, hence the marketing agencies should take the necessary steps to improve the transportation facilities.
9. Encouragement of scientific grading system.

   Areca cultivators grade the produce arbitrarily, and customarily by themselves at their level, as a result they will get low prices. It is therefore necessary the marketing agencies should undertake necessary steps to encourage scientific grading of the produce by the growers so as to receive good financial benefit.
10. Introduction of centralised tender system at the marketing yard. The tender box is opened in the respective commission agents mandi, immediately after the business and the prices quoted by traders, are announced. This will have an adverse effect on the prices quoted by the traders in the remaining mandis, later in the same day. Therefore centralised system to be followed properly and the prices quoted should be announced at a time. Though the central system is followed but it should be improved still.
11. Encouragement for export of arecanut.

    At present small quantities of arecanut is exported to other countries, compared to the production in India. It is therefore necessary to see that both central and state governments encourage exports by providing necessary assistance to export agencies and traders.

12. Fixation of minimum price for arecanut by the government.

    Arecanut price is always subject to wide fluctuation and there is no stability and certainty. Even the growers irrespective of the category of farmers in the study area opined that government should fix minimum price for arecanut in the procuring season. Hence the government must fix the minimum price for arecanut for this produce so as to protect the interest of the arecanut growers from the uncertainties.

13. Vigilance is necessary on the working of the co-operative societies.

    Though co-operative marketing societies are playing a significant role in arecanut marketing, the cases of misappropriation are often common. The government must exercise strict control upon the working of co-operative societies, the board of directors must be vigilant, sincere, prompt in discharging their duties. Thereby safeguarding the interest of the grower and also the respect of the co-operative society.

14. Establishment of 'Arecanut Publicity Board' by the Government.

    For popularising arecanut both within and outside the country it is essential to establish a publicity board and it must make efforts to popularise arecanut in foreign markets either as scented supari form or in any other form acceptable for the consumers without blending harmful ingredients with good packing and marketing infrastructure. Thereby it boosts the arecanut growers economy.

8 SUMMARY, CONCLUSIONS AND RECOMMENDATIONS

246

A brief summary of the findings derived in the previous chapters are presented here to draw appropriate conclusions and suggestions.

The story of arecanut chewing dates back to antiquity. Reference to arecanut is found in Rigveda Mandala (10) Suktha (145) more than 4000 years ago. Innumerable references are found in several ancient Sanskrit texts to the areca palm, the arecanut and its uses. Among most important one quoted is being Anjana Charitha by Sisumayana (B.C. 1300) and also references are made in Sisupalavadha by famous Sanskrit poet (650 B.C. not later than 900 B.C.) and Amarakosha etc.

In Ajanta caves in central India from 2nd century B.C. to 9th centry A.D. certain extremely artistic picture of areca palm is made in cave no. 17. In padmapani cave areca palm provides a backdrop to Bodhisattava Padmapani in cave no.1.

The five natural aromatics connected with betel chewing is mentioned in ancient texts of ayurvedic medicine Dhanvantari Nighantu, are which includes piper chaba, puga, clove, nutmeg, camphor. Arecanut is rich in several essential nutrients and it is supported by the research work carried out by the central Food Technological Research Institute, Mysore.

The medicinal values of arecanut is immense and is used in the following ailments. Urinary stones, Heart burn, Jaundice, Flutulence of the abdomen, Abdominal colics, Dysentry, Diarrhea, Leucoderma, Leprosy, Cough with phlegm Anamia, Nasal ulcers, used as an universal antidote in emergencies, as an antihelminthic in dogs.

The arecanut palm, Areca catechu Linn is the source of common masticatory nut popularly known as arecanut, betel nut or supari. It is extensively used in India by all sections of the people as a masticatory, and is an essential requisite for several religious and social ceremonies. Consequently arecanut occupies commercial, economic, religious, cultural and medicinal importance in India. The arecanut palm occupies a prominent place among the cultivated crops in the states of Karnataka, Kerala and Assam are the largest producers of arecanut in India, other producing states are West Bengal, Maharastra and Andhra Pradesh.

Many of the arecanut farmers have this crop as the only source of income. In this context diversifying arecanut farming with other crops such as banana, pepper, cocoa, clove etc. which are all high cash value crops which will be more helpful for the farmers.

The cultivation of areca palm providing livelihood more than 5 lakh farm families in Karnataka, majcrity of these are small farmers and landless labourers. It provides assured employment opportunity to the extent of 5 crore mandays is created in its cultivation annually in India.

In Karnataka the total area under arecanut cultivation in 1998-99 was 98.047 hectares and arecanut is being cultivated in Dakshina Kannada(22.13%), Shimoga (19.54%), Chickmagalur Uttara Kannada (9.92%) out of 98,047 hectares of areca land in 1998-99.

The percentage of area under arecanut cultivation has increased by 0.796% in Dakshina Kannada, 16.00% in Uttara Kannada and 49.26 % in Shimoga district between 1990-91 to 1998-99.

Shimoga district recorded the highest increase in area under arecanut cultivation in the last decade (1990-91 to 2000-01) as compared to other districts.

In the intention of getting an additional income in the first stage the areca growers choosed growing banana as an intercrop and in the second stage pepper and cocoa as mixed crops.

The returns from intercrop and mixed crop will help the areca farmers to overcome the cost incurred in the areca cultivation and mixed cropping does not effect the yield of main crop rather it is beneficial.

Apart from the income from banana as an intercrop, pepper and cocoa as mixed crops, value added arecanut products such as ghutka has given a real boost to the arecanut economy in India.

When the era of value addition started large scale of industrial processing of arecanut higher with diversified products in attractive packets and labels such as scented supari, pan masala, herbal supari, kaju supari and ghutka flooded the Indian retail market.

This enhanced the choice and convenience for the consumers as a result of which the consumption of arecanut especially in northern states such as Uttara Pradesh, Gujarath, Delhi, Maharashtra increased by many folds.

As the value addition is the stated objective under our agricultural development policy, this in the case of arecanut is viewed as a step in the right direction. This impact enhanced greatly the earning capacity of arecanut farmers in India.

Out of total production of arecanut in India 50% goes towards the preparation of ghutka and scented supari, 47% for panbeedas and remaining 3% for home consumption. One estimate says that around 2 crore people are consuming these products in India.

In a span of just 15 years from 1985 to 2000, area under arecanut cultivation in Karnataka has almost doubled and the increase in price for rawnuts has increased by 500%. It enabled even small farmers with below 01 hectare under arecanut to earn an assured income sufficient enough to lead descent living.

Average price for white chali variety reached as high as Rs. 13,000 qtls in the year 2000, the average yield of around 10 qtls. the farmers in the district could easily realise a net income of around Rs. 50,000 to Rs. 70,000.

As a result, the consumer durable such as two wheelars, TV, refrigerators, four wheelars which are otherwise confined only to the Urban upper middle class become common household items in the regions growing arecanut.

India is the largest producer of arecanut in the world. India stands first both in area (57%) and production (53%) of arecanut in the world. In India, Karnataka state stands first both in the area and production of arecanut when compared to other states.

In Karnataka among the 27 districts Shimoga district stands first in area under areca cultivationin 2002. In addition to this, Shimoga district recorded the highest increase in area under arecanut cultivation in the last decade (1990-91 to 2000-01) as compared to other districts.

Apart from this Shimoga district comprise both traditional and non traditional areas of arecanut cultivation as compared to other districts. Further, Shimoga district very well represents all the stages of areca gardens (first, second and third stages) as compared to other districts. The above reasons made us to select Shimoga district as case study.

The Shimoga district for administrative purpose is divided into seven taluks and two sub divisions. Sagar subdivision and Shimoga sub division in which Sagar and Shimoga taluks were selected for the study as the traditional and non traditional areca gardens respectively.

From each sample taluk, four villages were selected. The major arecanut growing villages, having all the stages (first, second and third) and all the categories of farmers (small, medium and large) were selected for the study. From each village 25 sample farmers were selected randomly from each village equally from different farm categories and also from different stages of areca gardens.

Assuming the life span (economic bearing)of the areca palm as 50 years the present study has divided this period into three stages.

1. First stage (1 to 7 yrs.)
2. Second stage (8 to 40 yrs.)
3. Third stage (40 to 50 yrs.)

In all 48 first stage gardens, 36 second stage gardens and 16 third stage gardens were selected from each taluk

The farmers of the sample villages were divided into three categories as small. (up to 1 hectare), medium (1.01 to 2 hectares) and large farmers (above 2 hectares). This criterion is adopted by IRDP.

In order to study marketing Sagar and Shimoga markets were selected. The study has been carried out with the following objectives.

1. To study the cost of cultivation of arecanut among different categories of farmers in all the three stages.
2. To study the returns of arecanut among different categories of farmers in all the three stages.
3. To assess evaluation of investment in areca garden among different categories of farmers.
4. To study cost and returns of intercrop in the first stage/ mixed cropp in the second stage in areca gardens among different categories of farmers.
5. To study the marketing, price spread effect of arecanut.
6. To make suitable policy recommendations in the light of analysis to influence the public policy.

Hypothesis

The following hypothesis have been tested in the study.

1. The cost of cultivation of arecanut is more among large farmers as compared to medium and small in all the three stages in Shimoga district.
2. The returns of arecanut is more among large farmers as compared to medium and small in all the three stages in Shimoga district.
3. The large areca farmers are benefited more by cultivating intercrop / mixed crop as compared to medium and small in Shimoga district.
4. Arecanut plantation is economically viable among all the categories of farmers in Shimoga District.

To ascertain the influence of arecanut cultivation on the cultivation practices and socio-economic status of the arecanut farmers is made and it is evident from the analysis for the district as a whole and in both the taluks, the large farmers' socio economic status is better when compared to medium and small farmers.

Between the taluks all the categories of farmers of Sagar taluk is better when compared with the conditions of Shimoga taluk.

The cultivation practices of sample areca cultivators in the study area exhibits the different methods of cultivation adopted, types of irrigation, variety of seedlings, intercrops and mixed crops, method of processing, grading all these will have an impact on cost of cultivation and yield.

The method of cultivation in traditional areca growing area is markedly different from the methods adopted in non-traditional areca growing area.

The heavy monsoon, the broken hilly nature, steep and narrow valleys alternating with jungles and slopes are the special characteristics of malnad tract when compared to Shimoga taluk where arecanut gardens occupy large area of levelled fields and the rainfall is less. The important difference in cultivation is that of no prominence given to irrigation channel and almost discarding the drainage channels. The cultivation of these gardens is neither so elaborate nor systematic as in the areca gardens of traditional taluk.

The weeding, light digging followed by application of fresh earth and farm yard manure, mulching, selection of seeds makes the difference between the traditional and non-traditional growing area.

All the sample farmers in both the taluks will grow banana as a intercrop in the first stage basically for the shade and for the improvement of subsoil moisture and to get some additional income, but in the second stage pepper and cocoa will be grown as mixed crops in traditional and non-traditional area respectively in their areca gardens to get substantial additional income, which will help the areca farmers in the study area to maintain the areca garden in the second stage.

The majority of sample farmers in the study area will market their produce through APMC, Co-operative societies and few of them sell their produce in the local markets.

The sample farmers of Sagar taluk are more efficient in adoption of cultivation practices and marketing of arecanut as compared to sample farmers of shimoga taluk.

In agriculture cost of cultivation definitely has its impact on yield from crop. Here an attempt has been made to estimate the cost of cultivation of arecanut garden in different stages with the help of information provided by the sample farmers of the study area in Shimoga district.

To establish an arecanut garden it requires huge amount of investment, as it is a perennial crop. Areca palm takes seven years to establish and start bearing economic yield in the gestation period. During this period i.e. in gestation period, banana is grown as an intercrop mainly to provide shade to the young areca palm and to get some early returns in the study area. The banana suckers will be removed once the areca palm attains four years of age.

In the second stage of the arecanut garden i.e., 8-40 yrs in the study area the farmers grow pepper and cocoa as mixed crops to get additional income.

As it is already mentioned earlier that arecanut is a perennial crop, the cost of cultivation consists of establishment cost and maintenance cost. In the first stage of the garden it is the establishment cost which constitute considerable proportion of cost and at later stages it will be maintenance cost which becomes important, but both of them will have a bearing on yield from the crop. Hence the relative role of establishment cost and maintenance cost need to be examined so as to see which cost is most influential in determining the yield. For this purpose the analysis of cost of cultivation among different categories of farmers in two taluks is considered in the present study.

The establishment cost is one time investment on arecanut garden. The amount of establishment cost sometime determines the healthy growth of a plant and its yield. Thus it is necessary to examine it.

In the present analysis establishment cost consists cost incurred on land levelling, fencing, openwell, pumpsets, sprinkler, conveyor pipes, processing yard, interest on fixed capital, land revenue seedlings, red earth etc.

The maintenance cost consists items like wages paid to labourers, hiring costs of bullocks and machines, cost on chemical fertilizers, farm yard manure, green leaves, pesticides and insecticides, irrigation cost etc.

In the gestation period the total establishment cost of Sagar and Shimoga taluks and in the entire district the share of the first year establishment cost is highest because expenses made on irrigation infrastructure which includes open wells, pumpsets, sprinklers, conveyor pipes, pumphouse and for intensive labour is high.

The cost incurred on labour cost which includes activities like land levelling, digging of pits, planting the seedlings, irrigating the garden, application of organic manures and chemical fertilizers etc.

In the first year, the expenses incurred on hired machines is high for the preparation of land, whereas in Sagar taluk it is still higher as compared to Shimoga taluk because of geographical conditions.

Expenses made on nursery of seedlings have considerable impact on the economic bearing of the areca garden subsequently investment made from second year to sixth year on irrigation of the garden manuring, plant protection chemicals which inevitably includes labour cost also.

In the life of areca palm the sixth and seventh year is considered as the penultimate year before which bears nuts hence fertilizers will be applied more in quantity. Hence in the gestation period the share of establishment cost as well as maintenance cost is considerably high as compared to second and third stages among all the categories of farmers.

In the gestation period, the average amount of investment per hectare in the study area is Rs.2,11,969.00 more than half of this constitutes maintenance cost. The establishment cost accounts for 37% of the total investment. The amount of investment per hectare varies among different categories of farmers. The percentage gap between establishment cost and maintenance cost is not as much as it is for the entire district. In case of large farmers per hectare investment, is more than the overall average for the district. Whereas in case of medium and small farmers category the average investment per hectare is less than the overall average investment. The investment made by the medium farmers is slightly more than the small farmers.

It is clear from the data that the proportion of maintenance cost is found increasing as the size of holding decreases. In other words, in case of small farmers the proportion of maintenance cost is more than the establishment cost. This ratio decreases with increasing size of holding. It means maintenance cost is more and establishment cost is less in case of small farmers and this gap declines with increasing size of holdings.

The talukwise comparison of the volume of investment depicts a different picture. In Sagar taluk the per hectare investment is much above the overall investment in the study area whereas in case of Shimoga taluk it is very much below the overall position. It may be concluced that farmers in Sagar taluk are investing more as compared to farmers of Shimoga taluk.

But in Shimoga taluk the percentage Share of establishment cost is more than the maintenance cost but this ratio is less in Sagar taluk that means establishment cost is less than the maintenance cost in Sagar taluk.

Within the taluk the percentage share of establishment vs maintenance cost varies between different farm categories. For example, in Sagar taluk the share of maintenance cost is more than establishment cost. This share decreases as size of holding increases. It is evident that there is not much difference between small and medium farmers as regards the share of establishment and maintenance cost.

But it is totally different in case of large farmers where in the percentage share between the two costs is not much. For this it may be concluded that in Sagar taluk in case of small and medium farmers more money is spent in maintenance of areca farms than on establishment. Whereas large farmers in the same taluk spend relatively more on establishment of the areca farms. Such variation will have some impact on the yield from the palm.

In Shimoga taluk the investment picture is altogether different as compared to Sagar taluk. In this taluk percentage share of establishment cost is more as compared to Sagar taluk. It is on higher side in case of large farmers categories wherein the proportion of establishment cost is more than the maintenance cost.

This is the distinct feature of large farmers category in Shimoga taluk which is not found in the entire study area.

It is clear that the average per hectare investment is highest in Sagar taluk, and much less in Shimoga taluk when compared to entire study area. Another special feature of investment in the study area is that per hectare investment by large farmers is much above the overall average investment for the study area in both taluks.

Among them it is found to be highest in Sagar taluk followed by the District and Shimoga taluk. Even the small and medium farmers in Sagar taluk are found investing more as compared to Shimoga taluk and the District.

In Sagar taluk in the first stage the large farmers invests more as compared to medium and small farmers. The total maintenance cost is also more when compared to total establishment cost among all categories of farmers.

In the maintenance cost all the categories of farmers made more investment on human labour followed by organic manures, cost on irrigation, interest on working capital, bullock power, on hired machines and plant protection chemicals.

In the establishment cost medium and large categories of farmers made more investment on irrigation infrastructure, followed by land levelling red earth, fencing, land revenue, interest on fixed capital, processing yard, seedlings.

Whereas in small farmers category in the total cost the share of seedlings is little higher than land revenue, interest on working capital and processing yard.

The expenditure made on total maintenance cost is high among large farmers as compared to other categories of farmers. Large farmers have made more expenditure on human labour, chemical fertlizers, manures, irrigation cost with interest on working capital, plant protection chemical as compared to medium and small farmers. The total establishment cost is high among large farmers as compared to remaining categories of farmers. Because they have made more investment on irrigation infrastructure that too sprinkler and conveyor pipes.

Whereas in Shimoga taluk the total establishment cost is higher than the maintenance cost among large farmers category as compared to other categories of farmers as they have made more investment on irrigation infrastructure.

In the maintenance cost small farmers have made more investment on human labour followed by irrigation and interest on working capital, organic manures with chemical fertilizers, bullock power, hired machines and plant protection chemicals whereas medium and large farmers have made more investment on human labour, irrigation cost, interest on working capital, bullock power in combination with hired machines, farm yard manure, green leaves, chemical fertilizers and plant protection chemicals.

In the establishment cost all the categories of farmers invested more on irrigation infrastructure i.e. openwell, pumpsets, sprinkler, conveyor pipes, pumphouse followed by land levelling, red earth, fencing, land revenue in combination with interest on fixed capital, processing yard and seedlings.

The expenditure made on total maintenance cost is high among large farmers as compared to other categories of farmers because they made more expenditure on all components of maintenance cost.

In the district in the total establishment cost all the categories of farmers have made more investment on irrigation infrastructure, land levelling, red earth, fencing, land revenue, interest on fixed capital, processing yard in this order.

All the categories of farmers in their respective maintenance cost made more expenditure on human labour, organic manure, chemical fertilizer, irrigation cost and interest on working capital, bullock power, hired machines and plant protection chemicals in this sequence.

In the second and third stages in Sagar taluk large farmers invested more as compared to medium and small. The total maintenance cost is more as compared to total establishment cost.

In the maintenance cost all the categories of farmers made more investment on human labour followed by organic manures, chemical fertilizers, irrigation cost, interest on working capital and plant protection chemicals.

All the categories of farmers in their respective establishment cost have made more investment on red earth, interest on fixed capital and land revenue which is comparatively negligible.

The expenditure incurred on total maintenance cost is high among large farmers as compared to remaining categories of farmers as larger farmers invested more on all components of maintenance cost.

In considering the total establishment cost, among large farmers it is high compared to other categories of farmers because of the same reason, where the investment is more on red earth, interest on fixed capital and land revenue.

Whereas in Shimoga taluk in second and third stage large farmers invested more when compared to remaining category of farmers. Further in comparison with the maintenance cost the establishment cost is negligible among all the categories of farmers.

In the maintenance cost, small, medium and large farmers have made major investment on human labour followed by irrigation cost, interest on working capital, organic manures, chemical fertilizers and plant protection chemicals.

In the total maintenance cost the expenditure made is high among large farmers category as compared to other categories of farmers, because of large farmers made more investment on various components in the maintenance cost.

In the entire study area within the maintenance cost all the three categories of farmers invested more expenditure on human labour, organic manures, chemical fertilizer, irrigation cost with interest on working capital and plant protection chemicals in that order.

Large farmers made more investment in both the stages as compared to medium and small categories of farmers.

In conclusion the overall investment in both the taluks declined considerably from second to third stage of areca garden among all the categories of farmers.

In the gestation period the areca palms are in growing stage and they will not yield any income till they, attain 4 to 5 years and they start bearing economic yield from the sixth year. During this period farmers have to invest on areca garden without any remuneration. Therefore, to supplement their investment most of the farmers grow an intercrop. Such intercrop not only bring income to farmers but also act as shade to the young areca plants. Basically banana will be grown as a intercrop to give shade to the areca plants in turn they will get income from the intercrop.

Therefore an assessment is made to see how much money is invested on intercrop and what is the return from such an intercrop an analysis will enable us to know, how far the intercrop will help farmers economically.

The average amount of investment on intercrop per hectare in the study area is Rs. 44,760.83. The amount of investment per hectare varies among different categories of farmers. For eg. in case of large farmers the per hectare investment is more than the overall average for the district.

The talukwise comparison shows that in Sagar taluk the per hectare investment is much above the overall investment in the study area.

With respect to Shimoga taluk it is very much below the overall position. From this it may be concluded that farmers in Sagar taluk are investing more as compared to Shimoga taluk. From the analysis made it is clear that the average per hectare is highest in Sagar taluk and much less in Shimoga taluk when compared to entire study area.

A special feature of investment in the study area is that per one hectare investment by large farmers is much above the overall average investment for the study area in both the taluks. Among large farmers' category it is found to be highest in Sagar taluk followed by district and Shimoga taluk

Even the small and medium farmers in Sagar taluk investing more as compared to Shimoga taluk and the district. It is evident from the analysis that investment by small, medium and large farmers in Sagar taluk is much more than the same in other taluk and the district as a whole.

In Sagar taluk the investment per hectare made by small farmers is almost equal to the investment made by large farmers in Shimoga taluk. It evidently shows the average investment by all categories of farmers in Sagar taluk is much more than the Shimoga taluk.

It is evident that small farmers in Shimoga taluk are found investing least on intercrop as compared to others and further cost of cultivation of intercrop showed increasing trend with the increase in the size of farm holding.

Mixed crop is grown in the second stage in the study area. This crop is grown under the shade of areca palm. For this farmers spend some extra amount and it will bring some additional income to farmers. Hence an assessment is made on the cost of cultivation of these crops and the yield from this crop so as to see the benefit of cultivating arecanut by the farmers.

The average amount of investment per hectare on the mixed crop in the study area is Rs. 31,405.83. The investment per hectare varies among different categories of farmers. For instance large farmers per hectare investment is more than the overall average for the district and also it is clear from the analysis made that the investment increases as the size of holding increases.

In Sagar taluk the per hectare investment is much above the overall investment in the study area whereas in case of Shimoga taluk it is very much below the overall position. From this it may be concluded that farmers in Sagar taluk are investing more as compared to farmers of Shimoga taluk.

In the analysis made it is clear that the average per hectare investment is highest in Sagar taluk at the same time it is less in Sagar taluk when compared to entire study area. A special feature of investment in the study area is that the per hectare investment by large farmers is much less in Shimoga taluk when compared to entire study area.

Another unique feature of investment in the study area is that the per hectare investment by large farmers is much above the overall average investment for the entire study area in both the taluks.

Among large farmers it is found to be highest in Sagar taluk followed by the district. The medium farmers are found investing more as compared to small category of farmers in Shimoga taluk and the district.

It may be concluded that the investment made by small, medium and large farmers in Sagar taluk is much more than the same in other taluk and the district as a whole.

It is observed in Sagar taluk, the per hectare investment made by small farmers is almost equal to the investment made by medium farmers in Shimoga taluk.

It clearly shows the average investment made by all categories of farmers in Sagar taluk is much more than the farmers of Shimoga taluk.

It is also clear that small farmers in Shimoga taluk are found investing least on mixed crop as compared to others.

The following observations are made why large farmers in the study area of both taluks in all the three stages invest more as compared to medium and small.

The cost of cultivation depends upon the method of cultivation. The cost of cultivation is considerably high among large farmers as compared to medium and small in all the three stages. Higher investment made on cultivation definitely has its impact on the yield of areca garden. Large farmers adopt planned and scientific cultivation practices followed by better management. The large farmers' socio-economic background is high with higher educational status and contacts and with, good mass media participation and above all better withstanding capacity in unforeseen conditions and in times of price fluctuations.

Usually large farmers made more investment on irrigation infrastructures, on sprinklers, conveyor pipes with good manuring practices associated with mulching.

Large farmers' resource use management is better than medium and small. They will make use of plant and animal wastes to increase the yield per hectare and even the liquid manuring after filtering will be given to the garden through sprinklers. At the same time they will maintain the fertility of the soil by green leaf manure, mulching and conduct soil testing and counseling with agricultural experts etc. with scientific manuring and good irrigation practices. Further they will take atmost care to increase economic bearing of areca garden and they will keep the garden cool and tidy by maintaining soppina betta and gomala and planting trees at the edge of the garden to withstand the winds and from the sunscorch.

From the analysis it is proved that farmers of Sagar taluk are investing more as compared to farmers of Shimoga taluk because the cost of investment incurred on preparation of land for establishment of the areca garden, seed nursery, irrigation infrastructure, proper manuring, mulching and human labour. Apart from that selection of suitable area for establishment of the areca garden, fencing, selection and rising of areca nursery, proper preparation of pits followed by trenches, drainages in and around the garden for the flow of excess sepage and rain water, deweeding, periodical manuring, mulching, giving red earth, using slurry as a liquid manure and will be fed to the garden throw sprinklers. The recycling of plant and animal wastes, moreover proper economic usage of land area by adopting intercropping and mixed cropping for economic feasibility. They will take almost care in preventive measures against pest and diseases periodically.

Apart from this the involvement of human labour in the agricultural practice for manual works in the agricultural practices taken into account. Because human labour is the most important factor which is of primary importance in increasing the production in traditional agriculture. The basic input in production process is human labour.

In Sagar taluk human labour involvement is high because for the following reasons. They are involved is land levelling, fencing, trench, drainage in and around the areca garden, seednut selection, raising and maintaining the nurseries, digging of pits, planting, irrigation maintenance of the garden, application of manures, fertilizers, plant protection chemicals, likewise cultivation activities and supervision etc.

Areca cultivation in Sagar taluk is the way of life as there were cultivating areca since a very long time, and there is no scope for alternative crop to grow apart from areca except intercropping and mixed cropping due to geographical and climatic conditions. Hence they are taking proper care regarding the areca crop.

At the same time some observations is made to bring out the salient features why low investment is made by the farmers of Shimoga taluk as compared to counterparts farmers of Sagar taluk.

Basically farmers of Shimoga taluk are not traditional growers of areca they have not adopted systematic plant cultivation practices in selection of site, proper fencing, selection of nut variety, raising of nursery etc. basically the farmers of Shimoga taluk are the paddy and sugarcane growers, but in recent decades those fields are presently converted into areca garden in the recent decades.

As arecanut is exclusively seed propagated crop. Being a perennial crop it is essential that adequate care is bestowed in the selection of proper planting material.

Four important factors to be observed in selection and raising of arecanut seedlings.

1. Selection of mother palm.
2. Selection of seed nuts.
3. Selection of proper technique in germination and raising seedlings.
4. Selection of seedlings.

There is no proper drainage and trenches. Agricultural (cultural) operations are not followed intensively.

There is no soppinabetta and gomala is not existing in shimoga and moreover the land owners are all absentee landlords because the supervision will be done from their managers or local farmers.

The important factor is the crop is not suitable to local soil and climatic conditions. Due to the fluctuations in areca prices the farmers of Shimoga taluk do not give sole attention towards the establishment and maintenance cost as they are getting main income from other sources. Because they are all professionalists either in medical, in engineering or merchants, contractors, lecturers, and retired officials. Hence the income from areca cultivation is secondary to them.

In the present study correlation co efficient is carried out to check for multicolliniarily among the important variables to know.

(i) Whether there is any correlation between the variable.

(ii) Whether the correlation is positive or negative.

Sagar Taluk

The correlation co efficient of maintenance cost among various farmers category in Sagar taluk is made. It reveals that all the variables in the equation are highly positively correlated with the total maintenance cost. This indicates that all the variables influences the total maintenance cost.

Within the total maintenance cost all the variables are positively correlated with each other at 1% level of significance. In Sagar taluk all categories of farmers made more investment on total maintenance cost, in which the dominant variables are human labour, farm yard manure, green leaves, chemical fertilizer, cost on irrigation with interest on working capital, bullock power, hired machines and plant protection chemicals.

The large farmers in Sagar taluk have made more investment on farm yard manure, green leaves, chemical fertilizers as compared to medium and small farmers in the study area.

Human labour is the highly dominant variable in the maintenance cost among all the categories of farmers, as they are involved in the application of farm yard manure green leaves and chemical fertilizers etc.

Shimoga Taluk

Statistical analysis with respect to the correlation co-efficient of maintenance cost among various farmers category in Shimoga taluk shows that total maintenance cost is positively correlated with all the variables in the equation at 1% level of significance.

Within the maintenance cost all the variables are positively correlated with each other with 1% level of significance.

In Shimoga taluk, in the maintenance cost the dominant variables are human labour, irrigation cost, farm yard manure, chemical fertilizers, bullock power, machines hired, plant protection chemicals respectively.

As in Sagar taluk in Shimoga taluk also human labour is the dominant variable in the maintenance cost.

The District

In Shimoga district the statistical analysis with respect to correlation co-efficient of maintenance cost among various farmers category reveals that, the maintenance cost is positively correlated with all the variables in the equation at 1 % level of significance.

Within the maintenance cost all the variables are positively correlated with each other at 1% level of significance.

In Shimoga district in the maintenance cost the most dominant variable is human labour. Next dominant variables are farm yard manure green leaves, chemical fertilizers, irrigation cost, bullock power, machines, hired, plant protection chemicals respectively.

In conclusion from the analysis made, there is significant correlation between the variables among the various farmers category in both the taluks in the study area and highly positive correlation is existing between the variables in the maintenance cost.

Multiple Regression is applied to analyse the significance of different variables in the present study and how these variables influence the total maintenance cost. At the same time it will enable us to understand which is the dominant variable in determining the yield of areca and intercrop/mixed crop.

Sagar Taluk

In Sagar taluk multiple regression of maintenance cost among various farmers category is applied.

The analysis reveals that among small, medium and large farmers category all the variables are dominant at 5% level of significance in the maintenance cost. The R square value for small and medium farmers is 99 % each and for large farmers 100%.

In the maintenance cost dominant variables are human labour farm yard manure, green leaves, chemical fertilizers, cost on irrigation, interest on working capital, bullock power, hired machines plant protection chemicals which implies that expenditure incurred on each component in the maintenance cost has significant role in enhancing returns of arecanut as well as returns of intercrop / mixed crop.

Human labour is the most dominant variable in the maintenance cost.

Shimoga Taluk

In Shimoga taluk it is clear from the statistical data that among all the category of farmers all the variables are dominant at 5% level of significance.

The R square value is 99% each for small and medium farmers, 100% for large farmers.

The dominant variables are human labour, farm yard manure, green leaves, chemical fertilizer cost on irrigation, interest on working capital, bullock power , hired machines, plant protection chemicals.

As witnessed in Sagar taluk here also human labour is the highly dominant variable in the maintenance cost.

It evidently shows that the expenses incurred on each component in the maintenance cost has a significant bearing on the returns of areca and returns of intercrop/mixed crop.

The District

In the district, the statistical data reveals that among all the categories of farmers all the variables are dominant at 5% level of significance.

The R square value is 99% each for all the categories of farmers. Within the maintenance cost human Labour is proved to be highly significant variable.

Within the farmers category the investment per hectare is more among large farmers in both the taluks as compared to medium and small farmers because large farmers are taking several cultivation operations to maintain the garden in good condition. Within the taluk maintenance cost is highly dominant in Sagar taluk because all the components of the maintenance cost are dominant as compared to Shimoga taluk.

After the cost analysis an attempt is made about the yield and returns of arecanut in the study area.

Yield of any field crop which is the average amount of produce per unit area is simple and definite in conception but biologically is very complex and is influenced by many factors.

Normally, type of soil, crop husbandry, season, quality of seed materials, incidence of pests and diseases, management of agricultural practices effect on the yield of crop. Arecanut being a perennial crop unlike annuals the yield is further subjected to the influence of the age of the areca palm.

Successful cultivation operation is an individual problem. It involves many physical and economic factors. The success of any particular farmer is determined largely by the resources available and his willingness to work industriously and his ability to manage farms in such a manner so as to get maximum returns.

A farmer must involve himself diligently to his work to be a successful farmer. In addition he must be a skilled manager. Within this background the evaluation of returns of arecanut per hectare with respect to various stages in traditional as well as non-traditional areas of Shimoga district is made.

In the present study during the gestation period i.e. at the end of 6th and 7th year areca palm starts yielding and in the second stage yield will go on increasing year after year and in third stage yield will slightly decline.

It is clear from the analysis in the study area large category of farmers are getting better yield when compared to medium and small farmers.

With respect to Sagar and Shimoga taluks here also large farmers are in better position compared to medium and small. In taluk wise comparison in the study area, farmers of Sagar taluk are getting better yield as compared to farmers of Shimoga taluk. It is evident from the analysis, returns of arecanut in the first stage is Rs. 54,204.17 per hectare. The total returns of arecanut per hectare in the district varies among all the categories of farmers.

For instance, in case of large farmers the returns of arecanut per hectare is more than the overall for the district, while in the case of medium and small farmers category the average returns of arecanut per hectare is less than the total returns of the returns of the district. However in comparison the total returns of arecanut is slightly higher among medium farmers category than the small farmers category.

In the study area the taluk wise comparison of total returns shows that in Sagar taluk it is much above the district average, where as in Shimoga taluk it is very much below the district average total returns.

When both the taluks are taken into consideration on an average the total returns per hectare is more among large farmers category than medium and small farmers category.

Further, large farmers are getting more returns in comparison with the overall average of the district. While in the case of medium and small farmers on an average the total returns is less than the overall average total returns.

It is clear from the above analysis that on an average, the total returns is highest in Sagar taluk as compared to Shimoga taluk and also the entire study area due to the higher investment made by the farmers of Sagar taluk as compared to farmers of Shimoga taluk.

In addition farmers in Sagar taluk adopt scientific methods of cultivation as compared to farmers of Shimoga taluk. Further, the soil and climatic condition in Sagar taluk are more favorable to arecanut cultivation. That is the reason as to why farmers of Sagar taluk get better returns.

In the second stage farmers can get maximum returns from arecanut garden and make some profits. Therefore, the analysis of returns in the second stage will throw light on the economic feasibility of arecanut cultivation.

Large farmers category in the study area are getting higher yield in comparison to medium and small farmers.
When compared to the farmers of Shimoga taluk and the district, the farmers of Sagar taluk are getting higher yield.
The returns per hectare in the study area is Rs. 2,16,170.66. The total returns of the district of arecanut per hectare varies among different categories of farmers.

In case of large farmers the per hectare total returns of arecanut is more than the overall average for the district, whereas in case of medium and small farmers category the average returns of the arecanut per hectare is less than the overall average.
However, the total returns of arecanut of medium farmers category is slightly more than the small farmers category. It is clear from the analysis the total returns is found increasing as the size of landholding increases.

Between the taluk wise comparison of the total returns depicts a different picture. In Sagar taluk the per hectare total returns is much above the overall total returns in the study area, whereas in case of Shimoga taluk, it is very much below the overall position.

From this it may be concluded that farmers in Sagar taluk are getting more total returns as compared to farmers of Shimoga taluk.

Within the district in both the taluks the total returns per hectare is Rs. 2,46,797 and Rs. 1,85,544.33 respectively. In case of large farmers the per hectare total returns is more than the overall average for the respective taluks. Whereas in case of medium and small farmers category the average total returns per hectare is less than the overall average total returns.

However, the total returns of medium farmers is slightly more than the small farmers. From the analysis it is clear that the average per hectare total returns is highest in Sagar taluk and much less in Shimoga taluk as compared to the entire study area.

Large farmers in both the taluks are getting more returns than medium and small farmers due to

1. Higher investment per hectare,
2. Planned and Scientific cultivation practices.
3. De-weeding periodical manuring with red earth, proper irrigation management with sprinklers, mulching operations, proper periodical maintenance of drainages and trenches, disease palms will be removed and after proper processing new sapling will be planted.

All these operations will be carried out properly and meticulously in Sagar taluk, whereas in Shimoga taluk the above mentioned operations are not followed strictly. Hence, returns is comparatively low among large farmers in Shimoga taluk as compared to large farmers of Sagar taluk.

As compared to the second stage the yield of areca palm shows a declining trend after 40 years due to the age of the palm and soil condition.

It is evident from the analysis that in the district as a whole and in both the taluks, large farmers are better position with respect to the yield when compared to medium and small farmers category. While in talukwise comparison the farmers of Sagar taluk are getting higher yield as compared to farmers of Shimoga taluk. Another special feature to be noted in this stage is in comparison with the second stage the yield is comparatively less among all the categories of farmers in the study area.

In spite of declining returns in the third stage as usual large farmers are getting comparatively higher returns, than the medium and small farmers in the study area, because of their high investment and better farm management. In both the taluks large farmers are getting more returns per hectare as compared to medium and small farmers category.

In the taluk wise comparison as observed in the first and second stages, here also the farmers of Sagar taluk are getting more returns as compared to Shimoga taluk and overall for the study area. Evidently it is due to high investment, better management, eco-friendly nature of the crop, scientific and planned cultivation practices adopted.

Between taluk-wise comparison shows that the Sagar taluk has proved to be more efficient in areca cultivation as compared to Shimoga taluk and even the district.

To know the economic feasibility of investment on arecanut cultivation over a period of fifty years in the study area total returns, net returns, returns over total maintenance cost, returns per Re. Unit cost is calculated.

It is evident from the analysis that the total returns, net returns, returns over total maintenance cost. Returns per Re. Unit cost in the study area varies among different categories of farmers. In the entire district that the total returns, net returns, returns over total maintenance cost, returns per Re unit cost is high in large farmers as compared to medium and small.

In both the taluks the total returns, net returns, returns per Re unit cost, returns over total maintenance cost is high among large farmers category. Further, as compared to the entire district large farmers are getting more total returns, net returns, returns per Re unit cost whereas in case of medium and small farmers category the total returns, net returns, returns over total maintenance cost and returns per Re unit cost is less.

The taluk wise comparison shows that in Sagar taluk total returns, net returns, returns over total maintenance cost, returns per Re unit cost is much above the overall position in the study area, whereas in Shimoga taluk it is very much less than the overall district average.

The above analysis shows that total returns, net returns, returns over total maintenance cost, returns per Re unit cost is highest in Sagar taluk as compared to Shimoga taluk and also for the entire study area.

Considering the long pre bearing age of 6-7 years the farmers in the study area grow intercrop to get some subsidiary income from intercrop and also as a shade to the tender areca palm, which will improve the quality and condition of sub soil moisture.

In the entire district and in both the taluks large farmers are more beneficial in cultivating intercrop as compared to medium and small farmers.

Between the taluks intercrop cultivation is more remunerative to the farmers of Sagar taluk as compared to farmers of Shimoga taluk.

Mixed crop grown in the second stage in the study area. Pepper will be cultivated by the farmers of Sagar taluk and cocoa by the farmers of Shimoga taluk as a mixed crop. Mixed crop brings additional income to farmers hence it is worth analysing the income received from mixed crop so as to see to what extent it helps to farmers in recovering cost of cultivation incurred on areca garden in that stage or to what extent the income from mixed crop can subsidise the cost of cultivation during the second stage. This analysis will through light on economic benefit of cultivating mixed crop in the study area.

For the district as a whole net returns received from mixed crop among small farmers is Rs. 32,270 which is about 78.08% of the total cost incurred on arecanut cultivation in the second stage. In case of medium farmers category the net returns received from the mixed crop is Rs. 43,972.50 which is more than the total cost of cultivation incurred on arecanut cultivation in the second stage. In large farmers category the net returns received from mixed crop is Rs. 58,290 which is very much higher than the cost of cultivation of arecanut.

The overall position for the district shows that the net returns received from mixed crop is Rs. 44,844.17 which fully covers the entire cost of cultivation of areca garden during the second stage. From this it may be concluded that the income received from mixed crop gives substantial relief to farmers in the study area.
In Sagar and Shimoga taluk also the cultivation of mixed crop is quite beneficial among all the categories of farmers.

Agriculture plays a vital role in providing employment for rural folk. Areca cultivation provides a major employment generation for the rural community in Shimoga district. The garden provides work throughout the year, since it involves various cultivation operation like land levelling, fencing, pit preparation, nursery rising, planting of areca seedlings, de-weeding, mulching, manuring, irrigation management, maintenance of drainages and trenches, plant protection activities, harvesting, processing, watch and ward, transportation and allied activities.

Human labour is the dominant variable in the maintenance cost and also in determining the returns of arecanut. In the present study the involvement of human labour in the areca cultivation is evaluated.

In the first stage the total labour employment in mandays is more among large category as compared to medium and small in both the taluks of the study area due to intensive cultivation practices adopted. Between the taluks total labour employment (mandays) is high among all the categories of farmers of Sagar taluk as compared to the farmers of Shimoga taluk and it is even more than the overall average of the district due to meticulous cultivation practices.

As compared to the first stage, in second and third stages in the study area employment of human labour is less because only maintenance of the areca garden will be followed.

By and large it may be concluded that areca cultivation is more labour intensive in nature. This will help in solving the problem of rural unemployment in the study area.

Hence encouraging the farmers in arecanut cultivation will serve as an effective step in solving the problem of unemployment in the study area.

An analysis on returns of arecanut is made, the correlation co efficient is carried out to verify multicolliniarity among the dependent variables to know.

(i) Whether there is any correlation among the variables.

(ii) Whether the correlation is positive or negative.

The correlation co efficient of dependent variables with respect to returns of areca, intercrop/mixed crop, establishment cost and maintenance cost, cost of cultivation of intercrop/mixed crop among various farmers category is taken into account.

Sagar Taluk

It is clear from the analysis that in all the categories of farmers the cost of cultivation of intercrop/mixed crop is highly negatively correlated at returns of intecrop/mixed crop and also the returns of arecanut at 1% level of significance.

This indicates that over a period of time cost of cultivation declines as the returns increase.

In all the categories of farmers the returns of intercrop / mixed crop is highly negatively correlated with all the variables in the equation with 1% level of significance except returns of arecanut. Because banana as an intercrop increases the returns of arecanut as it will improve the sub soil moisture and also helpful to increase the pH level of the soil.

Among all the categories of farmers returns of arecanut is highly negatively correlated with all the variables in the equation at 1% level of significance except maintenance cost for small and medium farmers their correlation is low negative. Because, over a period of time cost of cultivation of arecanut decline but at the same time returns of areca increase.

Establishment cost is highly negatively correlated with returns of intecrop/mixed crop and returns of arecanut at 1 % level of significance among all the categories of farmers. Because in the areca gardens the initial investment is high but, in the second and third stage the component of establishment cost is very much negligible in the total cost. Establishment cost declines substantially over a period of time.

Among all the categories of farmers maintenance cost is highly negatively correlated with the returns of intercrop/mixed crop and also with the returns of arecanut at 1% level of significance. The reason is over a period of time maintenance cost declines substantially stage by stage but the returns arecanut increases considerably up to the end of second stage of the areca garden. In the third stage, returns of arecanut slightly declines. Due to this reason maintenance cost is perfectly negatively correlated with returns of intercrop/mixed crop and also with returns of arecanut.

Among all the categories of farmers the maintenance cost is also highly positively correlated with establishment cost with 1% level of significance. Hence, maintenance cost has direct relationship with establishment cost. But, the relation is inverse with respect to intercrop/mixed crop.

Shimoga Taluk

Correlation co-efficient of dependent variables of various farmers category in Shimoga taluk in made with respect to returns of arecanut, returns of intercrop/mixed crop, maintenance cost, establishment cost, cost of cultivation of intercrop/mixed crop. It is evident from the data that the returns of intercrop/mixed crop is highly negatively correlated with all the variables in the equation at 1% level of significance among all the categories of farmers except for returns of arecanut which has highly positive correlation in case of medium and large farmers but low positive correlation for small farmers.

As the intercrop/mixed crop helps to increase the yield of areca palm it is positively correlated with returns of arecanut at 1 % level of significance.

Among all the categories of farmers cost of cultivation of intercrop/mixed crop is negatively correlated with returns of intercrop/mixed crop and with returns of arecanut at 1 % level of significance. Because, over a period of time cost declines and simultaneously returns increase.

Among all the categories of farmers returns of arecanut is negatively correlated with all the variables in the equation at 1 % level of significance. Because, over a period time the cost declines returns increase.

Whereas establishment cost is positively correlated with the maintenance cost at 1% level of significance among all the categories of farmers, because in each and every stage there is direct relation between the establishment cost and the maintenance cost. Among all the categories of farmers maintenance cost is negatively correlated with returns of intercrop/mixed crop and also with returns of arecanut at 1 % level of significance. Because, the cost of maintenance made on areca garden declines gradually at the same time areca yield per hectare increases.

The District

Correlation co-efficient of dependent variables with respect to returns of arecanut, returns of intercrop/mixed crop, maintenance cost, establishment cost and cost of cultivation of intercrop/mixed crop an analysis is made.

It is clear from the data that among all the categories of farmers the returns of intercrop/mixed crop is negatively correlated with all the variables at 1% level of significance except for returns of arecanut banana which is grown as an intercrop will improve the subsoil moisture and also helps to maintain the pH level of soil. Thereby improve returns of areca.

Likewise pepper as a mixed crop will also influence on the yield of areca and does not compete with the nutrients of the manure given to the areca palm.

The additional income received from the intercrop/mixed crop gives relief to the farmers in the study area.

Whereas cost of cultivation of intercrop/mixed crop is negatively correlated with returns of intercrop/mixed crop and also with returns of arecanut, at 1% level of significance among all the categories of farmers.

This shows that over a period of time cost of cultivation declines and the returns increase.

Returns of arecanut is negatively correlated with all the variables at 1% level of significance. Because, over a period of time cost of cultivation of arecanut declines and at the same time returns increase. But in case of small and medium farmers their correlation is low negative.

Establishment and maintenance costs are negatively correlated with the returns of intercrop/mixed crop and also with returns of arecanut at 1 % level of significance. Whereas establishment and maintenance costs are positively correlated with each other at 1 % level of significance among all the categories of farmers.

In conclusion, in the entire district and also in both taluks in large farmers categories returns of arecanut, returns of intercrop/ mixed crop is highly negatively correlated with the maintenance cost and the establishment cost and cost of cultivation of intercrop /mixed crop as compared to medium and small farmers which indicates large farmers are more beneficial.

Between the taluks, in Sagar taluk returns of intercrop/mixed crop and returns of arecanut is highly negatively correlated with the maintenance cost and establishment cost and with cost of cultivation of intercrop/mixed crop which implies that farmers of Sagar taluk are more beneficial as compared to farmers of Shimoga taluk and the entire district.

The results of correlation co efficient further subjected for verification by the multiple regression with respect to returns of arecanut and linear regression with respect to returns of intercrop /mixed crop is made.

Sagar Taluk

Multiple Regression of returns of arecanut among various farmers category is made, from the data it is evident that among all the categories of farmers the establishment and maintenance costs are dominant at 5% level of significance in determining returns of arecanut, which shows the expenditure incurred on establishment and maintenance costs are significant in enhancing returns of areca. Within the maintenance cost, dominant variables are human labour, farm yard manure, green leaves, chemical fertilizer and cost on irrigation.

R square value for medium and large farmers is 98% each and for small farmers it is 96%. This indicates the R square is found to be fairly high among all the categories of farmers in Sagar taluk, indicating a fact that it fits in well with the data.

Further, it is clear from the statistical data that large farmers are more beneficial as compared to medium and small farmers.

Shimoga Taluk

Multiple Regression analysis on returns of arecanut among various farmers category in Shimoga taluk is made.

It is evident from the data that among all the categories of farmers, in determining the returns of arecanut establishment and maintenance costs are significant at 5% level of significance.
In the maintenance cost human labour, farm yard manure, fertilizers and irrigation cost are dominant variables.
R square value for small, medium and large farmers is 11%, 39% and 71% respectively.

The R square value is found to be fairly high among large farmers category as compared to medium and small farmers.

It is proved from the statistical data, that the expenses incurred on establishment and maintenance is significant in determining the returns of areca and also it is evident from the analysis that large farmers are more beneficial as compared to medium and small farmers.

The District

Multiple Regression analysis on returns of arecanut among various farmers category is made.

It is clear from the data, among all the categories of farmers, in determining the returns of arecanut establishment as well as maintenance costs are significant at 5% level of significance.
Which clearly indicates the investment made on establishment and maintenance has significant influence on the areca yield.

The maintenance cost is dominant in all the three stages. Within the maintenance cost the dominant variables are human labour, farm yard manure, green leaves, chemical fertilizer, cost on irrigation.

R square value for small, medium and large farmers category is 11%, 30% and 76% respectively. The R square value is fairly high among large farmers as compared to medium and small farmers category.

In the gestation period large farmers made more investment on irrigation infrastructure that too on sprinklers and conveyor popes as compared to medium and small farmers category.
Large farmers made more investment on maintenance cost in all the three stages as compared to medium and small farmers.
In conclusion it is clear from the above statistical analysis that in the entire district and also in both the taluks, large farmers are benefited as compared to medium and small farmers.

Between the taluks, the farmers of Sagar taluk proved to be more beneficial as compared to farmers of shimoga taluk.

Sagar Taluk

Linear Regression dependent variable (returns of intercrop/mixed crop) among various farmers categories in Sagar taluk is made. It is clear from the data that among all the categories of farmers cost of cultivation of intercrop/mixed crop is significant at 5% level of significance with the returns of intercrop/mixed crop.

It implies that cost of cultivation of intercrop/mixed crop influence significantly in determining the returns of intercrop/mixed crop. Further, among all the categories of farmers there is 99% of variation is existing between the variables, (R square value is 99%) which implies that all the categories of farmers in Sagar taluk is proved to be beneficial in intercrop/mixed crop cultivation.

Shimoga taluk: Linear Regression on returns of intercrop/mixed crop among various farmers category in Shimoga district is made.

It is clear from the data that in Shimoga taluk also among small, medium and large farmers category the cost of cultivation of intercrop/mixed crop is significant at 5% level of significance, with returns of intercrop/mixed crop, which implies that the cost of cultivation of intercrop/ mixed crop influences significantly in enhancing the returns of intercrop/mixed crop. The R square value for medium and large farmers category is 99% each, whereas for small farmers it is 99%.

The District

Linear Regression of returns of intercop/mixed crop among various farmers categories in the district is made.

It is evident from the data, that the cost of cultivation of intercrop/ mixed crop is significant with the returns of intercrop/ mixed crop at 5 % level of significance. Because farmers in Sagar taluk are giving equal prominence to the cultivation of intecrop/ mixed crop. As a result returns are more.

The R square value is 22%, 64% and 94% for small, medium and large farmers category respectively which indicates clearly that large farmers are more beneficial as compared to medium and small farmers in the study area.

From the above statistical analysis made it is clear that in the entire district and in the both the taluks large farmers evidently benefited more than medium and small farmers category.

Between the taluks, farmers of Sagar taluk proved to be more remunerative in intercrop/mixed crop cultivation as compared to farmers of Shimoga tatuk and the entire district. In the marketing aspect a brief note on price movement and growth in areca plantation is mentioned.

There is high co relation between plantation and price with prices picking up arecanut gained importance as a cash crop. Increasing in prices attracted farmers. Lot of paddy, sugarcane areas especially in Shimoga taluk were concerted into arecanut gardens, when this was the trend people other than - traditional growers were also started investing in arecanut plantations.

Later when prices started falling down the growers stopped investment on new arecanut plantations.

Such price correlation with crop area and plantation is found in all agricultural commodities, whenever prices increase for any commodity farmers shift to that crop.

Co-operative marketing societies play an important role in the marketing of arecanut in bulk and assist their members in selling their produce whenever they wish. These societies provide facilities like provision of credit facilities, storage facilities etc.

There are three important co-operative marketing societies functioning in the Shimoga district are,

1. Central Areca and cocoa marketing co-operative society Limited (CAMPCO)
2. Maland Areca marketing co-operative society Limited (MAMCOS)
3. Arecanut processing and sales co-operative society Limited. (APSCOS).

CAMPCO is a joint venture effort of the state governments of Karnataka and Kerala and was establishment in 1973. The CAMPCO was started by the state government of Kerala and Karnataka in order to protect it is popularly known as CAMPCO.

The few main objectives of the institutions.

1. To procure arecanut from member growers and if necessary from other growers on agency basis or on outright purchase basis.
2. To arrange for their sale of arecanut to the best advantage of its members.
3. To provide credit facilities.
4. To export the produce
5. To promote scientific research and manufacture of semi-finished, finished produce of arecanut, MAMCOS.

It is one of the oldest marketing society of the sample district started in 1939. The head office is situated in Shimoga.

The main objectives of the MAMCOS are,

1. To provide good market for the arecanut grower members.
2. To provide credit facilities, storage facilities, fertilisers etc to its members.
3. To export arecanut out of state.

   Apart from these facilities it provides useful literature about arecanut production.

1. Cultivation, processing to its members.
2. Provides implements for the purpose of spraying chemicals.
3. It organises seminars workshops and on arecanut production and development.

APSCOS, Sagar

It is also one of the reputed and oldest society established during 1973 in study area at Sagar with Hosanagar, Sagar and Sorab taluk growers as its members.

APSCOS also is having many objectives.

1. On marketinng, processing, grading of arecanut just like CAMPCO.

Agricultural Produce Marketing Committee (APMC)

Regulated APMC also started by the Government at Shimoga in the APMC yard. Thus the establishment of the co-operative marketing societies because a boon to arecanut cultivators in the study area.

It is very interested to note that the prices of arecanut donot always fall within the economic principles. In principle the price moves forward or backward with the change in supply or demand. More surprisingly, there are instances in areca trade the price has risen or fallen even though the supply is more or less constant. However this sort of wild variation in prices of arecanut has become almost regular feature in the market. This has widely affected the small and medium farmers categories who entirely depend upon the areca income for their livelihood.

The white variety of arecanut which is got from ripe arecanut after sundrying for 40-45 days in the common most variety.

Major market for Red in Shimoga. Sagar market is for Red and White.

The growers will do primary grading at their level but the traders will do further grading of the arecanut based as quality, colour, size and demand of the market. Red variety of areca is mainly used for preparation of gutkha, panmasala and scented supari and few quantity is consumed by direct chewing.

The sales procedure and proceedings in APMC is highlighted in the marketing chapter. The price behaviour of arecanut and its reason for price fluctuation delt is the marketing chapter.

The price spread effect in the local market from growers to consumers in the study area is worked out.

In Sagar market the price spread effect is less from grower to consumer because the wholesales, retailers quote less profit margin as compared to Shimoga market.

With regards to imports during 1950 arecanut production in the country was not sufficient to meet the international requirements. This reflected in the import of areca in huge quantities to India.

In 1994-95, India started importing arecanut due to increase in domestic consumption. However compared to the total Indian production of arecanut import is negligible as per the DGCIS statistics about 29,227 tonnes, Rs.850 million of arecanut was imported during the year 2000-01.

When prices of arecanut suddenly picked up in 1999-2000. The prices became unaffordable to the Indian consumers mainly for the price of value added products. As a result candestine import started because, imported arecanut is inferior to Indian quality and it was very cheap and mainly used for manufacturing Gutkha.

To protect the interest of domestic industry Government of India took major initiatives by raising duty on arecanut from 35% to 100%. Thus the traders were using unofficial ways for import.

The imported arecanut from Indonesia, Malaysia, Mayanmar, arrives at Kolkata port for exports to Nepal. From Nepal this arecanut is transported to Nepal by road and it is again brought to Kolkota market or Siliguri market through Dhalbari border.

The estimated imports from Nepal border to India in the year 2000-01 is around 14,500 tonnes, This arecanut is moved to Kolkota, Uttarapradesh, Bihar for other parts of the country for gutka manufacturing.

It has been observed that the quality of imported arecanut is inferior and tasteless. Hence it was mainly used gutkha and panmasala manufacturers, and also some of the traders mix the imported arecanut with chali or white variety of the domestic market.

In this regard Government has to take stringent action against the cladnderstine imports from other countries if not it effects the prospects of domestic arecanut in India.

In the marketing with respect to the exports of the country, the bulk of production of arecanut in India is consumed within the country. However, small quantity of arecanut is exported abroad, as per the DGCIS statistics export is ranging between 100 to 800 tonnes over a period of fifty years. During 2000-01 India exported 639 tonnes (62-9 million) of arecanut mainly to UAE, UK, Maldives, Canada, Singapore, Bangaldesh, USA and to other countries.

During the survey conducted by DGCIS it has been abserved arecanut is exported to Bhutan and Bangladesh from fuentsholing town a border town of West Bengal and Assam considering this estimated export of arecanut from India during 2000-01around 4000 tonnes.

In the marketing chapter proper conclusions and suggestions were given to facilitate the marketing and safeguard the interest of all the farmers category of the study area. One the basis of the results of the present study the following conclusions are drawn.

1. Arecanut is highly remunerative crop in the entire study area and in both the taluks and this was the reason behind rapid area expansion of areca cultivation of both the taluks, despite the high establishment cost in the first stage of the areca garden.
2. The results of the study indicates that the investment on arecanut cultivation is economically feasible and financially sound-irrespective of category of farmers in the study area.

   However the results of the investment evaluation (NPV, IRR, B:C Ratio, pay-back period) reveals that, if any priority tof be asigned in the development of areca gardens the first priority goes to large farmers category followed by medium and small farmers category.
3. The size of land holding is a vital element in determining the management capacity of the farmer.

   Large farmers are more economical in working and conductive to greater efficiency because all the technical advantages is open to large farmers are not open to small and medium farmers.

   Large farmers enjoy economics of cultivation yield and returns, management and marketing. In turn these economics will help in reducing cost of the farm and increases the efficiency.

   Economics of cultivation will be reaped by large farmers on account of

   1. Use of upto date human and machine labour.
   2. Advantages of skilled and unskilled labourers in areca cultivation.
   3. Maintenance of the infrastructure.
   4. Proper utilisation of by products.
   5. Usage of more effective utilisation of available source of their farm yield.

   Hence the investment on large gardens are more profitable.
4. As arecanut is a perennial crop, it starts bearing economic yield from, sixth year onwards and the farmers has to make heavy

investment in the forst stage. Banana has grown as an intercrop basically to give shade to the young areca sapling. Banana suckers will be removed when areca palm attains four years. Banana gives an additional income in the gestation period it will help the farmer to meet some part of the expenses made on the investment, and also provides employment generation for the rural yolk.

Likewise, mixed cropping grown in the second stage in Sagar and Shimoga taluks. Peper is cultivated in Sagar taluk while cocoa is cultivated in Shimoga taluk as mixed crop respectively.

Mixed crop brings additional income to farmers. The income received from the returns of mixed crop will subsidise the cost of cultivation of areca garden during second stage. The income varies for different farmers category in the study area. Hence we recommend to grow intercropand mixed crop in areca gardens to get some economic relief (benefit) to the farmer.

5. Arecanut is a commercial crop and arecanut cultivation is highly capital intensive at the same time it is high employment oriented also. It provides direct employment to large no. of rural folk as well as indirect employment to many who are in its processing, marketing and trading activities.

   It provides more than five crores of mandays of employment annually in its cultivation. It provides basic necessities for the persons who are involved in areca cultivation and marketing.

   The areca gardens provides work throughout the year since it involves various agricultural operations like land levelling, fencing, for pit preparation, nursery rising, planting of areca seedlings, intercrop, and mixed crop cultivation, de-weeding, mulching, manuring, in irrigation infrastructure, for plant protection activity, harvesting, watch and ward, transportation, marketing upto the consumer level.

   Arecanut cultivation provides employment for both skilled and unskilled labourers. The large farmers category provides highest mandays of employment followed by medium and small farmers category.

6. Arecanut cultivation in the entire study area and in both the taluks helped in boosting the farmers economy and also enhanced the social and economic position of the farmers.

7. In the study area system of irrigation mark the progress of people. Water management is important in agriculture. The success of agriculture depends mainly on how timely and adequately the water is used. And the requirement of areca cultivation.

The conservation of water and its judicious and economic use is very important. As areca is a perennial crop the farmers adopt more scientific techniques and intensive cultivation and enables the farmers to use best quality at the right time and to reap bigger margins of profit.

Loss of water occurs in conveince and distribution system, non-uniformity in the spread of water over the field, perculation below the root zone and sugarcane run-ff is common in the canal system. Hence sprinkler system of irrigation is advantageous, and it is superior over the conventional irrigation system and it is helpful in getting more yield.

In the study area large farmers installed sprinkler irrigation system though it requires more investment.

The inputs like human labour, farm yard manure, green leaves, chemical fertilizers, plant protection chemicals are used efficiently by large farmers category in the study area and they are getting good returns and they are economically benefited.

Hence we recommend to small and medium farmers to use all the above inputs in a proper and efficient manner to get good yield and in turn to get remunerative returns.

Suggestions

In Karnataka use of arecanut and its cultivation constitute a distinct agricultural practice and it is also one of the important commercial crop compared to other economic crops. Areca palm received adequate attention by large farmers of study area as far as possible in the following aspects. So as to get good economic yield. These following aspects is also applicable for small and medium categories of farmers to follow to get good and remunerative returns.

Arecanut is cultivated in varieties of soils and climatic conditions but the yield and economic bearing of arecanut is governed by the following points.

Climate

(i) Altitude is very important since at a higher altitude the winter temperature is too extreme for the crop it adversely effect on yield of areca and its returns and the quality of fruit is not good.

At a higher altitude it effects the germination of seed of arecanut as well as the dry Kernal i.e. chali.

It grows well below 850 meters of the see level because the germination of nut and preparation of the weight of the Kernal is good.

(ii) *Temperature:* The palm florishes within the temparature range of 14^{0}C to 36^{0}C. Extremes of temperature are not good for the healthy growth of the palm. Because its causes heavy damage to the foliage and even the death of the areca palm.

(iii) *Rainfall:* The area palm flourishes in tracts of rainfall especially in Malnad but not so well in maidan parts. It grows but the yield is less. It grows well in traditional areas as it is suitable for areca cultivation. It is suitable to local soil and climatic conditions. In traditional areas hence we recommend small and medium farmers of non-traditional belt to consider this factor before investing on areca plantations.

NURSERY

Arecanut is exclusively seed propagated perennial crop. It is essential that adequate care is to be taken in selection and rising of areca seedlings.

1. Selection of mother palm.
2. Selection of Seednuts.
3. Selection of proper techniques and germinating and rising seedlings.
4. Selection of seedlings.
5. Selection of mother palm. the characters of the mother plam is age at which the first bearing start and regular bearing habit, with larger number of leaves and shorter internode and high fruit set are the criteria for the selection fo mother palm. Seednut selection.

Nuts to be selected from fully ripe nuts from the middle portion of the middle branch selection of seedlings.

NURSERY

Establishment of the Garden

Selection of the Site and Layout

Arecanut essentially a garden land crop and thrives best in humid areas protected well against hot sun burn and heavy wind. The palm does not withstand either drought or water stagnation. The site selected should therefore have adequate irrigation facility during the dry period.

The soil should be well drained and must have drainage facilities.

Areca palm is very delicate and cannot withstand with the extremes of temparature and exposure to direct sun. So it is essential that the site selected for rising areca garden should have protection either by way of hollocks or tall evergreen trees around the garden.

This is the reason that the traditional gardens are located in valley of hillslopes which are protected by forest trees growing all round. It is a typical site of malnad tract of Karnataka this should noted well by non-traditional areca farmers.

Spacing

Spacing depends primarily on the depth and fertility of the soil. It reflects on the yield of the areca palm.

Depth of Planting

Depth of plantingdepends upon the sub-soil moisture and height of water table. Areca palm does not with sand water stagnation, hence drainages in the fields to be provided and deep planting is preferred. Deeper planting provides a firm anchorage to the roots and also provides a larger volume of the space for the spread of roots.

Year after year fresh nodes exposed above the pit it has to be covered up in the course of annual operations of the manuring and intercultivation.

Season of planting

(Usually in May-June or September-October) the planting of seedlings in the permanent sites is done best in May-June or Septrember-October.

Drianage

Perfect drianage system and protection from suncorch is very important. It is essential to provide one drianage channel for every two rows of palms to drain the excess water.

At the beginning of the monsoon each year these drains are to be cleaned to have an easy flow for the stagnant or seepage water.

Shading

Young seedlings to be protected to the direct exposure of sun by providing shade of either arecanut or coconut leaves or by rising a shade crop of banana during the early years, it also helps the farmers to get some income in the gestation period.

GARDEN MANAGEMENT

Cultural operations followed by the cultivators in an elaborate and programmed system done in twice a year for digging the operations like digging, spread of farm yard mannure, de weeding, the interspaces of areca garden with green or dry leaves, it prevents the water evaporation from the ground recently dug protects rains and forms humus and manure to the soil and it suppress the weed growth.

Manuring

Green leaves, farm yard manure to be applied in large doses annually. Along with cattle manure, green leaves use of tank silt or earth from the paddy fields together with farm yard manure to be used. In malnad soppina betta is maintained.

Application of chemical fertilizers is split doses is also important.

Irrigation

The areca palm is very sensitive to drought. The methods of irrigation plays a important role in cultivation of areca gardens. In recent years sprinkler irrigation is in practice by large farmers.

Drip or trickle irrigation is gaining importance.

Harvesting

The stage of harvesting depends upon the type of produce to be prepared for the consuming markets.

One type prepared out of immature green nuts. other from ripe nuts.

Majority at which the fruit is harvested and the season of harvest affect the quality of the processed nut considerably.

All these above points are invariably followed by large farmers in the study area in getting good yield and substantial returns hence we recommend the above factors to be followed by small and medium farmers category to get good and remunerative returns, which will enhance the socio-economic status of the small and medium farmers and in turn price fluctuations.

In the study area, the small, medium and large categories, out of their respective yields are traditionally preparing 50% of Grade 1, 34% of Grade 2 and remaining 16 % of Grade 3. Here we suggest to prepare more percentage of grade 1 in their respective yields so as to fetch income in terms of returns.

The large farmers are in better position is getting yield and returns and it should not be confined large farmers category only at the same time the small and medium category of farmers has to reap the substantial benefit by implementing the above cultivaion practices intensively and meticulously.

The large farmers are in better position in getting yield and returns and it should not be confined to large farmers category only at the same time the small and medium category of farmers can reap the substantial benefit by implementing the above cultivation practices intensively and meticulously.

Recommendations

In the light of various difficulties and constraints faced by arecanut growers including the CAMPCO Ltd. regarding, Fall in the arecanut price and other issues related to arecanut, following salient features or recommendation are mentioned below.

As on today arecanut is mainly used for masticatory purpose. It is commonly used with lime and betelleaf for chewing. It is also consumed as processed arecanut in the form of Gutkha, panmasala and panparag, which are hazardus to health.

Arecanut as a crop neither contributes to food and nutrition security of people nor as any significant foreign exchange carring potential. However, the reported medicinal values of arecanut and other alternative uses need to be explored profitably for the sustenance of arecanut farmers in future. It is quite essential to develop technologies for value added products through products development in terms of pharmacentical, industrial and cosmetic values.

Keeping in view of the liberalisation of trade, removal of quantitative restrictions (QRS) in the WTO regime the prevailing arecanut price is which lower (55 to 78%) in the international market than the domestic price and the possibility of import of arecanut cannot be ruled out even after increasing the levy duty from 35% to 100% to safeguard the interests of farmers. Similarly, the export price is much lower than the domestic price and so there is remote chance for Indian arecanut to be exported.

However, there is an urgent need to increase the productivity of the crop by doubling the yield and reducing the unit cost of production in order to be competitive in the world market.

With this background the following recommendations given below, which need to be implemented scrupulously.

1. Seednuts and seedlings are to be distributed from govt. nurseries/ ICAR institutions / Central State Forum Nurseries. (only for replanting of old plantation with higher yielding varieties and not for any new area planting.)
2. Proper steps to be taken by the state Govts. to create awareness among the farmers about possible impact of the indiscriminate expansion of area over a period of time and the need to have sustainable income.
3. For the increase of productivity of the existing plantations, which are young or old drip irrigation may be instituted. It is gaining momentum nowadays.
4. Cropping system should the profitability of arecanut +cocoa, areca + pepper on areca, areca with pepper, clove and nutmeg which need to be popularized to get sustainable income from mixed cropping instead of monocropping.

   Farmers who are adopting such cropping systems get higher income and additional employment potential. This needs popularisation through demonstration and agricultural universities has to intervene in this respect.
5. There is an urgent need to design suitable harvest in devices and appropriate small dryers and grading machines which will go a long way for reducing the difficulty in harvesting, cost of harvest and this will also helps to go for on farming process.

For this research and development organisations like ICAR, has to design suitable appropriate devices.

6. Technical and financial assistance for the entrepreneurs to encourage and promote alternate uses of arecanut by products from arecanut stem, leaf sheath formaking disposable plates, cups, caps, unbrellas, photo frames etc.
7. Since the price fluctuation in arecanut is predictable and violent, there is need to work out a strategy for providing price support in order to safeguard the traditional arecanut growers to get sustainable income.

   Areca marketing seems to be complicated system. Large number of intermediaries are involved besides a few co-operative organisations like CAMPCO and other co operative societies in other states. The CAMPCO network only procure 10% of production.
8. One of the high risk to the farmers is lack of storage facilities either at CAMPCO or in any other co-operative societies, hence subsidy may be given for constructing airted, humidity controlled godowns at different places. This pattern of assistance is available with NHB, which may be extended to the co operative societies in corporate sectors.
9. As CAMPCO is a well organised society in the marketing of arecanut and having vast experience in marketing arecanut they should expand their activities in other states as it is helpful to the areca farmer.
10. The CAMPCO being an apex body, it is necessary that CAMPCO should take up a detailed survey on industrial, medicinal uses of arecanut.
11. The import duty on arecanut was increased from 35 to 100% to safeguard the interest of the farmers by the Govt of India. However, instances are reported that arecanut is brought as a dry fruit. Arecanut should not be covered under dry fruit category. Appropriate action may be instituted so that the unscruplous import should not take place.
12. Alternative uses of Arecanut.

    Important aspect of Arecanut and its alternative uses are listed below, it may boost the farmers economy and it will open up a new way in marketing and makes the areca cultivation sustainable.

Apart from the use of Arecanut as a masticatory and with the introduction of by products got from modern ways of living the various parts of the areca palm can be made use of for different purpose.

From Nuts

The by products from nuts can be used for tanning leather.

1. In leather industry.
2. As a writing ink
3. As an adhesive in playboard manufacture.
4. As a textile dye.
5. In purification of sugar juice. As a safe food colouring agent etc.

From Husk

- From fibre, for making thick board, flufficushions and non-woven fabrics.
- For preparing hard boards and plastics.
- Pulping and paperboards.
- Wrapping papers can be prepared from areca pulp and bamboo.

From Leaf Sheath

- For making paper boards for packing purpose
- Through away cups and plates.
- Ply boards.
- For teachers for long-distance transport, it cutdowns the use of softwood timber for this purpose.
- Used as picture mounts, can be used as decorative panels of wooden almirahs and teapoys.
- Used as a cheap substitute for leather in house chapples and as a cheap summer wear chappals.
- Used in briefcases, bags, spectacle cases, tea and coffee trays, office file boards and flaps, and in the manufacture of match boxes and can be used for packing glass wear and fragile articles by converting sheaths into packing wool.
- Test is on in the use of thermal and electrical insulations.

From Arecanut Stem and Leaf

Areca stem can be used as a building material.

Due to its hardness and golden yellow colour the timber can be used in stationary articles like rulers, shelves, waste paper baskets, the sharpened stem used for husking coconuts,

- Nails made of areca stem widely used in furniture industry.
- From leaves are good source of organic manure.

The future of arecanut and arecanut base industry depends on the extent to which an economically feasible alternative use for the different constituents of the areca palm could be developed early.

In the field of arecanut marketing co-operative institutions such as CAMPCO have played an important decisive role in recent years in the states of Karnataka and Kerala.

The technology for the utilisation of different parts of areca palm etc if developed it would not be difficult to start small scale industry at the village level in turn it gives employment generation in cultivation and by-product aspects. Though arecanut production and its related activities are reckoned as a major industry, it is a fact that no efforts at any time have been made for popularising use of this commodity.

In view of the numerous uses for which arecanut has been put to, it is to be assumed that it will have an impact in future also, possibly through developing a suitable alternative technology for its utilisation.

BIBILOGRAPHY

BOOK

Ashok Kumar (1995), Economic Development and Mukter Mittal Planning in Third World. Pub by: Anmol Publications Pvt Ltd. New Delhi pp. 1-17,123-152.

Bhise V.B (1998), Economic Reforms and Ninth Five Year Plan, Pub by: Anmol Publications Pvt Ltd, 4374/4b, Ansari Road, Daryaganj, New Delhi pp. 1 to 25.

Gerald M.Meier (1995), Leading Issues In Economic Development Pub by: Oxford University, Press, Bombay. pp. 327,395

Gillis Perkins Roemer (1996), Economic of Development Snodgrass Pub by: W.W.Norton and Company, Newyork. pp. 155-190.

Hans W. Singer. (1998), Growth, Development and Trade Pub by: Edward Elgar U.K, USA. pp. 3-45.

Inder K Alagh (1990), Land and Man. Pub by: Har Anand Publications, Delhi pp. 36-52

Michael P. Tudaro (1995), Reflection on Economic Development Pub by: Edward Elgar Publishing Ltd. England. pp. 241-260.

AGRI ECONOMICS

Albert Berry. and William. R. Cline. R. (1979), Agrarian Structure and Productivity in Developing Countries. Pub by: The Johns Hopkins, University Press. Baltimore and London pp. 5-29.

Ashok Rudra (1967), Relative Rates of Growth, Agriculture and Industry. Pub by: University of Bombay. Series No.14, pp. 1 to 12

D.S Anathi (1984), Productivity and Growth in The Indian Economy. pp. 3 to 46.

J .Ashton and S.J Rogers (1969), Economic Change and Agriculture. Pub by: Oliver U. Boyd Edinburgh and Landon. p. 66.

The American Economic Association (1969), Reading in the Economics of Agriculture. Pub by: George Allen Unwind Ltd., Ruskin Honse, pp. 37, 64, 89.

Abdul Munir (1991), Agricultural Productivity and Regional Development. Pub by: Manak Publications Pvt Ltd., p. 113.

Andrew Pearse (1980), Seeds of Plenty Seeds of Want Social and Economic Implication of the Green Revolution, Pub by: Clarin Don Press Oxford., pp. 80, 105, 118.

Adlowe L. Larson (1953), Agricultural Marketing in a Specialized Economy. Pub by: Prentice Hall, INC New York, pp. 30, 49, 57, 67, 87.

S.S Acharya and M.L.Agarwal (1994), Agricultural Marketing in India. Pub by: Oxford and IBH Publishing co-Pvt Ltd., pp. 1 to 170.

A.N Agarwal (1951), Indian Agriculture and its Problem. Pub by: Ranjit Printers and Publishers, pp, 1 to 25.

Ajay Kumar Bhattacharya (2001), Community Participation and Sustainable Forest Development, Global Perspective Pub by: Concept Publishing Company New Delhi, p. 82.

Brajendra Nath Banergee (1987), Industry, Agriculture and Rural Development and Indian Science Pub by: B.R. Publishing Corporation, Delhi, pp. 108-148 & 149-161.

H. Banerji (1974), Supply and Demand for Agricultural Products, Calcutta, Pub by: Progressive Publishers, pp. 19-29.

C.E.Bishop And W.D.Toussiant (1964), Introduction to Agricultural Economic Analysis Pub by: New York, John Wiley & Sons INC, Landon, pp. 68-72.

Berkely Hill (1980), An Introduction to For Students of Agriculture Pub by: Pergaman Press, p. 120.

Baeigh Barlowe (1958), Land Resource Economics Pub by: Practice Hall INC., p. 112.

Bruce F. Johnston and Peter Kilby, (1975), Agriculture and Structural and Transformation, Pub by: Oxford University Press, Landon. p. 328.

Birla Institute of Scientific Research (1980), Technological Changes in Agriculture. Pub by: Union books, Pvt Ltd. New Delhi, pp. 13, 23.

D.S. Bawa (1976), Rural Project Planning Methodology and case studies, Pub by: D.S. Bawa R-17, Heuz Khaz, Enclose New Delhi, pp. 44-57

Colin Clark M.R. Haswell (1967), The Economics of Subsistence Agriculture, Pub By: Macmillan, Landon, St Matins' Press, New York, pp. 78-110

Carl Eicher and Lawrence witt (1970), Agriculture in Economic Development, pp. 1 to 120

D.S.Chauhan (1966), Studies in utilization of Agricultural Land, Pub by: - Shiva Lal Agrwala & Company, pp. 75-175

Chopra.R.N. (1985), Green Revolution in India, Pub by: Intellectual Publishing Home, New Delhi, pp. 9 to 91.

R.L Cohen (1957), The Economics of Agriculture, Pub by: -Digs Well Place James Nishet & Co. Ltd Cambridge at The University Press, p. 23.

Cofton.R Dharton.J.R (1965), Subsistence Agriculture, Economic and Development, Pub by: - Aldine Publishing Company, Chicago, pp. 12, 209, 363.

Deniel Titorner Basile Kerblay (1966), The theory of Peasant Economy, The American Economic Association Pub by: - Richard, Irwin, INC.

David.L.Debertin (1986), Agricultural Production Economics, Pub by: - Macmillan Publishing Company, New York, pp. 62-79.

L.N. Dutta (1997), Agricultural Production Efficiency and Farm Sage., Pub by: - University, Publishing Company, Ranchi, pp. 111.

Donald .J. Epp John. W. Maldone (1981), Introduction to Agricultural, Economics, Pub by: - Rutledge New, Fetter Lane, London, pp. 1 to 70.

Dale. C.Dahl and Jerome W. Hammid (1977), Market and Price Analysis and Pub by: - Megraw Hill Book, Company, pp. 1 to 70.

Earl Otheady (1965), Agricultural Policy Under Economic Development, Pub by: - IOWA State, University Press, IOWA, USA. pp. 3 to 76

Easter Boserup (1965), The Conditions of Agricultural Growth, Pub by: - George Allen and Unwind Ltd Landon, pp. 23-26

Earl . O.Theady John.L.Dillon (1964), Agricultural Productions Functions, Pub by: - Iowa State University Press IOWA, pp. 142, 218

Eddy Finely (1994), International Agriculture and Pub by: - Delmar Publishers, Robert R. Price INC Newyork, pp. 51 to 75

Forster .G.W (1953), Farm Organization and Management, Pub by: - Prentice Hall INC Newyork, pp 8, 12, 147

Gupta .S.C. (1962), Producers Response to Changes in Prices and Marketing Policies a Case, Study of Sugarcane and Paddy, in Eastern UP, Pub by: - Asia Publishing House, New York, pp. 3 to 29

Gupta .A.P. (1948), Marketing of Agricultural Produce in India Pub by: - Vora & Co-Publishers Pvt Ltd. Bombay, pp 14 to 92

Gadgil .D.R. (1948), Economic Effects of Irrigation, Pub by: - Okhale Institute of Politics and Economics, pp. 1 to 34.

Geoffrey.S.Shephard (1952), Agricultural Price and Income policy Pub by: - The IOWA State College Press Ames, IOWA, pp. 69-73

Harold G.Halcrow (1955), Contemporary Readings in Agricultural Economics, Pub by: - Prentice Hall INC, Newyork, pp. 42,54, 195, 202, 214

John .W.Meller (1967), The Economics of Agricultural Development, Pub by: - Cornell University, Press, pp. 289, 291

Joshi .G.N. (1992), A Study of ResourceTransfers from Agriculture, Pub by: - Commonwealth, Publishers, Newdelhi, India, pp. 31, 70, 121.

Jain .S.C. (1971), Principles and Practice of Agricultural Marketing and Prices, Pub by: - Vora & Co Publishers Pvt Ltd., Bombay, pp. 221

John Donald Black (1953), Introduction to Economics for Agriculture, Pub by: - The Macmillan Company, Newyork, pp. 17 to 31

Komal kumar Jain (1990), Growth of Instability in Agriculture, Pub by: - Himalayan Publishing House, pp. 223-270

Karl Brandt (1944), The Reconstruction of World, Agriculture, Pub by: - George Allen and Unwin Ltd, Landon, pp. 1944, 36.

Kahlon A.S. (1980), Economics of FKaram Singh Management in India, Theory and Practice, Pub by:- Ltd. Bangalore, pp. 16 to 23

Indian Society of Agricultural Economics (1990), Agricultural Development, Policy Adjustments and Reorientation, Pub by: - Oxfore & IBH, Publishing Co Pvt Ltd., pp. 133,

Khem Singh Gill (1993), A Growing Agricultural Economy Technological Changes Constraints and Sustainability, Pub by: Oxford and IBH, Publishing Co Pvt Ltd., New Delhi,

Meti. T.K (1989), Agricultural Growth and Non-Agricultural Growth, Dynamics of National Development, Pub by: - Gain Publishing, House, New Delhi

B.B.Mukherjee (1960), Agricultural Marketing in India, Pub by: - M.N.Jha for Thacker Spink & Co.

Mamilal B. Nanavati (1960), The Indian Rural Problem and J.J. Anjoria Pub by:- Indian Society of Agricultural Economic

Nadkarni .M.V (1980), Marketable Surplus and Market Dependence, A Study of a Millet Region, Pub by: - Allied Publishes Pvt Ltd Bangalore, pp. 95-112

Nakkiran.S. (1980), Agricultural Farming and Rural Banking in India, An Evaluation, Pub by: - Rainbow Publications, Coimbatore, pp. 1 to 9, 10 to 18, 27 to 34

Norman Efferson .J (1953),, Principles of Farm Management, Pub by: - MC-Graw Hill Book Company, INC pp. 16, 32, 47, 69.

Rajamani A.N. (1970), Conditions Necessary for Agricultural Growth, Pub by: - Educational Publishers, Agra, pp. 31-39.

Robertson C.A (1971), An Introduction to Agricultural Production Economics and Farm Management, Pub by: - TATA McGraw- Hill Publishing Company Ltd., New Delhi, pp. 20-40

Ravindra Nath Ghosh (1977), Agriculture in Economic Development, Pub by: - Vikas Publishing House Pvt Ltd., pp. 74.

Ramesh Chand (1999), Agricultural DiversificationIn India, Pub by: - Mittal Publications, New Delhi, pp. 57 and 165

Rajgopal (1990), Agri-Business and Enter, Pub by: - Anmol Publications, pp. 53 to 73

Richard L. Kohls and Joseph.N.Uhl (1980), Marketing of Agricultural Product, Pub by: - Macmillan Publishing Co., INC, London, pp. 3 to 21.

Sankayan. P.L. (1988), Introduction to the Economics of Agricultural Production, Pub by: - Prentice Hall of India Pvt Ltd., New Delhi, pp. 6-25.

Shah.C.H. (1960), Conditions of Economic Progress of Farmers Pub by: - The Indian Society of Agricultural Economics Bombay, p. 25

Sadhu.A.N and Amarjith Singh (1989), Fundamentals of Agricultural Economics, Pub by: -Himalaya Publishing House, p. 186

Singh S.P. (1973), Cuter-State Relations in Agricultural Development, Pub by: - Vikas Publishing House Pvt Ltd, Delhi, pp. 226, 329.

Suardrtrum.K.F. (1980), Agricultural Marketing for Co-poetries. Pub by: - allied Publishers, Private Ltd. Bangalore, pp. 122-130

Theordore.W.Schultg (1963), Transforming Traditional Agriculture, Pub by: - Yale University Press, London. pp. 110-127.

Theordore.W.Schnlty (1964), Economic Crisis in World Agriculture, Pub by: - The Universally of Michigan Press, pp. 69-96

Vyas.V.S. and (1997), Policies for a Agricultural Pradeep Bhargava Development. Pub by: - Rawat Publication, Jaipur. pp. 30-87

Williard.W.Cochrane (1974), Agricultural Development and Planning, Pub by: - Pager Publicity, New York, pp. 1-15

William.H.Nichollas (1947), A Terrifically Analysis of Imperfect Competition with Special Application to the Agricultural Industries, Pub by: - The ZWA, State Collages Ames, Iowa,

BOOKS ON ARECANUT

Bavappa K.V.A., Nair .M.K, Prem Kumar.T (1982), The Areca Nut plan (Area Catechu Linn) Pub by: - K.V. Ahmed Bavappa, Director, CPCRI, Kasargod, Kerala, India

Hegde .K.M. (1993), Areca Nut Cultivation in North Canara, Pub by: - District Areca and Spices Growers Association.

Dr. T.K.Prabhakara Shetty, Prof. B.L.Vishveshwara Gowda. (2003), Areca Nut Cultivation and Its Alternative Use., Pub by: - UAS, Bangalore, Areca Nut Research Center, Regional Research Station, Shimoga

Shama Bhat. K., Radhakrishna Nair. C.P (1985), Areca Nut Research and Development, Pub by: - K.V. Ahamed Bavappa, Director CPCRI, Kasargod, Kerala, India.

Arecanut (2002), Govt of Karnataka Dept of Horticulture, Shimoga

Cost of Cultivation of Horticultural Crops (2001), Govt of Karnataka Dept of Horticulture, Pub by: - Horticulture Information Center, Bangalore

Sen Gupta.B (1946), Manufacture of Catechu,

Areca Nut Cultivation (2000), Agricultural Expert Institution, Bangalore, Shimoga, Devision (Unit)

Golden Jubilee (1990), MAMWS, Shimoga Sornier Mamws

Singara (2000), Diamond Jubilee Sovenier, Mamcos, Pub by: - Mamcos, Shimoga

Rajatha Singara (1998), Silver Jubilee Slovenlier, Campo Co. Pub by: - Campco, Mangalore

Seminar On Areca Nut (1999), Special Suvenier, Org by, APMC Bangalore, APMC Shimoga, Sagara.

Workshop On Areca Nut (1995), Special Svenier, Org by, APMC, Dept of Agricultural Marketing Govt of Karnataka & Development Board for Cocoa, Areca & Spices Products, Govt of India

Stastistics of Shimoga (2001-02), District Statistical Office, Shimoga

Agricultural Progress A Glance (2001-02), Pub by:- Govt of Karnataka and Dept of Agricultural, Shimoga.

JOURNALS ON AGRI - ECONOMICS

M.M.Bhalerao (1992), Input use Efficiency in Indian, Sant kumar Agricultural A study of Vegetables and D.N.Prasad and Oilseeds Indian *JL.of Agri, Eon,* July-Sept 1992, Vol 47, No,3, p. 486.

Binod Ch Monhanty (1992), Study of Resource Efficiency on Groundnut Productivity in Orissa, July-sept 1992,Vol 47, No 3 pp. 496

Chhotan Sing (1992), Resource use Efficiency and Productivity on Different Forms in Salem District, Tamil Nadu. Indian *JL. of Agri. Econ,* Vol 47, No.3 July-Sept 1992, p. 488.

Chahal and G.S.Mander (1992), An Economic Analysis of Resource use Efficiency in Punjab. Indian *JL. of Agri. Econ,* Vol 47, No,3, July-Sept 1992, pp 545

K.S.Dhawan and R.S.Prihar (1992), An Economic analyses of Efficiency of Different Crops in Utilization of Factor of Production is Punjab. Indian *JL. of Agri, Econ,* Vol 47, No, 3, July-Sep.1992 p. 493.

Elsamma Job (1992), Input use Efficiency in Paddy Cultivation in Andhra Indian *TL of Agril, Econ,* 1992. p. 498.

Dinesh Chandra (1992), Resource use Efficiency on Different Irrigation Systems In Ghazibad Dist. Uttar Pradesh. Indian *JL. of Agril. Econ*, Vol 47, No, 3 July Sept 192, 494.

Idnani.N.L. K.K.Duben and B.L. Mishra, (1992), Resource Productivity and A Locative Efficiency in Soybean Production. Indian, *JL of Agril Econ*, Vol 47, No,3 July-Spt,1992 p. 490

Hannmantha Rao.H. (1992), Contribution of Irrigation to Factor Productivity in Agriculture. Indian, *JL, of Agri Econ*, Vol 47, No. 3, July-Sept, 1992, p. 497.

Ikbal Singh (1997), Irrigation Water Efficiency Through Conjunctive uses of Surface and Ground Water in Upper Ganga Canal Command Area. Indian, *JL. of Agril, Ecn*, Vol 47, No, 3 July-sept 1997, p. 489

Joginder Singh, I.S. Chatha and Bhajan Singh (1992), Rational of Fertilizer use in Indian Agriculture: Indian *JL of Agril Econ*, Vol 47, No 3

Kazi .M.S.Rahim and Nurshad Ali (1992), Technological Gaps as the Determents of Yield Gaps in Rice Varieties in Birbhun District. Indian, *JL of Ag.Econ*, Vol. 47, No, 3, July-Sept 1992, P. 545.

P. Lalitha Sudha and V.T. Raju (1992), Resource Productivity and Resource use Efficiency on Gingerly Farms of Visakapatnam District of Andra Pradesh, Vol 47, No 3, July-Sept-1992, p. 495.

Madhusudan Ghosh (1992), Resource use Efficiency is a Rice Based Agricultures Indian, *JL of Agric. Econ*, Vol 47, No, 3 July-Sept 1992, p. 495.

Mahita and Madhusudhan rao (1992), Resource use Efficiency in Paddy Cultivation in Andra Pradesh, Indian, *JL of Agric, Economics*, Vol 47 No, 3 July- Sept 1992 p. 498.

P.K.Muraleedharan (1987), Resource use Efficient in Kole Lands in Trichur District (Kerala) Indian, *JL of Agric, Economics*, Vol. 42, No, 4, Oct-Dec 1987, pp. 378-386.

M.R.Naidu and G.Tirupathaiah (1992), Resource use Efficiency and Resource Allocation in Ground Nut farms of Vizianagaram District of Andra Pradesh, Indian, *JL of Agric, Economics*, Vol. 47, No, 3, July-Sept, 1992, p. 488.

T.N.Prakash Srijay Devaraj Urs And Lalith Achoth (1998), Impacts of Co-operative on Market Structure and Prices, The Case of Central Areca Nut and Processing Co-operative (CAMPCO) Ltd., Karnataka, Indian in of *Agri Econ.*, Vol. 53. No, 3, July-Sep, 1998

B.M.Sharma S.K.Goel And Sharma (1992), Input use Efficiency on Tractor and Bullock Operated Farms in Aligarh District of Uttar Pradesh, Indian, *JL of Agric, Econ.*, Vol 47, No, 3 July-Sept. 1992, p. 487.

B.D.Shukla, Dinesh Kumar Bhasti and R.K.Jha (1992), Input use Efficiency in Indian Agriculture A Study of Pulse, Crops. Indian *JL of Agri, Econ.*, Vol. 47, No, 3 July-Sept 1992 p. 493.

V.S. Satyapriya (1992), Industrial Factors and Marketing Behaviors A Study of Three Major Areca Nut Markets in Karnataka. Indian, *JL of Agri, Econ*, Vol 47, No, 3, July-Sept, 1992, pp. 179-184.

G. Subramanyam (1986), Labor Demand and Supply Responsiveness of Cotton in Madurai District, Tamil Nadu. Ind, *JL of Agric Econ.*, Vol 41, No 2, April- June 1986, pp. 155-163.

K. Sain (1992), Relative Efficiency of Input, Use in the Cultivation of some Food Crops. and Commercial, Crops., Indian, *JL of Agric, Econ*, Vol 47, No 3, July-Sept 1992, p. 491.

C.L.Thakur N.K. Raghuwanshi and K.G. Choubey (1982), Fertilizer use Efficiency for the Production of Irrigated Wheat In Rice Wheat Zone of Madhya Pradesh. Indian, *JL of Agric, Econ.*, Vol 47, NO 3, July-Sept 1982.

M. Upender (1992), Production Elasticity and Returns to Scale on Different farm size Groups A Sample Study, Indian, *JL of Agric, Econ*, Vol 47, No, 3, July-Sept, 1992. p. 492.

JOURNALS ON ARECANUT

Ananda .K.S, Anuradha Sane, Choudhary B.S., Sane. A (2000), Growth and Yield Performance of Areca Nut Varieties in Malnad Region of Karnataka, *Journal of Plantation Crops.* Vol, 28 No 2 pp. 105-109.

Ananda K.S, and Thampan .C (1999), Promising Cultivars and Improved Verities of Areca Nut (Areca Catches Linn) Indian *Journal of Areca nut, Spices and Medicinal Plant*, Vol 1 No 1, pp. 24-29,

Azad .A.K. Ghare.G.H, Aziz Ahmed, Biswas .M Biswas M. Hussain AKM. Ahmed A Hussain A.K.M. Subhadrabandhu. S(1992), Effect of Sunshine on Growth, Reproductive Character and Scoring Damage of Areca Nut Palm ev, Mangala International Symposium on Tropical Fruit: Frontier in Tropical Horticulture No, 321, pp. 449-454,

Abdul Khader .K.B Kumar .P.H (1982), More Cero this way (Improved And Management Practices of Areca Nut, India.) Intensive Agriculture, (India) Vol. 20, pp. 8-10

Abdul Khader .K.B (1982), Drip -a New Method of Irrigation in Areca Nut (betel Nut - India) Indian Farming, (India) V, 32 (9), pp. 25-26

Abdul Khader K.B (1982), Drainage and its Importance in Areca Nut (Betel Nnut-India), Indian Farming (India) V, 32 pp. 35-37.

Bhat .V.R. (2000), Adverse Effect of Neem Oil on Areca Nut Fruit Setting. Indian, *Journal of Areca Nut, Spices and Medicinal Plants* Vol 2 No, 1 pp. 1-5

Bucky . M (1996), Teak And Areca Nut Colonial State Forest and People in the Western Ghats (South India), Publications lu Department le Science Socials, 1800-1947, XiX+ 255

Bhagavan .S Bhat .K.S (1989), An Appraisal of Mixed Cropping Trial on Areca Nut and Cocoa, *Journal of Plantation Crops,* Vol 17 No 1, pp. 10-17.

Bhalerao .M.M. (et-al) (1990), Pattern and Intensity of Resource use in Intercrops of Areca Nut, Narendra Deva, *Journal of Agricultural Research,* Vol 5 No 1 pp. 34-37

Bavappa . K.V.A (1982), Areca Nut Research and Development -a Success Story, (Betel Nut -India) Indian, Farming (India) Vol 32 (9) pp. 3-5

Bopaiah . B.M (1981), Beneficial Aspects of Growing Legumes as Inter or Mixed Crop. In Areca Nut Plantation, Indian, Cocoa Areca Nut and Spices , *Journal, India,* Vol 5 (2) pp. 33-35

Bhat K.S (1978), Agronomic Research in Areca Nut -a Review (Areca Catechu Linn) *Journal of Plantation on Crops.* Vol 6 (2) pp. 67-80.

Chandha. KL. (1998), Improvement in Tree Fruit and Plantation Crops. Indian, *Journal of Horticulture.* Vol. 55 No. 4, pp 265-296

Chowdappa.P. Biddappa. C.C. Sujatha.S. (1999), Efficient Recycling of Organic, Organic Wastes in Areca Nut (Areca Catechu) and Cocoa Plantation Through, Vermicornpostionh Indian, *Journal of Agricultural Sciences,* Vol 69, No, 8, p. 563-566

Dayanand Sharma.OP. Fageria.M.S. Maniram. (1999), Influence of Phosphorus and Sculpture on Nutrient Uptake and Quality Seed Production of Fenugreek, Indian, *Journal of Areca Nut Spices and Medicinal Plants.* Vol 1 No 4, pp. 127-145,

Das.P.K. (1982), Areca Nut marketing in India, (Betel-Nut) India Farming (India) Vol 32 (9), pp. 48-51,

Gowda.T.H. Lrnapathy.PM. Usha.J.K. (1999), A Note on the New Tiny Inflorescence Caterpillar Batrachedra near Arenoseila Walker, on Areca Nut, Walker, on Recount. Current Research, UAS Bangalore 28, pp. 7-8, 113-114,

Gowda.T.H. Uapathy P.M. Usha.J.K. (1999), Areca Nut Moth Batrachendra sp, nr, Arenosella Walker. (lepidopteron) Momphidere a New Pest of Argument in Southern Plains of Karnataka, Indian, *Journal of Arcanum, Spies and Medicinal Plant,* Vol 1 No 4. pp. 121-122,

Guruswanmy.K.T. and Krishnamurthy.N. (1994), Characterization of Soils Collected from Profiles in Yellow Leaf Desire-Affected Areca Nut Gardens in Taluk (Karnataka), India, *Journal of Agricultural-Sciences,* Vol 7 No 1, pp. 73-75

Giriappa.S. (1995), Plantation Economy in India. Vii+ 15,tpp, 32 ref.

Gurumurthy.K.T. and Baiger.M.K. (1993), Yellow Leaf Disease in Arecanut, UAS, Bangalore. pp. 6-8, 89-91,

Giriappa.S. (1994), Areca Nut Production and Marketing in India, ix + 15opp.

Hegde.H.G. Gangadharappa.P.M. Hegde N.K. (1997), Effect of Fertilizers on Yield of Areca Nut and Black Pepper Mixed -Cropping System. Karnataka, *Journal of Agricultural Sciences,* Vol 10 No, 1, pp.. 262-264

Hunter.D. and Zuhair M. 1996), Coconut, Areca Nut and Spice Crops in the Maldives, Status and Prospects, *Journal of Plantation Crops.,* Vol 24, No. 1, P. 1-8,

Ibrahim.K.K. Satheeshan.K.N. Rajagopalan.A. Neema.V.P. (1996), Evaluation of Pepper Cultivars, Cultures for Mixed Cropping in Areca Nut gardens. Indian, Cocoa, Areca Nut and Spices, *Journal,* Vol P; 20, No. 4,

Joseph Kumari.T. Skaria.B.P. (1999), Medicinal Plants in Pest Control, Indian *Journal of Areca Nut Spices and Medicinal Plants.*

John.T. (1995), Coca Development in India, Position Paper. Indian Cocoa, Areca Nut and Spices *Journal,* Vol 19 No. 4, pp. 133-135

Jose.C.T. Khadek.B.A. Mathew.J. (1995), Plant Competition in Cocoa and Areca Mixed Cropping System, Indian, Cocoa, Areca Nut and Spices, *Journal,* Vol 19 No.1, P 11-13

Joshi.R.M. Borude.S.G. Thakare.G.G (1995), Economics of Production of Areca, Nut in Raigad Maharashtra, District of Indian Cocoa, Areca Nut and Spices, *Journal,* Vol, 19 No. 1 pp. 14-17,

Kumar.T.P. Vasantha Kumar.K. Aipe.K.C. Kumarna.K. George.S.P Manmohandas.T.P Anith.K.N. (1999), Studies on Yielding Behaviors of Black Pepper Panniyur-1 Indian, *Journal of Areca Nut Spices and Medicinal Plants.* Vol. No. 3, pp. 88-90,

Korikanthimath.V.S, Rajendra Hegde, Ravindra Mulge. Hosamani.N.M. Mulge.R. Hgde.R. (1998), Mixed cropping of Areca Nut and Cardamom-Compatibility and Yield Pattern. Karnataka, *Journal of Agricultural Sciences,* Vol, 11 No. 3

Korikanthimath.V.S.Hiremath. Gm. Hegde.R. Mulge.R. Hasmani. M.M. (1998), Comparative input Utilization Pattern in Mono/s Mixed Cropping of Areca Nut with Cardamom. *Journal of Maharashtra Agricultural Universities.* Vol. 22, No. 2, pp. 210-212.

Korikanthirnath V.S. Hosamani.M.M. Hegde.R. Mulge.R. (1997), Economics of Mixed Cropping of Cardoons in Areca Nut Gardens, *Journal of Spices and Aromatic Crops*. Vol, 6 No.2, pp. 107-113,

Kumar.SNS. and, Nambiar.KKN. (1996), Management of Anabe-Disease of Areca Nut. Scientific Horticulture, 5; pp. 57-61,

Krishnaswarny.J. (1995), Marketing of Cocoa in, India, Indian Cocoa, Areca Nut, Spices, *Journal*, Vol, 19 No. 4 pp. 136-138,

Korikanthimath.V.S Rajendra Hegde Hegde.R. (1994), Cardamorn and Areca Nut Mix-Cropping Systems, Indian Cocoa, Areca Nut and Spices *Journal*, Vol. 18 No. 4, pp. 109-112,

Loganthan.S. Marimuthu.S. Ramarethinam.S. (2000), A Survey of Phytophagous Mites in Areca Nut Plantations in Combater District of Tamil Nadu, Insect Environment, Vol, 6 No. 2, pp. 67-68,

Latha bastine, Palaniswamy.K Bastine.L. (1996), Financial Analysis of Irrigation Investments in Small Holder Areca Nut Cultivation in North-Kerala. *Journal of Plantation Crops*, Vol 24, No. 1, pp. 66-69.

Mehandale.R.K. Mahaldar.S.R. Magdum MA (1999), Effects of Application of Potash in Soil and Spraying of Borax on Nut Splitting in Areca Nut, Indian *Journal of Areca Nut, Spices and Medicinal Plants*, Vol, 1 No, 3, pp. 85-87

Madhusudhanan.K. and Chandramohanan.R. (1997), Cultivation of Pheurotus Sajor-aju (fr), Singer on Areca Wastes, Standardization of Substrata, Preparation During Summer and Rainy Seasons, Mushroom Research, Vol, 6 No 2, pp. 75-78,

Mahesha.A. Khader KBA. Ranganna.G. (1990), Consumptive use and Irrigation Requirement of Areca Nut Plan, Indian, *Journal of Agricultural Sciences*, Vol. 60 No, 9 pp. 609-611

Murthy.K.N and Mohan.K.V.J. (1982), Varietal Improvement in Areca Nut. Indian Farming, (India) Vol 32 (9), pp. 7-11

Mohapatra.A.R. Sannamarappa.M. Braham.R.N. Bhat No.T. (1982), Green manure crops for Areca Nut Gardens, Indian, Farming (India), Vol 32 (9) p. 27,

Mohapatra.A.R. (1977), Soil Fertility Research in Areca-Nut: a Review, *Journal of Plantation Crops*. Vol.5 (2) p.. 114-120

Prakash.T.N. Urs.S.D. Lalith-Achoth. (1998), Impact of Co-Operative on Market Structure and Prices The Case of Central Areca Nut and Cocoa Marketing and Processing Co-operative (Camp Co) Ltd Karnataka, Papers Real At the Fifty-eight Annual Conference of the Indian Society of Agricultural Economics. Mahatma Puale Krishi Vidyapeath, Rahuri, Maharashtra, India. Indian, *Journal of Agricultural, Economics*, Vol 53 No 3, pp. 333-343,

Ponnama.K.N. and Solomon.J.J. (1998), Yellow Leaf Disease of Areca Palms-Critical Studies on Transmission with the Vector, Protester, Moister, Westwood, *Journal of Plantation Crops.*, Vol, 26 No.1, pp. 75-76

Prakash.T.N. Achoth.L. Mallikarjunaiah.K.G. (1989), Processing and Marketing of Areca Nut in Karnataka an Economic Analysis, Indian Coca-Areca Nut and Spices, *Journal,* Vol 12 No. 4, pp. 109-112,

Padmanabhan.H.C. (1979), Cardamorn-as an Intercrop in Areca Nut (India), Vol 12(8) pp. 9-11,

Ray.AK Reddy.DVS Sairam.CV Gopalasundaram.P. (2000), Performance of Area Based High Density Multispecies Cropping System, Under Different Levels of Fertilizers, *Journal of Plantation Crops.* Vol. 28, No.2, pp. 110-116

Ravinctran Tc Selvan Mt Sivaraman.K. (1999), Production, Marketing and Development Programmes of Areca Nut in India, *Indian, Journal of Areca Nut, Spices and Medicinal Plants.* Vol 93 No. 8, pp. 339-347

Remold.M. (1998), Pepper Production Prospects in India. Planters Chronicle, Vol 93 No. 8. pp. 339-347

Rajagopalan.A. Satheeshan.K.N. Mammoty.K.P. (1995), Selection of Quality Seedlings in Areca Nut a Case Study, Indian, *Journal Cocoa, Areca Nut and Spices.* Vol 19 No. 3, pp. 94-95

Reddy .V.M. Ravi Bhat Bhat. R (1994), Cropping system in Areca Nut Indian, Cocoa, Areca Nut and Spices, *Journal,* Vol 18, No 1, pp. 13-15,

Roy .A.R. Yadukumar .N.. Singh .R.K. (1983), Growing pepper on Areca Nut Mango and Silk Cotton Trees, Indian Farming (India) Vol 33 (3), pp. 30-32.

Reddy M.K. Saraswathy.N Chandramohana (1978), Diseases of areca Nut in India, A Review and Further Considerations, *Journal of Plantation Crops.,* Vol 6(1) pp. 28-43

Sujatha .S and Haris .A.A (2000), Root Distribution as Influenced by Different Methods of Irrigation, In Young Areca Nut Plans *Journal of Plantation Crops.*, Vol 28 No2, pp. 117-112

Sujatha .S. Ravi Bhat, Reddy V.M Haris A.A, Bhat .R(1999), Respone of High Yielding Varieties of areca Nut to Fertilizer Levels in Coastal Karnataka. *Journal of Plantation Crops* Vol 27 (3), pp. 187-192 .

59)Sundaraju .P Sudha .S, Mehta .U.K (1998), Nematode Management in Areca, Nut and Areca Nut Based Farming, System. Nematology, Challenges and Opportunities in 21st Century, Processing of the

Third, International Symposium of Afro-Asian Society of Nematologists, Sugarcane Breading Institute (ICAR) Coimbature, India April 16-19, 1998, pp. 190+92

Singh .S.P (1996), Sustaining profitability of Coconut and Areca Nut plantations. Advances in Horticulture and Forestry. 5, pp. 81-86.

Singh .R.K. and Baranwal V.K. (1993), Areca Nut Based High Density Multiple Spices Cropping System, For Northern Region of West Bengal, Indian Cocoa, Areca Nut and Spices *Journal*. 16, pp. 3-4, 97-100

Singh R.K. Bhale rao.H.M.M Reddy M.N.M (1985), Economics of Areca Nut Cultivation in West Bengal, Indian Farming, (India) Vol 36 (1) pp. 31-34

Satyapriya.V.S (1984), Institutional Factors and Marketing Behavior a Study of Three Major Areca Nut Markets in Karnataka (India) Indian *Journal of Agricultural Economics,* Vol 39 (3) pp. 347-352

Saraswathy .N. (1982), Recycling of Areca Nut Waste (Betel-nut, India) Indian Farming, Vol 32 (9), pp. 47-51

Sannamarappa .M (1976), Effect of Tillage Operations in, Areca Nut Plantations of ' Maidan ' Parts of Karnataka on the Productivity of Palms (India), *Journal of Plantation Crops,* Vol 4(2), pp. 58-59.

Thomas.K.G. (1978), Crop Diversification in Areca Nut Gardens. Indian Areca Nut, Spices and Cocoa, *Journal,* Vol 1(4) pp. 97-99

Vishwanath N.S. and Narappanavar.S.R. (1994), Production, Marketing & Export Potential of Areca Nut in India, Indian, Cocoa, Areca Nut and Spices *Journal* Vol 18 No.4 pp. 113-116

Vishwanath.N.S. And Narappanavar .S.R. (1994), Grading of Areca Nut in India -a Study. Bihar, *Journal of Agricultural Marketing,* Vol 2 ,No 4, pp. 371-380

Vijayakumar .B.G. Devaraju.G.V, Balasimha .D Khader.KBA, Ranganna.G (1991), Influence of Weather on Areca Nut and Cocoa Yield, *Journal of Plantation Crops.* Vol 19 No 1, pp. 33-36

Vigneshwara .V (1991), CAMPCO in Areca Nut and Cocoa, Marketing in India Problems and Prospects. Indian, Co-operative, Review Vol 28 No 4, pp. 352-368

Vigneshwara .V (1990), Marketing of Areca Nut need for a Consumer Based Approach, Indian, Cocoa, Areca Nut and Spices, *Journal,* Vol 14, No 2, pp. 52-54.

Velappan.E And George .C.K (1982), Areca Nut Production in India, Indian Cocoa, Areca Nut and Spices, *Journal* (India) Vol 6(2) pp. 27-30.

Velappan .E (1992), Measures to Enhance Returns from Areca Nut

Gardens. Indian Cocoa, Areca Nut and Spices, *Journal*. Vol 5 (3), pp. 55-58.

Yadava.R.B.R. Kumar .K.V. Murthy .K.N. (1977), Correlation Studies in Areca Nut (Areca Catechu Linn) Proceedings of the National Academy of Sciences, (India) Vol 47 B (3) pp. 226-230.

AGRICULTURAL REPORTS

Reports of The Ccommission for Agricultural, Costs and Prices for the Crops, Sown during 2000-01 Season, (2001-01), Dept of Agriculture and Co-operation. Ministry of Agriculture, Govt of India, New Delhi, P, 135-379

Indian Agriculture (2003), Vikas Singhal, Indian Economic, Data Research Center, pp. 753-764

Crop Out Put Projections for States by Agr-climate Sub-Regions (Based on an Inter Regional Area Allocation Model) (1994), Agro-Climatic Regional Planning Uunit, Planning Commission, Thatte Hill Ahmedabad, India, pp. 12-35

Agro-Climatic Regional Planning at State Level, Profiles, Issues, Strategies, Programmers Appu Working, Paper No.5 July 1991 (1991), Agro-climatic Regional Planning, Unit. Planning Commission, Ahmedabad, India, pp. 105-119

National Seminar on Agro-climatic Regional, Planning. Held on 5th and 6th, March 1990 at Ahmedabad, Appu Special Issue dec 1990 (1990), Agro-Climatic Regional, Planning Unit. Planning Commission, Ahmedabad, India.

State Focus paper 2005-06 Karnataka, National Bank for Agriculture and Rural Development Karnataka, Regional Office Bangalore, pp. 95-104.

REPORTS

Report of the Expert Committee (2001), Dept. of Agriculture and Cooperation, Ministry of Agriculture, Govt. of India on Areca Nut.

Report on the Areca Nut, Proccessing and Marketing, Co-operative Society Ltd., Apscos, Sagara, 2000

Annual Report, Apms, Shimoga, Apms, Shimoga 1988-89, 89-90, 90-91.

Annual Report Apmc, Sagara (1998-99), Apmc, Sagara,

Annual Report Mamcos, Shimoga (1999-2000), Mamcos, Shimoga

Annual Reoprt CAMPCO, Mangalore (2001-02), CAMPCO, Mangalore

THESIS AND DISSERTATIONS

Gajanana.T.M. (1985), An Analysis of Supply Response, of Areca Nut in

Karnataka, 1985, MSDCAG, Dissertation, Dept of Agricultural Economics UAS Bangalore.

Hegde.D.A. (1987), Impact of Price Behavior on Areca Nut Plantations and Growth in Karnataka. A Case study of North Kanara District Dept of Economics, Karnatak University, Dharwad.

Hegde N.K. (1998), Crop Diversification Studies in Areca Nut (Areca Catech Linn) Plantation. PHD thesis, Dept of Horticulture, UAS, Dharwad.

Prasanna.D.G. (1998), Financial Feasibility of Investment Under Drip and Traditional Methods of Irrigation in Areca Nut Orchards of Shimoga District, Karanataka, 1998 MSC Ag Dissertation Dept. of Agricultural, Economics, UAS, Dharwad,

Vishwanath.N.S. (1987), Impact of Price Behavior on Areca Nut plantations and Growth in Karantdaka, 1987 Phd Thesis Dept of Economics, Karantaka University, Dharwad.